Blockchain Fundamentals for Web 3.0

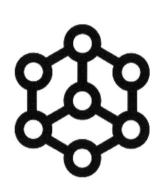

Blockchain Fundamentals for Web 3.0

Mary C. Lacity
&
Steven C. Lupien

An imprint of The University of Arkansas Press
Arkansas, USA

An Epic Books publication
(Imprint of The University of Arkansas Press)

Cover design:
SB Publishing

Editor & layout designer:
Steve Brookes
SB Publishing
Stratford-upon-Avon, UK
www.sbpublishing.org

Cover artwork image:
Kryptós Gráfo – The Hidden Secret
by Sammy Hexter-Andrews, 2022
www.track5art.com

Authors:
Mary C. Lacity
Steven C. Lupien

Published in 2022 by:
Epic Books (an imprint of University of Arkansas Press)

ISBN: 978-1-68226-225-2

Printed and bound in the USA by University of Arkansas Press

Contents

Contents

PART III: Road to Maturity

Figures and Tables

Figures

Figures and Tables

Figures and Tables

Tables

Foreword by Caitlin Long
Founder & CEO of Custodia Bank

Satoshi Nakamoto, the inventor of Bitcoin, is one of the most important systemic thinkers in human history.

A systemic thinker is a polymath—an expert who works across disciplines, spotting connections others may not see by going broad as well as deep. For example, a systemic thinker may see that Michelangelo's David has more in common with Dante's Divine Comedy than it does with Bernini's David, despite both statues of David studying the same Biblical subject. Why? Dante and Michelangelo were Renaissance creators whose works displayed the humanism, symmetry, order and clean lines of the Renaissance. By contrast, Baroque creators, such as Bernini or Mozart, favored ornate detail over simplicity as well as movement over stability. Systemic thinkers learn to spot such patterns horizontally—patterns that even the greatest experts in each vertical may not be able to see.

Satoshi Nakamoto is a true polymath—one of the greatest, if not the greatest, systemic thinker of our time. Satoshi's invention, the Bitcoin blockchain, was cross-disciplinary. Satoshi solved a computer science problem long considered unsolvable by computer scientists, by applying knowledge from outside computer science. To create Bitcoin, Satoshi applied elements of economics, psychology and behavioral science to cryptography and distributed systems.

A blockchain is a new type of database technology. Speaking simplistically, a blockchain allows multiple parties to see the same data at the same time and trust that it's valid. A blockchain is a 'golden copy' of information upon which all users can rely. It is shared technology infrastructure.

What problem does blockchain technology solve? Expressed in practical terms, on the one hand, blockchain solves the duplication/reconciliation problem—when parties don't trust each other, they need to keep and reconcile their own copies of data. Expressed in philosophical terms, on the other hand, blockchain solves the trust problem. To establish trust, today we use an army of auditors; accountants; trustees; lawyers; transfer agents; registrars; county clerks; asset custodians; and myriad other forms of third-party validators, and sometimes we throw in a central counterparty to stand in between, and then we duplicate and reconcile the same data across each of these parties. Until blockchain came along, there was no avoiding all this—it was the cost of establishing trust. But it's a tremendously inefficient and resource-intensive way to create trust. Blockchain is a database architecture that can streamline these processes massively. It's a cheaper way to create trust.

A true blockchain is decentralized. This means there is no system administrator. There is no gatekeeper. There is no central target for hackers to attack.

Some of you may find the analogy to Google Docs helpful. When students use Google Docs to write a term paper, they share the same document with multiple parties at the same time and can see their colleagues editing it in real-time. But there's a problem. Google controls the data, and you have no way of knowing whether Google tampered with it. A blockchain is 'like Google Docs but without Google'—because no party has a controlling role in a true blockchain. No one owns the network because every participant in the network owns it.

Now let's talk about Bitcoin, the first blockchain. Satoshi Nakamoto actually didn't invent anything new in 2008. Rather, Satoshi combined several existing advances in a way no one had combined them before, and the advances cut across disciplines—spanning math (i.e., cryptography), computer science (i.e., distributed systems/peer-to-peer networking) and economics (i.e., game theory). The use of game theory was Satoshi's real genius—Satoshi reinforced the technology with asymmetric incentives.

For example, it's expensive to add transactions to Bitcoin's ledger, but cheap to verify them once they've been added, thereby making it very easy to enforce property rights within this system. It's prohibitively expensive to attack the Bitcoin network—it would cost billions just to re-write this morning's transaction history—but cheap for individuals to participate in the network by simply downloading the open-source Bitcoin software to become a network node.

15

But most importantly, unlike every other form of money used in human history, growth in the value of bitcoin doesn't cause more bitcoin to be produced. Growth in the value of gold causes more gold to be mined or growth in the value of the dollar enables the Federal Reserve to print more of them. Rather, growth in bitcoin's price ONLY makes the network more secure. There will never be more than 21 million bitcoins, regardless of how high its price goes. As more people join the Bitcoin network, it simply becomes more immune to attack.

And Bitcoin has never been hacked successfully. It is almost certainly the most secure technology system ever built. Wait, you might be thinking, what about the hacks I've read about? Those hacks happened within insecure applications built on top of the Bitcoin blockchain. The underlying Bitcoin blockchain itself—the base ledger layer—has NEVER been successfully hacked. And it's worth $560 billion on the day of this writing, so there's quite a hacker's bounty! Bitcoin's success from a cybersecurity standpoint is even more notable when you learn that Bitcoin is not protected by a firewall. It lives in the wilds of the Internet and hackers constantly try but fail to penetrate it. Why? Remember, Bitcoin works because it's a beautiful balance of technology and economic incentives—hackers would spend a lot more money to hack it than they would gain from doing so.

It took a systemic thinker—with top-notch skills in cryptography and computer science and a keen understanding of game theory, monetary history and human behavior—to concoct such a beautifully-balanced system. And in doing so, Satoshi solved a problem that the computer science field had tried to solve for decades, called the Byzantine Generals Problem. Put simply, how would generals fighting on a Byzantine battlefield know that messages they received from other generals during battle weren't tampered with during their journey across the battlefield? This was considered by many to be an unsolvable problem in the computer science specialty of distributed systems, but Satoshi solved it. Perhaps if computer scientists had spent more time talking to economists and behavioral scientists all along, it might have been solved a lot sooner!

Authors' Acknowledgements

Many people informed and shaped this research program. We are especially thankful to all of the thought leaders and pioneers interviewed for this research. We hope this book fittingly trumpets their visions and achievements.

We have many people to thank at our respective institutions.

The Blockchain Center of Excellence at the University of Arkansas. In June of 2018, Mary became the Director of the Blockchain Center of Excellence (BCoE) at the Sam M. Walton College of Business (WCOB) at the University of Arkansas. It was an opportunity of a lifetime to work with fellow blockchain enthusiasts including Professor Matt Waller, the Dean of the Walton College; Professor Rajiv Sabherwal, Chair of the Information Systems (ISYS) Department; Professor Paul Cronan, Director of Management Information Systems (MIS) graduate programs; and Dr. Zach Steelman, Associate Professor of IS (and resident blockchain guru). They laid the groundwork for the BCoE. From there, the BCoE grew to include the exceedingly capable team: Kathryn Carlisle, BCoE Senior Managing Director; Professor Dan Conway, BCoE Associate Director; Professor Remko Van Hoek from Walton College's Supply Chain Management department; Professor Carol Goforth from the School of Law, and Andrea Morgan, ISYS Department Assistant. A special thanks to Srividya Yellepeddi and Tchetahan 'Nato' Silué, two rock-star Professional MIS students who helps with BCoE activities in 2021-2022.

The BCoE's mission is mission to make the Sam M. Walton College of Business a premiere academic leader in research and education of blockchain-enabled technologies and digital ecosystems. We believe that future professionals with skills and knowledge in blockchain-enabled technologies and digital ecosystems will transform businesses and society into more efficient, sustainable, and profitable networks. Twelve Executive Advisory Board Member firms contribute to the mission, namely, Accenture, ArcBest, EY, FedEx, FIS, Golden State Foods, IBM, J.B. Hunt Transport Services, McKesson, Microsoft, Tyson Foods, and Walmart. Many of the insights for this book came from the BCoE's Executive Advisory Board workshops. See https://blockchain.uark.edu/

The Center for Blockchain and Digital Innovation (CBDI) at the University of Wyoming. The CBDI is an interdisciplinary center focused on emerging technologies to foster innovation, economic development, and education. The CBDI is shared by the College of Business, College of Engineering and Applied Science, College of Agriculture and Natural Resources, and the School of Energy Resources; it is also working with the state's community colleges. The CBDI is working with government and industry partners on several projects, including SheepChain ranch management system, ESG tokenization of carbon credits, tokenization of environmental credits, including Sage Grouse habitat preservation, and clean water credits as well as blockchain-based healthcare filing system.

Many thanks to State of Wyoming for providing us with American Rescue Plan Act to Recovery funding to support this project. We also thank EPIC Publishing, SB Publishing, and the University of Arkansas press. Our gratitude to Matt Waller for launching the EPIC book series and for his vision, kindness, and leadership. SB Publishing, whose editing and production services bring our best work to market faster than any traditional publishing route, has been a great partner for years. Thank you to Mike Bieker, Director of the University of Arkansas Press, for understanding and accommodating the unique needs of business publications.

Mary expresses her heartfelt gratitude to her family and friends: *"Thank you to my parents, Dr. Paul and Joan Lacity; my son, Michael Christopher; my sisters, Karen, Diane (always close) and Julie, and dear friends, Michael McDeviitt, Beth Nazemi, and Val Graeser for your unwavering support and humor. Christine Emma Cotney Benson, thank you for entertaining me during my many research trips to New York City. Finally, to the man who makes all this worthwhile, Jerry Pancio, my past, present, and future."*

Steve expresses his thanks: *"I will start by thanking my daughter Abigail and my partner Caitlin for their love and guidance. Both drive me to be my best every day and are pillars of support. I'd like to thank Chris Land—a truly talented lawyer that understands digital assets like no one else—and University of Wyoming Deans Rasco, Wright, and Krutka for their inspiration and vision for blockchain education. Also, thanks go to Wyoming Governors Mead and Gordon who provided leadership when few understood the power and impact of this new asset class. Finally, my thanks to the legislators of Wyoming whose courage drove them to see possibilities that other states are still trying to comprehend and the people of Wyoming who live the 'Cowboy Code' every day."*

Publication Credits

Excerpts from earlier versions of our work have been revised, updated, and cited for this guide:

- Chen, Z., and Lacity, M. (2021). The Emergence of Web 3.0: Tokenization and the Internet of Value, Blockchain Center of Excellence White Paper Series, BCoE-2021-02, University of Arkansas.

- Lacity, M., and Carmel, E. (2022). Implementing Self-Sovereign Identity (SSI) for a digital staff passport at UK NHS, Blockchain Center of Excellence, University of Arkansas Research Paper Series.

- Lacity, M. (2022). Blockchain: from Bitcoin to the Internet of Value and beyond, Journal of Information Technology, forthcoming.

- Van Hoek, R., Larsen, G., and Lacity, M. (2022). RPA in Maersk procurement—applicability of action principles and research opportunities, International Journal of Physical Distribution & Logistics Management, 52(3).

- Lacity, M., and Van Hoek, R. (2021). What We've Learned So Far About Blockchain for Business, Sloan Management Review, 63(3), pp. 48-54.

- Lacity, M., and Van Hoek, R. (2021). How Walmart Canada Used Blockchain Technology to Reimagine Freight Invoice Processing, MIS Quarterly Executive, 20(3), pp. 1-15.

- Lacity, M. (2021). Fake news, technology and ethics: Can AI and blockchains restore integrity? Journal of Information Technology Teaching Cases.

- Van Hoek, R., and Lacity, M. (2021). How the Pandemic Is Pushing Blockchain Forward, Harvard Business Review, Summer Issue, p, 52-53.

- Lacity, M. (2020). Crypto and Blockchain Fundamentals, Arkansas Law Review, 73.

- Lacity, M. (2020), Re-inventing Talent Acquisition: The SmartResume® Solution, Blockchain Center of Excellence Case Study Series, BCoE-2020-01, University of Arkansas.

- Lacity, M., and Conway, D. (2020). Authenticating real news with ANSAcheck, a blockchain-enabled solution developed by ANSA and EY, Blockchain Center of Excellence White Paper Series, BCoE-2020-02, University of Arkansas.

- Van Hoek, R., and Lacity, M. (April 27, 2020), How the Pandemic Is Pushing Blockchain Forward, Harvard Business Review, https://hbr.org/2020/04/how-the-pandemic-is-pushing-blockchain-forward

- Lacity, M. (2019). An Overview of the Internet of Value, Powered by Blockchains. Blockchain Center of Excellence white paper, BCoE-2019-03, University of Arkansas.

- Lacity, M., Zach, S., Paul, C. (2019). Blockchain Governance Models: Insights for Enterprises. Blockchain Center of Excellence white paper, BCoE-2019-02, University of Arkansas.

- Lacity, M., Zach, S., Paul, C. (2019). Towards Blockchain 3.0 Interoperability: Business and Technical Considerations. Blockchain Center of Excellence white paper, BCoE-2019-01, University of Arkansas.

- Lacity, M. (2018). A Manager's Guide to Blockchains for Business, SB Publishing, Stratford-Upon-Avon.

Contributors

Anouk Brumfield is responsible for the strategy, organization, and business performance globally of IBM Blockchain Services. She is focused on delivering accelerated client value in the advisory & creation of new business models and intelligent workflows, powered by blockchain services, AI & hybrid cloud. She is known for driving global businesses and strategic growth initiatives in a profitable & scalable way, inspiring change and delivering brand breakthrough for clients & IBM. She has built winning and empowered teams whose results are recognized by analysts as market leading & market making.

Kathryn Carlisle is the Senior Managing Director of the Blockchain Center of Excellence in the Sam M. Walton College of Business and course instructor for Introduction to Cryptocurrency. Kathryn founded Sow Ventures, a web3 consulting and investment business, that enabled her to lead blockchain and crypto product design, manage communities, educate clients, and launch pilot projects with startups and nonprofits since 2017. She is a Little Rock native who has been studying and investing in crypto personally since 2014. Kathryn holds a Master's of Digital Currency from The University of Nicosia in Cyprus, the first institution in the world to offer this degree, and she is also a proud Alumni of the University of Arkansas, where she received a dual-degree in International Business and Spanish Language. Kathryn leads the Blockchain Center of Excellence in outreach, operations, and crypto education.

Erran Carmel is a Professor of Information Technology at the Kogod School of Business at American University in Washington D.C. He is a former dean. Carmel is known for his expertise on the globalization of technology work especially global outsourcing and has written three books and well over one hundred articles. Recently he has been studying Digital Health Passports, Self-Sovereign Identity, and Tokens.

Dale Chrystie is business fellow and blockchain strategist for FedEx. He also serves as chairman of the BiTA Standards Council, and is a member of the Blockchain Research

Institute. He was awarded the inaugural Enterprise Blockchain Award in Enterprise & Industry Leadership and is a global thought leader on the business and strategy aspects of blockchain and Web3. His focus on 'coopetition' in the blockchain space continues to challenge conventional wisdom and typical corporate and regulatory culture, and his perspective in that space appears in academic and other publications. He is a proud graduate of the University of Arkansas.

Dan Conway is teaching professor and associate director of the Blockchain Center of Excellence at the University of Arkansas. He is active in US blockchain standards efforts and is on the CognitiveWorld think tank for AI.

Melanie Cutlan leads Accenture's Technology Incubation Group and Blockchain practice, focusing on shaping solutions with emerging technologies across distributed systems, XR, Quantum, and Robotics to bring companies into the future. Melanie has a role on the board of the Hyperledger Foundation and has been quoted in publications including the Silicon Republic, CoinDesk, Irish Independent, PYMNTS.com, BrandLab, and LedgerInsights. Melanie is a gifted and sought-after speaker, helping to bring complex topics to life at events including Consensus, Hyperledger Global Forum, SIBOS, Global Blockchain Summit, International Association of Outsourcing Professionals, International Women's Day, and Women in Technology. Her Accenture publications cover a wide array of topics helping to guide leaders - from building value chain resilience to charting the course toward a more sustainable future.

Dino Farinacci is a software engineer by trade and a technology visionary by passion, advancing the state of the art in computer networking. As one of the first Cisco Fellows, Dino holds over 40 Internet and Networking related patents and has been a major IETF contributor for nearly 30 years with ~50 RFCs and Internet Drafts published. Dino is the founder of lispers.net, a non-profit engineering organization, where he now focuses on design and deployment of the LISP protocol for IoT, cryptocurrency, 5G mobile networks, satellite networks, and contact tracing applications.

Authors' Acknowledgements

Carol Goforth is the Clayton N. Little Professor of Law at the University of Arkansas (Fayetteville). She, along with Yuliya Guseva, is the author of Regulation of Cryptoassets (2d Ed., West Academic 2022), as well as more than a dozen published articles dealing with regulation of cryptoassets and transactions. She is a regular commentator on the subject, with her observations and opinions being quoted in Forbes, Fortune, Reuters, and CoinTelegraph, among others.

Caitlin Long is Founder & CEO of Custodia Bank. Caitlin is a 22-year Wall Street veteran who has been active in bitcoin and blockchain since 2012. In 2018-20 she led the charge to make her native state of Wyoming an oasis for blockchain companies in the US, where she helped Wyoming enact 20 blockchain-enabling laws. From 2016-18 she jointly spearheaded a blockchain project for delivering market index data to Vanguard as chairman and president of Symbiont, an enterprise blockchain start-up. Caitlin ran Morgan Stanley's pension solutions business (2007-2016), held senior roles at Credit Suisse (1997-2007) and began her career at Salomon Brothers (1994-1997). She is a graduate of Harvard Law School (JD, 1994), the Kennedy School of Government (MPP, 1994) and the University of Wyoming (BA, 1990).

Remko Van Hoek is a full professor of practice in the supply chain management department of the Sam M. Walton College of Business. He is also executive director of the CSCMP Supply Chain Hall of Fame which is hosted by the Walton College as a service to the supply chain profession and is an advisor to several companies. Prior to joining the Walton College he worked in procurement and supply chain executive roles around the world for several companies, including Disney, Nike and PwC and he taught the UK, the Netherlands and Belgium.

Yorke Rhodes is Director of Transformation, Blockchain at Microsoft where he leads company efforts in blockchain and web3. In 2015 he Co-founded Blockchain @Microsoft and set the company on a course from enterprise blockchain to its current day curiosity in web3. Blockchain is not his first innovation wave rodeo. From early in his career he rode the PC wave, client server computing & databases, & client server email. In 2000 he set out to conquer wireless internet with roles at startups, Goldman Sachs and IBM. In 2008 he started in digital marketing and spent several years in ecommerce mobile & web before rejoining Microsoft to focus on cloud. An NYU adjunct Professor of E-commerce Marketing in their master's degree program, he also holds a BS in Computer Science from NYU.

Sandra Ro serves as CEO of the Global Blockchain Business Council, the leading global industry association for blockchain and digital assets. As a proponent of 'human-centric tech,' Sandra advances responsible innovation and inclusion as an angel investor, board director, advisor, guest lecturer, media commentator and cofounder of social impact and tech start-ups. From investment banking and currency markets to blockchain technology, Sandra has spent her career advocating using digital tools to solve big societal problems. She holds an M.B.A. from London Business School, studied Computer Science at Columbia University, and earned a double B.A. degree from Yale University.

Chen Zur leads EY's US Blockchain practice. He is a technologist, a leader, and a principal in EY's Technology Consulting Organization. He is committed to developing and promoting the state of the art of web 3.0 and blockchain technology, in collaboration with his colleagues, clients, and the community. He strongly believes Web 3.0, and public blockchain technology will enable us to build a fairer and more open world and will fundamentally change the way we (individuals and organizations alike) manage our digital identity, store value, and exchange it between us. It is his purpose to work together with EY's clients and ecosystem partners through these exciting times, understand, develop, and adopt blockchain-based solutions, and better deal with this era of rapid technological change and disruption.

The book's cover art

Kryptós Gráfo – The Hidden Secret
by Sammy Hexter-Andrews

The artist—Sammy Hexter-Andrews

Sammy is an abstract artist from Hampshire in the United Kingdom. Passion for art and the desire to create is what keeps Sammy's mind racing with ideas for her artwork. She works in a variety of mediums, so, when viewing Sammy's portfolio for the first time you could easily be under the impression that the artworks presented are the creations of several artists. The diversity in her styles is breathtaking—explosive abstract art paintings and contemporary mixed media collage art are just two of the styles you will discover when you delve into Sammy's work.

Sammy's cover art for this book was commissioned by the authors, and the original piece is acrylic/mixed media on canvas. The painting truly captures the evolution of blockchain as we move inexorably towards Web 3.0.

See Sammy's art at **www.track5art.com**.

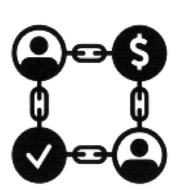

PART I

Blockchain Foundations

Chapter 1

Restoring Trust with Blockchains

What's inside: Globally, we have a crisis of trust in our governments and institutions. This chapter explains the movements to establish trust through the decentralization of value, identity, and data ownership. These movements are part of 'Web 3.0', the idea that individuals rather than institutions should control and benefit from online social and economic activities. Blockchain technologies are the digital infrastructure for these movements. Blockchain technologies are designed for peer-to-peer online activities, with no central control. Many view blockchains as the best solution to some of world's most pressing problems, from income disparity to climate change.

Learning objectives:

- Describe the role of decentralization in restoring trust in social and economic activities
- Compare the 'Internet of Information' with the 'Internet of Value'
- Compare centralized/federated identity models with self-sovereign identity (SSI)
- Compare surveillance capitalism with individual data ownership and monetization
- Explain how blockchains enable an 'Internet of Value', SSI, and individual data ownership and monetization

1.1. Trust is the foundation of a well-functioning society

"The root problem with conventional currency is all the trust that's required to make it work. The central bank must be trusted not to debase the currency, but the history of fiat currencies is full of breaches of that trust. Banks must be trusted to hold our money and transfer it electronically, but they lend it out in waves of credit bubbles with barely a fraction in reserve."

Satoshi Nakamoto, inventor of Bitcoin[1]

Although this is a book about technology, we are going to start our learning journey with the very human notion of trust. Trust is the foundation of a well-functioning society. High levels of trust in social institutions and economic markets promotes stability, prosperity, security, and wellbeing. Low levels of trust in social institutions and economic markets promotes instability, hardship, insecurity, and ill-being.[2]

We can conceive of trust as a sort of mental calculus that pervades every relationship we have. Take a moment to think about the relationships in your life. Whom do you trust and why? What are the limits of your trust in each relationship?

Trust can be defined formally as *"the degree to which subject A has confident positive expectations that object B will fulfil its obligations in context C to limit L".*[3] For example, perhaps you (subject A) trust your neighbor (object B) to collect your mail (context C) while you are on vacation (limit L), but you do not trust them to open your mail and pay your bills, thus your trust is contextual and limited. In this example, the object of trust is another individual, i.e., another single human being who is your neighbor.

We also apply the mental calculus of trust to formal institutions, like companies, government agencies, universities, hospitals, charities, and religious organizations. Which institutions do you trust and why? Perhaps you trust your university to provide a quality education for four years. Perhaps you trust your election commission to count your vote in every election. Perhaps you trust your charity to allocate your donation of $100 to those it promises to help.

The object of trust could also be a community—defined as *'a group of people who come together for a common purpose/interest'*—such as a neighborhood watch, an open-source software community, or a computer gaming community. In contrast to an institution, a community is not a legal entity. Which communities do you trust? Perhaps you trust your neighbors to watch over your property. Perhaps you trust a Reddit community to answer your questions on your favorite computer games.

Let's flip the question to: whom do you *distrust* and why? Distrust can be defined formally as *'the degree to which subject A has confident negative expectations that object B will fulfil its obligations in context C to limit L'*. Distrust in social institutions and economic markets results in fear and anxiety. In the quote above, we see that Satoshi Nakamoto, the inventor of Bitcoin, distrusts banks.[4] We will learn that one of Bitcoin's main features is to ground trust for economic activities in an incentivized community rather than in institutions.

We can also apply the mental calculus of trust to technologies. Which social media sites do you trust to connect you with family, friends, and interest groups? Which e-commerce platforms do you trust to buy and sell goods and services? Which online payment services do you trust to pay your debts?

When a technology is the object of trust, we need to consider two contexts for trust: trust in the technology's functionality, such as the technology performs as expected, and trust in the governance of the technology. Since all technologies are created, operated, and used by human beings, humans govern it. Your trust in the Facebook application to keep you connected to friends is a separate mental calculus than trust in the Facebook company (now 'Meta') to govern the application in your best interests. Research shows that people trust technologies based on many technical and governance factors, including the technology's reputation; transparency (understanding how data is collected, processed, stored, and used); ease of use and perceived usefulness; the quality of the services; the performance in terms of availability, response time, and reliability; the costs in relation to benefits; the perceived risks, positive past experiences, and the reputation of its creators and operators.[5]

Thus far, we have argued that trust is the foundation for well-functioning social institutions and economic markets. While we hope that you are fortunate enough to trust many individuals, institutions, communities, and technologies, when we widen the aperture of trust to a global scale, the levels of trust are quite low in many places. Global surveys tracked the percentage of people from 1993 to 2004 who agreed with the statement, *"most people can be trusted"*. Sweden consistently ranked highest with over 60 percent of the respondents agreeing; the United States (US) hovered around 35 to 38 percent; Peru was among the lowest with under 10 percent.[6] More recently, the 2021 Edelman Trust Barometer found that the majority of 33,000 global respondents believe that government leaders (57 percent), business leaders (56 percent), and journalists (59 percent) are purposely misleading people by saying things they know are false. Based on an overall trust index that measures competency and ethical behaviors, Edelman reported significant drops in the index from 2020 to 2021. For example, in the two largest economies, the US's trust index dropped 18 points and China's dropped by 5 points. According to the authors, the survey reveals *"a widespread mistrust of societal institutions and leaders around the world."*[7] Many people hope to restore global trust by decentralizing activities with the help of blockchain technologies.

1.2. Restoring trust with blockchain-based solutions

Many people believe that the decentralization of economic and social activities is the best way to restore global trust. Decentralization is the dispersion of functions and power to the many. Decentralized activities discourage abuses of power and ideally promote more inclusive participation, unity around decisions, and individual empowerment, freedom, and privacy. Since most of our modern social and economic activities happen online, decentralized activities need a decentralized digital infrastructure, thus the creation of blockchain technologies.

Blockchains are the digital infrastructures that support decentralized activities. Blockchains are networks of computers where processing and storage of data is dispersed across a network, with no master computer (see Figure 1.1). Each connected computer is called a 'node' in the network. A node is an independent computing entity that communicates with other nodes in a network to work together collectively to complete transactions and to store them in a shared system of record, called a ledger. Communication among the nodes is peer-to-peer.

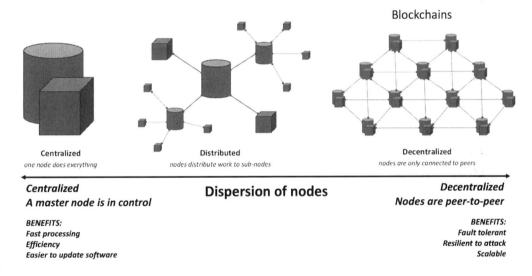

Figure 1.1: Three network architectures[i]

Source: Adapted from https://i.stack.imgur.com/hDDzg.png

---

i The terms 'distributed' and 'decentralized' are not consistently used in practice. Some people label the 'distributed' picture in Figure 1.1 as 'decentralized' and label the 'decentralized' as distributed. Whatever the label, blockchains look like the right-most network in the figure.

Decentralized architectures are resilient to cybersecurity attacks because the attack surface is diffused across many locations. The only way to infiltrate the network is to commandeer more than 50 percent of the processing power of nodes. Cybersecurity gets stronger as more nodes are added to the network because hackers will need to attack more nodes.[ii] Scalability is another benefit—just add more machines to the network to get more computing power. While architectural decentralization offers quite a bounty of business value, but there are downsides as well.[iii] Processing is slower compared to a centralized network because results need to be diffused and checked by the other nodes in the network. Software cannot be updated unless the majority of nodes agree to adopt it—it takes a lot of coordination to make any changes.

The governance of blockchains may or may not be decentralized, but in general, the most popular blockchains like Bitcoin and Ethereum, are governed by communities, not by institutions. Chapter 2 covers governance issues more deeply. So, in general, the technology and the governance are decentralized, yet all the users agree on the activities that occurred in the application. Vitalik Buterin, co-inventor of Ethereum, wrote, *"blockchains are politically decentralized (no one controls them) and architecturally decentralized (no infrastructural central point of failure) but they are logically centralized (there is one commonly agreed state and the system behaves like a single computer)."[8]*

Blockchain-enabled solutions have been developed to restore global trust to address some of the world's most pressing problems (see Figure 1.2).

---

ii Caveat: this is a high-level description written for non-specialists. In actuality, the safety of the network also relies on n-versioning of software (i.e., the same logic programmed in different languages), node independence (i.e., operated by different parties) and a variety of hardware implementations.

iii Moreover, Brewer's Theorem states that when some nodes are down in a distributed network, the network can either be designed to be available or consistent. In most blockchain networks, the choice is availability over consistency unless the community rallies to stop processing. So blockchains tolerate some short-term inconsistency to gain the benefits of availability. This is explained in Chapter 3.

Global problem	Example of a blockchain-enabled solution	Example(s) covered in
How can we restore trust in economic exchanges of value without relying on governments and corporations?	• Bitcoin was the first blockchain solution to address this problem.	Chapters 1–3.
How can we provide financial services and identities for the 1.1 billion people who currently lack them?	• Stellar aims to increase access to financial services for all. • Self-sovereign identity (SSI) solutions aim to provide identities and verifiable credentials for all.	Chapters 5 and 8
How can we close the income disparity gap so that people can more equitably share in the profits from their efforts?	• Beefchain aims to solve this for ranchers. • Several non-fungible token (NFT) blockchain solutions aim to directly compensate artists, athletes, and other content creators.	Chapters 4 and 7
How can we improve our global supply chains to eliminate forced labor, prevent counterfeits, reduce waste and ensure product quality and safety?	• The IBM Food Trust, Everledger, MediLedger, TradeLens and VeriTX tackled these issues.	Chapter 7
How can we protect our infrastructure from cybersecurity attacks?	• Blockchains are designed to be tamper-resistant, fault tolerant, and always available.	Chapters 1, 3 and 10
How can we stop fake news while protecting the integrity of our elections and freedom of speech?	• ANSAcheck provides a first important step against fake news by preventing imposter news.	Chapter 9

Figure 1.2: How blockchain-based solutions are restoring trust to solve global problems

As we learn more about blockchains, it's important to make one thing clear: readers should not trust a blockchain application just because it uses blockchain technologies. Scammers run 'pump and dump' schemes that leave inventors rich, and investors broke. Governments and private companies try to take centralized control, which is counter to the aims of decentralized power. For example, Scott Galloway, Professor of Marketing at New York University, was very vocal against Facebook's plans for a cryptocurrency because he does not trust the company to govern it with the best interests of users in mind.[9] Readers should apply the same mental calculus of trust to blockchain applications as they do any technology.

Figure 1.2 mentions specific blockchain-based solutions for specific problems. We can generalize what blockchains aim to achieve in terms of the next evolution of the Internet, for what many people commonly call 'Web 3.0'.

1.3. Blockchains as the architecture for Web 3.0

For the first few decades of the Internet's existence, it wasn't easy for the average user to find information online. We had to wait until the World Wide Web (WWW) and web browsers were created in the 1990s. The first generation of the WWW, called Web 1.0, made searching for information online much easier. However, it was still difficult for the average person to generate content. With the advent of social media and more user-friendly platforms, users could finally create content with ease on the Internet, bringing us to Web 2.0. We are still in the Web 2.0 era today.

While Web 2.0 has many advantages, it also has several disadvantages. We rely on trusted third parties to establish trust online—they hold a lot of power. We use a bolted-on identity model based on accounts and passwords—they are onerous, controlled by institutions and vulnerable to cybersecurity attacks. Tech giants are monetizing online activity and manipulating our behaviors—isn't it time for individuals to reclaim control?

Web 3.0 is the idea that decentralization of the WWW will solve these problems. The term is credited to Gavin Wood, co-founder of Ethereum.[10] Blockchain technologies are a key enabler of Web 3.0. To understand why many people want a Web 3.0, it's important to understand where the Internet came from, where we are today, and where we are headed. We tend to look back on the Internet's history and see it as a purposeful evolution, but the history of the Internet is fraught with competing technologies, happenstances, and political battles. For readers interested in a deep understanding of the history of the Internet, we have recommended sources in the endnotes.[11] For most readers, the abbreviated history summarized in Figure 1.3 and in the text below will be enough to meet our larger purpose of answering the question: why do people want Web 3.0 and how do blockchains help?

	Early Internet	Web 1.0	Web 2.0	Web 3.0
Approximate dates	1960s – 1990	1991 to 2004	2004 to present	2009 to present
Compound innovations led to:	• Machine-to-machine connections	• Easy searching	• Easy searching • Easy content generation • TTP-facilitated value exchange	• Easy searching • Easy content generation • Peer-to-peer value exchange

Examples of Innovations	1969 ARPANET
	1982 TCP/IP
	1983 DNS
	1989 Dial-up
		1990 HTML
		1991 WWW
		1993 WWW browsers
		1994 Amazon
		1995 Ebay
		    Craigslist
		1997 Netflix
		1999 Napster
			2003 MySpace
			    Second Life
			2005 Facebook
			2006 Youtube
			2007 Twitter
			2010 Instagram
			2011 WeChat; Snapchat
			2016 TikTok
				2009 Bitcoin
				2014 Ripple
				2015 Ethereum
				    Stellar
				    Everledger
				2018 IBM Food Trust
				    Tradelens
				2018 Brave browser 1.0
				2020 ANSAcheck
				    Mediledger

Figure 1.3: Eras of capabilities on the Internet

The dawn of the Internet

The Internet traces its roots to ARPANET, a computer network designed by the United States Defense Advanced Research Projects Agency (DARPA) to share information among researchers who already knew and trusted each other. The University of California Los Angeles, the University of California Santa Barbara, the University of Utah and Stanford University were the first institutions to be connected to it in 1969.

As more computers were added and as other networks emerged (ARPANET was not the only one), a standard way to connect computers was needed. Two DARPA scientists—Vint Cerf and Robert Khan—did just that when they developed the Transmission Control Protocol/Internet Protocol (TCP/IP) in the 1970s, which became a standard in 1982. TCP/IP is still the Internet's primary protocol used today. TCP/IP takes a copy of a message from the sending device, breaks the message into packets, and routes them to their destination device where they are reassembled. Make a mental note: *the Internet communicates information by sending copies*.

How do devices find each other? TCP/IP provided a way to identify the growing number of *machines* connected to the network of networks. Every device connected to the Internet has a unique IP address. For example, the IP address for the University of Arkansas server is 130.184.0.0/16; the IP address for the University of Wyoming server is 129.72.56.233. IP addresses are not easy to remember. The Domain Name Service (DNS) was another important milestone. Invented in 1983, it maps an IP address to something more user friendly, like 'uark.edu' for the University of Arkansas and 'uwyo. edu' for the University of Wyoming. IP addresses and DNS are for machine-to-machine identification. Internet standards do not identify the humans who are sending messages from those machines. This is why we use accounts and passwords. Make a mental note: *the Internet lacks an identity layer*.

Web 1.0: the 'READ' era

For the first few decades of the Internet's development, it wasn't easily accessible or readable to the average user. Then in 1990, Tim Berners-Lee, a scientist at European Organization for Nuclear Research (CERN), developed HyperText Markup Language (HTML). CERN launched the World Wide Web (WWW) a year later, marking the dawn of Web 1.0—the read era—which approximately occurred from 1991 to 2004. Web browsers like Mosaic released in 1993, Netscape and Microsoft Explorer in 1994, and Google in 1998, made it easier to find information online. Today, we easily search 'uark.edu' and 'uwyo.edu' with WWW browsers using the Uniform Resource Locators, https://www.uark.edu/ for the University of Arkansas and http://www.uwyo.edu/ for the University of Wyoming.

After the browsers, the centralized platforms came. Jeff Bezos founded Amazon in 1994 as an online bookstore. Although Amazon was not the first electronic commerce site, it heralded the coming explosion of business-to-consumer (B2C) commerce.[12] eBay and Craigslist, both launched in 1995, popularized consumer-to-consumer (C2C) commerce, thus creating online marketplaces for people to buy and sell goods and services using centralized platforms. Netflix launched in 1997. Napster, released in 1999, launched a centralized platform for peer-to-peer file sharing. As more consumers gained confidence in transacting on the Web, online banking finally took off.[iv] By 2001, the Bank of America had 3 million online customers.[13] During Web 1.0, it was still difficult for the average person to generate content.

Web 2.0: the 'READ' and 'WRITE' era

Social media platforms brought us Web 2.0—known as the read and write era. Major social media platforms were released: MySpace and Second Life in 2003; Facebook in 2005; YouTube in 2006; Twitter in 2007; Instagram in 2010; WeChat and Snapchat in 2011; and TikTok in 2016. Users could finally create content with ease on the Internet. The Web 2.0 era began in about 2004. Although we are still in this era today, Web 3.0 has already started—with Bitcoin, in 2009— and more is on the way.

By year end 2021, the consumer e-commerce market reached nearly $5 trillion, and business-to-business e-commerce reached $7.4 trillion.[14] Over 4.48 billion people worldwide used social media, representing 57 percent of the population. We generate 2.5 quintillion bytes of data every day![15] That is 2,500,000,000,000,000,000 bytes per day. Thus, the Internet is being used to generate a massive amount of information and to transact a massive amount of economic activity, but it's mostly controlled by institutions. Make a mental note: ***the Internet is controlled by institutions.***

Web 3.0: the 'READ', 'WRITE', and 'EXECUTE' era

Web 3.0 is the idea that we will use the Internet for reading, writing, and execution, but that users will control and monetize their activities by decentralizing the WWW with blockchain technologies. Returning to our mental notes, we investigate three movements leading us to a decentralized Web 3.0:

---

iv The first home banking service was offered in 1980 to customers of the United American Bank. Customers had to buy a custom MODEM made by RadioShack to use the services. MODEMs are a way to convert the digital signals used by computers to the analog signals used by telephone lines. The service cost each customer $30 per month. It reached only a few thousand users and died out after a takeover.

- The Internet communicates information by sending copies: Web 3.0 aims to evolve from an 'Internet of Information' to an 'Internet of Value'.
- The Internet lacks an identity layer: Web 3.0 aims to evolve from centralized and federated identity models to self-sovereign identity (SSI).
- The Internet is controlled by institutions: Web 3.0 aims to evolve from tech-giant 'surveillance capitalism' to individual data control and monetization.

We'll take a deeper dive into each of these movements and the early blockchain-based applications heralding their arrival.

1.4. From an 'Internet of Information' to an 'Internet of Value'

With the 'Internet of Information', we noted that *copies* of information are routed over the Internet. If you email a friend, you keep the original email, and your friend receives a copy of the email. With Web 3.0, we have an 'Internet of Value' where people transact value and data directly with each other, without relying on trusted third parties like banks. Data is made unique, i.e., money and other assets. However, we cannot send copies of value like we send copies of information. The pivot to an 'Internet of Value' requires innovative solutions to some very old problems—like double-spending, identity, credentials, bookkeeping and a medium of exchange (i.e., money!)—as well as to newer problems like cybercrime. Before blockchains, we rely on institutions to solve these problems. After blockchains, we rely on technologies like cryptography, distributed ledgers, digital assets, smart contracts, and community governance to solve these problems.

Bitcoin, the first blockchain application released in January of 2009, is the first solution that moves us from an 'Internet of Information' to an 'Internet of Value' where people transact value, i.e., money and other assets, directly with each other. The importance of Bitcoin cannot be overstated. It is THE reference point for understanding blockchains. Every student should know Bitcoin's story because all subsequent blockchains are an extension of or a departure from the original Bitcoin blockchain.

Satoshi Nakamoto, the inventor of Bitcoin, was the first to meaningfully solve the first problem listed in Table 1.1: How can we restore trust in economic exchanges of value without relying on governments and corporations? Nakamoto—a pseudonym used by an unknown person or persons who remains unknown to this day—imagined a world where people could safely, securely, and anonymously transfer value directly with each other (1) without using government-issued currencies; (2) without relying upon trusted third parties (TTPs) like banks or brokers; and (3) without the need to reconcile records across trading partners. Their innovation was Bitcoin, described in a white paper posted to a cryptographic mailing list on October 31, 2008.[16]

The timing of Bitcoin was no accident. After the 2008 Global Financial Crisis—possibly the greatest economic disruption since the Great Depression of 1929—people became increasingly distrustful of financial institutions. Movements like Occupy Wall Street ranted against wealth inequality and the influence of large financial institutions on government policy. People rallied against the government's power to control money. Bitcoin has its roots in Libertarian and Cypherpunk values, which aim to create social and political change by circumventing governments and large financial institutions through privacy-enhancing technologies.[17]

Satoshi Nakamoto's nine-page white paper specified the technical requirements for the 'Internet of Value'. What's remarkable is that Nakamoto used existing algorithms, but Nakamoto assembled them in a way to do something entirely new.[18] Quite simply, Nakamoto proposed *"a purely peer-to-peer version of electronic cash [that] would allow online payments to be sent directly from one party to another without going through a financial institution."*[19] Bitcoin achieves this by tackling some very old problems with algorithms and behavioral incentives (See Figure 1.4). Let's begin with the 'double spend' problem, the risk that value might be sent twice (or more).

Problems with establishing trust in an exchange of value	TTPs and Governments	Bitcoin
Double spending and other counter-party risks (e.g., counterfeit assets; illegitimate ownership)	Trusted third parties (TTPs) mitigate counter-party risks	Computer algorithms and an incentivized community mitigate counter-party risks
Bookkeeping errors and reconciliations	Each party keeps and reconciles their own records	A digital ledger (called a blockchain) that is verified, transparent and immutable is shared, so reconciliations are not needed
Mediums of exchange	Parties use fiat money, regulated by soveign governments	Parties use a cyptocurrency, governed by software and an incentivized community
Cybersecurity threats	Each party protects its IT permimeter or relies on a TTP to do it for them	Cryptography and other computer algorithms secure the data and network

**Figure 1.4: Trusted-Third Parties & Governments *vs.* Bitcoin:
Different solutions to old and new problems**

Counter-party risk mitigation

To transact *value,* i.e., money, over the Internet, one cannot send a copy. Instead, after the transfer of value is complete, the sender should no longer have the money, the recipient should. Today, a messy network of global financial systems and regulators prevent double spending. They also mitigate other counter-party risks—the risk each trading party bears that the other party will not fulfill its contractual obligations. Banks, credit card companies, money transmitters, notaries, lawyers, and other trusted third parties (TTPs) provide independent 'truth attestations' such as notarizing signatures; verifying identity; verifying ownership; authenticating assets; and attesting those agreements have been properly executed. TTPs provide these and many other vital services to facilitate trade (the advantages), for which they earn significant transaction fees (a major disadvantage). Transaction costs for remittances are typically between two and eight percent of the value of the transaction.[20] Before an 'Internet of Value', the process to transact value is expensive, and it is often opaque in that tracking transactions can be difficult.

Bitcoin solved the double spend and other counter-party risks by automating some of the services normally done by TTPs and by engaging a community to perform other services. For an automation example, Bitcoin (and many blockchain applications that followed) rely on cryptographic private-public key pairs to verify account ownership; whoever is in possession of the private key is assumed to be the legitimate owner of the account[v] (explained more deeply in Chapter 3). Bitcoin's software easily verifies that only the person with the private key could have submitted a transaction from that account.

Validating transactions to prevent double spending was a bit trickier to solve without trusted third parties. Senders cannot be trusted to verify that they have enough cryptocurrency in their accounts to fund their transactions. An independent verifier is needed, but Nakamoto did not want to rely on traditional financial institutions to provide the validation. Here was Nakamoto's brilliant solution: reward other people in the network (called 'miners'[vi]) with newly issued bitcoins to validate all the recently submitted transactions. The economic incentives of the Bitcoin network motivate validators to play by the rules.[vii]

---

v 'Address' is a more accurate term, but for now, readers can think of a Bitcoin address as a bank account without the need of a bank.

vi The Bitcoin protocol is based on a gold mining metaphor. Just as gold miners *work* using physical resources to excavate gold from gold mines, bitcoin miners *work* using computer resources to release new bitcoins; Bitcoin, like gold, has a limited supply, making it a rare commodity. Just as it gets harder to mine gold as a gold mine is depleted, bitcoin releases fewer new digital coins over time.

vii Nakamoto (2008) wrote this about the economic incentives to motivative miners to behave honestly: *"If a greedy attacker is able to assemble more CPU power than all the honest nodes, he would have to choose between using it to defraud people by stealing back his payments, or using it to generate new coins. He ought to find it more profitable to play by the rules, such rules that favour him with more new coins than everyone else combined, than to undermine the system and the validity of his own wealth."*

Bookkeeping. We also have the ancient challenge of bookkeeping. We need a record for every transfer of value upon which all parties agree. Before an 'Internet of Value', every party manages its own systems of records (software and data, including ledgers that track debits and credits) or relies on a TTP. Parties, each with their own version of the transaction, must reconcile information about the transaction. Reconciliations are expensive and time-consuming. Once reconciled, there is nothing to prevent trading partners from modifying records after the fact; partners cannot be confident they are dealing with the same historical record of transactions through time. Therefore, we have millions of people with accounting skills working on processing everyday receipts and payables.

Nakamoto solved the bookkeeping problem by moving from party-level record keeping to shared record-keeping. The Bitcoin network maintains a digital ledger, called a *blockchain*, to serve as the universal bookkeeping record to track debits and credits (see Figure 1.5). Trading parties no longer need to reconcile records because every party agrees 'this is what transpired'.

The ledger is distributed to all the host computers (i.e., nodes) that run the Bitcoin network. Anyone can view the Bitcoin ledger using a Bitcoin explorer.[viii] There were over 14,000 public Bitcoin nodes (and many more private nodes) by 2021, each with its own identical copy of the ledger.[21] The nodes in the Bitcoin network constantly reconfirm the ledger to make sure no party tampers with the records after-the-fact. If anyone cheats, the other parties' nodes automatically ignore it.

---

viii For example, https://www.blockchain.com/explorer

Debit side: The sender sent a fraction of a bitcoin from this account (called an address)

Credit side: The receiver now has the value deposited in their account (called an address)

13XSrVkweo5Dzm3yuykFw4P63N63MA6bTd	0.19206072 BTC	➡	1HU1LDBXUg73f2ro2e2dB3XY8cFoYLFgZZ	0.18706072 BTC
Fee	0.00500000 BTC			

Miner's fee: The sender offered a fee to miners to add their transaction on the ledger

Figure 1.5: An example of a transaction stored on Bitcoin's public ledger

Medium of exchange

We also have the ancient problem of an acceptable medium of exchange. Money was invented over 10,000 years ago to facilitate trade. Money serves three functions: as medium of exchange for purchases and payment of debts; as a common measure of value; and as a store of value that aims to retain its worth over time. Primitive moneys included whale's teeth, shells, and stones. Metal coins were invented in about the 6th century BC and paper currency in about 1,000 AD.[22] Today, we have government-issued currencies, of which the United Nations recognizes 180 as legal tender.[23] Most sovereign currencies are now *fiat*, backed solely on the promises of governments rather than by gold reserves as was common in the past.

Granted, fiat currencies have several advantages. Fiat currencies have defined laws and regulations, so individuals and enterprises know how to be compliant when using them. Many currencies are reasonable stable stores of value that hold their worth over time (of course there are exceptions like the Venezuelan bolívar fuerte). People understand fiat currencies as a unit of measure; if a soda costs $1.25, you have a mental model of its value. However, fiat currencies have several disadvantages. Governments can mint fiat money at will, causing inflation and can change regulations on a whim (see

Nakamoto's quote above). Governments can also freeze, seize, or restrict access to one's assets.[24] Criminals can counterfeit currencies, and according to one website, the most counterfeited currencies are the Chinese yuan, United States dollar, United Kingdom pound, Indian rupee, New Zealand dollar, and Mexican peso.[25]

Rather than using a government-issued currency, Nakamoto created a new *cryptocurrency*—a digital currency secured by cryptography[26] that makes it nearly impossible to counterfeit. Moreover, Bitcoin's monetary policies are programmed in the software. Specifically, Bitcoin's software capped the total monetary supply at 21 million bitcoins; scarcity contributes to Bitcoin's value. Bitcoin has an automatic monetary distribution schedule. The last bitcoin will be released in the year 2140.[27]

Cybersecurity

Lastly, cybersecurity is a newer problem that needs to be overcome to realize the 'Internet of Value'. If we are sending value over the Internet, how do we prevent someone from stealing it? Or stealing our identity? Today, individuals rely on Internet providers, financial institutions, software providers, retailers, and other institutions with whom they transact to protect their identities and assets. Enterprises either secure their own information technology (IT) perimeters or outsource to a TTP. It's a daunting task for whoever is responsible for cybersecurity. Scams included 'phishing', where a cyber thief poses as somebody you trust; tech support fraud, where someone pretends to be from an IT department and needs access to your account; extortion, where someone seizes control of your digital assets and demands a ransom; and payroll diversion, where someone hijacks your paycheck and deposits it in their account. According to the US Federal Bureau of Investigation (FBI), cybercrime cost victims $4.2 billion in losses in 2020.[28] Attacks keep getting more widespread and dangerous. The 2020 Russian government-sponsored SolarWinds attack cost governments and businesses nearly $100 billion.[29]

Bitcoin uses several sophisticated algorithms to secure the data and the network. Readers will learn about private-public-key pairs, hashing algorithms, and consensus algorithms used to secure the data stored on the blockchain ledger in Chapter 3.

Bitcoin's legacy

Bitcoin is important because it is the most visible on-going, live experiment for an open, public, secure, non-governmental, and non-TTP reliant application, pointing us towards an 'Internet of Value'. All are welcome to participate. Millions of people use it—over 100 million Bitcoin wallets have been created.[30] Tens of thousands of people help secure it by being miners. Bitcoin proves that the 'Internet of Value' is technically feasible and that a shared digital ledger is highly secure.

However, Bitcoin, like all innovations, has limitations and there is room for improvement. Bitcoin has a higher price volatility compared to other major fiat currencies, leading to innovations like stable coins. (Although our friend Professor Dan Conway counters that Bitcoin is completely stable, it's the US dollar that fluctuates wildly!) Bitcoin has limited functionality—it is just a payment system to send and receive bitcoins; it cannot do much else. Ethereum, Cardano, Polkadot, Solana, and other blockchain platforms overcame this limitation by allowing users to build and operate their own decentralized applications. Bitcoin is rather pokey, only capable of processing about two to six transactions per second (TPS). Innovations in 'layer 2' solutions that run on top of Bitcoin (and other platforms) speed processing and reduce transaction fees. Bitcoin is not user-friendly, so most people end up relying on a trusted third party anyway, called an exchange, to transfer their bitcoins. Bitcoin's protocol, called proof-of-work, is highly secure, but the miners who operate computers to secure the Bitcoin network consume *a lot* of electricity. New protocols are more energy efficient, like proof-of-stake. Bitcoin was designed as a standalone application, which is a long way off from a seamless, interoperable 'Internet of Value'. Interoperability solutions aim to connect blockchain networks. In this book, readers will learn about these innovations and more. Bitcoin started it all.

To summarize, Bitcoin was the first application that restored trust in economic exchanges of value without relying on governments and corporations. Bitcoin accomplishes this feat with a decentralized technology architecture, i.e., a blockchain, and with decentralized human control via the miners. While Nakamoto was working on Bitcoin, a separate community was working on self-sovereign identity (SSI).

1.5. From centralized/federated Internet identity models to SSI

We noted that the Internet was designed without an identity layer. TCP/IP provides a way to identify the machines connected to the Internet, but the standards do not verify the individuals or organizations who are sending messages from those machines.

Governments and organizations needed to know who is using devices, leading us to the first era of identity on the Internet, known as the **centralized identity model** (see Figure 1.6). Centralized identity models are account based, requiring users to create logon IDs and passwords. Accounts and passwords date back to the 1960s when multiple people were sharing the same computer.[31] It has several limitations. Most crucially, the centralized model gives institutions control over a user's credentials.[32] Even when users 'delete' an account, all they have done is revoke their access privileges, as it is up to the institutions to decide when an account is deleted from their databases. This also means that our credentials are not portable across webpages. The proliferation of accounts and passwords is another limitation of the centralized model. By 2015, the average United Kingdom (U.K.) Internet user had 118 online accounts; by 2017, the average United States (U.S.) Internet user had 150 online accounts.[33] Beyond the users' inconveniences, governments and organizations also spend a vast number of resources managing accounts and passwords. According to a 2020 report, a single password reset costs, on average, $70.[34]

More recently, some organizations invite users to access multiple sites through a single account managed by companies such as Facebook, Google, Amazon, LinkedIn, and others (see Figure 1.6), called the **federated identity model**. While the federated model reduces the number of accounts users need to manage, it creates larger attack surfaces. One of the reasons that the SolarWinds attack was so widespread was because hackers stole federated logon credentials to access many systems. Federated accounts also increase institutional power over users' data and monetize user data for their own advantage.

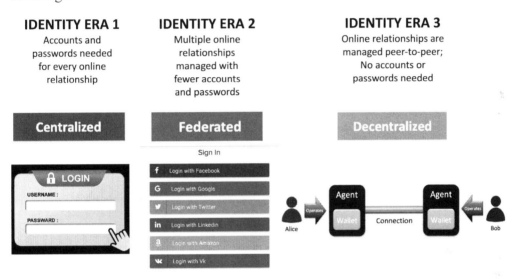

Figure 1.6: Three eras of identity on the Internet

Source: Adapted from Preukschat and Reed (2021)

An account to establish online identity is only one type of credential. Most individuals have many credentials.[ix] Governments, for example, issue credentials about an individual's legal name, citizenship, and legal status by issuing birth certificates, passports, and marriage licenses. Another example: universities, medical associations, and hospitals issue a medical doctor's credentials about someone's qualifications (e.g., an academic medical degree), competencies (e.g., infectious diseases specialist), access rights (e.g., permission to access the hospital's dispensary), or authorizations (e.g., authority to perform surgeries).

---

ix **Credentials**: attestations made by authorized issuers about subjects.

Many people believe there is a better way to establish identities and credentials, leading us to the third identity era on the Internet: the **decentralized identity model** for self-sovereign identity (SSI).[x] SSI aims to empower individuals to control their own identities/credentials, thus the term 'self-sovereign'. SSI aims to provide a way for more people who currently lack identities to prove their residency, skills, and experiences. It offers a new way to prevent hackers from stealing credentials (i.e., identity theft). SSI replaces usernames and passwords with peer-to-peer relationships and provides verification of credentials within seconds. Blockchains play a role in SSI, primarily by becoming the public key infrastructure (PKI) for verifying that only authorized parties can create, hold, and verify credentials. We devote all of Chapter 8 to the SSI model and its first applications.

1.6. From 'surveillance capitalism' to individual ownership and monetization

"Remember the Golden Rule. Whoever has the gold makes the rules."

Brant Parker and Johnny Hart, *Wizard of Id*[35]

We noted that institutions control the Internet. Besides owning and controlling our economic activities and identities via accounts and passwords, giant tech companies own and monetize our data. It turns out that our online activities are incredibly valuable. Billions of individuals knowingly and willingly trade their data for free services, without realizing the extent to which they are being monitored and manipulated. Company's algorithms watch and process what we do to make predictions on our behaviors, such as what we will purchase, and sell this knowledge to advertisers.

---

[x] We must clarify the term '**identity**'. Scholars from the many disciplines, such as philosophy, ethics, psychology, and sociology, consider 'identity' to be an inalienable human right, a psychological construct defined by self, and/or a social construct defined by one's social groups. From these perspectives, governments and organizations do not provide individuals with identities. Instead, governments and organizations provide individuals with credentials. A better labeling of the SSI movement, in our opinion, is 'self-sovereign *credentials*' (or to be more accurate, 'self-sovereign *verifiable credentials*'), but alas, SSI is the entrenched term, and we shall proceed with that nomenclature.

Shoshana Zuboff, Harvard Business School Professor, coined the term, 'surveillance capitalism' to describe how companies use our data for the sole purpose of making a profit. She believes that surveillance capitalism is an existential threat to our human liberty, autonomy, and well-being. In her book, titled ***The age of Surveillance Capitalism: the fight for a human future at the new frontier of power***, she wrote, *"The stakes could not be higher: a global architecture of behavior modification threatens human nature… the focus has shifted from machines that overcome the limits of our bodies to machines that modify the behavior of individuals, groups, and populations in the service of market objectives."*[36]

Algorithms have also been used to manipulate our beliefs and behaviors, such as spreading false news on social media to manipulate election outcomes. For example, the British political consulting firm, Cambridge Analytica, was hired by major politicians to manipulate voters, primarily by posting 'fake news', defined as the deliberate spread of verifiably false information.[37] The *Independent* reported in 2020 that Brittany Kaiser, prior business development director of Cambridge Analytica, claimed that the elections in at least 68 countries included many of the same disinformation tactics seen during the US presidential election and the UK's Brexit vote in 2016.[38]

Zuboff believes we need better answers to the questions: Who gets to know? Who gets to decide? Who decides who decides? She sees a reclamation of democracy as the antidote. Other people believe laws and regulations are the antidote. For example, Scott Galloway, Professor of Marketing at New York University, believes the US government should apply antitrust laws to break up tech giants.[39]

Blockchain-based solutions are also options to address some of these issues. On the topic of fake news, ANSAcheck provides a first important step against fake news by preventing imposter news, a type of fake news story that appears to be from a legitimate news agency. Developed by Agenzia Nazionale Stampa Associata (ANSA)—Italy's top news wire service—and Ernst & Young, the solution posts stories to the Ethereum blockchain so that readers can verify that the story came from ANSA. ANSAcheck is covered in Chapter 9.

The Brave web browser serves as an example of shifting a high percentage of advertising revenues from tech platforms to individuals. Brave blocks all advertising and web tracking, but users can activate a feature that directly compensates them for watching adds online. Users can earn 'basic attention tokens', called BAT, a cryptocurrency that runs on Ethereum. Advertisers purchase BAT to upload advertisements to the Brave platform. When a user watches an add, 70 percent of the BAT that the advertiser paid for is transferred to a user's digital wallet and 30 percent goes to the Brave Software, the company that owns the platform. Figure 1.7 shows that after downloading and configuring the Brave browser, the user earned .01 BAT for clicking on a webpage, worth a bit over one cent in US dollars.[40] In 2021, the *New York Times* rated the Brave web browser as the best privacy browser.[41] By year end 2021, Brave had 46 million monthly users and advertisers from 187 countries.[42]

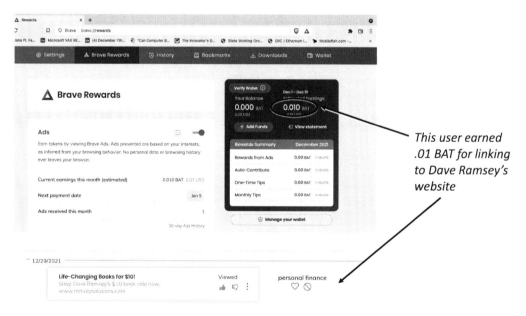

This user earned .01 BAT for linking to Dave Ramsey's website

Figure 1.7: The Brave web browser compensates users for paying attention to advertisements

1.7. Conclusion

Trust is the foundation for well-functioning societies, yet global surveys show high levels of distrust for governments and institutions. We have argued that the decentralization of economic and social activities is a way to restore global trust, and that blockchains can serve as the digital infrastructure. We have also made a crucial distinction between the technology decentralization and the decentralization of the governance of technology. Blockchain technology is decentralized because each computer node in the network is a peer, with no single computer in charge. Blockchain governance may or may not be decentralized; each blockchain network has its own governance mechanism. In the next chapter, we explore the governance of the technology more closely.

Citations

[1] Quote is from: https://satoshi.nakamotoinstitute.org/posts/p2pfoundation/1/

[2] Lewicki, Roy J., et al. "Trust and Distrust: New Relationships and Realities." *The Academy of Management Review*, vol. 23, no. 3, Academy of Management, 1998, pp. 438–58, https://doi.org/10.2307/259288.

[3] Scheutz, S., Steelman, Z., Kuai, L., and Lacity, M. (2022). Trust in the IT artifact: a systematic review. University of Arkansas working paper.

[4] Scholars view trust and distrust as distinct social constructs. Low distrust is not equivalent to high trust. Low distrust may be characterized by low levels of fear, skepticism, or cynicism whereas high levels of trust are characterized by high levels of hope, faith, and confidence. See Lewicki, Roy J., et al. "Trust and Distrust: New Relationships and Realities." *The Academy of Management Review*, vol. 23, no. 3, Academy of Management, 1998, pp. 438–58, https://doi.org/10.2307/259288.

[5] Scheutz, S., Steelman, Z., Kuai, L., and Lacity, M. (2022). Trust in the IT artifact: a systematic review. University of Arkansas working paper.

[6] Esteban Ortiz-Ospina and Max Roser (2016) - "Trust". Published online at OurWorldInData.org. Retrieved from: 'https://ourworldindata.org/trust' [Online Resource]

[7] Esteban Ortiz-Ospina and Max Roser (2016) - "Trust". Published online at OurWorldInData.org. Retrieved from: 'https://ourworldindata.org/trust' [Online Resource]

[8] Buterin, V. (2017). The meaning of decentralization. https://medium.com/@VitalikButerin/the-meaning-of-decentralization-a0c92b76a274

[9] CNN. NYU professor's warning about Facebook's cryptocurrency. https://edition.cnn.com/videos/tech/2019/07/08/galloway-facebook-libra-cryptocurrency-buyer-beware-first-move-sot.cnn

[10] https://en.wikipedia.org/wiki/Web3

[11] These are recommended resources for history of computers, the Internet and social media:

Campbell-Kelly, M., & Garcia-Swartz, D. (2013). The history of the internet: The missing narratives. Journal of Information Technology, 28(1), 18-33.

Netflix documentary, The Social Dilemma, https://www.netflix.com/title/81254224

Professor Michael Parks, University of Houston: http://auckland.bauer.uh.edu/students/parks/phoundry/phoundry.htm

[12] According to Markoff (2005), the first e-commerce transaction occurred on ARPANET in 1972 for the purchase of marijuana by a Stanford university student. Markoff, J. (2005). What the Dormouse Said, Penguin Publishing, New York.

[13] https://en.wikipedia.org/wiki/Online_banking

[14] Insider Intelligence (2021). Worldwide ecommerce will approach $5 trillion this year. https://www.emarketer.com/content/worldwide-ecommerce-will-approach-5-trillion-this-year

GlobalNewswire (2021). Business-to-Business (B2B) E-commerce Market Size. https://www.globenewswire.com/news-release/2021/11/02/2325466/0/en/Business-to-Business-B2B-E-commerce-Market-Size-to-Grow-Over-18-70-CAGR-to-Reach-USD-18-57-Trillion-by-2026-Globally-Facts-Factors.html

[15] Bernard Marr, How Much Data Do We Create Every Day? The Mind-Blowing Stats Everyone Should Read, https://bernardmarr.com/how-much-data-do-we-create-every-day-the-mind-blowing-stats-everyone-should-read/

[16] Nakamoto, S. (2008). Bitcoin: A Peer-to-Peer Electronic Cash System. p. 1. https://bitcoin.org/bitcoin.pdf

[17] Lacity, M. (2018). *A Manager's Guide to Blockchain for Business: From Knowing What to Knowing How*, SB Publishing, Stratford-Upon-Avon.

[18] Before Bitcoin, there were other digital cash ideas and experiments. Nick Szabo, the inventor of smart contracts, conceived of decentralized digital cash in 1998 as 'Bit Gold' (Szabo 1998), but it was not implemented. David Chaum launched DigiCash in 1990—the first live cryptocurrency of significance. While an important breakthrough, DigiCash was centrally controlled in that the company's system performed the validations. Nakamoto (2008) synthesized several innovations, such as the idea of a public ledger by Wei Dai; timestamping by Massias et al., Haber and Stornetta, and Bayer et al.); cryptographic Merkle trees for security by Professor Merkle; digital currencies like Hashcash by Back, and proof-of-work consensus to keep copies of the public ledger in sync by Dwork and Naor. Nakamoto brought these prior inventions together to create a peer-to-peer payment application.

See:

Back, A. (2002). "Hashcash - a denial of service counter-measure," http://www.hashcash.org/papers/hashcash.pdf.

Chaum, D. (1982). Computer Systems Established, Maintained and Trusted by Mutually Suspicious Groups, University of California, Berkeley.

Dai, W. (1998). "b-money," http://www.weidai.com/bmoney.txt

Dwork, C., and Naor, M. (1993), Pricing via processing: Combatting Junk Mail, Retrieved September 18, 2021 from http://www.hashcash.org/papers/pvp.pdf

Haber, S. and Stornetta, W. (1991). "How to time-stamp a digital document," Journal of Cryptology, 3(2), pp. 99-111, 1991.

Haber, S. and Stornetta, W. (1997). "Secure names for bit-strings," In Proceedings of the 4th ACM Conference on Computer and Communications Security, pp. 28-35

Massias, H., Avila, X. and J.-J. Quisquater, "Design of a secure timestamping service with minimal trust requirements," In 20th Symposium on Information Theory in the Benelux, May 1999.

Merkle, R. (1980). "Protocols for public key cryptosystems," In Proc. 1980 Symposium on Security and Privacy, IEEE Computer Society, pp. 122-133.

[19] Nakamoto, S. (2008). Bitcoin: A Peer-to-Peer Electronic Cash System. p. 1. https://bitcoin.org/bitcoin.pdf

[20] The World Bank estimated that sending remittances cost an average of 7.99 percent of the amount sent; "Navigating the world of cross-border payments," http://www.iqpc.com/media/1003982/57107.pdf

The administrative costs for tracking containers in the global supply chain was roughly 22 percent of the retail costs according to Anderson, J., & Van Wincoop, E. (2004). Trade Costs. *Journal of Economic Literature, 42*(3), 691-751. Retrieved from http://www.jstor.org/stable/3217249

[21] The actual number of Bitcoin nodes is difficult to track because some nodes operate behind fire walls. This site tracks 'reachable' nodes: https://bitnodes.earn.com/

[22] https://en.wikipedia.org/wiki/History_of_money

[23] Sawe, B. (2018). How Many Currencies Exist in the World? *WorldAtlas,* worldatlas.com/articles/how-many-currencies-are-in-the-world.html.

[24] For example, the Greek banks would not allow account holders to withdraw more than 60 euros a day in 2015; Associated Press (June 28, 2015), "The Latest: Strict limits on bank withdrawals will not apply to foreign credit cards," *US News,* https://www.usnews.com/news/business/articles/2015/06/28/the-latest-greece-wants-ecb-to-keep-giving-emergency-help

[25] April 6, 2018. The world's most counterfeited currencies, https://www.lovemoney.com/www.lovemoney.com

[26] *Cryptography* is "a method of protecting information and communications through the use of codes so that only those for whom the information is intended can read and process it" https://searchsecurity.techtarget.com/definition/cryptography

[27] https://en.bitcoin.it/wiki/Controlled_supply

[28] US Federal Bureau of Investigation (2021). Internet Crime Report, https://www.ic3.gov/Media/PDF/AnnualReport/2020_IC3Report.pdf

[29] Combs, V. (June 28, 2021). Cybersecurity study: SolarWinds attack cost affected companies an average of $12 million, TechRepublic https://www.techrepublic.com/article/cybersecurity-study-solarwinds-attack-cost-affected-companies-an-average-of-12-million/

[30] Mitchell, E. (2021). How Many People Use Bitcoin in 2021? https://www.bitcoinmarketjournal.com/how-many-people-use-bitcoin/

[31] For a history of accounts and passwords, see: McMillan, R. (2012). The World's First Computer Password? It Was Useless Too, Wired Magazine, https://www.wired.com/2012/01/computer-password/.

[32] Preukschat, A. and Reed, D. (2021). *Self-Sovereign Identity: Decentralized digital identity and verifiable credentials*. Manning Publications, Shelter Island.

[33] See:

   Allen, C. (2016). The Path to Self-Sovereign Identity. Retrieved July 12, 2021 from http://www.lifewithalacrity.com/2016/04/the-path-to-self-soverereign-identity.html

   Caruthers, M. (2018). World Password Day: How to Improve Your Passwords. Dashlane Tech News. Retrieved July 10, 2021 from https://blog.dashlane.com/world-password-day/

[34] Douglas, A. (2020). Are Password Resets Costing Your Company? Retrieved November 3, 2021 from https://www.bioconnect.com/are-password-resets-costing-your-company/

[35] From the Wizard of Id comic strip, "Remember the Golden Rule," 1964. https://economicsociology.org/2015/08/28/remember-the-golden-rule-whoever-has-the-gold-makes-the-rules/

[36] Zuboff, S. (2019) The Age of Surveillance Capitalism. New York: Public Affairs

[37] Zuboff, S. (2019) *The Age of Surveillance Capitalism*. New York: Public Affairs.

[38] Wood V (2020) Fake news worse during election campaign than Brexit referendum, whistleblower says. *The Independent*, 27 January. Available at: www.independent.co.uk/news/uk/politics/brexit-fake-news-2019-election-facebook-cambridge-analytica-brittany-kaisar-eu-referendum-a9304821.html (accessed 6 April 2021).

[39] Galloway, S. (2017). The Four: The Hidden DNA of Amazon, Apple, Facebook, and Google. New York: Portfolio/Penguin.

[40] The value of BAT may be monitored here: https://coinmarketcap.com/currencies/basic-attention-token/markets/

[41] Chen, B. (March 31, 2021). "If You Care About Privacy, It's Time to Try a New Web Browser". *The New York Times*.

[42] Brave's platform statistics and token activity may be found at https://brave.com/transparency/

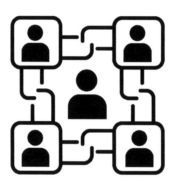

Chapter 2

Blockchain Governance: Who's the Boss?

What's inside: While a blockchain architecture is decentralized, the governance of a blockchain may or may not be decentralized. In this chapter, we examine decision-making rights over blockchains—the humans who have power to make decisions. By the end of this chapter, readers will have a deeper understanding of the many decisions to be made, the eight governance models designed to make them, and how trade happens before and after a blockchain-based solution.

Learning objectives:

- Compare the benefits and risks of (de)centralized governance
- Identify eight governance models and provide one example of each
- Describe the complexity of governance decisions
- Explain how partners transact before and after a shared blockchain application

2.1. Good boss, bad boss

You've likely been assigned to team projects in school or at work. The team is supposed to work together to accomplish a goal. Which teams were successful, and why were they successful? Which teams struggled, and why? Reflect on your answers by grounding them in the context of decentralization (a team with no leader) and centralization (a team with a leader).

Decentralization disperses the performance of activities and the power over decisions to the many. Teams that are truly peer-to-peer lack a leader; no one is the 'boss'. Everyone has autonomy and an equal opportunity to contribute their opinions, gifts, and talents. The major benefits of decentralization include low abuses of power, more inclusive participation, unity around decisions when everyone votes, individual freedom to act according to one's will, and privacy to act without being monitored (see right side of Figure 2.1). While these benefits are obvious, there are downsides to consider.

Teams with no leaders, i.e., with no centralized control, can result in an absence of a shared vision on what should be done, decisions can take a long time to be agreed upon, efforts may be duplicated, slackers may slow progress, and the team may find it difficult to assemble the fragmented works of individuals into a coherent whole.[1] Think of an orchestra without a conductor—how can the musicians stay synchronized?

Teams with a competent leader—that is, with a bit of centralized control—can often make decisions faster; progress work faster (quick execution); efficiently allocate work to avoid duplication of effort (high efficiency); punish slackers—or better yet, inspire them to meaningfully contribute; and provide clear control and accountability. Team members have someone to rely upon to take responsibility for the overall success of the team. These are the benefits of centralization under a competent leader (see left side of Figure 2.1).

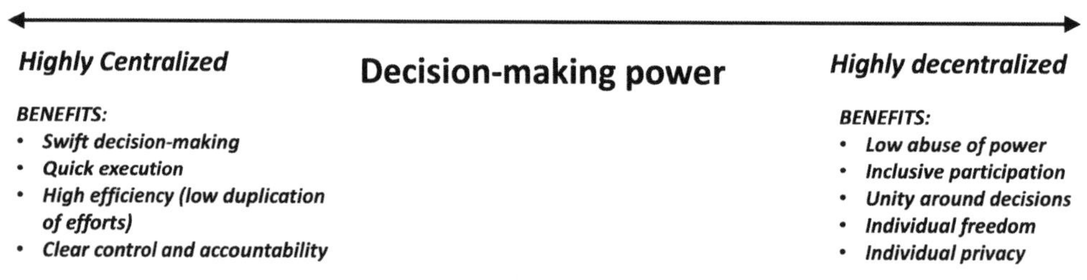

	Decision-making power	
Highly Centralized		*Highly decentralized*
BENEFITS:		*BENEFITS:*
• *Swift decision-making*		• *Low abuse of power*
• *Quick execution*		• *Inclusive participation*
• *High efficiency (low duplication of efforts)*		• *Unity around decisions*
• *Clear control and accountability*		• *Individual freedom*
		• *Individual privacy*

Figure 2.1: The benefits of centralized and decentralized decision-making power

So which is better, a team with or without a leader? The answer reverts to our calculus of trust. If you, (subject A), have confident positive expectations that a leader (object B) will fulfil her obligations to act in the overall best interests of the team (context C) for this project (limit L), your team is better off with a leader. If you don't trust someone to lead, you are better off keeping control decentralized.

Centralization runs aground when leaders abuse power; pursue their own interests at the expense of others; exclude participation from individuals who do not agree with them (no inclusivity); stifle opinions (no unity around decision); crush the will and actions of others (lack of freedom); and invade their privacy though over-monitoring. These are the major concerns expressed by the global blockchain community, and why, on balance, many open-source communities favor decentralization—not only of the network architecture, but of the governance as well. In contrast, some communities (often governments and business enterprises), favor more centralized governance.

In summary, centralization and decentralization of decision-making power have benefits and downsides. We are now ready to apply the learning to the specific context of blockchains.

2.2. Blockchain governance models

Blockchain governance defines the decision-making rights pertaining to a blockchain-enabled solution. Decision making rights might be held by benevolent dictatorships; oligarchies; stakeocracies; federations; representative meritocracies; meritocracies; and/or democracies. These governance models have varying degrees of (de)centralization, and as we learned in Figure 2.1, offer various benefits and risks. In Figure 2.2, we map eight blockchain governance models along the decision-making power continuum. Thus, a benevolent dictator who controls everything is the most centralized blockchain governance model; a democracy where every person gets an equal vote is the most decentralized. Each governance model is described below and in Table 2.1.

Figure 2.2: Blockchain Governance Models

A **benevolent dictator** is single person or single organization that solely holds decision making rights. The community must trust the person or organization to make decisions based on the best interests of the community. Initially, Satoshi Nakamoto over the Bitcoin whitepaper and Bitcoin Core, and Vitalik Buterin over the idea for Ethereum, are examples of benevolent dictators over public blockchains.[2] These projects succeeded because the earliest of adopters—typically other like-minded coders—trusted the founders' intentions, even in the interesting case of Bitcoin where the identity of Nakamoto isn't known. Nathanial Popper, reporter for the *New York Times*, wrote, *"Satoshi's anonymity, if anything, seemed to increase the level of faith in the system. The anonymity suggested that Bitcoin was not created by a person seeking personal fame or success."*[3] As we will see, these benevolent dictators moved quickly to disperse their powers.

Traditional enterprises prefer to call this governance model a **neutral facilitator** or **founder-led** model. For example, Chronicled founded MediLedger in 2017, a blockchain-enabled platform for the pharmaceutical sector designed to comply with drug regulations enacted in the United States, Europe, Asia and South America. Chronicled is the neutral facilitator over MediLedger. Susanne Somerville, CEO of Chronicled and co-founder of MediLedger, said, *"A neutral facilitator, who can establish trust among parties, can serve as a benevolent dictator—at least initially—because they are incentivized to solve the problem for everyone."*

Governance model	Who has voting/decision rights?	Blockchain examples
Benevolent Dictator	A single person holds decision making rights, even when seeking input from others	• Initially, Satoshi Nakamoto, over the Bitcoin whitepaper and Bitcoin Core • Initially, Vitalik Buterin over the idea for Ethereum • Initially, Chronicled over MediLedger
Oligarchy	A few people or institutions hold decision making rights, even when seeking input from others	• Satoshi Nakamoto willingly gave Martti Malmi and Gavin Andresen access rights to update Bitcoin's website and source code • Buterin cofounded Ethereum with Mihai Alisie, Amir Chetrit, Charles Hoskinson, and Anthony Di Iorio, and soon brought on Joseph Lubin, Gavin Wood, and Jeffrey Wilke[4] • we.tade was founded and launched by a consortium of European banks
Stakeocracy	'Pay to Play'; People/institutions' votes are weighted by the size of their investment	• The Libra Association initially referred to its decision-making process as 'proportional power', where voting powers of the council will be proportional to their stake. The initiative was rebranded as the Diem Association; It sold its assets to Silvergate Bank in 2022.
Federation	Decentralized groups specialize on parts of the project while coordinating with a central group	• The Hyperledger Foundation's overarching structure is a set of specialized projects
Representative Meritocracy	People/institutions who have proven their merit are eligible to be elected to a council based on votes from other meritorious members	• The Hyperledger Foundation's Technical Steering Committee is governed by 15 elected people from a pool of active contributors
Meritocracy	Power is held by people based on one's ability	• The Bitcoin community (miners, developers, and investors) vote on Bitcoin Improvement Proposals (BIPs) based on the merit of the proposal • The Ethereum community votes on Ethereum Improvement Proposals (EIPs)
Democracy	Any participant can vote	• Bitcoin and Ethereum miners 'vote' by either installing or failing to install changes to the source code
Steering/ Advisory Committee	Committees typically support other governance structures by providing advice and guidance	• IBM Food Trust has an Advisory Board • MedliLedger uses Steering Committees, one for each solution

Table 2.1: Blockchain Governance Models

Blockchain Governance: Who's the Boss?

If launched by a few partners, blockchain governance likely begins as an **oligarchy,** where power rests with a few. Both Bitcoin and Ethereum quickly moved from benevolent dictators to oligarchies. Satoshi Nakamoto willingly gave Martti Malmi and Gavin Andresen access rights to update Bitcoin's website and source code. In April of 2011, Nakamoto walked away from Bitcoin by sending an email that read, *"I've moved on to other things"* and that Bitcoin was in good hands.[5] Buterin cofounded Ethereum with Mihai Alisie, Amir Chetrit, Charles Hoskinson, and Anthony Di Iorio, and soon brought on Joseph Lubin, Gavin Wood, and Jeffrey Wilke.

Most private blockchains are being developed by a core group of companies, sometimes referred to as the 'minimal viable ecosystem' (MVE). By its very nature, an oligarchy represents a negotiated treaty among the founding partners, maximizing their shared benefits. These partners—often comprising competitors as well as trading partners—form an entity charged with developing and enforcing the rules for the initiative. we.trade, a blockchain-enabled platform for trade finance, is one example. It began as an agreement among seven banks to build a minimal viable product (MVP). They eventually added members and launched a joint venture in 2018. (Chapter 6 provides a more detailed case description of we.trade.)

'Staked' oligarchies, which we call **'stakeocracies',** is a governance model where people pay to become part of the oligarchy. The Libra Association, which was initiated by Facebook in 2019, was an example. Council members (initially 28 firms) were expected to buy *at least* $10 million in Libra Investment Tokens. The Libra Association referred to its decision-making process as 'proportional power', where voting powers of the council would be proportional to their stake, but with a cap to prevent an overtaking of the association.[6] By 2020, the Libra Association lost some of its founding members— including PayPal, Mastercard, eBay, and Vodafone—after regulators expressed deep concerns, particularly over Facebook's influence as the initiator of the project. Many people were also concerned that Calibra (Facebook's digital wallet for libra coins) would have an unfair competitive advantage.[7] In December of 2020, the Libra Association was changed to the Diem Association to distance the project from Facebook.[8] The Diem Association was a member-based association *"dedicated to building a blockchain-based payment system that supports financial innovation, inclusion, and integrity"*.[9] The Diem Association was governed by the Diem Association Council, with one representative per member. At the start of January 2022, the Council had 26 members, but it disbanded and sold its assets later that month. (Facebook, by the way, changed its wallet's name from Calibra to Novi in May of 2020 and the company name to Meta in November 2021.[10])

Federations allow decentralized groups to specialize on parts of the project while coordinating with a central group to integrate solutions. The Hyperledger Foundation's overarching structure is a set of specialized projects. However, the Hyperledger Foundation's Technical Steering Committee is governed by what can be called a **representative meritocracy**, where people have to prove their merit to be eligible for election to a committee based on votes from other meritorious members. Working group leaders for Hyperledger's projects submit the names of the active contributors and all active participants vote to elect the 15 leaders. The 15-person Technical Steering Committee has decision rights over the admission of new projects, rules over projects, and status of projects (incubation/active).[11]

With a **meritocracy,** power is held by people based on their ability and goodwill. The aim is to elicit multiple views from informed stakeholders, debate views in open forums, and then stress-test ideas to find the best solution. Anyone, for example, can propose ideas to improve Bitcoin by submitting a Bitcoin Improvement Proposal (BIP). The whole Bitcoin community (miners, developers, and investors) can vote on the proposal based on its merit. By 2022, 386 BIPs had been submitted, of which 41 had been finalized.[12] Bitcoin.org helps to coordinate the community's efforts. Ethereum runs a similar process. People can suggest Ethereum Improvement Proposals (EIPs) for the Ethereum platform, including core protocol specifications, client application programming interfaces (APIs), token standards, and contract standards. By 2022, over 400 EIPs had been submitted, with 80 finalized. Ethereum.org helps with coordination.

A **democracy** is the most decentralized form of governance, where one participant each gets one vote. That's why many people like the fact that Bitcoin and Ethereum miners 'vote' by either installing or failing to install changes to the source code. Focusing on Bitcoin, once proposals are reviewed and supported by Bitcoin developers, miners may be asked to vote using the following process: *"The proposal itself typically sets the requirements for agreement and adoption. For example, the proposal may say that a certain change requires the approval from a super-majority of miners (a typical number is 95%) during a given period (measured in blocks). Miners signal their support for a proposal by adding a line to the blocks they solve. Once the threshold is achieved, the proposal is said to be locked in, and it is activated at a predetermined later date."[13]* However, a miner's vote is non-committal. It's more akin to a political pole as to how one intends to vole in an election. *"It is possible for proposals to secure support from many miners and still be dropped. An example was the 2017 proposal called SegWit2x, which secured support from 100% of miners but was later dropped due to lack of consensus among different Bitcoin stakeholders."[14]*

In addition to the governance structures covered above, enterprise blockchains often use a **steering committee** or an **advisory committee.** These committees may or may not have decision-making rights, but are nonetheless influential in guiding, recommending, and providing expertise on the development of the blockchain. Often used in conjunction with centralized governance structures, steering/advisory committees help ensure that decisions are transparent (at least to the members). The IBM Food Trust and MediLedger rely on such committees for direction.

The IBM Food Trust is a blockchain platform for global food supply. It was commercially available in October of 2018. It aims to improve food safety, food freshness, and supply chain efficiency while reducing food fraud and food waste. The IBM Food Trust has an advisory council. The first nine members were Walmart; Dole; Nestlé; Kroger; Carrefour; Danone; Driscoll's; Golden State Foods (GFS); and GS1. According to its website: *"An Advisory Council comprised of a range of industry representatives helps set the rules of engagement for the blockchain community, ensuring that the solution benefits all."*[15] Council members *"share, learn, discuss, prioritize and address the opportunities and challenges relevant to the food industry globally. They actively learn from each other and the market to provide meaningful direction to IBM Food Trust."*[16]

MediLedger has a steering committee that serves as the final word on any issue that could not be resolved with working teams, project managers, or the network owner. So, in this example, the steering committee *does* have decision-making rights.[17]

Within a blockchain-based solution, some decisions might be governed with one model and other decisions governed by another, forming a **governance portfolio.** For example, a steering committee might oversee data policies while a neutral facilitator oversees validation nodes. Moreover, the governance portfolio will likely evolve over time. Most blockchain-enabled applications/platforms/projects are launched by one entity or by a few partners. Initially, the founder or founding partners have full control over the suite of governance decisions, mainly because there is no one else to delegate power to yet. If governance remains centralized as is often the case with private blockchains, it needs to be trusted and transparent to the other participants. As we saw with Bitcoin and Ethereum, founders of public blockchains typically aim to disperse power quickly.

We have covered eight governance models, but what exactly are they governing? Next, we explore the types of decisions that need to be made in a blockchain network.

2.3. Blockchain governance decisions

"Distributed ledgers present a dual challenge for companies, one that is arguably 20 percent technological and 80 percent governance."

Marie Wieck, former General Manager, IBM Blockchain[18]

For an entire blockchain ecosystem, the scope of human influence and decision-making rights is complex. Some of the major governance decisions include the mission/vision; the funding model; rights of participation; rights of validation; rights of overrides; governance residence; rights around data and business rules; software license management; software version control; regulatory compliance, and legal liability. No wonder Marie Weick (see quote above) stated that governance, at least for most companies, takes 80 percent of the effort! For our purposes, we cover just six areas:

1. **Mission/vision:** What is the mission/value of the blockchain-based solution?
2. **Funding model:** How is software development and operations paid for?
3. **Rights of participation:** Who can submit transactions?
4. **Rights of validation:** Who is allowed to operate the validator nodes in the network?
5. **Rights of overrides:** Who is authorized to roll back the ledger in the instance of egregious errors?
6. **Governance residence:** What governance, if any, is on chain so that majority-rule decisions are automatically adopted verses off-chain governance that requires human negotiation?

2.3.1. Mission

A formal mission statement should express the aspirations and values of the blockchain. A blockchain's mission should be used to guide governance choices. Furthermore, a compelling mission can keep members engaged—particularly when facing significant obstacles—and can inspire others to join the network. In general, *a mission should appeal to a greater good beyond the founders.* Table 2.2 includes examples of blockchain mission statements.

Blockchain	Description	Mission
Bitcoin.org	Bitcoin.org was originally registered and owned by Bitcoin's first two developers, Satoshi Nakamoto and Martti Malmi. Today it is an independent open-source project with contributors from around the world.	• Inform users to protect them from common mistakes. • Give an accurate description of Bitcoin properties, potential uses and limitations. • Display transparent alerts and events regarding the Bitcoin network. • Invite talented humans to help with Bitcoin development at many levels. • Provide visibility to the large-scale Bitcoin ecosystem. • Improve Bitcoin worldwide accessibility with internationalization. • Remain a neutral informative resource about Bitcoin.[19]
Ethereum.org	Ethereum.org is a public, open-source resource for the Ethereum community that anyone can contribute to.	*"To be the best portal for Ethereum's growing community."*[20]
Chronicled, founder of MediLedger	A blockchain-enabled network solution for pharmaceutical industry	*"To streamline trading partner interactions across the healthcare industry to better serve providers and patient."*[21]
IBM Food Trust	A blockchain-enabled solution for food industry	The IBM Food Trust: *"creating a smarter, safer, more sustainable food system for all."*[22]
Diem Association	The association overseeing the Diem token, reserve, and software	Diem's mission was *"...To build a trusted and innovative financial network that empowers people and businesses around the world. Provide people everywhere access to safe and affordable financial services. So people everywhere can live better lives."*[23]
Stellar Development Foundation	Non-profit foundation overseeing the Stellar protocol	*"Creating equitable access to the global financial system."*[24]

Table 2.2: Sample blockchain mission statements

71

Once founders have an idea and mission statement for a blockchain-based solution, they need to figure out how to finance it. How will developers be incentivized to spend time on system design and coding? Once launched, how will the maintenance and ongoing operations of the network be incentivized? In the world of blockchains, economic incentives are considered the most effective.

2.3.2. Funding model

Blockchains need funding for software development and ongoing operations.

For enterprise blockchains like MediLedger, the IBM Food Trust, and TradeLens, founders often fund the development themselves because they see significant business benefits in developing the blockchain-based solution. Maersk, for example, paid for the development of the TradeLens platform. After the launch, TradeLens began charging customers a transaction fee per ocean shipping container to financially support the platform. Depending on the functionality a user needs, transaction fees ranged from $8.00 to $22.00 per ocean container.[25]

For blockchain startups, traditional funding through angel and venture capital investors remains popular, but raising money for blockchains saw new financing mechanisms such as Initial Coin Offerings (ICOs), Security Token Offerings (STOs), Initial Exchange Offerings (IEOs), and Initial DEX Offering (IDOs) (see Table 2.3 for a comparison). All these models create a new crypto token; people buy the tokens in anticipation that the token's value will appreciate, or perhaps, because they view the mission as worthy of a donation. Many startups funnel most of the funds into a non-profit foundation to compensate developers and to retain reserves to grow the network in the future. Other startups are scams that intend to make the founders wealthy at the expense of investors.

	ICOs	STOs	IEOs	IDOs
Commonality	Projects raise funds by issuing a new crypto-token			
Fundraising managed by	The project's developers	Capital investor firms	A cryptocurrency exchange	Smart contract on a decentralized exchange
Investors	Anyone	Accredited investors only	Customers of the exchange	Anyone
Pre-screening	None in countries where ICOs are not regulated	Full pre-screening; compliant and fully regulated	The exchange screens projects before they are willing to risk their reputation	None
Relative investor risk	Highest	Lowest	Medium	Highest

Table 2.3: Comparison of ICOs, STOs, IEOs, and IDOs

Initial Coin Offerings (ICOs). With an ICO, people exchange money (typically bitcoins) for new coins released by the project's founders. Investors buy the coins, but not shares in a company. *Mastercoin* was the first ICO, which raised $5.5 million in 2014. *Ethereum* was the second ICO, raising $18 million in 2014.[26] The largest ICOs include:

- *EOS,* a blockchain platform to build and launch smart contracts, raised $4.1 billion;
- *Telegram Open Network* raised $1.7 billion to build a peer-to-peer messenger app;
- *Dragon Coin* raised $320 million for a decentralized currency for gambling;
- *Huobi* raised $300 million for its Singapore-based cryptocurrency exchange;
- *Hyundai Digital Asset Currency* (HDAC) raised $258 million for an Internet of Things (IoT) contract platform;
- *Filecoin* raised $257 million to store files on a distributed network analogous to the way Bitcoin stores transactions; and

- *Tezos* raised $232 million to put more governance around blockchains to prevent forks such as occurred at Ethereum (a story told later in this chapter).[27]

When regulators around the world started intervening, the ICO market fell precipitously.[28] In 2019, ICOs raised only $371 *million* compared $7.8 *billion* worldwide 2018.[29] In the US, the Securities and Exchange Commission (SEC) deemed that many of the ICO projects' tokens were securities, and thus subject to all SEC regulations.[30] While ICOs fell in popularity for a while, two new funding models rose in popularity: Security Token Offerings (STOs) and Initial Exchange Offerings (IEOs).

Security Token Offerings STOs are legally compliant, licensed ICOs which protect investors against fraud. The value of the token is based on the company's valuation. STOs are only available for accredited investors who do not need as much protection as non-accredited investors. For example, Mark Cuban, the American billionaire entrepreneur, can afford to take higher risks on new projects than the average investor. In the US, the SEC regulates who qualifies as an accredited investor based on their net worth and financial sophistication.

Initial Exchange Offerings (IEOs) are a funding round conducted on a cryptocurrency exchange, which is a trusted third party. Investors fund their exchange wallets with coins and use those funds to buy the fundraising company's tokens. All US exchanges now comply with FinCen anti-money laundering (AML) and Know Your Customer (KYC) regulations and also vet the fundraisers, making IEO investments less risky than ICOs. Binance, Huobi, OKEx, and BitMax are examples of exchanges with IEO services.[31] In January 2022, there were 37 active IEOs across platforms.[32]

Initial DEX Offering (IDOs) is one of the newest funding models. This model allows startups to raise money on a decentralized exchange by launching a new cryptocurrency, managed by a smart contract, with no third parties involved. The advantage is built-in liquidity, which means that investors can quickly trade the coins in the market at a price reflecting its current value pools without depending on intermediaries.[33] The disadvantages are that the smart contract needs to be well-coded to prevent hacks, there are significant investor risks since offerings are not vetted by independent third parties (like the SEC). So far, the amounts raised by an IDO are significantly less than the other models, but the number of IDOs is quite high.[34] On Coinmarketcap.com, the number of upcoming IDOs at the start of 2022 was in the hundreds. The most popular IDO platforms in 2021 were BSCPad (IDO platform on Binance), GameFI (built on Solana), Seedify, TrustPad, and DAO Maker.[35]

Other funding models are quickly emerging as well. A **Wallet Holder Offering (WHO)** drops coins directly into users' digital wallets; A **Strong Holders Offering (SHO)** is limited to investors who can hold crypto assets for extended periods of time. An **Initial Game Offering (IGO)** creates non-fungible tokens (NFTs) for gaming projects. **An Initial Farm Offering (IFO)** allows pre-sale events for IDOs.[36] The level of financial innovations cannot be overstated, but many new instruments are risky. How do you spot a scam? For the casual investor, Techcrunch contributor Deep Patel identified these red flags to detect scams:

- the early release of coins goes primarily to the founders, not investors or miners;
- the founders are anonymous or have little credible experience;
- the project's white paper is missing details;
- the project has no clear timelines;
- the project claims the programming code will be open sourced but it does not exist on GitHub—the de facto repository for open-sourced blockchain source code.[37]

In short, *caveat emptor*!

2.3.3. Rights of participation and validation

Rights of participation define who is allowed submit transactions to a blockchain network. **Rights of validation** define who is allowed to run validator nodes in the blockchain network. At a very high level, rights of participation are either open to the public or private; rights of validation are either permissionless (anyone may operate a validator node) or permissioned (an individual or institution needs permission or must be selected/voted upon to run a validator node). Plotting these two dimensions yields four types of blockchain networks (see Table 2.4):

1. Public-permissionless
2. Public-permissioned
3. Private-permissionless
4. Private-permissioned

However, there are nuances; EOS, for example, distinguishes between node validators—which anyone may run—and block producers, which must be voted upon by the community. Next, we examine the four types of blockchains in more detail.

Permissionless (Anyone)		Who can operate a validator node?	
		Permissioned (Requires permission, selection, or election)	
Who can submit transactions?	**Public** (Anyone)	**Public-permissionless** · Bitcoin • Ethereum • Cardano • Monero • EOS (node validators)	**Public-permissioned** · Ripple • EOS (block producers)
	Private (requires keys to access)	**Private-permissionless (new)** • Nightfall Protocol • Baseline Protocol	**Private-permissioned** • MediLedger • IBM Food Trust • TradeLens

Table 2.4: Types of blockchain networks

With public-permissionless blockchains, anyone can participate, and anyone can run validator nodes. Bitcoin, Monero, Ethereum, Cardano, EOS, and Solana are popular public-permissionless blockchains. Anyone with access to the Internet can observe a public blockchain to see all the transactions that have taken place over time (see Table 2.5 for blockchain explorers). To transact on public-permissionless blockchains, users need some sort of application interface (such as a digital wallet). Anyone may become a node operator by downloading the source code (see Table 2.5 for instructions). Permissionless blockchains need strong incentives to attract independent, 'well-behaving' validator nodes. Bitcoin and Ethereum incentivize good behavior by awarding cryptocurrencies to miners.

Blockchain (launched)	Native Digital Asset (Crypto-currency Symbol)	Blockchain explorer website to observe all transactions	Instructions to download code to operate a node
Bitcoin (2009)	bitcoins (BTC)	https://blockexplorer.com/	https://developer.bitcoin.org/devguide/mining.html
Monero (2014)	Monero (XRM)	https://moneroblocks.info/	https://web.getmonero.org/get-started/mining/
Ethereum (2015)	ether (ETH)	https://etherscan.io/	https://eth.wiki/en/fundamentals/mining
Cardano (2017)	Ada (ADA)	https://explorer.cardano.org/en	https://cardano.org/stake-pool-operation/
EOS (2018)	EOS	https://eostracker.io/	https://developers.eos.io/manuals/eos/v2.0/nodeos/usage/node-setups/index
Solana (2019)	SOL	https://explorer.solana.com/	https://solana.com/validators

Table 2.5: Public-Permissionless Blockchains

With public-permissioned blockchains, anyone can transact, but node validators are selected or elected. Ripple and EOS are examples (see Table 2.6).

Blockchain	Native Digital Asset (Cryptocurrency Symbol)	Website to observe all transactions	List of Validator Nodes
Ripple	Ripple (XRP)	https://xrpcharts.ripple.com/#/transactions	https://livenet.xrpl.org/network
EOS	(EOS)	https://bloks.io/#transactions	https://bloks.io/#producers

Table 2.6: Public-Permissioned Blockchains

Ripple is a decentralized, real-time settlement global payments system. Anyone can transact on the Ripple network by using a digital wallet or engaging a gateway partner, which are mostly financial institutions. Institutional customers use an application programming interface (API)—a piece of software that connects two software applications—to connect to the Ripple network via a Ripple Gateway. When institutions join the Ripple network, they can select which nodes they want to perform validation checks, or they can accept the default list maintained by Ripple, which is called a Unique Node List (UNL). Ripple maintains its own validator nodes around the world.[38] Without the incentives of mining, Ripple asks intuitions to run a validator node when they join the system to help secure the network. On January 8, 2022, the Ripple Network had 135 validator nodes, with 34 recommended on the UNL.

EOS was developed to keep all of the advantages of a public blockchain platform—open, secure, decentralized; but without the latency, scalability, and resource intensity. Anyone can transact on EOS. Anyone can operate a validator node if they meet minimal criteria.[39] However, only 21 'block producers' can add blocks. The owners of EOS cast votes for block producers in proportion to their stake.[40] The validator nodes with the most votes become a 'delegate'. The algorithm takes turns selecting a leader from among the panel of delegates for a current time period. After the time period elapses, another round of voting occurs to select the next panel of delegates.[41] Delegates are rewarded with transaction fees. Blocks are produced about every 500 milliseconds, with each of the 21 producers getting a turn. On the day of this writing in 2022, the 21 block producers were located in China (7), Cayman Islands (4), Singapore (3), Australia (1), BVI (1), Canada (1), South Korea (1), Japan (2), Ukraine (1), and one unknown.

Private-permissioned blockchains require authorization to participate and to operate validator nodes. Private-permissioned blockchains rely upon a front-end gatekeeper to enforce the rights of access (see Figure 2.3).

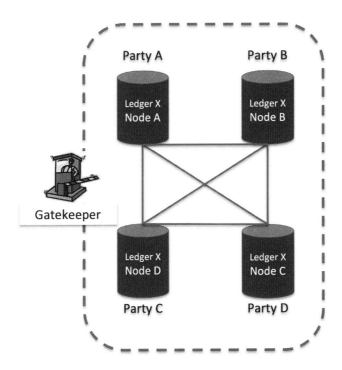

**Figure 2.3: A permissioned blockchain with a gatekeeper
to enforce the rights of access**

Unlike a trusted third-party that sits in the middle of transactions, the gatekeeper is like a security guard that checks a badge before allowing entry. It has no ability to alter the ledger or to stop smart contracts from executing.[i] The gatekeeping function may be governed collaboratively by the trading partners or by a single enterprise, such as a regulatory authority that issues licenses for participation: *"existing participants could decide future entrants; a regulatory authority could issue licenses for participation; or a consortium could make the decisions instead."*[42] Once participants are past the gatekeeping function, they enter the distributed blockchain application.

Many private-permissioned blockchains also allow participants to select validator nodes and to create private channels with their own private ledgers. There are typically 'public' data that all approved network participants can view and 'private' data that only the parties to the transaction can submit and view. Quorum—the permissioned version of Ethereum—is an example (see Figure 2.4). In other protocols, like Hyperledger Fabric, there are no 'public' views, only channels for private views that must be configured and approved for each participant in the network.

Private-permissioned blockchains are the most common enterprise blockchain solutions because they provide assurances of confidentiality, fast settlement times, resource efficiency, and regulatory compliance. MediLedger, the IBM Food Trust and TradeLens serve as examples of private-permissioned blockchains.

MediLedger. MediLedger's first project focused on compliance with the US Drug Supply Chain Security Act of 2013. The act requires that all participants in the US pharmaceutical sector track and trace sellable units for certain classes of pharmaceuticals from manufacturers to pharmacy on one interoperable electronic system. Qualified participants (such as licensed manufacturers and pharmacies) may join the network.

---

i   This is true provided that the organization that serves as the gatekeeper operates fewer than 50 percent of the nodes; If a gatekeeper does operate 50 percent or more of the nodes, there is little point in using a blockchain except under specific circumstances, such as an intra-organizational blockchain across divisions.

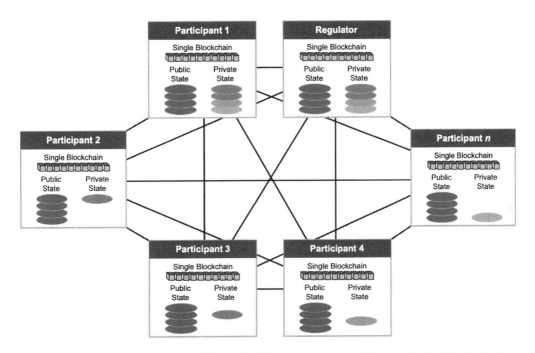

Figure 2.4: Quorum has public and private states stored on a single blockchain
Source: Crosman 2017 [43]

Any qualified participant may operate a node, but it is likely that smaller players will engage a cloud provider or service provider to operate a node on their behalf. The validator's identity is known, thereby staking the organization's reputation on preserving the network.[44] Its 26 working group members include McKesson; Pfizer; AmerisourceBergen; Cardinal Health; FedEx, GS1; Walgreens and Walmart.[45]

IBM Food Trust. The IBM Food Trust platform relies on 'trust anchors' for validation. Trust anchors receive a full copy of the encrypted ledger but cannot view the transaction unless data owners grant access.[46] Initially, trust anchors were operated by IBM in IBM's cloud, but as the network grows, more participants will run trust nodes and possibly on other cloud environments.[47] As of 2021, the platform had over 27 million transactions on more than 25,000 stock keeping units (SKUs), and more than 300 members adding data to the system. Major enterprise adopters include Walmart; Carrefour; Smithfield; Topco; Golden State Foods; and Nestlé.

TradeLens. Developed by Maersk and IBM, TradeLens is an industry platform—released in 2018, after years of development—used to track shipping containers in the global supply chain.[48,49] TradeLens also relies on 'trust anchors'. Trust anchors participate in consensus to validate transactions, host data, and assume a critical role of securing the network. Maersk (via IBM's cloud environment) operates nodes, as well as Hapag-Lloyd and Ocean Network Express (ONE).[50] As of June 2021, it had over 300 members, including major shippers, ports, and terminal operators. As of January 2022, TradeLens had processed 2.8 billion events on over 53 million containers.[51]

Private-permissionless blockchains. A private-permissionless blockchain is best described as a 'virtual private blockchain', like a virtual private network (VPN) that is connected to the public Internet, but data remains private from anyone not authorized to see the transaction. Private-permissionless blockchains launch a smart contract on a permissionless network that restricts access and use to specific public keys.[52] In 2019, Ernst & Young (EY) took a major step to making it a reality when it launched Nightfall on Github.[53] Nightfall is a set of protocols that provides private transactions on public Ethereum. Paul Brody, head of EY's Blockchain Technology, said, *"Blockchain technology holds tremendous promise to bring in a new era of transparency, accountability and efficiency in business. I am working to make sure that happens and, in particular, to ensure that open, decentralized and truly public blockchains are successful."* [54]

The next big release was the Baseline Protocol, in 2020, when 14 companies released the open-source project. The Baseline Protocol is a standard for synchronizing states across different systems of record over the Internet, using a public blockchain as a common frame of reference. The idea is that trading partners keep their data in their own systems of record but use a public blockchain like Ethereum to guarantee that records match across the trading partners' systems. Initially, Baseline uses Ethereum for hashing and ordering events to show partners that their data is in sync, but the protocol can be used with other blockchains. [55] While the protocol is still new as of the beginning of 2022, its founding members, including EY, Microsoft, and ConsenSys, describe it as using blockchains as 'middleware'.[56]

2.3.4. Rights of overrides

Rights of overrides define who is authorized to roll back the ledger in the instance of egregious errors, i.e. who has the power to create a hard fork. A hard fork is a permanent, divergent path of a blockchain. *A hard fork is a highly contentious issue because it means that a blockchain ledger loses its property of immutability.* In public blockchains, hard forks typically occur under two circumstances. First, someone may create their own blockchain or digital asset by copying and modifying source code. Second, hard forks can occur when the blockchain community disagrees on the rules of the next version of the protocol. For example, Bitcoin forked into Bitcoin and Bitcoin Cash when miners disagreed over a proposed upgrade in 2017. Bitcoin Cash was created to allow block sizes of up to 8 megabytes (MB), whereas Satoshi Nakamoto coded the Bitcoin Core to cap block sizes at 1 megabyte. In 2018, Bitcoin Cash split again over disagreements with extending the block size further. One branch became Bitcoin Cash (32 MB block size limit) and one branch became Bitcoin Cash SV (128 MB limit).[57]

In another example, Ethereum split into Ethereum and Ethereum Classic when the community disagreed about remediating the DAO hack. The DAO (Decentralized Autonomous Organization) is perhaps blockchain's most ominous heist because its perpetrator(s) didn't steal private keys from a digital wallet stored off a blockchain, which is how most thefts occur. Rather, the perpetrator(s) exploited a weakness in a smart contract launched on the Ethereum blockchain. The DAO was deployed in May of 2016. Despite the concerns some people voiced—like Professor Emin Gün Sirer of Cornell University—about the weaknesses in the code, money poured in.[58] The DAO raised $150 million worth of Ethereum's native digital asset (ether), during its 28-day funding window, exceeding anyone's expectations, as this represented 15 percent of the ether money supply. In June of 2016, a hacker (or hackers) exploited a weakness in the smart contract's code. He, she or they began draining the DAO's funds. The Ethereum community was powerless to stop it, as smart contracts run autonomously. The hacker syphoned $50 million in ether into another account. Vitalik Buterin, the co-founder of Ethereum, called for a complete stop in trading until the problem could be addressed. The price of ether fell immediately from $20 to $13.[59]

What should be done? Opposing views swarmed in: Vitalik Buterin wanted to *"freeze the account"*, which would require new code that had to be run by at least 50 percent of the nodes. Stephan Tual—Ethereum's Chief Compliance Officer—argued that the blocks should be unwound and that all the stolen ether should be returned to the investors' accounts.[60] Some members of the open-source community insisted that ***nothing should be done***. The blockchain was not breached; the coders of the smart contract did a poor job, so they should suffer the loss. Chat rooms were ablaze with analogies to the US federal government bailing out the banks during the Global Financial Crisis of 2008, and accused the Ethereum Foundation of acting like a government. The decision was made to let miners vote, weighing their votes by their hashing power. The miners voted for a hard fork, a permanent divergence in the Ethereum blockchain. The blocks were rolled back, and the stolen ether was returned. Those miners who refused to follow the fork proceeded mining with the original code, leaving us with Ethereum (fork followers) and Ethereum Classic (non-fork followers), where the thief can still cash out.

These stories from public-permissionless blockchains are highly relevant to permissioned blockchains. Clear procedures should exist for 'pulling the emergency brake' by forking the ledger. The Diem Association, for example, had the power to create a hard fork with a two third supermajority of votes.[61]

2.3.5. Governance residence

"I argue that 'tightly coupled' on-chain voting is overrated, the status quo of 'informal governance' as practiced by Bitcoin, Bitcoin Cash, Ethereum, Zcash and similar systems is much less bad than commonly thought, that people who think that the purpose of blockchains is to completely expunge soft mushy

human intuitions and feelings in favor of completely algorithmic governance (emphasis on 'completely') are absolutely crazy...''

Vitalik Buterin, inventor of Ethereum[62]

"Most of our success is a lot of hard work; in the blockchain space, we talk about automatically executing smart contracts, but I spend a lot of time dealing with attorneys and good old-fashioned paper contracts to onboard participants."

Aaron Lieber, Head of Offering Management, TradeLens, IBM

Governance can be off-chain, on-chain, or a combination of both. Human beings manage off-chain governance, and it is the structure with which we are all familiar. People govern cities, states, nations, institutions, clubs, consortiums, alliances, software, etc. While there may be encoded 'rules'—constitutions, bylaws, or contracts—people can change the rules, be it by vote, persuasion, or coups. As such, ***off-chain governance is alterable, allowing the governance model to evolve over time.*** Most blockchain governance is managed off-chain, whether its decisions over source code patches or updates, protocol changes, or membership changes. Given that governance structures tend to evolve, it seems ***off-chain governance is the lower-risk option.***

On-chain governance is a newer option; ***on-chain governance is unalterable without a significant software fork or intervention approved by the majority of the participants***. It's meant to provide a guarantee—a programmed-in commitment, as it were—to how decisions will be made in the blockchain network now and in the future. EOS is its most visible poster child. It launched its blockchain network with guaranteed democratic voting rights. Whereas Bitcoin and Ethereum miners vote on changes, EOS shifted the decision rights from developers and miners to users. The EOS system has suffered from low voter turnout. In July 21, 2019, for example, only 63,000 of 1.3 million EOS account holders participated in 1,030 votes taken since its launch. Few EOS users have the time or expertise to investigate trustworthy nodes. By 2020, block producers paying for votes became a normal practice, so an EOS user's vote goes to the highest bidder.

Some people view the vote-buying behavior as a natural part of market forces in the new token economy. Other people are outraged. Vitalik Buterin is in the latter camp: *"Bribery is, in fact, bad. There are actually people who dispute this claim; the usual argument has something to do with market efficiency."*[63]

Other blockchain networks with on-chain governance include DFINITY (a blockchain-based cloud computing project aiming to reduce the costs of cloud computing); Tezos (a blockchain-based project aiming to improve smart contract safety); and Decred (a cryptocurrency like bitcoin but with on-chain governance). ***The arguments for on-chain governance are guaranteed inclusion and decentralization. The arguments against are unanticipated consequences; the inability to adapt; ill-informed voters; and low voter turn-out.*** [64,65]

By now, readers should have a better insight into Marie Wieck's quote: *"Distributed ledgers present a dual challenge for companies, one that is arguably 20 percent technological and 80 percent governance."* We've only covered some aspects of governance here, namely, the mission/vision; funding models; rights of participation; rights of validation; rights of overrides; and governance residence. There are other issues, including rights around data, business rules, software licenses, software version control management, regulatory compliance, and liability that potential blockchain adopters also need to consider.

So far, we've discussed (de)centralization of blockchain architecture in Chapter 1 and blockchain governance in this chapter. We've learned that there are pros and cons for each. Next, we bring these ideas together to show how partners trade before and after a blockchain.

2.4. Trade before and after a blockchain

Let's consider a simple ecosystem with five parties to compare the differences in how parties transact with centralized architectures and governance and decentralized architectures and governance. Suppose four of the five entities—these could be individuals or institutions—buy and sell goods with each other (see the left side of Figure 2.5).

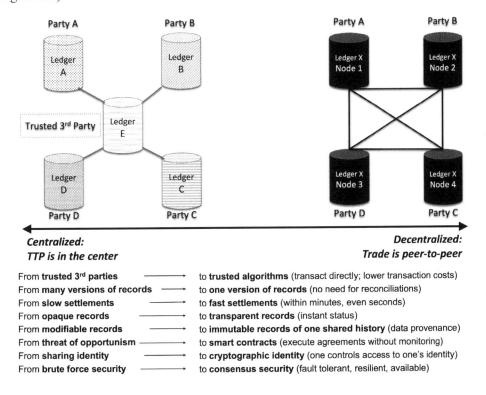

Figure 2.5: Trade before and after a blockchain-based solution

The four trading partners mitigate counter-party risks by engaging a trusted third party to provide truth attestations, that is, to verify information about the parties, assets, and transactions. The trusted third party provides vital services to facilitate trade; that is why our four trading parties rely upon it. The TTP provides **clear control and accountability**. The trading parties have an identifiable institution to address questions, concerns, or complaints. Additionally, trading partners **can alter agreements** as new information becomes available or as circumstances change. However, the TTP can command significant fees for such services. Let's assume the four trading parties pay, on average, five percent of the value of each transaction to the TTP for these services. As a benchmark, in more complex scenarios like remittances and global supply chains, **transaction costs can be high,** between eight and 22 percent of the value of the transaction.[66]

In our simple scenario, the network is centralized, with the TTP at its center, routing information to and from the four trading partners. Each party also maintains its own independent information to compare with what the TTP sends. (Think of it as keeping track of your own purchases and comparing your paper receipts with the credit card statement you receive from the bank.) Each party maintains its own systems to record debits, credits, and other data on their private ledgers (represented by different patterned database icons in Figure 2.5). Each party benefits from controlling their own software and ledgers—each party can swiftly and unilaterally execute decisions. Each party can modify its records and alter its software as it sees fit. But there are downsides to independent record keeping in the context of trading relationships. In our little ecosystem, each party spends significant resources protecting their IT perimeters against cybersecurity attacks, which we called **brute force cybersecurity defense**. Among the four trading partners and one TTP in our scenario, there are five **versions of the truth** which need to be reconciled. Even after reconciliation, nothing prevents a party from re-writing history after-the-fact. Because each party can modify its own records, partners cannot be confident they are dealing with the same historical record of transactions through time, thus hindering the ability to uniformly trace the origin of an asset and every change to its status over time (called 'data provenance'). Reconciliations, in turn, slow settlement times. In a more realistic scenario than an ecosystem with just five parties, such as trade finance, the knotwork of players involved—customers, suppliers, banks, customs, transporters, and warehouses—may take weeks to settle transactions.[67]

Moreover, each party has **low transaction visibility**; each party can only see the transactions coming in and out of its own organization—the rest are opaque. Each party has to work with the trusted third party to assess the status of a transaction. In more complex scenarios, some parties spend days or weeks tracking down the status of a transaction. Consider cross-border payments; when a manufacturer in one country sends payment to a supplier in another country, the manufacturer and the supplier's financial institutions, national payment systems, and corresponding banks process the transaction. Parties to an exchange have no access to the status of the transaction, the fees being charged, or even which institution controls a transaction as it works its way through the knotwork.

The threat of 'vendor opportunism'—the idea that vendors may pursue their self-interests with guile, may withhold information, or may not comply with the terms and conditions of the agreement—always exists.[68] Therefore, trading partners **spend a lot of resources monitoring agreements** to make sure that trading partners are behaving as promised.

In short, before a shared blockchain application, each party maintains its own records and relies on trusted third parties to provide truth attestations. The trusted third parties add significant value and parties like having control over their own data, but the entire setup prompts disputes; requires onerous reconciliations; commands high transaction fees; provides little transaction transparency; is slow to settlement transactions; and creates cybersecurity vulnerabilities. Blockchain applications aim to overcome these limitations.

Returning to our scenario, the right side of Figure 2.5 shows how the same four parties could transact if they decide to share a blockchain application. The parties have agreed to a governance framework that addresses the mission, rights of participation, rights of validation, rights of overrides, software update control, and a funding model. They have agreed to the data structures, data processing rules, and have selected an open-source, permissioned code base upon which to build the application. They agree to a democratic governance model where each party has equal voting rights and require a super-majority of 3 out of 4 to make governance decisions.

Each party agrees to operate an independent computer node in the network. Each independent node runs the same software and maintains an identical copy of the digital ledger. Only the authorized parties can interpret the data on the ledger.

One notes that after a shared blockchain application, there is no need for a trusted third party; instead, the blockchain application uses cryptography and computer algorithms to perform truth attestations. This allows **trading partners to transact directly**. While the parties pay for and govern the shared software, the overall **transaction costs should be lower** by eliminating the TTP.

Transactions are only added to the ledger if they are valid; it's a confirm-before-commit process instead of post-then-confirm-later process. As such, parties can rely on **one version of the truth**, so there is **no need for reconciliations**, enabling **faster settlement times.** The transactions can settle in sub-second to sixty minutes, depending on which consensus algorithm is used in the blockchain application. With one **transparent**, shared version of the truth, parties of an exchange can instantly determine the status of a transaction by reading the ledger. Furthermore, transactions on the shared distributed ledger are **immutable**, thus every party can be confident they are always dealing with the same historical data, guaranteeing consistent **data provenance**. Rather than solely rely on paper contracts, verbal agreements or handshakes, parties can rely on **smart contracts** that automatically execute the terms of agreements without oversight. No more monitoring and worrying that trading partners are not fulfilling their obligations. Moreover, blockchain applications promise **heightened security** because the architecture is decentralized.

However, as we learned above, there are downsides to decentralized trading systems. Table 2.6 summarizes the advantages and disadvantages of centralized and distributed trading systems.

Without a trusted third party, the risk profile will be altered. Smart contracts are only reliable if the terms and conditions can be explicated, but in a world filled with

	Centralized systems	Decentralized systems
Architecture	Each party centrally owns its own systems of records (software and data, including ledgers) and involve trusted third parties to mitigate counter party risks.	Trading partners join a blockchain network. Each party operates a node that runs the same software and has its own copy of the ledger that is guaranteed to be sync with other copies in the network.
Governance	Governance is centralized	Governance may or may not be centralized
Advantages	<ul><li>Trusted third parties absorb counter-party risks</li><li>Trusted third parties are accountable</li><li>Each firm controls its internal systems to modify records and to alter software as each sees fit</li><li>Trading partners can adapt terms of an agreement to meet changing circumstances</li></ul>	<ul><li>Trading partners transact directly without needing a trusted third party</li><li>Lower transaction costs</li><li>With shared data, there is no need for reconciliations</li><li>Fast transaction settlement times</li><li>Instant status of transactions</li><li>Data provenance</li><li>Execute agreements without oversight</li><li>Cybersecurity is fault tolerant, resilient, and always available</li></ul>
Disadvantages	<ul><li>High transaction costs</li><li>Disputes over information between trading partners require reconciliation</li><li>Slow transaction settlement times</li><li>Lack of transparency across trading partners</li><li>Trading partners may alter records after the fact, making data provenance unreliable</li><li>Trading partners may not act in good faith</li><li>Each firm spends a lot of resources on cybersecurity</li></ul>	<ul><li>Without a trusted third party, the risk profile changes</li><li>No single point of accountability; who does one seek remediations from in cases of fraud or malicious acts?</li><li>Records cannot be overwritten unless the majority of nodes agree</li><li>Software cannot be updated unless the majority of nodes agree</li><li>Smart contracts are not easily modifiable if circumstances change</li></ul>

Table 2.6: Trade before and after a blockchain application

uncertainty and ambiguity, coded agreements are not always possible. In our scenario, a party would need to appeal to two other parties to seek remediations from in cases of fraud or malicious acts. Normal software upgrades also need to be coordinated among the parties.

In our example, the trading partners built a platform for their own use, but custom software is expensive to maintain, and if they intend to scale the solution to other trading partners, the newcomers may resist—why would they trust the network? Will new members get locked into this solution? How many networks will each party have to join? As public blockchains mature, a more realistic choice in the future would be for the four trading partners to launch a smart contract on a public network, thus avoiding infrastructure costs, fear of vendor lock-in, and scalability challenges, perhaps using the Baseline Protocol discussed above. Each party will keep their own data in their systems of record and use the blockchain to verify the records agree across parties.

2.5. Conclusion

While blockchains are designed to automation transactions without relying on a trusted-third party, we've learned that humans still play major roles in governing blockchain-based solutions. We discussed eight governance models: benevolent dictatorships; oligarchies; stakeocracies; federations; representative meritocracies; meritocracies; democracies; and advisory boards. We covered six governance decisions in detail: the mission/vision; funding model; rights of participation; rights of validation; rights of overrides, and governance residence. We've learned that trading with a blockchain has many benefits, but also some downsides to consider. Overall, blockchains can be trusted if there are enough independent nodes in the network to secure it (decentralized architecture) and if the decision-making powers are dispersed among an incentivized community (decentralized governance) or if the few people in power are trusted and transparent (centralized governance). In the next chapter, we will look at the component parts of a blockchain application.

Citations

[1] Sample articles on team leadership, leaderless teams, and teams effectiveness:

R. Paul, J. R. Drake and H. Liang, "Global Virtual Team Performance: The Effect of Coordination Effectiveness, Trust, and Team Cohesion," in IEEE Transactions on Professional Communication, vol. 59, no. 3, pp. 186-202, Sept. 2016, doi: 10.1109/TPC.2016.2583319.

Feng, Y., Hao, B., Iles, P. and Bown, N. (2017), "Rethinking distributed leadership: dimensions, antecedents and team effectiveness", Leadership & Organization Development Journal, Vol. 38 No. 2, pp. 284-302. https://doi.org/10.1108/LODJ-07-2015-0147

McDaniel, S. H., & Salas, E. (2018). The science of teamwork: Introduction to the special issue. American Psychologist, 73(4), 305–307. https://doi.org/10.1037/amp0000337

Ovans, A. (2012). When No One's in Charge. Harvard Business Review, https://hbr.org/2012/05/when-no-ones-in-charge

[2] Popper, N. (2015), *Digital Gold*, HarperCollins, New York, p. 82.

[3] Popper, N. (2015), *Digital Gold*, HarperCollins, New York, p. 82.

[4] https://en.wikipedia.org/wiki/Ethereum

[5] Kay, G. (November 28, 2021). The many alleged identities of Bitcoin's mysterious creator, Satoshi Nakamoto, https://www.businessinsider.com/bitcoin-history-cryptocurrency-satoshi-nakamoto-2017-12

[6] The Libra Association, https://libra.org/en-US/association-council-principles/#overview

[7] Fisher, C. (July 15, 2019), *US Treasury has serious concerns Libra could be used for terrorism*, https://www.engadget.com/2019/07/15/facebook-libra-cryptocurrency-us-treasury-department-concerns/

Alexandre, A. (August 5, 2019), *UK Data Protection Watchdog Raises Concerns Over Facebook's Libra*, CoinTelegragh, https://cointelegraph.com/news/uk-data-protection-watchdog-raises-concerns-over-facebooks-libra

[8] Kastrenakes, J. (December 1, 2020). Libra cryptocurrency project changes name to Diem to distance itself from Facebook. The Verge, https://www.theverge.com/2020/12/1/21755078/libra-diem-name-change-cryptocurrency-facebook

[9] https://www.diem.com/en-us/about-us/

[10] Porter, J. (May 26, 2020). Facebook renames Calibra digital wallet to Novi. The Verge. https://www.theverge.com/2020/5/26/21270437/facebook-calibra-novi-rename-digital-wallet

[11] Hyperledger Foundation (October 26, 2020). Introducing the expanded 2020-2021 Hyperledger Technical Steering Committee. https://www.hyperledger.org/blog/2020/10/26/introducing-the-expanded-2020-2021-hyperledger-technical-steering-committee

Hyperledger Foundation (September 6, 2017), *ABCs of Open Governance*, https://www.hyperledger.org/blog/2017/09/06/abcs-of-open-governance;

[12] Bitcoin Improvement Proposals. https://github.com/bitcoin/bips

[13] Ferreira, D., Li, J., and Nikolowa (2019), *Corporate Capture of Blockchain Governance*, London School of Economics Discussion paper DP13493, Financial Economics and Industrial Organization.

[14] Ferreira, D., Li, J., and Nikolowa (2019), *Corporate Capture of Blockchain Governance*, London School of Economics Discussion paper DP13493, Financial Economics and Industrial Organization.

[15] https://www.ibm.com/blockchain/solutions/food-trust/food-industry-technology

[16] What is the Advisory Council? https://www.ibm.com/blockchain/solutions/food-trust/food-industrytechnology#1797811

[17] Lacity, M., Zach, S., Paul, C. (2019). *Blockchain Governance Models: Insights for Enterprises.* Blockchain Center of Excellence white paper, BCoE-2019-02, University of Arkansas.

[18] Wieck, M. (December 11, 2019). 2019 Saw the End of Blockchain Tourism, Coindesk, https://www.coindesk.com/2019-saw-the-end-of-blockchain-tourism

[19] https://bitcoin.org/en/about-us#owntxt-title

[20] https://ethereum.org/en/about/

[21] Chronicled (April 27, 2021). Chronicled Announces New MediLedger Working Group To Solve Medicaid Duplicate Discounts. https://www.prnewswire.com/news-releases/chronicled-announces-new-mediledger-working-group-to-solve-medicaid-duplicate-discounts-301277657.html

[22] https://www.ibm.com/blockchain/solutions/food-trust

[23] https://www.diem.com/en-us/

[24] Stellar Development Foundation Mandate, https://www.stellar.org/about/mandate/ https://www.stellar.org/foundation?locale=en

[25] https://www.tradelens.com/pricing

[26] Griffith, E. (May 5, 2017). Why Startups are Trading IPOs for ICOS, *Fortune Magazine*, http://fortune.com/2017/05/05/ico-initial-coin-offering/

[27] Higgins, S. (July 13th 2017). $232 Million: Tezos Blockchain Project Finishes Record-Setting Token Sale, *Coindesk*, https://www.coindesk.com/232-million-tezos-blockchain-record-setting-token-sale/

[28] https://www.icodata.io/stats/2019.

[29] https://www.icodata.io/stats/2019.

[30] Shin, L. (December 4th 2017). $15 Million ICO Halted By SEC For Being Alleged Scam, *Forbes Magazine*, https://www.forbes.com/sites/laurashin/2017/12/04/15-million-ico-halted-by-sec-for-being-alleged-scam/-1728c7141569

[31] Winslet, T (2019). "Top 3 Initial Exchange Offerings (IEOs) to Watch in the Crypto Market," *The Daily Hodl*, https://dailyhodl.com/2019/04/11/top-3-initial-exchange-offerings-ieos-to-watch-in-the-crypto-market/

[32] https://coincodex.com/ieo-list/

[33] Aureliano, L. (April 23, 2021). IDO Watch List - Top Upcoming Token Crowdsales in 2021. https://www.yahoo.com/now/ido-watch-list-top-upcoming-132049902.html

[34] CoinTelegraph. (November 23, 2021). Initial DEX offering (IDO): A beginner's guide on launching a cryptocurrency on a decentralized exchange. https://cointelegraph.com/funding-for-beginners/initial-dex-offering-ido-a-beginners-guide-on-launching-a-cryptocurrency-on-a-decentralized-exchange

[35] Cordin, E. (Dece,ber 13, 2021). 10 Best IDO Launchpads For Crypto Projects in November 2021 https://theislandnow.com/blog-112/best-ido-launchpads/.

[36] Caroline, J. (December 16, 2021). What Are WHO, SHO, IEO, IGO, IFO, IDO Fundraising Models? https://www.coinspeaker.com/guides/what-are-who-sho-ieo-igo-ifo-ido-fundraising-models-2/

[37] Patel, D. (December 7th 2017). Six red flags of an ICO scam, *Techncrunch*, https://techcrunch.com/2017/12/07/6-red-flags-of-an-ico-scam/

[38] To view all of Ripple's nodes, go to https://livenet.xrpl.org/network; To see the unique node list UNL), see: https://livenet.xrpl.org/network/validators

[39] To operate an EOS validator node, an individual or organization must have a public website URL, at least one social media account, and ID on Steemit, sufficient hardware, plans to scale hardware, plans to benefit the community, telegram and testnet nodes, a roadmap, and a dividend position. Source: Ben Sigman (May 8, 2018), EOS Block Producer FAQ, https://medium.com/@bensig/eos-block-producer-faq-8ba0299c2896

[40] To view the 21 EOS validator nodes and block producers, see https://bloks.io/vote

[41] Delegated Proof of Stake, https://lisk.io/academy/blockchain-basics/how-does-blockchain-work/delegated-proof-of-stake

[42] Jayachandran, P. (May 31, 2017). The difference between public and private blockchain, https://www.ibm.com/blogs/blockchain/2017/05/the-difference-between-public-and-private-blockchain/

[43] Crosman, P. (April 28, 2017). JPMorgan defection underscores tough blockchain choices, *American Banker*, https://www.americanbanker.com/news/jpmorgan-defection-underscores-tough-blockchain-choices

[44] POA Network, *Proof of Authority: Consensus Model with Identity at Stake*, https://medium.com/poa-network/proof-of-authority-consensus-model-with-identity-at-stake-d5bd15463256

[45] https://www.mediledger.com/

[46] What are Key Responsibilities for a Trust Anchor? https://www.ibm.com/blockchain/solutions/food-trust/food-industry-technology#1797811

[47] IBM Press Release (October 23, 2018). *IBM and Microsoft Announce Partnership Between Cloud Offerings*, https://www.pbsnow.com/ibm-news/ibm-and-microsoft-announce-partnership-between-cloud-offerings/

[48] TradeLens Overview (October 2, 2018), https://shipbrokers.fi/wp-content/uploads/2018/10/jeppe-kobbero-tradelens-presentation.pdf

[49] Jensen, T. (December 12, 2018), *Blockchain Strategize Digital Infrastructuring: Blockchain technology bridging the Document Platforms towards real business value in Maritime Supply Chains*, Pre-ICIS Workshop, San Francisco.

[50] TradeLens Press Release (June 24, 2021). HAPAG-LLOYD AND OCEAN NETWORK EXPRESS COMPLETE TRADELENS INTEGRATION. https://www.tradelens.com/post/hapag-lloyd-and-ocean-network-express-complete-tradelens-integration

[51] TradeLens posts a real-time dashboard of activities here: https://www.tradelens.com/platform

[52] Daniels, A. (October 18, 2018). The Rise of Private Permissionless Blockchains, *Medium*, https://medium.com/ltonetwork/the-rise-of-private-permissionless-blockchains-part-1-4c39bea2e2be

[53] Nightfall, https://github.com/EYBlockchain/nightfall

[54] https://www.ey.com/en_us/people/paul-brody

[55] https://docs.baseline-protocol.org/

[56] Allison, I. (September 14, 2021). Boring Is the New Exciting': How Baseline Protocol Connected With 600 Corporates. https://www.coindesk.com/business/2020/08/26/boring-is-the-new-exciting-how-baseline-protocol-connected-with-600-corporates/

[57] The Bitcoinist, *Bitcoin Cash ABC vs. Bitcoin Cash SV-Examining the Bitcoin Cash War*, https://bitcoinist.com/bitcoin-cash-abc-vs-bitcoin-cash-sv-examining-the-bitcoin-cash-hash-war/

Clifford, T. (November 14, 2018), *"Crypto civil war' slams bitcoin, but it won't last,"* says BKCM's Brian Kelly, CNBC.

[58] Segal, D. (June 25, 2016), *Understanding the DAO attack*, http://www.coindesk.com/understanding-dao-hack-journalists/

[59] Segal, D. (June 25, 2016), *Understanding the DAO attack*, http://www.coindesk.com/understanding-dao-hack-journalists/

[60] Segal, D. (June 25, 2016), *Understanding the DAO attack*, http://www.coindesk.com/understanding-dao-hack-journalists/

[61] https://www.diem.com/en-us/white-paper/#the-libra-association

[62] Buterin, V. (2017), Notes on Blockchain Governance, https://vitalik.ca/general/2017/12/17/voting.html

[63] Buterin, V. (March 28, 2022). Governance, Part 2: Plutocracy Is Still Bad https://vitalik.ca/general/2018/03/28/plutocracy.html

[64] Buterin, V. (2017), Notes on Blockchain Governance, https://vitalik.ca/general/2017/12/17/voting.html

[65] Frankenfield, J. (October 25, 2021). On-Chain Governance. https://www.investopedia.com/terms/o/onchain-governance.asp

[66] The World Bank estimated that sending remittances cost an average of 7.99 percent of the amount sent; "Navigating the world of cross-border payments," http://www.iqpc.com/media/1003982/57107.pdf

The administrative costs for tracking containers in the global supply chain was roughly 22 percent of the retail costs according to Anderson, J., & Van Wincoop, E. (2004). Trade Costs. *Journal of Economic Literature, 42*(3), 691-751. Retrieved from http://www.jstor.org/stable/3217249

[67] For example, the European Central Bank reported that the average time to settle cross-border credit transfers was 4.8 working days in 1999. McKinsey found little progress by 2015, as the average settlement times were still between three to five business days.

European Central Bank (September 1999), "Improving Cross-border Retail Payment Services: The Eurosystem's view", https://www.ecb.europa.eu/pub/pdf/other/retailpsen.pdf

McKinsey (2015), "Global Payments 2015: A Healthy Industry Confront Disruption," http://www.mckinsey.com/~/media/mckinsey/dotcom/client_service/financial services/latest thinking/payments/global_payments_2015_a_healthy_industry_confronts_disruption.ashx

[68] Williamson, O., (1991). Comparative economic organization: the analysis of discrete structural alternatives. *Administrative Science Quarterly*, 36 (2), 269–296.

Chapter 3

The Blockchain Application Framework

What's inside: In this chapter, we peek under the hood of a blockchain application. The component parts include a distributed ledger, a native digital asset, cryptography, a consensus mechanism, smart contracts, a code base, a use case and user interfaces. We map Bitcoin to illustrate the framework. We track a Bitcoin transaction from start to finish to illustrate how the component parts function as an integrated whole. By the end of this chapter, readers will have a deeper appreciation of the variety of blockchain applications.

Learning objectives:

- Identify the different components of a BC application
- Compare and contrast digital ledger structures
- Compare and contrast monetary policy options for cryptocurrencies
- Compare and contrast consensus protocols
- Differentiate among the types of smart contracts
- Map Bitcoin to the Blockchain Application Framework
- Explain a Bitcoin transaction from start to finish

3.1. Introduction

In this chapter, we develop a framework to explain the component parts of a blockchain application. A blockchain application comprises protocols, code bases, use cases, and application interfaces (see Figure 3.1). For a given blockchain application, **protocols** serve as the blueprints. A blockchain application has blueprints for the distributed ledger, native digital assets, cryptography, consensus, and smart contracts. Protocols are normally explained in a white paper so that potential adopters can understand the purpose and design choices made. Once rules are established, protocols are programmed into **code bases**, like Bitcoin core, Ethereum core, EOS, Hyperledger Fabric, Corda, Quorum, Chain or Multichain. Code bases are published as open-source software, typically on Github. From there, a code base can be adapted for a particular **use case**, like tracking items in a supply chain, cross-border payments, decentralized finance (DeFi) or voting. Finally, all blockchain applications have **interfaces** where users access the system.

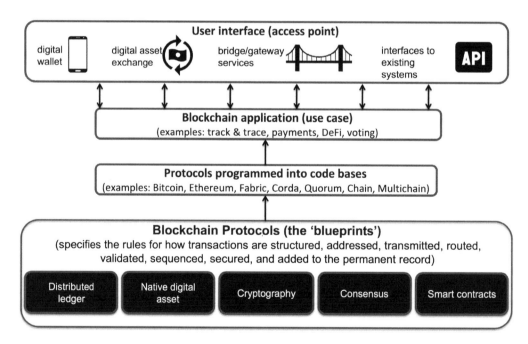

Figure 3.1: The Blockchain Application Framework

We learned in Chapter 1 that Bitcoin was the first blockchain application; it is a decentralized network with a single primary application, namely, peer-to-peer payments. Ripple launched in 2014 and Stellar launched in 2015; both are blockchain networks with a single primary application, namely, currency exchanges for global payments. The launch of Ethereum in 2015 heralded the era of blockchain platforms. Now, most new public blockchain applications are launched on top of an existing platform by coding a new smart contract. Developers piggyback on top of the network that has been programmed for them, allowing them to take advantage of the existing network infrastructure. In addition to Ethereum, popular blockchain platforms include Polkadot, Cardano, Solana, Avalanche, EOS, and Binance Smart Chain.

For private blockchain applications, developers must build the network to launch the application, but existing code bases help to speed the process. Private blockchains are commonly built using Hyperledger Fabric, Corda, or Quorum code bases. For example, Walmart Canada's DL Freight and the IBM Food Trust are built in Fabric; both applications are featured in subsequent chapters.

In this chapter, we explain each component in more detail, then illustrate the framework by mapping Bitcoin to it. By the end of this chapter, readers will be able to map any blockchain application to the framework and understand the trade-offs of different choices among its component parts. We'll have succeeded if by the end of the chapter, readers can comprehend the meaning the following definition of a blockchain application:

A blockchain application is a peer-to-peer (decentralized) network for validating, timestamping, and permanently storing transactions on a shared *distributed ledger*. *Digital assets*, native to each blockchain application, are programmable, exist only in digital form, and come with rights of use. *Consensus* algorithms validate transactions, update the ledger, and keep copies of the ledger in sync. *Cryptography* helps to secure the network. Most blockchains use *smart contracts* that apply rules to automatically execute transactions based upon pre-agreed conditions.

3.2. Distributed ledgers

A ledger is a record of transactions. Your monthly bank account statement is an example of a report from your bank's ledger. A bank statement lists all the receivables coming into your account (credits) and payments you made (debits) in a timed sequence. The summation of all transactions over time results in your account balance. A blockchain application has a ledger that records all debits and credits for each account, or to be more precise, for each public 'address'. Blockchain ledgers also store and execute smart contracts, so a blockchain ledger is more complex than a simple bank account statement.

Why use a ***distributed*** ledger? Why not use a super secure spreadsheet or a traditional database? Spreadsheets and traditional databases are controlled by one party who can decide to add, modify, or delete records, and who can approve or deny access to others. A blockchain ledger is peer-to-peer technology, meaning that the parties share independent copies that are synchronized. After entries are validated and added to the ledger, no one party can modify it, delete it, or deny the other party access to it.

Protocols define the structure of the distributed ledger. The most common structure is a ***chain of blocks***—thus the name 'blockchain' (see Figure 3.2). With a blockchain structure, recently approved transactions are sequenced and collected into a block. Each block comprises a header and a set of sequenced transactions. The block header includes a pointer to the previous block of transactions, forming a chain of sequenced blocks over time, all the way back to the first block, called the 'genesis block'. Bitcoin, Ethereum, Quorum and Hyperledger Fabric structure their digital ledgers as blockchains.

Distributed ledger structured as a chain of blocks:

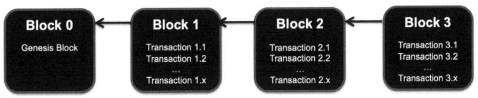

Distributed ledger structured as a continuous ledger with account balances and current transactions:

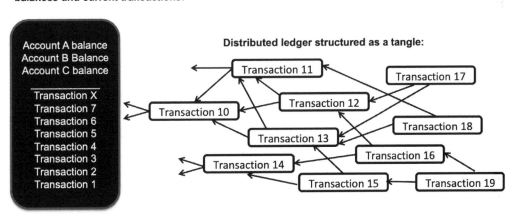

Figure 3.2: Examples of three distributed ledger structures

Another common structure is a ***continuous stream of transactions***, one after the other, through a process of continual ledger close. A completely new ledger is created every few seconds in such a way that the most current version could be reconstructed from all the prior versions. Ripple and Stellar use this structure. Their ledgers are more complex than Bitcoin's ledger because they maintain account settings, balances, trustlines and different types of transactions like sell offers, payments, and cancel offers. The account balances are updated with the most recent set of validated transactions. Figure 3.3 shows how a ledger gets updated.

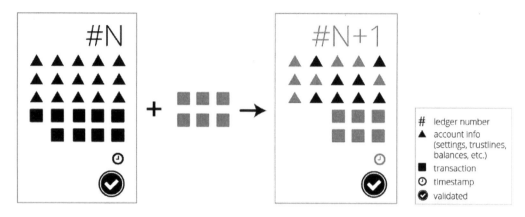

Figure 3.3: Ledger structure for a continuous ledger process

Ledger #N+1 updates the account balances with all the recently approved transactions since ledger #N

Source: https://casinocoin.org/build/concept-consensus.html

IOTA structures its distributed ledger as a ***tangle*** of transactions.[1] Each new transaction has to use its computing resources to validate two other transactions. Serguei Popov, the author of the IOTA white paper explains:

> *"The main idea of the tangle is the following: to issue a transaction, users must work to approve other transactions. Therefore, users who issue a transaction are contributing to the network's security. It is assumed that the nodes check if the approved transactions are not conflicting. If a node finds that a transaction is in conflict with the tangle history, the node will not approve the conflicting transaction."[2]*

Figure 3.4 is an example of Tangle's ledger. Each circle represents a transaction. Readers may explore the tangle on https://explorer.iota.org/mainnet.

Different structures have tradeoffs between security and speed of transaction settlement. In general, the chain of blocks is the most secure; the tangle is the quickest.

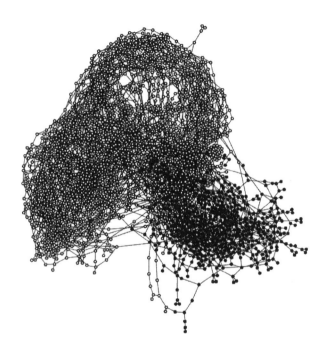

Figure 3.4: IOTA's tangle structure: each circle represents a transaction

Source: http://tangle.glumb.de/

One of the key features of any digital ledger is that it is 'append only', meaning that the ledger gets bigger and bigger over time. The question arises: Won't these ledgers eventually become too large to process? Nakamoto considered this issue and addressed it by restricting a block size to 1 megabyte (MB), basing the calculation on Moore's Law.[i] Nakamoto wrote, *"By Moore's Law, we can expect hardware speed to be 10 times faster in 5 years and 100 times faster in 10. Even if Bitcoin grows at crazy adoption rates, I think computer speeds will stay ahead of the number of transactions."[3]*

---

i Moore's Law estimates that computers double their processing capacity every two years. Moore's Law was made by Gordon Moore, the co-founder of Intel. Specifically, he observed that the number of transistors on an integrated circuit doubles every 2 years.

3.3. Native digital assets

A protocol defines the uses of a blockchain application's native digital asset—an asset that is programmable, exists only in digital form and comes with rights of use. There are a growing number of types of digital assets. Alex Tapscott, co-founder of the Blockchain Research Institute, for example, identified nine types of digital assets:

- **cryptocurrencies** (digital money);

- **protocol tokens** (tokens native to a platform like Ethereum or Cosmos);

- **governance tokens** (provide holders with decision making rights for Decentralized Autonomous Organizations (DAOs));

- **non-fungible tokens** (NFTs) that represent unique assets; exchange tokens that are native to exchange platforms (like Binance);

- **securities tokens** that represent stocks, bonds, and derivative;

- **stable coins** that are pegged to fiat currencies;

- **natural asset tokens** that are pegged to commodities like gold;

- **central bank digital currencies** (CBDCs) that are crypto versions of fiat currencies. China is taking the lead in CDBCs.[4]

The array of options is dizzying—over 16,000 native digital asset types were being traded as of January 2022.[5] Since we are still at the beginning of our learning journey, we will simplify the complexity by focusing on five common *functions* of digital assets.

3.3.1. Functions

Native digital assets function as money (cryptocurrency), tokens of value, participant compensation, resource efficiency, and network security (see Figure 3.5).

| Cryptocurrency | Token of Value | Participant Compensation | Resource Efficiency | Network security |

Medium of exchange for the payment of debts
Common measure of value (unit of account)
Store of value that should retain worth over time

Figure 3.5: Common functions of native digital assets

1. Cryptocurrency: As a currency, a native digital asset serves the same functions as fiat money, namely as a medium of exchange for the payment of debts; as a common measure of value; and as a store of value that should retain its worth over time. As we learned in Chapter 1, we call these *cryptocurrencies*—digital currencies that are secured by cryptography, which makes them nearly impossible to counterfeit.

2. Token of value: Native digital assets also function as 'crypto-tokens' to represent anything of value.[ii] A crypto-token is a digital token that is secured by cryptography. Crypto-tokens can be used to represent *fungible* (non-unique) assets, such as loyalty rewards and airline frequent flyer miles in which one token is interchangeable with another. Stable coins are also examples of fungible crypto-tokens; stable coins peg the crypto-token to a stable asset outside of the blockchain network, such as pegging a digital token to a fiat currency or to commodity like gold or a barrel of oil. Crypto-tokens can be used to represent *non-fungible* (unique) assets where the token represents a particular asset in the real world. These are called non-fungible tokens (NFTs). For example, a unique token could be created to represent a particular diamond, a particular medical device, a particular plot of land, or a particular work of art. Subsequent chapters will dive more deeply into stable coins and NFTs.

---

ii The terms 'token' and 'cryptocurrency' are often used interchangeably. However, some people describe a 'cryptocurrency' as native to the blockchain platform and a 'token' as a new asset launched on a platform using a smart contract. For example, the 'cryptocurrency' ether is native to the Ethereum network, whereas a Cryptokitties are 'tokens' launched by a smart contract on the Ethereum platform.

3. Participant compensation. Blockchains rely on participants to operate nodes to validate transactions and to constantly re-check the integrity of the ledger's records. For many public blockchains, native digital assets are a way to compensate participants for securing the network. Bitcoin, Ethereum 1.0 and Monero, for example, reward validator nodes with native digital assets.

4. Efficient network usage. Native digital assets can be used to discourage people from over-using a shared resource by requiring or encouraging senders to include a fee to submit transactions to the network. Ethereum, for example, uses its native digital asset 'ether' to pay for specific actions on the blockchain network. The fee is called a 'gas fee', and the fee varies based on the computational intensity of the transaction and on the busyness of the network. Bitcoin's fee is optional, but miners' computers are highly unlikely to select a transaction with no fees. One can think of it this way: does a waitress have any incentive to serve a customer who has told her he will not tip?

5. Network security. Additionally, native digital assets serve as a countermeasure to Denial of Service (DoS) attacks, as a malicious actor trying to spam millions of transactions would run out of funding.[6]

3.3.2. Programmability

Native digital assets are programmable—it's one of blockchain's superpowers. Let's first consider the programmability of fungible tokens (cryptocurrencies). Whereas the US Federal Reserve[iii] determines monetary policy for the US dollar, anyone can create a native digital asset and decide upon its monetary policies. There are multiple ways to create your own digital asset. Initially, new coins were created by downloading the Bitcoin Core, altering the programming code, and launching a 'fork' (see Glossary) to Bitcoin. These are called 'altcoins' because they are alternative coins to Bitcoin. Today it is more common to launch a new digital asset by using a smart contract on an

---

iii The US Federal Reserve consists of a seven-member board of directors and 12 regional banks. The regional institutions are owned by commercial banks and they only do business with the US Treasury and other member banks, not with the public at large.

existing platform like Ethereum. When a new token is launched, the native digital asset's monetary policies and functionality are pre-programmed. Basic monetary policies to consider include the money supply, token distribution, transferability, and divisibility (see Table 3.1). It's fascinating to consider how one might craft a monetary policy that results in a valuable digit asset. What policies would you choose?

		Fiat Example	Crypto Examples		
	Basic options	**US Dollar**	**Bitcoin (BTC)**	**Ethereum (ETH) 1.0**	**Binance (BNP)**
Token supply	Fixed/Unfixed	Unfixed	Fixed at 21 million	Not fixed	Fixed at 200 million
Token distribution	Distribute to commercial banks; Mining rewards, IXOs, air drops	Distribute to commercial banks	Mining reward only	ICO; mining; grants	ICO
Rights	Transferable/non-transferable	Transferable (laws apply)	Transferable	Transferable	Transferable
Divisibility	Whole or divisible	Divisible (cent)	Divisible (satoshi)	Divisible (wei)	Divisible (jager)

Table 3.1: Monetary policies for US Dollar and three cryptocurrencies

Token Supply. Tokens may have a fixed supply or an unfixed supply. You might choose a fixed supply if you are primarily concerned with creating value through scarcity. You might select an unfixed supply if you want to adapt the supply in the future to combat inflation or deflation.

The US dollar has an unfixed supply of money. The US Federal Reserve (Fed) has several ways to alter the money supply through its relationships with commercial banks, such as dictating the percentage of deposits the banks must keep in reserve and the rates at which banks can borrow money from the Fed. Lowering the reserve ratio or interest rate increases the money supply. The Fed can also increase the money supply by buying back treasury bonds, which puts more cash in circulation. The Fed reports monthly upon the total money supply using several formulas. For example, the M1 formula includes currency in circulation and checking account balances. The M1 money supply dramatically increased during the COVID-19 pandemic (see Figure 3.6).

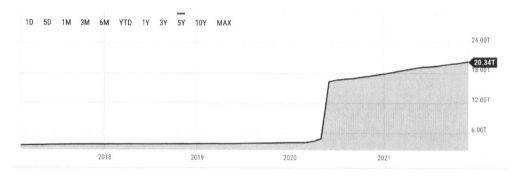

Figure 3.6: US money supply (M1) 2017-2021

Source: https://ycharts.com/indicators/us_m1_money_supply

Bitcoin is an example of a fixed money supply. Nakamoto was very concerned about the powers of the Fed, and invented Bitcoin in part to prevent inflation. Recall Nakamoto's quote from Chapter 1, *"The central bank must be trusted not to debase the currency, but the history of fiat currencies is full of breaches of that trust."*[7] Nakamoto, we noted, fixed Bitcoin's total money supply at 21 million bitcoins; there can never be more than 21 million bitcoins (BTC). In an email to Mike Hearn, Nakamoto explained further: *"If you imagine it being used for some fraction of world commerce, then there's only going to be 21 million coins for the whole world, so it would be worth much more per unit."*[8]

Ethereum's token, called ether (ETH), is an example of a non-fixed money supply. At its launch in 2014, 72 million ether were created, with 60 million allocated to the public for sale at its ICO and 12 million allocated to the Ethereum development fund. New coins are released with each new block to reward miners.[9] According to Ethereum's monetary policy, *"Ethereum does not have a fixed supply because a fixed supply would also require a fixed security budget for the Ethereum network. Rather than arbitrarily fix Ethereum's security, Ethereum's monetary policy is best described as 'minimum issuance to secure the network".*[10]

Like Bitcoin, Binance also decided upon a fixed money supply for its coin, BNB. The total BNB supply was capped at 200 million coins.

Token distribution. Tokens need to be put into circulation. The Fed distributes US dollars via the reserve ratios, discount rates, and open market operations discussed above. When creating a cryptocurrency, options include mining (releasing new coins every time a block is added to the ledger), applying to a foundation set up by the founders (like the Ethereum development fund or Stellar Foundation), air drops (depositing money into users' wallets), IXOs (e.g., ICO, IEO, STO, IDO) or a combination.

Bitcoin distributes coins through the process of mining. Every time a miner successfully adds a new block to the distributed ledger, a programmed number of coins is released from the total money supply into circulation by putting it in the miner's wallet address. Bitcoin releases new coins, on average, every ten minutes. Bitcoin's mining reward halves every 210,000 blocks; initially miners were awarded 50 bitcoins per block. In 2022, the bitcoin block reward is 6.25 bitcoins. The mining reward will drop to 3.125 bitcoins on May 3, 2024.

Ethereum used/uses a combination of ICO, mining, and grants from the Ethereum Foundation to distribute ether. Ethereum sold more than 50 million ether during its 2014 ICO, of which 10 percent went to Ethereum's founders and 10 percent to the non-profit, the Ethereum Foundation.[11] Ethereum also distributes new coins through mining. Unlike Bitcoin's fixed mining reward schedule, Ethereum does not have a set schedule but instead relies on Ethereum Improvement Proposals (EIPs), explained in the previous chapter, to alter the mining reward. The original mining reward was 5 ETH per block in 2015, which was reduced to 3 ETH in 2017 and to 2 ETH in 2019. The average time it takes to mine an Ethereum block is around 13-15 seconds.

Binance distributed its entire money supply of 200 million BNB upfront. One hundred million BNBs were distributed to the public during its ICO in 2017. Eighty million BNPs were distributed to its founders; and 20 million BNB were distributed to angel investors.[12] The protocol does not release new coins when a validator node creates a new block. Instead, transaction senders offer fees to the validator nodes.[13]

Airdrops are another way to get a cryptocurrency into circulation. Founders simply send coins directly into users' wallets, either with or without their permission. Founders only need public addresses, which they can find by searching the distributed ledger. If you decide to create your own cryptocurrency, we urge readers to always request permission before doing an airdrop. While receiving free coins may be viewed as a pleasant surprise, it violates the ethical principle of user control over their own assets. Moreover, it may have tax or other legal consequences that the recipient should have the right to consider. Sometimes founders airdrop coins into famous people's known public addresses without their permission, then brag that the influencer 'owns' their new coins. Founders have airdropped new coins into Vitalik Buterin's wallet, which he often burns or donates. For example, he donated the unwelcomed airdrop of 50 trillion Shiba Inu coins (SHIB) to the India COVID Relief Fund in 2021.[14]

In contrast to adding coins to the money supply, *burning tokens* removes them from the money supply, typically by sending it to a public wallet 'eater address'. An eater address is an address that is visible to the public but it is coded to be frozen—coins can be deposited but never withdrawn.[iv] One reasons to burn fungible tokens is to increase the scarcity, thus increasing its value. Binance, for example, intends to burn half of its BNB money supply over the next ten years. Another common example is burning an NFT to remove it from circulation.[15] Although less common, tokens may be programmed to be *non-burnable*. HelloCoins, for example, are non-burnable (although workarounds are discussed in online forums[16]).

---

iv For example one 'eater address' on Ethereum is: 0x000000000000000000000000000000000000dEaD

Rights of use. Once a person owns a token, its digital rights define what the owner is allowed to do with the token. A specific token might be ***transferable*** to other people. For example, US dollars are transferable, but ruled by laws to make sure the transfer is legal to prevent financial terrorism, money laundering, etc. Cryptocurrencies like BTC, ETH, and BNB are transferable.

Non-transferable tokens cannot be given or sold to other people, such as a person's identity token, professional license token or a vote token.

Divisibility. Tokens may be ***whole*** or ***divisible***. Let's first consider fungible assets. If divisible, the creators specify the number of decimal places. The US Dollar is divisible by a hundred; the smallest unit is called a 'cent' (100 cents equal one US Dollar). Bitcoin (BTC) is divisible down to eight decimal places. The smallest bitcoin unit is called a 'satoshi' (100 million satoshis make up one bitcoin). Ether (ETH) is divisible up to 18 decimal points, and its smallest unit is called a 'wei', named after the cryptographer Wei Dai. Like Bitcoin, BNB is divisible up to 8 decimal points, and its smallest unit is called a 'jager', named after one of its managers.

Let's now consider non-fungible tokens. Many NFTs are whole, i.e., non-divisible, essentially meaning that only one person can own the NFT at a time. Many artists, for example, create non-divisible NFTs to document ownership for their works of art. But newer models are emerging where NFTs can be divisible, allowing for ***fractional ownership of assets***. In 2021, a decentralized community of investors used a smart contract to pool their crypto to make a bid on one of the 13 original copies of the US Constitution (see Figure 3.7).

**Figure 3.7: The power of fractional ownership:
Community bid to buy US Constitution**

Source: https://icodrops.com/wp-content/uploads/2021/11/ConstitutionDAO_cover.png

Their smart contract, called ConstitutionDAO, was launched on Ethereum and raised over $20 million. Unfortunately, the community lost the auction to a bidder who bought it for $43 million. After losing, the community organizers posted, *"ConstitutionDAO (2021-2021) was a beautiful experiment in a single-purpose DAO. We now believe this project has run its course. The community has taken all actions that it was organized to accomplish: we raised capital, we bid at Sotheby's, and upon losing, we made full refunds available to the community as promised."[17]*

Other examples abound. An NFT for a real estate title could be divisible, allowing low-income investors to own some real estate anywhere in the world. Fractionalized ownership promotes inclusivity, one of the goals of Web 3.0. Imagine a time when a few million fans own a sports team, or when everyday art lovers share ownership of a Monet painting!

So far, we've stated several times that cryptocurrencies and crypto tokens are programmable digital assets that are secured by cryptography. It's now time to learn how cryptography works.

3.4. Cryptography

Blockchains rely heavily on cryptography, the science of securing data in the presence of third-party adversaries. There's quite a bit of imposing mathematics that secure blockchains, but here we will cover hexadecimal numbering system, hashes, and digital signatures.

3.4.1. Hexadecimal numbering system

Many blockchains rely on cryptography that is expressed in hexadecimals, otherwise known as base 16. The main advantage of a hexadecimal numbering system is that it is more closely related to the 8 bit byte computer architecture (2 hex = 1 byte). For those accustomed to the digital world (base 10), it takes a moment to realize that many blockchain data fields like addresses, transaction IDs, and block IDs are large numbers expressed in hexadecimal, which contain letters A, B, C, D, E, and F (see Table 3.2).

For example, this is a Bitcoin transaction ID, which is a *number* expressed in hexadecimal:

950ecd628c3630b0d7dec443eee2444d1dbb68a9a249c542d5d36e38df4e06ff

That number, converted to the decimal system is:

674207678126554680827895837823329084730098478281191329728549501352564 99226367[18]

The Bitcoin transaction ID above is created by taking inputs to the transaction—including sender's account address, receivers account address, miner's fee, and transaction amounts—by putting it through a hashing algorithm.

Decimal Base 10	Hexadecimal Base 16	Decimal Base 10	Hexadecimal Base 16
0	0	16	10
1	1	17	11
2	2	18	12
3	3	19	13
4	4	20	14
5	5	21	15
6	6	22	16
7	7	23	17
8	8	24	18
9	9	25	19
10	A	26	1A
11	B	27	1B
12	C	28	1C
13	D	29	1D
14	E	30	1E
15	F	31	1F

Table 3.2: Decimal to hexadecimal conversion

In addition to hexadecimal number systems, many blockchain applications also use Base58. Base58 uses the numbers 1 to 9, and all of the alphabet characters a to x and capital A to Z, except the 0, o, O, i, and I. The Bitcoin transaction ID above coverts to Base58 is:

29LdabXjZfCtXtbe9RG1ysXzkmnmpQLbMDHWU5AwhnDP9UKmgmHtc-Mbx6ZQonE9secWZ6swbfjZqHV3LkwmfhdFB

3.4.2. Hashing Algorithms

A hash is a mathematical algorithm for transforming one input into a different output. Given a specific input, the identical output will always be reproduced. A good hashing algorithm makes it practically impossible to determine the input value based on the output value, which is why hashes are called 'one-way' functions. Blockchains use hashes in many places to add layers of security. Public keys are hashed into addresses; addresses and amounts within a transaction are hashed to create a unique and secure transaction ID; transaction IDs within a block are hashed together multiple times to produce a Merkle Root that resides in a block header; and all the data in the block header is hashed to create a unique and secure block ID. SHA-256 is an example of a hashing algorithm.

SHA-256 is a secure, one-way hash function commonly used in blockchains. It was designed by the US National Security Agency. It takes any-sized input value and produces a 32-byte (i.e., 256 bit[i]) output value using hexadecimal notation. The output looks randomly generated, but the same input will always produce the exact same output. Figure 3.8 shows three examples. The first example transformed the name 'MaryLacity' into a 32-byte output. The second example, 'Marylacity', merely changed a capital 'L' to a small 'l', yet the output is completely different from the first example. The third example shows how a large block of text can still be transformed to a unique 32-byte output.[ii] It's quite remarkable!

---

i   A bit is a binary digit that can have a value of '1' or '0'; For example, the decimal number '256' is expressed as '100000000' in binary.

ii Astute readers may count what seems to be 64 characters, but hex uses two spaces to represent one character. '681794341783bb9b8e0c310ec316643bb3d1000766bdb5b32c63d3ffb7bad161' is best read as

'68 17 94 34 17 83 bb 9b 8e 0c 31 0e c3 16 64 3b b3 d1 00 07 66 bd b5 b3 2c 63 d3 ff b7 ba d1 61'

Example	Input (m)	SHA-256 Output H(m) in hex (base 16)
1	MaryLacity	681794341783bb9b8e0c310ec316643bb3d1000766bdb5b32c63d3ffb7bad161
2	Marylacity	de850a9d2f7d47163333ba3455cb94ea0209324470944df4c3d97dde99b5ad02
3	Dr. Mary C. Lacity is Walton Professor of Information Systems and Director of the Blockchain Center of Excellence in the Sam M. Walton College of Business at The University of Arkansas. She was previously Curators' Distinguished Professor at the University of Missouri. She has held visiting positions at MIT, the London School of Economics, Washington University, and Oxford University. She is a Senior Editor for MIS Quarterly Executive, a fellow of the Association of Information Systems	451217a5955fcb2146f807613ec2035c8d1ee276233ebc2e440950ea11ff900d

Figure 3.8: Three examples of the SHA-256 hash function

As a cryptographically secure one-way hash function, SHA-256 takes any size input and produces a unique 32-byte output.

Source: http://www.xorbin.com/tools/sha256-hash-calculator

Merkle root: Named after the US computer scientist, Ralph Merkle, the Merkle root is the result of a sequence of hashes between pairs of numbers. In blockchain applications, the numbers are pairs of transactions (see Figure 3.9). The process to calculate the Merkle root produces a very secure block because if a single digit is altered in any individual transaction, a subsequent calculation check of the Merkle root would reveal an alteration. For a given block, the Merkle root is added to the block's header.

3.4.3. Digital Signatures

A digital signature is the most important cryptographic feature to understand because if you don't protect the private key that is used to generate a digital signature, you risk losing your digital asset. Digital signatures have three functions: to ensure the sender is authentic, to ensure the transaction was not tampered with in transit, and to ensure the sender cannot later deny sending the transaction (non-repudiation).[19]

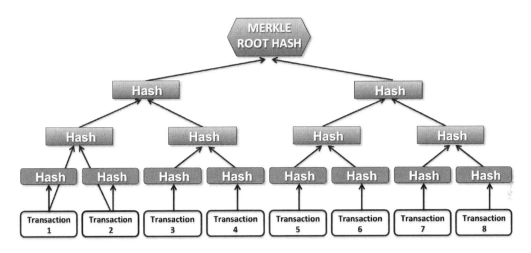

Figure 3.9: Merkle Tree

In this example, a block comprises 8 transactions. Each transaction is secured with a hash. Then, the transaction hashes are hashed again by hashing four pairs of transactions. Next, two pairs of the hashes are hashed. Then the last hash pair is hashed again, resulting in the root hash called the 'Merkle root'.

Here's how a digital signature works: A digital wallet generates a unique pair of numbers that are mathematically related, called a private-public key pair. The public key is the address we see stored on the blockchain (well actually, it's a hashed version of the public key—we'll explain that momentarily). The private key is stored off the blockchain. To move value out of the address stored on the blockchain, one needs to verify he or she owns the address by signing the transaction with their private key stored off the blockchain.

To digitally sign a transaction, the sender's wallet uses a computer algorithm (like ECC Digital Signature Standard) to create the signature. The inputs to the algorithm are the transaction data (called, 'the message') and the private key.[iii] The output is a number

---

iii It's more complicated than described here; the input also requires the starting point on the ECC curve.

called the 'digital signature'. Anyone can verify the signed message with three inputs: the transaction data, the digital signature, and the sender's public key. These numbers should reproduce the digital signature, proving that only the person with the private key could have created it (see Figure 3.10). It's more complicated than discussed here, but this a digital signature at a high level. To recap, a blockchain uses digital signatures to verify asset ownership and thus does not need to rely on a trusted third party to provide this function.

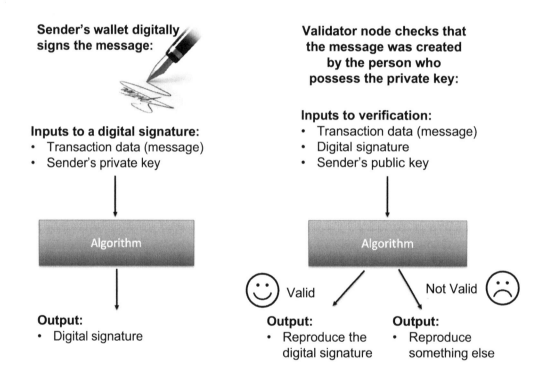

Figure 3.10: Proof of digital asset ownership using private-public key pairs

Advanced explanation. Blockchain applications commonly use **elliptic curve cryptography (ECC)** to generate the private-public key pairs. Basically, an ECC algorithm transforms a private key into a public key by bouncing around a large elliptic curve n number of times, where n is equal to the private key. The public key is the end point on the graph, i.e., a number with an x and y coordinate, after doing this process. It's theoretically impossible to figure out the private key if one only has the public key.

The specific elliptic curve used in Bitcoin is $y^2 = x^3 + 7$ (see Figure 3.11). This is called SECP256K1. If we give someone the starting point G and the ending point public key (x, y), one cannot easily determine the n (the private key)

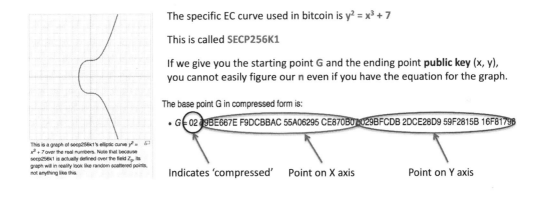

The specific EC curve used in bitcoin is $y^2 = x^3 + 7$

This is called **SECP256K1**

If we give you the starting point **G** and the ending point **public key** (x, y), you cannot easily figure our **n** even if you have the equation for the graph.

The base point G in compressed form is:

- G = 02 79BE667E F9DCBBAC 55A06295 CE870B07 029BFCDB 2DCE28D9 59F2815B 16F81798

This is a graph of secp256k1's elliptic curve $y^2 = x^3 + 7$ over the real numbers. Note that because secp256k1 is actually defined over the field Z_p, its graph will in reality look like random scattered points, not anything like this.

Indicates 'compressed'   Point on X axis   Point on Y axis

Figure 3.11: Elliptic curve cryptography creates private-public key pairs

The algorithm begins at base point G and moves across the graph trillions upon trillion of times equal to the private key to land on a final (x,y) coordinate that becomes the public key.

Source: https://en.bitcoin.it/wiki/Secp256k1

Figure 3.12 provides a specific example for creating a public-private key pair in Bitcoin. Suppose your friend, Jen, wants to send you some Bitcoin. You need to provide her with one of your public keys from your digital wallet. Here's how your digital wallet does it:

Your digital wallet generates a random number to serve as the private key. The private key is a very large number expressed in hexadecimal. Assume your wallet generated this private key:

DDA78BA47C7D3A1A49AA02E6C1CF7A30691603827E7DACE3C4EE63CA0D26DAE2ECC

To create the public key mate, the wallet uses the ECC algorithm; it bounces around the curve, $y^2 = x^3 + 7$, the number of times equal to the private key. ECC produces an (x,y) coordinate when the process is completed. In this example, your public key is temporarily in the form:

x = CDBE3A1BA0CC0E34F09886834DB0967B5E71EC9563050A4360C1DC66B371F883
y = D5B3EC7DAA354B0CF61E7EFF1ED863C88BA1E78D8AA405CC38B783DBDC9DD046

The (x,y) numbers are concatenated, and in front of that very large number, a '02' is added to indicate it is compressed. So the public key is now a very large number:

02CDBE3A1BA0CC0E34F09886834DB0967B5E71EC9563050A4360C1DC66B371F883D5B-
3EC7DAA354B0CF61E7EFF1ED863C88BA1E78D8AA405CC38B783DBDC9DD046

Next, the wallet transforms this large number into a smaller number. The public key is transformed into a Bitcoin address by hashing it twice; the second hash (RIPEMD160) shortens the first hash (SHA256) to produce a shorter address.[iv] So now, the wallet address, which begins with a 1, 3, or bc, depending on the algorithm used[v], reads as:

31uEbMgunupShBVTewXjtqbBv5MndwfXhb

This is the number you would give your friend, so she knows where to send the bitcoins.

---

iv This conversion is more complicated as it also includes checksums and Base256-toBase56 conversions.

v Legacy bitcoin addresses began with a '1'; Pay to Script Hash (P2SH) begins with a '3'; Native SegWit addresses begin with 'bc1q'; Taproot with 'bc1p'.

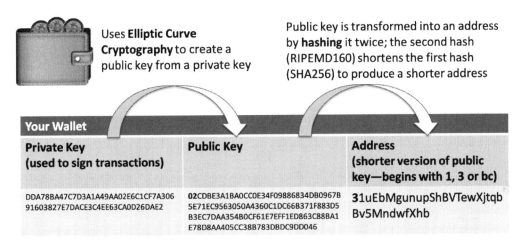

Uses **Elliptic Curve Cryptography** to create a public key from a private key

Public key is transformed into an address by **hashing** it twice; the second hash (RIPEMD160) shortens the first hash (SHA256) to produce a shorter address

Your Wallet		
Private Key (used to sign transactions)	**Public Key**	**Address** (shorter version of public key—begins with 1, 3 or bc)
DDA78BA47C7D3A1A49AA02E6C1CF7A306 91603827E7DACE3C4EE63CA0D26DAE2	**02**CDBE3A1BA0CC0E34F09886834DB0967B 5E71EC9563050A4360C1DC66B371F883D5 B3EC7DAA354B0CF61E7EFF1ED863C88BA1 E78D8AA405CC38B783DBDC9DD046	**31uEbMgunupShBVTewXjtqb Bv5MndwfXhb**

Figure 3.12: How a private key is transformed into a Bitcoin address

3.5. Consensus protocols

The **consensus protocol** is one of the most important protocols. It enables decentralization and defines the rules for making sure copies of the distributed ledger agree. A blockchain consensus protocol is often called a 'trust protocol'. However, the word 'trust' is narrowly defined to mean, 'trust that the records on the distributed ledger agree across copies.' There are many possible consensus protocols to define a process for reaching a consensus.

Let's first think about some possible methods for reaching consensus in an everyday scenario. Assume you are hanging out with three of your friends and you all want to order a pizza. When you pool your money, you only have enough funds to buy a large pizza with one topping. How do you decide which pizza topping to order? You and your friends might invoke several processes, i.e., protocols, for selecting the topping. Perhaps you agree that you all get an equal vote, but with four people voting, four toppings might be proposed, or tie votes (2-2) might occur, so you need another consensus method. Perhaps you and your friends have previously agreed to take turns picking a topping. It happens to be your turn, but you won't get to pick the topping again until your friends have ordered three more pizzas. This method is analogous to the consensus protocol known as Practical Byzantine Fault Tolerance (PBFT). Perhaps the choices are weighted by the amount of money each person pitched in—this method is analogous to the consensus protocol known as Proof-of-Stake (PoS). Perhaps you hold a contest—the first person who gets the order in online wins, and the rest of the friends stop ordering when the winner confirms the order was accepted by the restaurant. This is analogous to the Proof-of-Work (PoW) consensus used by Bitcoin and Ethereum 1.0.

Our pizza scenario is an example of the 'Byzantine Generals' Problem', a scenario that is referred to in many blockchain white papers.

The Byzantine Generals' Problem is a conceptual situation described by Leslie Lamport, Robert Shostak, and Marshall Pease (1982) to investigate how decentralized communication networks can reach agreement if some unknown number of nodes is faulty. They imagined a scenario where an army has set up divisions outside of an ancient city (i.e., before phones were invented). The only way the divisions can communicate is by sending a messenger (See Figure 3.13). To take the city successfully, all the divisions must attack at the same time. If only some of the divisions attack, they will be slaughtered. How can the entire army coordinate an attack when a messenger might be traitor or when a division commander might be a traitor? In their metaphor, a Byzantine General represents a computer node; most generals and messengers are loyal (i.e., not faulty) but some generals and messengers are traitors (i.e., faulty). Lamport et al. (1982) proved that the division generals could reach consensus provided two thirds of the people are loyal. Translating the metaphor to decentralized networks, decentralized networks can reach a consensus provided that two thirds (67 percent) of the nodes function properly.[20]

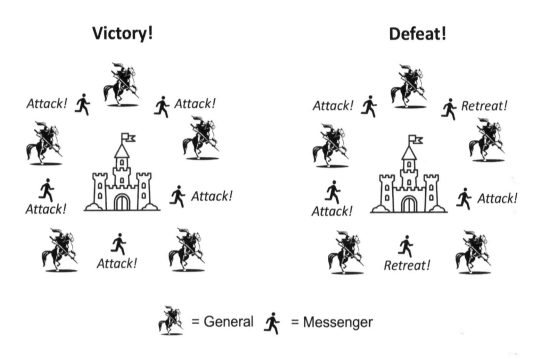

Figure 3.13: Byzantine Generals' Problem

The Byzantine Generals' Problem is a conceptual situation described by Lamport et al. (1982) to investigate how decentralized communication networks can reach agreement if some unknown number of nodes is faulty. In their analogy, a general is a node in the network. They found that 2/3 of the nodes must function properly to reach consensus, meaning 1/3 of the nodes could be faulty but the network still reaches consensus. In our picture on the left, all five generals received the attack message, leading to success. In the picture on the right, consensus is not reached; three generals attack and get slaughtered since two generals retreated (40 percent were faulty).

Many consensus protocols have been proposed, including proof-of-work; proof-of-stake; proof-of-activity; proof-of-burn; proof-of-authority; proof-of-space-time; proof-of-capacity; proof-of-listening; proof-of-elapsed time[21]; proof-of-attention; proof-of-importance; proof-of-luck—the list goes on.[22]

Although consensus protocols vary in their validation procedures, in general, all consensus protocols seek to verify legitimate transactions, reject unverifiable transactions, ignore faulty nodes on the network, and prevent modifications to the ledger. The process of validation begins when a new transaction is broadcast to the network. Computer algorithms on the other nodes verify legitimate ownership of the asset (based on the owner's digital signature with their private key) and check that the asset has not been given away before by scanning the digital ledger, thus preventing double spending. Which node gets to collect verified transactions, sequence them, and add them to the official ledger depends on the network's specific consensus protocol.

Three common *classes* of consensus protocols are 'proof-of-work' (used by Bitcoin, Ethereum 1.0, Dogecoin, Litecoin, Zcash and Monero), 'proof-of-stake' (used by Ethereum 2.0, Algorand, Cardano, Cosmos, Polygon, Solana, and Polkadot), and 'Practical Byzantine Fault Tolerance (PBFT)' (used by Ripple, Stellar, Hyperledger Fabric, Quorum, and Corda). Within the class of consensus, it's important to note that different blockchain applications using the same 'class' of protocol may vary from the descriptions below. For example, versions of PBFT include Reliable, Replicated, Redundant, And Fault-Tolerant (RAFT); Redundant Byzantine Fault Tolerance (RBFT)[23]; Delegated Byzantine Fault Tolerance[24]; and Federated Byzantine Agreement[25]—to name but a few.

Proof-of-Work (PoW) is a consensus protocol created by Cynthia Dwork and Moni Naor in 1993 to prevent junk email.[26] Satoshi Nakamoto adopted the 'proof-of-work' consensus protocol for Bitcoin in the 2008 white paper.[27] Nakamoto needed a way to find independent verifiers to validate transactions and add blocks to the blockchain without relying on trusted third parties. Nakamoto proposed to reward other nodes in the network with newly issued bitcoins when they validate all recently submitted transactions and create the next block. So that validator nodes take the task seriously, Nakamoto proposed a competition among computer nodes in the blockchain network to be the first to collect recently verified transactions into a block and then to find an acceptable block identification number (known as the blockhash) for the next block in the blockchain. It's not easy to find an acceptable number—it takes a lot of computing power to perform the brute force guesses to find a hash number that is less than the current mining 'difficulty' (explained below). The difficulty is part of the proof that the miner's computer did a significant amount of work to earn the block reward. The proof-of-work protocol creates a highly secure ledger, as an attacker would need to gain control of more than 50 percent of the processing power of the network, rewrite history and find all new hashes that adhere to the protocol before other nodes notice. The cons of the protocol include slower transaction settlement times and higher electricity consumption compared to other protocols.

Proof-of-Stake (PoS) is a consensus protocol created by Sunny King and Scott Nadal, in a 2012 white paper.[28] Instead of competing for coins, a validator node is selected in a semi-random way. It's called a 'proof-of-stake' because the members with the highest 'stake' offered as collateral are given priority in the selection algorithm. By locking their coins in a 'collateral' account, the validators are showing their good faith because they will lose their stake if they misbehave. PoS selection algorithms may bias the selection based on the largest account balances, holding the coins for the longest time period in a locked account, or other methods. Participants in the blockchain can estimate with some certainty which member will likely be the next validator. A proof-of-stake process uses much less energy than a proof-of-work process. It creates a highly secure ledger, as an attacker would need to gain control of more than 50 percent of the cryptocurrency to rewrite the ledger. However, critics claim it is less secure than proof-of-work because people with small stakes have little to lose by voting for multiple blockchain histories, which leads to consensus never resolving.[29] Also, some fear that with PoS, the rich will get richer and the poor will get poorer. The rich are more likely to stake their money and therefore be selected to create a block, thus increasing their wealth with more stake rewards, which might lead to central control of the network. Supporters of PoS disagree. For example, Ryan Adams argued that wealth grows proportionally. He wrote, *"the rich increase their wealth from 100 to 110, and the poor increase their wealth from 10 to only 11. However, since there are 10 poor stakers for every 1 single rich staker, the percentage share in the network does not change. Therefore, decentralization is not compromised."*[30]

Figure 3.14 compares PoW with PoS.

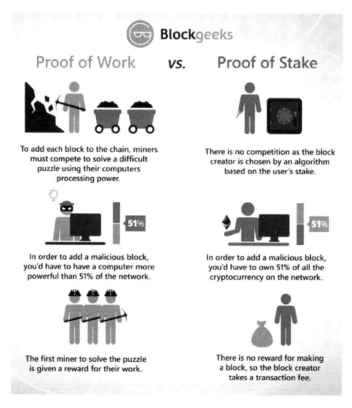

Figure 3.14: Proof-of-Work *vs.* Proof-of-Stake

Source: https://blockgeeks.com/wp-content/uploads/2019/05/proofofworkvsproofofstake-1.jpg

Practical Byzantine Fault Tolerance (PBFT) is a consensus protocol created by Miguel Castro and Barbara Liskov in 1999.[31] With PBFT, nodes need permission to serve as validator nodes, forming a member list. The nodes know each other, with each node operator staking their reputation that they will behave properly. Each round, a node from the member list is selected as leader (see Figure 3.15). A client node sends a request to the leader node to validate a transaction. The leader node multicasts the request to all the other authorized nodes. The authorized nodes execute the request independently and then send to each other and reply to the client. The client waits for a certain percentage of replies to confirm validation, typically waiting for 2/3 of the nodes to agree. The leader node changes for next round.

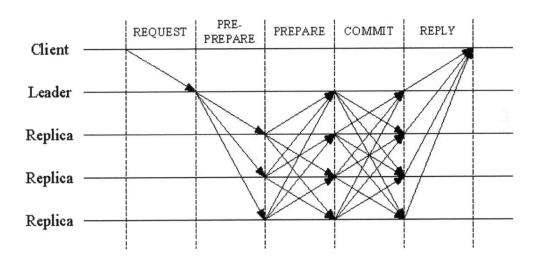

Figure 3.15: Practical Byzantine Fault Tolerance (PBFT) consensus process

Source: Castro & Liskov (1999) https://theintelligenceofinformation.files.wordpress.com/2017/02/ hotdep_img_1.jpg

PBFT consensus algorithms can process hundreds/thousands of transactions per second, with quick settlement times, and low resource consumption. However, PBFT is more centralized than PoW or PoS and settlement times will slow as more nodes are added. Also, anonymity is lost, as node operators are known. The loss of anonymity is an advantage for some applications that need to comply with regulations, but seen as a disadvantage by many public network advocates.

To recap, consensus protocols have tradeoffs between the number of transactions processed per second, settlement speed, resource consumption in terms of electricity consumed, security, and anonymity *vs.* confidentiality (see Figure 3.16).

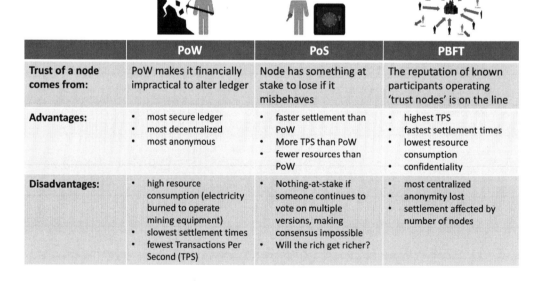

	PoW	PoS	PBFT
Trust of a node comes from:	PoW makes it financially impractical to alter ledger	Node has something at stake to lose if it misbehaves	The reputation of known participants operating 'trust nodes' is on the line
Advantages:	• most secure ledger • most decentralized • most anonymous	• faster settlement than PoW • More TPS than PoW • fewer resources than PoW	• highest TPS • fastest settlement times • lowest resource consumption • confidentiality
Disadvantages:	• high resource consumption (electricity burned to operate mining equipment) • slowest settlement times • fewest Transactions Per Second (TPS)	• Nothing-at-stake if someone continues to vote on multiple versions, making consensus impossible • Will the rich get richer?	• most centralized • anonymity lost • settlement affected by number of nodes

Figure 3.16: Advantages and disadvantages of PoW, PoS, and PBFT

3.6. Smart contracts

A smart contract, a concept developed by Nick Szabo in 1994, is *"a piece of software that stores rules for negotiating the terms of a contract, automatically verifies the contract and then executes the terms."*[32] Anything that can be coded with clearly specified rules, can be coded into a smart contract that is secured and permanently stored on a blockchain. Ethereum was the first major blockchain to include full smart contracting capabilities, thus escalating blockchains from peer-to-peer payment systems to platforms that can execute machine-to-machine agreements. By January 2020, over 1,000,000 contracts were running on Ethereum, but many of these were simple little contracts such as 'hello world'.[33] In 2022, the most widely used smart contracts were for decentralized exchanges (DEX), including Uniswap, SushiSwap, Bancor Network, Ether Delta and Airswap.[34]

The term 'smart contract' does not mean that the contract is a legally binding contract; it's more accurate to think of it as a small computer program that codifies agreed upon rules. Smart contracts' magic (and danger) is that once deployed, they execute automatically and cannot be stopped. Therefore, parties must decide in advance on all the terms of the agreement before deploying it. Smart contracts are commonly used to automatically move value around accounts based on agreed upon conditions. As we shall see, use cases abound: lotteries; voting; crowdsourcing; asset sharing (lookout Uber, Airbnb, and Spotify); asset tracking; identity management; bidding; rating; gaming; and gambling. In general, smart contracts can be classified as either deterministic or non-deterministic.

A deterministic smart contract means that the contract, once deployed on the blockchain, can execute autonomously without the need for any outside information. A lottery is a good example. A smart contract for a lottery could define the time period when people could send value to the smart contract public address to buy lottery tickets. The smart contract could specify how the winning lottery number would be selected, perhaps by taking the hash of a randomly selected block and awarding the address that is closest to that number as the winner. The smart contract could automatically transfer the money to the winning address. If the lottery was regulated, the smart contract could be coded to deduct taxes.

A non-deterministic smart contract means that outside information is needed to execute the contract. Horse race betting is an example. Like a lottery, a smart contract for horse race betting could be coded to define when people could send value to the smart contract account to place their bets. The rules for adjusting odds could also be mechanized in the contract. However, smart contracts for horse racing cannot run autonomously; they need outsiders (called '*oracles*') to inform the smart contract of the winning animal. Unlike trusted third parties, an oracle in this scenario does not control the funds, the smart contract does.

Autonomous execution of organizations. One special kind of smart contact is called a Decentralized Autonomous Organization (DAO):

> *"The idea of a DAO is to create a completely independent entity that is exclusively governed by the rules that you program into it and 'lives' on the chain. This is more than using the blockchain to manage a company: instead, the code is the entire company. And it cannot be stopped."*
>
> **Henning Diedrich, author of *Ethereum: Blockchains,
> Digital Assets, Smart Contracts, DAOs*[35]**

The concept of a DAO is intriguing. As the name implies, the idea is to create a new organization that runs automatically based on codified rules encrypted in a smart contract. It runs without anyone controlling it, and it cannot be modified or rescinded once it is launched. ***Think of a decentralized autonomous organization as a completely digital 'company' with no managers or employees.*** The 'owners' are the ones who transferred cryptocurrencies to the DAO's public address during an initial funding period. Their investments are subject to the rules of the contract, such as limiting when the balance can be liquidated.

We've already discussed the ConstitutionDAO. If you view the smart contract on the Ethereum ledger, you will see that the address balance is zero because the DAO refunded all the money, as promised, when they lost the bid.[36]

The most successful DAOs to date are decentralized exchanges like Uniswap, Aave, Maker, and SushiSwap. Not all DAOs have been successful. The coders of one particular DAO created such havoc, it resulted in a huge battle within the Ethereum open-source community, resulting in the community dividing Ethereum into Ethereum and Ethereum Classic. The story, covered in Chapter 2, is an important reminder of the difficulty of writing secure smart contracts and the challenges of shared governance when things go wrong.

Thus far, we have covered protocols for the distributed ledger; native digital assets; cryptography; consensus (to make sure everyone has the identical copy of the ledger); and smart contracts. All these rules must be specified and agreed upon before protocols are programmed into code bases.

3.7. Code bases

Open-source communities, consortia, private companies and individuals can program protocols into *code bases.* A code base is the set of programming instructions based on the blueprints, i.e., the protocols. To increase security, independent software teams should code the detailed functionality in different programming languages to improve fault tolerance and redundancy. For example, Ethereum protocols have been coded in various computer languages like Go, Rust, C++, Python, Java, Ruby, etc. The practice is called **n-versioning**.

Many code bases are managed by an open-source community who decides what changes can be made to the code base. Open-source code bases also allow people to download the code and play with the code in a test environment called a 'sandbox'.

Of course, Bitcoin was the first blockchain code base, but most businesses initially adopt open-source code bases for permissioned code bases, although many are experimenting with public Ethereum. HfS Research found that the top code bases for enterprises were Ethereum, Hyperledger Fabric, R3 Corda, Ripple and Quorum.[37] Multichain has also gained momentum by partnering with companies like Accenture, Cognizant, DeFi protocol Aave, and Mphasis to help build blockchain applications.

GitHub (bought by Microsoft in 2018) is a version-controlled repository hosting service that manages many open source blockchain code bases. Code bases are released in stages, such as alpha, beta, release candidate, and general availability. Upgrades are released and tracked using version control (see Table 3.3).

Code base	Released	Version as of January 2022
Bitcoin Core	Initial release: 2009	Bitcoin Core version 0.21.1[38]
Ethereum 1.0 (PoW)	General availability: 2015	Berlin and London upgrades were made in 2021[39]
Ethereum 2.0 (PoS)	Beacon Chain: 2020 (testnet)	ETH 2.0 Phase 1 scheduled for mid to late 2022
Cardano	Initial release: 2017	Cardano V1.33[40]
Quorum	Beta: 2017	Go-Ethereum v1.9.23[41]
Corda	Beta: 2017	Corda 4.7[42]
Hyperledger Fabric	Beta: 2017	Fabric v2.4.1[43]
Multichain	Pre-Beta: 2017	MultiChain v2.2[44]

Table 3.3: Code base release dates

3.8. Blockchain application use cases

Code bases can be used to develop *blockchain use cases,* i.e., applications. What makes a blockchain use case worthwhile? We have already discussed that distributed ledgers are preferred when centralized control is not wanted. Now let's refine the reasoning. 'Distributed databases' is an umbrella term that encompasses many different architectural designs where data is stored in multiple places and where agreement is maintained through computer algorithms that lock and time stamp records. Given that definition, we see that ***blockchains are distributed database systems, just of a special kind***. Whereas traditional distributed databases are centrally controlled so that a single organization can decide to alter records or access rules, blockchains are distributed—no one entity has the power to roll back or alter history. Under what circumstances is the distributed control of blockchains preferable to the centralized control of traditional databases? The answer depends on the 'trust boundary' (see Figure 3.17).

All the nodes in a traditional distributed database environment trust each other, and therefore fewer verifications are required.[46] Trust is not presumed among nodes in a blockchain distributed ledger, so every event must be checked and rechecked, which is one reason why traditional distributed databases are magnitudes faster than blockchains.[47] Other experts also point to the inclusion of smart contracts as a distinguishing feature and advantage of blockchains over distributed database systems.

There are countless circumstances when parties do not trust each other. Trying to account for the number of blockchain use cases is as pointless as asking, *"what can I use the Internet for?"* The possibilities are limitless. Figure 3.18 provides examples of use cases across industries collected from press announcements and Google alerts. Firms from the financial services industry were the first to take serious notice of blockchain's opportunities and threats, and therefore have explored more use cases than other industries. Insurance, healthcare, supply chain, media and entertainment and governments are quickly catching up, and new applications arise daily. Decentralized finance (DeFi) and metaverses are relatively new, but exploding in terms of investment and deployments. It's exciting to contemplate all the application use cases that will emerge that we cannot envision today. Perhaps YOU will be the person to create the next killer app!

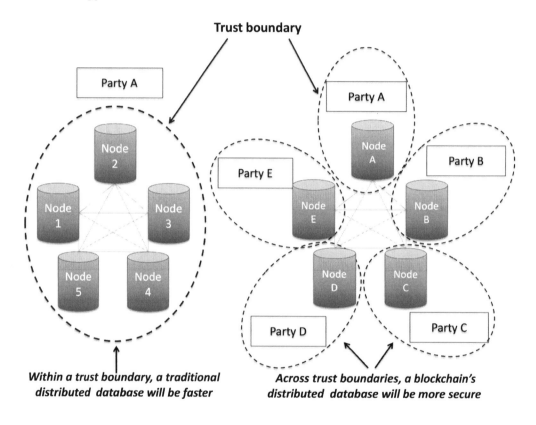

Figure 3.17: The 'trust boundary' as the distinguishing difference

Source: Adapted from Richard Gendal Brown[45]

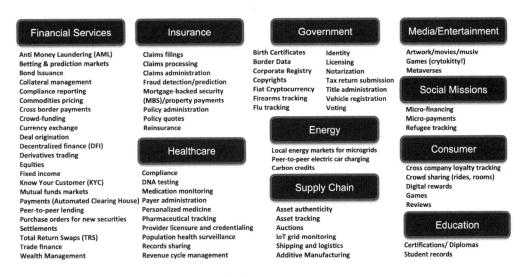

Figure 3.18: Blockchain use cases

Sources: various press announcements, Google alerts

3.9. The blockchain application interface ('access point')

To access public blockchain applications, users need a digital wallet they download themselves or go through an exchange like Coinbase, Kraken, or Binance. Beware: if you choose to use an exchange, you have introduced a centralized party, so you are no longer trading peer-to-peer. Using an exchange is termed, 'centralized finance' (CeFi). To access private blockchains, enterprise users typically interface through gateway services or build their own interfaces to existing systems using Application Programming Interfaces (APIs).

Interfaces are blockchains' main points of vulnerability. Nearly all of the hacks one hears about occur at the access points. We've already introduced the notion of a digital signature that comprises private-public key pairs. Hackers don't waste their time trying to calculate the private key because it's theoretically impossible to figure out the private key if one only has the public key (at least until Quantum computers are mainstream, see Chapter 10). Hackers find it much more lucrative to *steal* the private keys.

137

Many consumers do not realize just how vulnerable they are to theft or loss of their private keys. Many people keep their private keys in digital wallets stored on their mobile devices, again, not realizing that if the phone breaks or is lost or is hacked, they lose their private keys. As a general rule, private keys cannot be recovered—there is no help desk to call to retrieve them like when one forgets a password and no credit card company to report and recover damages from fraud. That said, new services are emerging that may help with recovery of private keys, but it is still early days and therefore difficult to find a provider with a strong historical track record. The safest places to store private keys are on a storage drive that is not connected to the Internet and, quite ironically, on a piece of paper that is locked in a fireproof safe.

Other people trust their centralized exchanges to store and protect their keys. However, hackers most commonly target exchanges because they can steal large numbers of private keys. One of the largest heists occurred in August of 2014 when 850,000 bitcoins worth $450 million at the time was stolen from the wallets managed by Mt.Gox, the largest Bitcoin exchange at the time. It's important to understand that such heists have not breached the blockchain itself. These heists happen outside the blockchain, that is, in the vulnerable access points to a blockchain.

Many exchanges now comply with regulations, including Know Your Customer (KYC) and anti-money laundering (AML) requirements. For example, Coinbase had money transmitter licenses from 45 US States and a New York State Virtual Currency License by 2019. Coinbase also has commercial criminal insurance that is greater than the value of digital currency maintained in online storage (98 percent of the private keys are stored offline). Increased compliance means a loss of user anonymity, a consequence counter to the Cypherpunk values of the initial Bitcoin adopters.

Thus far, we have explained all the component parts of a blockchain application. Hopefully by now, readers are comfortable with the notions of blockchains' protocols, code bases, use cases and application interfaces. We are now ready to map Bitcoin to the Blockchain Application Framework introduced, earlier, in Figure 3.1.

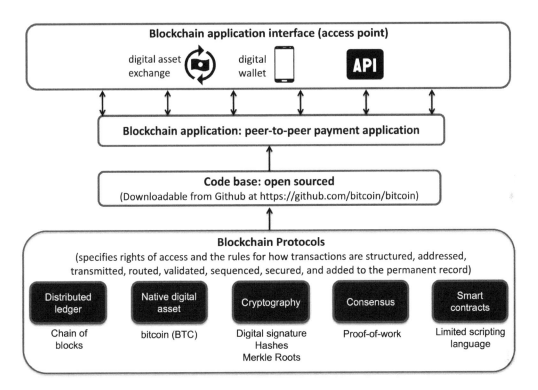

Figure 3.19: Bitcoin mapped to the Blockchain Application Framework

3.10. Mapping bitcoin to the Blockchain Application Framework

Like all blockchain applications, Bitcoin has its own protocols, code base, use case, and access points, which are mapped to the Blockchain Application Framework in Figure 3.19. Beginning at the bottom of the figure, Bitcoin's *distributed ledger* is structured as a chain of blocks. Bitcoin's *native digital asset* is a bitcoin (BTC). Bitcoin uses digital signatures (and other sophisticated *cryptographic* techniques) to authenticate asset ownership and to secure transactions. Bitcoin uses proof-of-work as its mechanism to ensure *consensus* across nodes in the network. Bitcoin participation access is open to the public and anyone can operate a validator node, i.e., it's permissionless. Bitcoin does not have what is called a 'Turing complete' (see Glossary)[48] *smart contracting* component (that innovation came later with Ethereum), but Bitcoin does have a scripting language that is intentionally restricted to increase security.

Moving up the framework diagram in Figure 3.19, the *code base* is called Bitcoin Core, and is maintained and supported by an open-source community. Anyway may download the code base from GitHub (https://github.com/bitcoin/bitcoin).

Bitcoin's *use case* is a peer-to-peer payment application; it is used to settle and store transfers of bitcoin on the distributed ledger.

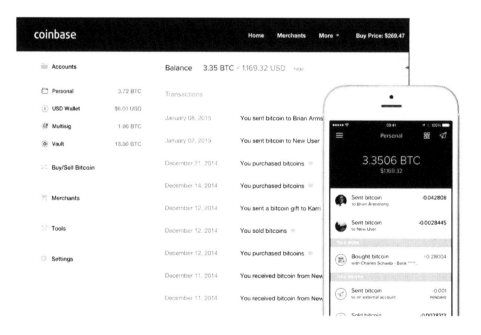

Figure 3.20: Example of a web-based and mobile digital wallet interface to Bitcoin

Source: https://www.coinbase.com/assets/home/global3-f9646244d66dd7c26191f091585db0f4feda2af3cad 7cfe63b0de080d1cd36c5.png

The *interface* to Bitcoin requires wallet software that stores the user's private keys off the blockchain. Wallet software makes it easy for users to transfer bitcoins (see Figure 3.20). Software developers can also access Bitcoin with over 125 APIs. For example, the API 'getBalance' triggers a remote call that returns the balance in a digital wallet.[49]

To get a better understanding of Bitcoin's transparency, immutability and anonymity, one may visit https://blockchain.com/explorer to see the most recent blocks (see Figure 3.21). One can also search the entire history of the blockchain by block number (called block 'height'), transaction ID or address (i.e., a hashed version of the public key).

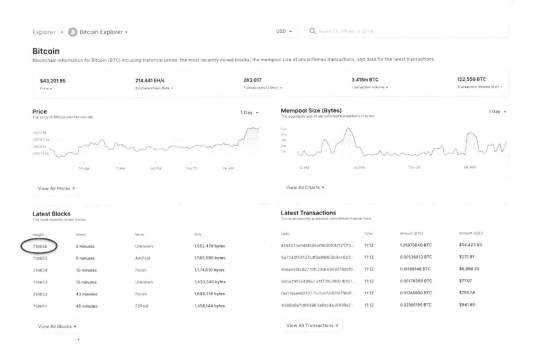

Figure 3.21: A screenshot of a website to view Bitcoin's blockchain

Block 71965 was the 'latest block' on January 20, 2022 at 11:12am UTC

Readers should now have more insight into the data stored on the distributed ledger for a Bitcoin transaction. Returning to a sample Bitcoin transaction introduced in Chapter 1 (see Figure 3.22), we now understand how the addresses are created. You can look up the transaction on the Bitcoin ledger:

https://www.blockchain.com/btc/address/13XSrVkweo5Dzm3yuykFw4P63N63MA6bTd

It was included in block 400000 that occurred on January 25, 2016. It's been confirmed 320,625 on the day of this writing, meaning that 320,635 blocks are now on top of it in the ledger.

Now that we understand the component parts of Bitcoin, let's better understand how the component parts work together to process a transaction.

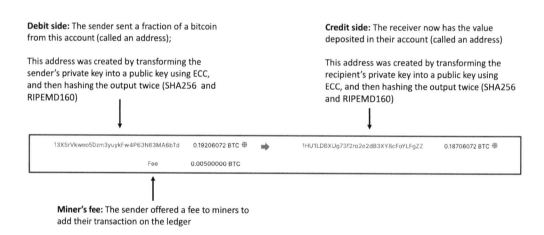

Figure 3.22: An example of a transaction stored on Bitcoin's public ledger

3.11. A Bitcoin transaction from start to finish

We've covered a lot of ground in this chapter. We've looked at the component parts of a digital ledger, native digital asset, cryptography, consensus protocol, smart contracts, code bases, use case and user interfaces. We next examine how the component parts work together to process a transaction, using Bitcoin as an example.[50]

Let's return to the scenario where your friend, Jen, wants to send you bitcoins (see Figure 3.23):

Step 1: You need to provide Jen with one of your public addresses from your digital wallet. You could call, write, text, or email Jen the Bitcoin public address we used above:

Your public address: 31uEbMgunupShBVTewXjtqbBv5MndwfXhb

Step 2: Jen uses her digital wallet to initiate the transaction. She wants to send you .001 bitcoins (worth about $35 on the day of this writing). She offers .00001 bitcoins (about 35 cents) as a transaction fee to the miners. Jen's wallet uses an address with enough funds to cover the amount being sent (.00101 bitcoins in total). (More than one address may be needed to cover the amount, but we will keep the example simple and assume Jennifer has one address that can cover the amount). Let's assume Jen's public address is:

Jen's public address: 38FvtF5xore37GduBTKQ5mYGHoHJJdRwKA

Her wallet generates a transaction with inputs and outputs. The input field contains just one 'from' address (Jen's public address) and total amount to be distributed to output addresses (.00101 BTC).[vi] The output field contains just one 'to' address (your public address) and the amount to go into your address (.001 BTC). The leftover is the miner's reward (.00001 BTC). The transaction is signed with Jen's digital signature.

---

vi If Jennifer's 'send' address has more than .001 bitcoins, her wallet will give her the change by pulling another one of her addresses and adding it to the 'output' part of the transaction.

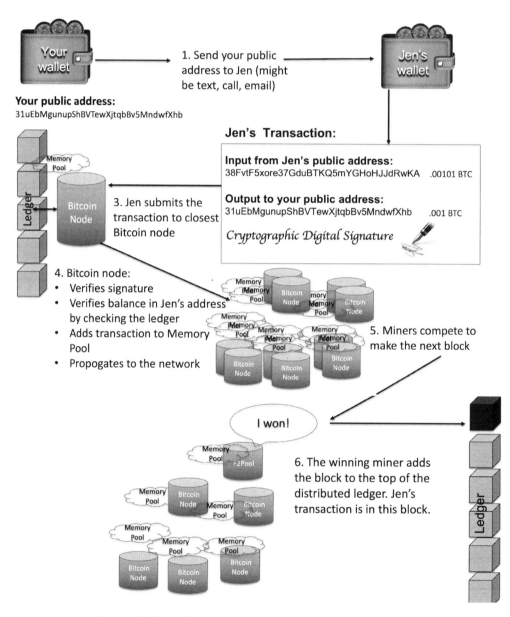

Figure 3.23: A Bitcoin transaction from start to finish

Step 3. Jen hits submit. The wallet sends the transaction to the closest node in the Bitcoin network using that node's IP address. The node verifies the digital signature and checks the digital ledger to make sure there are enough bitcoins in Jen's 'from' address(es) to cover the transaction. The miner's computer calculates an address balance by processing all the sequences of credits and debits to the address to make sure the address balance is great enough to fund Jen's transaction. This prevents the double spend.

After passing verification, the transaction gets added to the node's Memory Pool and it is propagated to the other nodes in the Bitcoin Network. In general, each node is directly connected to about eight other nodes, and quickly, the Bitcoin nodes can see all the valid transactions in the Memory Pool that are ready to be added to the distributed ledger.

While these new transactions are being verified and added to the Memory Pool, the mining nodes are also grabbing valid transactions from the Memory Pool to try to create the next block. The nodes select the transactions with the highest transaction fees first; the nodes grab as many transactions as can fit into the maximum block size (initially set by Nakamoto at 1MB per block, later increased by SegWit). Thankfully, the network is not busy today, so Jennifer's modest offer of 35 cents worth of bitcoin is enough for the miners to grab it.

Next, the miners' computers are frantically competing to write the next block. The first mining node to find an acceptable block identification number (known as the blockhash) to place on top of the distributed ledger is the winner. It's not easy to find an acceptable number—it takes a lot of computing power to perform the brute force guesses to find a hash number that is less than the current mining 'difficulty'.[vii] The difficulty is part of the proof that the miner's computer did a significant amount of work to earn the block reward. Figure 3.24 shows how it works.

---

vii A new block is mined every ten minutes on average. If miners start producing blocks faster than every ten minutes, the mining difficulty automatically increases to slow the process down. If miners start producing blocks slower than 10 minutes, the mining difficulty is decreased. The adjustment is made every 2,016 blocks (about every two weeks).

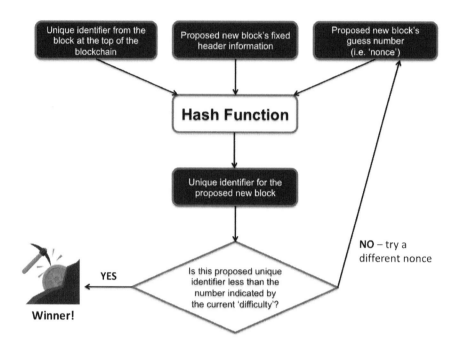

Figure 3.24: The 'proof-of-work' mining competition algorithm

A miner's computer takes the unique identifier (i.e., the blockhash) from the block at the top of the chain and hashes that number with the proposed next block's header of fixed information—the protocol version number, the root hash of the Merkle tree, the current time, and the difficulty—and a randomly selected number called a 'nonce'. The hash is then checked to see if it is less than the current mining difficulty. If the hash is greater than the target difficulty, the algorithm tries another guess. If it is less than the target difficulty, the miner wins the competition and is awarded newly created coins.

Let's assume F2Pool won the contest and broadcasts the new block that contains Jen's transaction. F2Pool receives a set reward of newly released bitcoins, which was 6.25 bitcoins as of 2022, plus the sum of all the small fees that people offered miners to include their transactions in the block, including Jennifer's 35 cents worth of bitcoins.

This total reward that goes to the miner is always the first transaction in a block. All the other nodes check the new block and the process starts again.

When can you be confident that the transaction has settled? Meaning, when will the entire Bitcoin network agree that your address, 31uEbMgunupShBVTewXjtqbBv5MndwfXhb, has .001 bitcoins in it? Bitcoin's settlement is probabilistic rather than deterministic. Although a new block is created on average every ten minutes, the actual settlement time is longer due to the possibility of a temporary divergence of the network. Sometimes two miners create the next block at the same time, resulting in two versions of the top of the ledger. For a short while, different nodes in the network work off different branches of the ledger until one branch is established as the longest and therefore the valid branch. To confidently consider a bitcoin transaction to be settled, it is generally recommended to wait until the transaction is six blocks deep, which on average takes an hour. Thereafter, you can be secure that the whole network agrees you own the bitcoin because it's locked in and visible for the world to see on the ledger.

3.12. Conclusion

In this chapter, we have learned that a blockchain application comprises protocols, code bases, use cases, and application interfaces. We took a closer look at the protocols associated with distributed ledgers, native digital assets, cryptography, consensus and smart contracts. Hopefully, readers can now comprehend the definition that opened this chapter:

> A blockchain application is a peer-to-peer (decentralized) network for validating, timestamping, and permanently storing transactions on a shared **distributed ledger**. **Digital assets**, native to each blockchain application, are programmable, exist only in digital form, and come with rights of use. **Consensus** algorithms validate transactions, update the ledger, and keep copies of the ledger in sync. **Cryptography** helps to secure the network. Most blockchains use **smart contracts** that apply rules to automatically execute transactions based upon pre-agreed conditions.

So far in our learning journey, we've learned about the 'why' of blockchains (i.e., it's the architecture for decentralization), the 'what' of blockchains as described in the application framework, and how a transaction works. In the next chapter, we will look at 'who' is investing in, creating and using blockchain technologies.

Citations

[1] Popov, S. (2017). *The Tangle*, IOTA whitepaper https://iota.org/IOTA_Whitepaper.pdf

[2] Popov, S. (2017), *The Tangle*, IOTA whitepaper https://iota.org/IOTA_Whitepaper.pdf

[3] Nakamoto answered questions about Bitcoin on email. His emails are available at: https://www.bitcoin.com/satoshi-archive/emails/mike-hearn/1/#selection-13.1-13.27

[4] Tapscott, A. (2021). Digital Asset Revolution: The Rise of DeFi and the Reinvention of Financial Services, A blockchain Research Institute Big Idea White Paper.

[5] https://coinmarketcap.com/all/views/all/

[6] Beck, A. (2002). *Hashcash - A Denial of Service Counter-Measure*, white paper   http://www.hashcash.org/papers/hashcash.pdf

[7] Quote is from: https://satoshi.nakamotoinstitute.org/posts/p2pfoundation/1/

[8] Here's why Satoshi Nakamoto set Bitcoin's supply limit to 21 million. https://thenextweb.com/news/heres-why-satoshi-nakamoto-set-bitcoin-supply-limit-to-21-million

[9] https://coinmarketcap.com/currencies/ethereum/

[10] Ethereum Monetary Policy https://docs.ethhub.io/ethereum-basics/monetary-policy/

[11] Cryptopedia (May 27, 2021). Ethereum and the ICO Boom. https://www.gemini.com/cryptopedia/initial-coin-offering-explained-ethereum-ico

[12] What is Binance Coin (BNB)? https://corporatefinanceinstitute.com/resources/knowledge/other/binance-coin-bnb/

[13] Binance Smart Chain Validator FAQs https://docs.binance.org/faq/bsc/val.html

[14] Seward, Z. (May 12, 2021). Vitalik's Regift of Unsolicited DOGE Knockoffs Sends Memecoin Prices Plunging. https://www.coindesk.com/markets/2021/05/12/vitaliks-regift-of-unsolicited-doge-knockoffs-sends-memecoin-prices-plunging/

[15] Barsby, O. (2022). BNB Burn Schedule: When Is The 18th Binance Coin Burn? https://www.gfinityesports.com/cryptocurrency/bnb-burn-schedule-next-binance-coin-burn-date-how-much-bnb-burned-meaning/

[16] How to burn non burnable ERC20? https://ethereum.stackexchange.com/questions/65916/how-to-burn-non-burnable-erc20

[17] https://www.constitutiondao.com/

[18] This website converts large numbers: https://www.mobilefish.com/services/big_number/big_number.php

[19] See https://www.hypr.com/digital-signature-standard-dss/

[20] Lamport, L.; Shostak, R.; Pease, M. (1982). The Byzantine Generals Problem", *ACM Transactions on Programming Languages and Systems*. 4 (3): 387–389.

[21] Proof-of-Elapsed-Time (PoET) was created by the Hyperledger Sawtooth project. https://www.hyperledger.org/projects

[22] Chan, R. (May 2, 2016). "Consensus mechanisms used in blockchains" posted on https://www.linkedin.com/pulse/consensus-mechanisms-used-blockchain-ronald-chan

[23] Hyperledger Foundation, *Hyperledger Architecture, Volume 1*, https://www.hyperledger.org/wp-content/uploads/2017/08/HyperLedger_Arch_WG_Paper_1_Consensus.pdf

[24] Connell, J. (June 2017), *On Byzantine Fault Tolerance in Blockchain Systems*, https://cryptoinsider.com/byzantine-fault-tolerance-blockchain-systems/

[25] Maziières, D. (2016), *The Stellar Consensus Protocol: A Federated Model for Internet-level Consensus*, White Paper, https://www.stellar.org/papers/stellar-consensus-protocol.pdf

[26] Dwork, C., and Naor, M. (1993). *Pricing via processing: Combatting Junk Mail*, http://www.hashcash.org/papers/pvp.pdf

[27] Nakamoto, S. (2008). *Bitcoin: A Peer-to-Peer Electronic Cash System*, https://bitcoin.org/bitcoin.pdf

[28] King, S., and Nadal, S. (2012). PPCoin: *Peer-to-Peer Crypto-Currency with Proof-of-Stake*, https://peercoin.net/assets/paper/peercoin-paper.pdf

[29] *Distributed Consensus from Proof of Stake is Impossible, posted by Andrew Poelstra on* https://www.smithandcrown.com/open-research/distributed-consensus-from-proof-of-stake-is-impossible/

[30] Adams, R. (December 2, 2021). Is Proof of Stake a Rich get Richer Scheme? https://newsletter.banklesshq.com/p/is-proof-of-stake-a-rich-get-richer#:~:text=Proof%20of%20Stake%20is%20NOT%20a%20%22rich%20get%20richer%22%20scheme

[31] *Practical Byzantine Fault Tolerance*, Proceedings of the Third Symposium on Operating Systems Design and Implementation, New Orleans, USA, February 1999, http://pmg.csail.mit.edu/papers/osdi99.pdf

[32] The Future of Blockchains: Smart Contracts, *Technode*, http://technode.com/2016/11/14/the-future-of-blockchain-technology-smart-contracts/

[33] This website tracks contract accounts running on Ethereum: https://etherscan.io/contractsVerified

[34] You may look at today's most active Ethereum smart contracts on https://etherscan.io/stat/dextracker.

[35] Diedrich, H. (2016). *Ethereum: blockchains, digital assets, smart contracts, decentralized autonomous organizations*, Wildfire publishing.

[36] To see the ConstitutionDAO, go to: https://etherscan.io/address/0x4f7ebf67b662bee6a764a2b79a3291f93d4be2df#readContract

[37] Fersht, P. (2018). The top 5 enterprise blockchain platforms you need to know about https://www.horsesforsources.com/top-5-blockchain-platforms_031618

[38] To track versions of Bitcoin Core, see: https://bitcoin.org/en/releases/0.21.1/

[39] To track changes to Ethereum, see https://github.com/ethereum/go-ethereum/releases

[40] To track versions of Cardano, see https://github.com/input-output-hk/cardano-node/releases

[41] To track versions of Quorum, see https://github.com/ConsenSys/quorum/tree/master/core

[42] To track versions of Corda, See: https://docs.r3.com/en/platform/corda/4.7/open-source/release-notes.html

[43] To track versions of Fabric, see: https://github.com/hyperledger/fabric/releases

[44] https://www.multichain.com/blog/2021/11/multichain-releases-2-2-with-nfts/

[45] Brown, R. (November 8, 2016) "On distributed databases and distributed ledgers", posted on https://gendal.me/2016/11/08/on-distributed-databases-and-distributed-ledgers/

[46] Diedrich, H. (2016). *Ethereum: blockchains, digital assets, smart contracts, decentralized autonomous organizations*, Wildfire publishing.

[47] Brown, R. (November 8, 2016) "On distributed databases and distributed ledgers", posted on https://gendal.me/2016/11/08/on-distributed-databases-and-distributed-ledgers/

[48] In layman's terms, "Turing Complete" means a programming language has a comprehensive instruction set; Bitcoin's scripting tool is not "Turing Complete" because it has no way to program logic loops, among other missing features. (See https://en.bitcoin.it/wiki/Script for Bitcoins command set.)

[49] This site explains Bitcoin's APIs: https://bitcoin.org/en/developer-reference#bitcoin-core-apis

[50] This site has more detailed information: Samarakoon, G. (2018). Bitcoin Fundamentals: Step by step explanation of a peer-to-peer Bitcoin transactionhttps://samarakoon-gayan.medium.com/bitcoin-fundamentals-a5d62fe98bac

Chapter 4

The Global Blockchain Landscape

What's inside: Now that we've learned HOW blockchains work, we are ready for a flyover of the global blockchain landscape. We'll look at the economic opportunity of news innovations in the crypto market, the investments and adoption of blockchain-enabled applications, and the stakeholders who enable/disable adoption, such as working groups/consortia, standards-making bodies, and regulators. Students interested in blockchain careers will find opportunities in startups, traditional enterprises, and open-source communities. The global blockchain landscape moves quickly, so readers will need to keep pace with developments by taking charge of their own learning journeys. This chapter is the starter tour.

Learning objectives:

- Explain the major events in the history of blockchains
- Explain the relationship between technology, standards, and regulations
- Identify influential investors, startups, and enterprises
- Identify major working groups/consortia
- Explain how standards are created
- Describe the legal and regulatory landscape for the United States and beyond
- Depict how blockchains have progressed on the maturity curve

4.1. Overview of the landscape

Thus far in our learning journey, we've learned that Web 3.0 aims to restore trust in online economic and social activities through the decentralization of the exchange of value, identity, and data ownership. We understand that blockchains are the architecture of decentralization, and how all the component parts work together to process exchanges of value without intermediaries. We've also covered the governance of blockchains—who holds decision making rights over blockchain networks. These lessons are foundational to understanding *how* blockchains work.

To achieve the vision of Web 3.0, we need contributions from inventors, startups, investors, working groups, traditional enterprises, standards-making bodies, regulators, academics, philanthropists, meet-up groups, technology journalists, politicians, lawyers, and more. Every reader, regardless of their background, can contribute in a meaningful way. The next steps are to increase our literacy of the language, history, and emerging concepts of blockchains and to increase our numeracy of the economic market size and potential.

In this chapter, our flyover of the global landscape incudes the crypto markets, leaders in investment and adoption, and other enablers of Web 3.0 (see Figure 4.1). We examine the explosion of innovations that followed Bitcoin, creating a global market worth trillions of dollars. Within this market, innovations include exchanges, stable coins, privacy coins and NFTs. These innovations are quickly combining with other technologies like Internet of Things (IoT), artificial intelligence, and virtual reality to create entirely new innovations like metaverses. Technologies will also combine in ways we cannot yet predict.

Technology innovation outpaces the formation of standards and the legal and regulatory guiderails we need for safe and equitable adoption. Standards aim to make technologies interoperable so that we can exchange assets seamlessly *across* blockchain networks, not just within them. We don't want to get trapped by a single supplier, called 'vendor lock-in'. Laws and regulations are also needed. Well-designed laws and regulations protect investors, consumers, and the environment without stifling innovation. Regulations from the State of Wyoming serve as our prime example of crypto-friendly laws that protect investors.

Again we stress that technology evolves rapidly but standards and regulations evolve slowly. We need more technologists to work on standards and to educate regulators; it may not be the most exciting work, but it's vital work to prevent technologies from damaging our well-being.

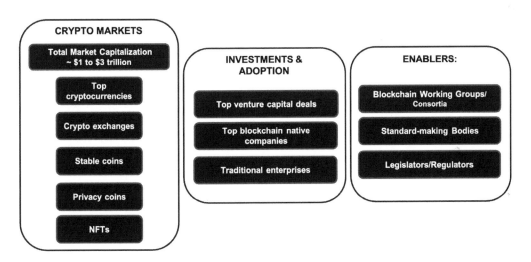

Figure 4.1: Global blockchain landscape

To make coverage of the global landscape engaging for readers, we share a series of 'top ten' lists. (Who doesn't love a top ten list?!) We've got lists for the top cryptocurrencies, privacy coins, stable coins, NFT markets, venture capital deals, blockchain startups, and the most active traditional enterprises exploring blockchain uses. The fun and challenges of this chapter are that it is out of date the minute we write it. As you read through the chapter, pause to investigate where markets have shifted, which players have risen or fallen, and which new trends that have emerged.

155

We conclude the chapter with Gartner's assessment of where blockchains are in the technology hype-cycle.

Ready? Let's dive in!

4.2. Global crypto market

On the day of this writing in February of 2022, CoinMarketCap lists over 17,000 cryptocurrencies. There are only 180 fiat currencies in the world serving as the sovereign currency for 195 countries, so cryptocurrencies considerably *outnumber* fiat currencies. What are these cryptocurrencies worth? The total market capitalization ('market cap') across all cryptocurrencies was $1.77 trillion on the day of this writing.[i] To put that $1.77 trillion number in perspective, consider the size of the crypto market in relation to the total value created in the world economy as measured by global Gross Domestic Product (GDP).[ii] World GDP was $85 trillion in 2021, meaning that crypto was two percent of the world's GDP—about the GDP for the country of Canada.

Although the cryptocurrency market can fluctuate by over a trillion dollars in recent years, the long-term trend is one of positive growth. Figure 4.2 depicts the global cryptocurrency market cap from 2013 to the first month of 2022. As the circles on the Figure 4.2 indicate, the market experienced three major crypto surges and plunges:

1. Late 2017 to early 2018. During the second half of 2017, the crypto market surged with the launch of many Initial Coin Offerings (ICOs), discussed in Chapter 2. The market reached nearly $800 billion dollars. By February 2018, the crypto market crashed, falling by more than $550 billion. Theories to explain the 2018 crash include:

---

i The market cap is calculated by multiplying the price per token in US dollars times the number of tokens in circulation.

ii Global GDP is the total value of all final goods and services that has been produced in the economy in a year.

- Fear of regulatory restriction, particularly in Asia and US
- Manipulation of the market by 'whales'
- The proper functioning of markets to reset prices from hyper-inflated values
- The belief that ICO issuers were fraudulent

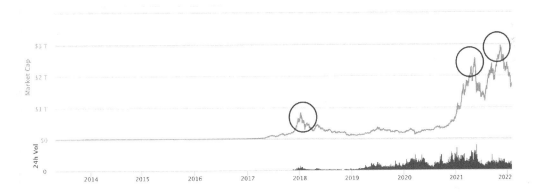

Figure 4.2: Market capitalization of cryptocurrency market 2013-2022

Source: CoinMarketCap

As far as the first theory, South Korean and Chinese government cracked down on virtual currencies, prompting other governments to consider banning virtual currencies. This caused uncertainty among crypto-holders, so they began exiting the market. The second theory asserts that Bitcoin's price was manipulated by one or more 'whales'—individuals with large bitcoin holdings of over $1 billion in value. Whales can sell a large enough portion of their bitcoins at a lower than market price to prompt a panic sell-off, which lowers the price further.[1] When the price falls low enough, the whales swoop in and buy more bitcoins at a reduced price. Prices rise soon after. Two university professors suspect that a single Bitcoin whale manipulated prices in 2017.[2] Another explanation: with Bitcoin rising in value by over 200 percent between October and December of 2017, along with other cryptocurrencies rising as well, analysts argued that the market became unsustainable due to the influx of new investors to the cryptocurrency market as a whole.[3] Despite its trillion-dollar swings, there is no denying that the crypto market is significant.

2. First half of 2021. The crypto market grew at a rapid pace in the first half of 2021, reaching over $2.5 trillion in May, followed by a plummet in summer. Several events led to the rise and fall. Tesla's decision to buy $1.5 billion worth of bitcoin in spring prompted a surge up; Tesla's decision three months later to no longer accept bitcoins as payments for its cars prompted a crash.[4] Elon Musk, CEO of Tesla, said he was concerned about Bitcoin's effect on the environment. The Chinese government, which had banned ICOs back in 2017 and banned cryptocurrency mining in 2019, finally banned all crypto trading in May 2021.[5] That announcement had a huge impact because China's crypto adopters were a large part of the market. Moreover, China's population represents over 18 percent of the world's population of 7.9 billion people and it is the world's second largest economy, so any of its policies affect global markets.

3. Second half of 2021. In the latter part of 2021, the market cap surged to an all-time high of $3 trillion in November. Some of the rise was attributed to the buzz around non-fungible tokens, but there were also many announcements from traditional enterprises escalating investments in the space, including Mastercard, Thailand's Siam Commercial Bank, Australia's CBA, JPMorgan Chase, and Citigroup.[6] Three months later, the market had fallen to $1.77 trillion. Causes include fear over inflation, rising interest rates, and Russia's threat to ban cryptocurrencies and mining.[7]

Now that we have looked at the overall market, let's zero in on a few of the top cryptocurrencies.

4.2.1. Top cryptocurrencies by market cap

Here's our first top-ten list: the top cryptocurrencies by market cap on this day in February 2022 were *Bitcoin* ($724 billion market cap), *Ethereum* ($319 billion); *Tether* ($78 billion); *Binance BNP* ($63 billion); *USD Coin* ($50 billion); *Cardano* ($34 billion); *Solana* ($30 Billion); *Ripple* ($29 billion); *Terra* ($20 billion); and *Polkadot* ($19 billion).[8]

Bitcoin continues to dominate the market, representing over 41 percent of the cryptocurrency market. It's also useful to know the age of these cryptocurrencies, as some of them have risen to the top ten in just a few years. Reorganizing the top ten list by release date: Bitcoin launched in 2009; Tether and Ripple in 2014; Ethereum in 2015; Cardano, Binance BNP, and Polkadot in 2017; USD Coin in 2018; and Solana and Terra in 2019.

Amongst the top ten list, five are the native digital assets of blockchain platforms that allow developers to deploy decentralized apps: Ethereum, Cardano, Solana, Terra and Polkadot. The last four platforms use proof-of-stake (PoS) consensus and generally hope to retain their dominance when Ethereum switches to PoS (anticipated in 2022). Ripple is a blockchain network for payments, settlements, asset exchanges, and remittances; we cover Ripple in the next chapter. Two stable coins (Tether and USD Coin) are among the top ten, explained below.

Market prices fluctuate considerably, sometimes rising or falling by hundreds of billions of dollars within a few weeks. Time to pause your reading. Go to https://coinmarketcap.com/ to see how the top-ten list has changed since this writing. Has Ethereum moved to PoS yet? Do Bitcoin and the platform coins still dominate?

We've discussed the market value of over 17,000 cryptocurrencies, but where did they come from? What do they all do? Next, we'll look at the brief history of altcoins, cryptocurrency exchanges, stable coins, privacy coins, and non-fungible tokens (see Figure 4.3).

4.2.2. Brief history of crypto

In previous chapters, we recognized Bitcoin as the first 'blockchain-based' cryptocurrency, but Bitcoin was not the first cryptocurrency. David Chaum launched DigiCash in 1990, the first live cryptocurrency of significance.[9] While an important breakthrough, DigiCash was centrally controlled in that the company's system performed the validations. Nakamoto resurrected Chaum's idea of digital signatures to verify asset ownership, but this time with distributed validation.[10] Nakomoto's aim was decentralization so that no government or institution could control it. Make a mental note: ***the point of cryptocurrencies is peer-to-peer exchanges of value—no trusted third parties are wanted or needed.***

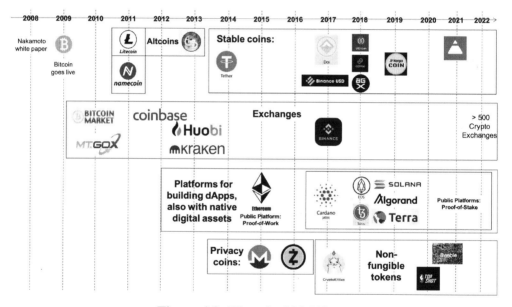

Figure 4.3: Historical highlights

After Bitcoin, new coins were often created by downloading the Bitcoin Core, altering the programming code, and launching a 'fork' (see Glossary) to Bitcoin. These are called 'altcoins' because they are alternative coins to Bitcoin. Early altcoins aimed to either improve on Bitcoin, such as increasing data storage, adding functionality, decreasing settlement times, or to serve different purposes such as funding a new platform.[11] Namecoin (NMC) and Litecoin (LTC)—both launched in 2011—are two early examples.

160

Namecoin was designed by the Bitcoin community to register names on the Bitcoin blockchain, allowing users to shorten their wallet address to a user-friendly domain name for channels like Twitter. Nakamoto supported the project.[12] One of its unique features is that Namecoin merged mining functions of Bitcoin and Namecoin to allow simultaneous mining of both coins, instead of making miners choose between the two. Namecoin still exists, but newer domain name registries like Ethereum Name Service (ENS) on Ethereum took off; Namecoin's market cap was only $24 million in February 2022.

Litecoin was created by Charlie Lee, a computer scientist from Google. Lee aimed to improve Bitcoin's settlement times by a factor of four; Litecoin creates a new block every 2.5 minutes instead of every ten minutes like Bitcoin does. Its money supply is 84 million litecoins, which is four times greater than Bitcoin's money supply. Most notably, it uses a different hashing algorithm ('Scrypt' rather than SHA-256), which at the time was designed to allow miners to mine litecoins without the need for specialized hardware.[13] Lee sold most of his litecoins in 2017, citing that he had too much influence over its price.[14] As of 2022, he still serves on the Board of Directors at the Litecoin Foundation. In general, Litecoin has performed well; it is typically among the top 25 cryptocurrencies by market cap, valued at $9 billion in February 2022.

Dogecoin (DOGE) was launched in 2013 based as an altcoin of Litecoin. Two software engineers, Billy Markus from IBM and Jackson Palmer from Adobe, started Dogecoin as a joke but it has sustained community support.[15] The name 'doge' coin comes from an Internet meme that featured a Shiba Inu dog. Its popularity soared in 2021 when Elon Musk (CEO of Tesla), Mark Cuban (billionaire entrepreneur), and Snoop Dogg (musician) started promoting it. It gained a 20,000 percent increase in one year![16] A flurry of new dog-themed cryptocurrencies were launched, including Kishu Inu Coin (KISHU), Dogelon Mars (ELON), Floki Inu Coin (FLOKI), and Baby Dogecoin (BABYDOGE) in 2021.[17]

Crypto exchanges. Initially, the only way to interact with the Bitcoin network was to become a miner to purchase bitcoin from Bitcoin ATMs, to manage one's own digital wallet, which requires technical competency and confidence in protecting one's private keys. Enter the crypto exchanges. Many people saw the need for an exchange where users could easily buy and sell bitcoins with fiat currency. However, if you buy and sell crypto on an exchange, you are relying on a trusted-third party! The exchanges collect transaction fees and takes custody of customers' private keys, the situation Nakamoto was trying to avoid. The use of an exchange is called centralized-decentralized finance, or '**CeDeFi**' for short, meaning that a centralized exchange sits between customers and decentralized blockchain networks. Many consumers find the convenience of exchanges a better option than managing their own crypto wallets.

The first Bitcoin exchange was *Bitcoin Market*, launched in March of 2010 by a Bitcoin Talk member using the pseudonym 'dwdollar'.[18] Soon after, Jed McCaleb (born in Fayetteville, Arkansas), launched the most infamous Bitcoin exchange called *Mt. Gox* in 2010. When his 'hobby' began taking all his time in 2011, McCaleb sold the site to Mark Karpelès.[19] Early exchanges operated under the radar of regulatory bodies, and many consumers were at risk for heists. Mt. Gox—and other exchanges that followed—were lucrative targets for hackers because exchanges controlled the users' private keys. One of the largest heists occurred in August of 2014 when 850,000 bitcoins, worth $450 million at the time, were stolen from the wallets managed by Mt. Gox.[20]

Today, there are over 500 cryptocurrency exchanges, including *Coinbase* (founded in 2012 in the US), *Huobi* (founded in China in 2013), *Kraken* (founded in 2013 in the US), *FTX* (founded in 2019 in the Bahamas), *Binance* (founded in China in 2017 but it has since moved to Malta).[21] Although exchanges are based in one country, many exchanges service customers world-wide. Kraken, for example, is available in 48 US states and 176 countries.[22] Many exchanges now comply with regulations, including Know Your Customer (KYC) and anti-money laundering (AML) requirements. For example, Coinbase had money transmitter licenses from 45 US States and a New York State Virtual Currency License by 2019. Coinbase also has commercial criminal insurance that is greater than the value of digital currency maintained in online storage (98 percent of the private keys are stored offline). Increased compliance means a loss of user anonymity, a consequence counter to the cypherpunk values of the initial Bitcoin adopters.

4.2.3. Stable coins

Most cryptocurrencies are like bitcoin in that they are native digital assets that exist inside the blockchain network. Stable coins are fungible crypto-tokens that are pegged to assets outside the blockchain network. Stable coins are most often tied to a fiat currency, most commonly to the US dollar, but also to the Euro, British pound, the Japanese yen, and others. Stable coins are 'stable' in that holders can always exchange them for the same value. Stable coins can also be pegged to a commodity like a gram of gold or a barrel of oil (see Figure 4.4).

Stable coins are primarily used to facilitate trades across cryptocurrency exchanges. Arbitrage traders need to quickly buy and sell crypto from multiple exchanges to generate a profit by taking advantage of the slightly different prices across exchanges. For example, at the moment of this writing, the price of bitcoin is $42,878 on the Binance exchange and $42,896 on Coinbase. If traders had to convert one cryptocurrency to US dollars before buying another cryptocurrency, they add transactions costs and lose speed. Holding stable coins allows them to trade immediately.[23]

Top ten stable coins. In February 2022, the ten stable coins with the highest market capitalization were Tether (USDT); USD coin (USDC); Binance USD (BUSD); TerraUSD (UST); Dai (DAI); TrueUSD (TUSD); Pax Dollar (USDP); Neutrino USD (USDN); Fei USD (FEI), and Tribe (TRIBE). These are all pegged to the US dollar. The total market value of all stablecoins listed on CoinMarketCap was $174 billion on February 3, 2022, representing about ten percent of the entire cryptocurrency market.[24] Let's examine some of them.

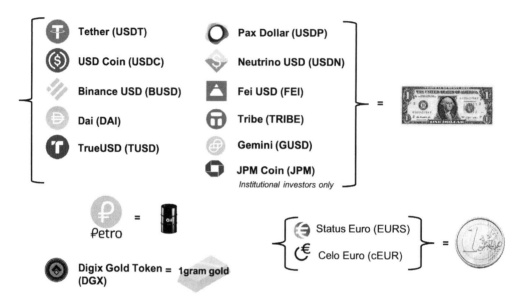

Figure 4.4: Stable coin examples

Tether **(USDT)** was the first stablecoin, launched in 2014, by a company called Tether Limited. The founders include J.R. Willett, Brock Pierce, Reeve Collins and Craig Sellars. Buyers exchange one US dollar for one tether coin, with Tether Limited allegedly storing each US dollar in a bank reserve. Crypto traders use tethers to take advantage of the price arbitrage across cryptocurrency exchanges as explained above.[25] Tether is actually multiple tokens, with versions running on Bitcoin, Ethereum, and TRON networks. Tether Limited has often been accused of not holding enough dollars in reserve and of manipulating the price of Bitcoin. It has repeatedly dodged demands for public audits and faced fines from the US Commodity Futures Trading Commission. Despite the controversy, Tether remains the favored stablecoin by crypto-traders as of February 2022.

Since Tether, other notable stablecoins were launched that were also pegged to the US dollar. These include USD Coin and Gemini, launched in 2018; JPM Coin in 2019;

Binance USD in 2019; and the proposed Facebook-backed Diem coin that was supposed to launch in 2022. However, the Diem Association sold its assets to Silvergate Capital Corporation on January 31, 2022, so its future launch is unlikely.[26]

The *USD Coin*—created by Coinbase and Circle—launched the coin as part of a consortium, promising transparency over its US dollar reserve management.[27] *Gemini* (GUSD) was founded by Cameron and Tyler Winklevoss; the Gemini coin is another 1-to-1 peg with the US dollar.[28] *JPM Coin* (JPM) is not available to the public, it's only for JPMorgan's institutional customers. JP Morgan uses its JPM Coin to facilitate institution-to-institution transfers; it is also pegged to the US dollar. When one JPMorgan client sends money to another JPMorgan client over the blockchain, it uses the digital coin to speed settlement times, which are immediately redeemed for US dollars.[29] Binance launched its stable coin, *Binance USD*, in 2019.

Besides pegging to fiat currencies, some stablecoins are pegged to commodities. For example, *DGX*, launched in 2018, pegs one coin to one gram of gold[30]; Venezuala's government pegged the *petro* to one barrel of oil in 2018 in an attempt to access international financing. This coin has been highly criticized by regulators from around the world.[31] Some stablecoins are pegged to other cryptocurrencies; *Dai,* launched in 2017, is pegged to the US dollar but it is backed also by *ether,* Ethereum's cryptocurrency.[32]

4.2.4. Privacy coins

Privacy coins aim to increase the privacy compared to Bitcoin, altcoins, and other cryptocurrencies that post wallet addresses and amounts on their distributed ledgers. We've already learned that any person with access to the Internet may view transactions stored on Bitcoin's digital ledger. The identities of the public address holders are not always anonymous. The two parties of the transaction often know each other, allowing them to follow all of the subsequent transactions associated with the addresses, which is why Bitcoin is considered to be 'pseudo-anonymous'. We also know some of the addresses associated with founders, since the first transactions put new coins in their wallet addresses. The world monitors the addresses presumed to be held by Nakamoto, who disappeared in 2011. So far, Nakamoto has not sold off bitcoins. The world also monitors some of the addresses associated with Vitalik Buterin, co-founder of Ethereum. Privacy coins aimed to prevent such monitoring.

Top ten privacy coins. On February 5, 2022, the top ten privacy coins by market capitalization were Monero (XRP), Zcash (ZEC), Oasis Network (ROSE), Decred (DCR), Secret (SCRT), Horizon (ZEN), Keep Network (KEEP), MobileCoin (MOB), Dusk Network (DUSK), and Status (SNT) (see Figure 4.5).

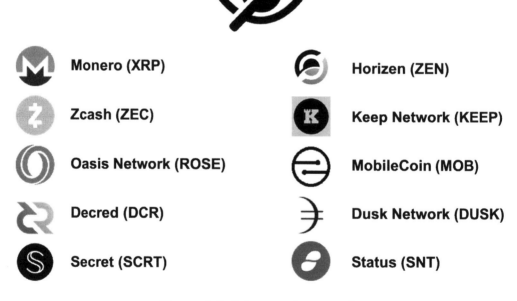

Figure 4.5: Privacy coin examples

The total market cap for all privacy coins was $10.6 billion dollars, less than one percent of the market cap for all cryptocurrencies. While the intentions of many founders of privacy coins seem noble, namely, to protect user privacy, they are also used as the preferred payment for ransomware, child pornography, illegal drug trades, and other illegal activities. Some exchanges do not trade privacy coins for fear of violating regulations or damaging crypto's image.[33] Let's examine a few examples of privacy coins.

Monero, Zcash, Oasis, and Secret are popular privacy coins. ***Monero (XMR)*** was created by seven people, but it is primarily associated with 'Nicolas van Saberhagen', a pseudonym used by the creator of the CryptoNote privacy protocol. Some people speculate on chat forums that Nicolas van Saberhagen and Nakamoto are the same person![34] Monero, launched in 2014, is a cryptocurrency with increased data obfuscation compared to Bitcoin using ring signatures[35] and stealth addresses. The public ledger hides addresses and amounts, yet still functions to prevent the double spend. We'll explain the mechanics in a subsequent chapter.

Zcash is another major privacy coin, launched in 2016. Designed by professors from Johns Hopkins, MIT, Technion, and Tel Aviv University and Zooko Wilcox-O'Hearn, a famous cypherpunk who worked on DigiCash with David Chaum. Zcash is based on Bitcoin's codebase, but the creators enhanced the code with cryptographic zero-knowledge proofs to allow users to mask their addresses.[36] We'll explain the mechanics of Zcash in a subsequent chapter.

The ***Oasis Network*** launched its privacy coin ROSE in 2020. ROSE is used to pay for transactions on the Oasis Network, *"a privacy-enabled blockchain platform for open finance and a responsible data economy."*[37] Professor Dawn Song from the University of California at Berkeley leads the project. She built the Oasis Network on the Cosmos protocol that uses Proof-of-Stake to allow both privacy and scalability. One of its privacy features is the ability for smart contracts to process end-to-end transactions using secure enclaves, meaning privacy happens at the hardware level.[38] A secure enclave *"provides*

CPU hardware-level isolation and memory encryption on every server, by isolating application code and data from anyone with privileges, and encrypting its memory. With additional software, secure enclaves enable the encryption of both storage and network data for simple full stack security. "[39]

The **Secret Network** (SCRT), launched in February of 2020, was also built using Cosmos. It is based on the ideas from an influential paper from faculty at the MIT Media Lab and Tel-Aviv University, called *"Decentralizing Privacy: Using Blockchain to Protect Personal Data."*[40] The secret network allows computations on encrypted data and includes the ability to create secret non-fungible tokens, secret cross-chain asset bridges, and secret DeFi apps.[41] The project was funded as a token sale of 'ENG' on Ethereum, which resulted in fines from the US Securities and Exchange Commission (SEC). Investors were able to swap ENG for SCRT, the native digital asset of the Secret Network.[42]

So far in our discussion, we've only written about fungible tokens, where each token is interchangeable with another of its class. Next we look at the growing non-fungible token (NFT) market.

4.2.5. NFTs

In Chapter 3, we defined a non-fungible token (NFT) as a digital token that represents a particular asset in the physical or virtual world; each NFT is unique! Smart contracts facilitate the creation, buying and selling of NFTs on a blockchain network. According to Bloomberg, the NFT market on Ethereum was $41 billion dollars in 2021.[43] Other popular NFT platforms include OpenSea, Axie Infinity, Rarible, Nifty Gateway, Decentraland, SuperRare, and Flow.[44]

It's important for NFT buyers to understand what they are purchasing. NFTs are programmable, so the terms may vary from ownership of an asset to limited uses such as the right to display the asset on social media, but the creator keeps copyright/ownership. So, in the NFT world, we must be careful to separate technical functionality (control over an NFT by possessing the private key) from legal ownership as defined by law and which varies by jurisdiction.

CryptoKitties was the first NFT smart contract to gain widespread adoption. It runs on Ethereum. Launched by Dapper Labs in 2017, it allows users to buy, trade, and breed virtual cats, each of which is unique and secured with an NFT. If you buy two CryptoKitties on the marketplace[iii], you can breed them to produce a new CryptoKitty; a new kitty with its own 'cattributes', secured with its own NFT. (If you only own one CryptoKitty, you can breed it with a public sire.) Owners can describe the personality of their CryptoKitty. For example, the description of Kitty number 540245, called Salaam, is, *"I've never told anyone this, but I once danced for a dog. My enemies describe me as 'brilliant'. It's... accurate. You can be my apprentice"* (see Figure 4.6). On the day of this writing, Salaam was for sale at .005 eth, or about $13.

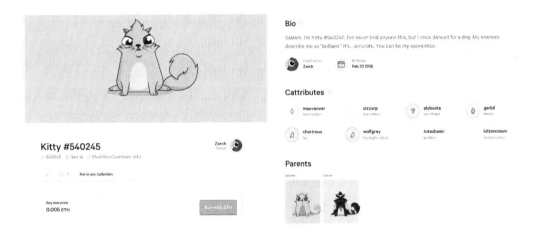

Figure 4.6: Saleem: A CryptoKitty for sale
Source: https://www.cryptokitties.co/kitty/540245

iii The CryptoKitties marketplace is here: https://www.cryptokitties.co/search?include=sale

To play the game, users need to have a digital wallet (like MetaMask) funded with enough ether to buy a Kitty and to pay gas fees to Ethereum miners to process sell, trade, or breed transactions. The smart contract processes the transactions and permanently stores them on Ethereum's digital ledger.[iv] It's important to realize that the digital image of the kitty is stored offchain and the art is owned by Axiom Zen (owners of Dapper Labs). So what good is an NFT? The NFT holder has possession of the private key that is needed to digitally sign transactions for buy, sell, and trade orders.

Cryptokitties became so popular in 2017 that the game created a backlog of tens of thousands of transactions on the Ethereum network. CryptoKitties started using 10 percent of Ethereum's network capacity by November of 2017.[45] CryptoKitties offers a few lessons. First, many new markets often start with gamers, who are looking for fun and who are less risk averse than average consumers. Second, it shows the market potential for virtual products—people are willing to use cryptocurrencies to pay for virtual things. Third, it shows the power of blockchain platforms because new NFT apps can be deployed for very little investment.

Let's look at a few other famous NFTs (see Figure 4.7). *Jack Dorsey*, founder of Twitter, sold his first tweet as an NFT for $2.9 million in 2021. He launched the NFT on the Valuables platform.[46] To date, Mike Winklelman—the artist known as *Beeble*—has the highest price paid for an NFT at $69 million for a digital collage of his work that included over 5,000 images. The 2021 sale was facilitated by Christie's, the UK auction house that has operated since 1766, which added legitimacy to the NFT market.

So what did the Beeble NFT buyer, Vignesh Sundaresan, actually buy? He bought a certificate of authenticity and the ability to display the entire image, but he did not buy the copyright to the art itself. Moreover, the buyer cannot divvy up and sell individual images in the collage, as Beeble retains that right. Sundaresan, can of course, sell

---

iv You can see the Cryptokitties smart contract on https://etherscan.io/address/0x06012c8cf97bead5deae2
37070f9587f8e7a266d

170

the NFT.[47] Besides this mammoth sale, Beeble has sold over 1300 NFTs of his digital artwork, with total sales exceeding $175,000,000 and counting.[48]

Figure 4.7: NFT examples: Beeple's collage, Jack Dorsey's tweet, and NBA Top Shots

Source: Part of Beeple's collage: https://cdn.voxcdn.com/thumbor/KMraJbkqzbkEAUuTqU5Tvt_1So 4=/0x0:3000x3000/1820x1213/filters:focal(1260x1260:1740x1740):format(webp)/cdn.voxcdn.com/ uploads/chorus_image/image/68948366/2021_NYR_20447_0001_001_beeple_everydays_the_first_5000_ days034733_.0.jpg

Many NFT owners are paying for the bragging rights, rather than legal ownership rights. For example, National Basketball Association (NBA) partnered with Dapper Labs to create and sell NFTs of digital collectibles of short videos called 'moments' from NBA basketballs games. The NFT platform is called ***Top Shots***. It launched in 2020. To be clear, the NBA owns the copyright to the videos; NFT buyers cannot alter or duplicate the video, but they can trade, sell, or give away the NFT.[49] By October 2020, NBA Top shots had sold $338 million worth of NFTs.[50] Top Shots is deployed on the Flow Blockchain, developed by Dapper Labs, to avoid the congestion that happened when

Dapper Labs deployed CryptoKitties on Ethereum.[v] The Flow Blockchain divvies tasks among consensus, verification, execution, and collection nodes to avoid bottlenecks. *"The NFT is mediated entirely by the Flow Blockchain, and Dapper Labs are unable to seize, freeze, or otherwise modify ownership of the NFT. Dapper Labs can, however, revoke your license to the intellectual property associated with the NFT—i.e., the associated NBA video highlight."*[51]

Illegitimate actors have scammed some NFT buyers. Since anyone can create an NFT, the person who creates an NFT may not be the legitimate owner of the asset.[52] For example, Nike sued StockX in February of 2022 for making and selling over 500 sneaker NFTs. StockX kept the sneakers in a vault, created the NFTs, and then sold them to customers. In some cases, the NFTs were selling for three times the value of the sneaker![53]

Streambed, a US startup, aims to address the current limitations of NFTs. The CEO, Jenna Pilgrim, says that NFTs are certificates of authenticity, but they are not worth anything without the accompanying rights contract. Her company is building a platform to create cryptographic links among the NFT, the rights contract and the metadata.[54]

Although it's early days, NFTs hold the promise of many new business and social models, such as fractional ownership of assets (see previous chapter), deeper engagements with customers (like NBA Top Shots) and counterfeit reduction, provided we find a way to vet NFT issuers. NFTs are a major enabler of metaverses, the three-dimensional virtual worlds where your avatar, virtual property, and other virtual assets will be issued and controlled by NFTs.

So far, we've covered the cryptocurrency and NFT markets. Next, we look at the investments in blockchains startups.

---

[v] To view the TopShot NFT smart Contract, see https://flowscan.org/account/0x0b2a3299cc857e29

4.3. Investment and adoption

Startups must be careful how they raise funds because they need to comply with regulations in the jurisdiction from which they operate. In Chapter 2, we introduced the *new* types of investment models, including Initial Coin Offerings (ICOs); Security Token Offerings (STOs); Initial Exchange Offerings (IEOs); and Initial Decentralized Exchange Offerings (DEXs). These models are exciting because startups can raise funds by selling new coins, i.e., new cryptocurrencies. In addition to these new funding models, startups also raise funds from traditional sources like angel investors, venture capital, and initial public offerings (IPOs) (see Figure 4.8).

Traditional fund raising models: **New fund raising models:**

- Early stage: investors provide cash in exchange for convertible debt or ownership equity

- Investors buy the coins, typically by sending money directly to a smart contract or to an account controlled by the startup

- Launched as fully SEC compliant investments (qualified investors only)

- Later stage: investors provide cash in exchange for ownership equity

- Investors buy the coins through a decentralized exchange

- A company's first offer to sell its stock shares to the **public**

- Investors buy the coins through a centralized exchange

Figure 4.8: Fund-raising models for startups

Angel investment. Have you watched the US television series, *Shark Tank*? On the show, celebrity investors like Mark Cuban, Kevin O'Leary, Daymond John, Barbara Corcoran, and Lori Greiner invest their own money in promising startups in exchange for equity ownership, convertible debt, and/or loans. The show offers insights into how angel investors make investment decisions by considering the product, business model, current market size, market potential, profitability, and characteristics of the entrepreneurs based on the entrepreneurs' 'pitches'. You also get a sense for the typical deal size of angel investing, under half a million dollars, typically in exchange for significant percentages of equity (about 10 to 40 percent). On TV, it looks like angel investors make decisions after 10 minutes of interactions, but the sharks spend 45 minutes to an hour with each contestant. Of the 40,000 entrepreneurs that apply each year to be on the show, only 150 entrepreneurs are selected to pitch to the 'sharks'.[55] On *Shark Tank*, the angel investors are primarily investing in physical products. In the crypto-space, investors are primarily investing in software and services (like exchanges).

FundWisdom maintains a list of angel investors focused on investing in blockchain/ crypto startups.[56] Satoshi Angels provides one example. Satoshi Angels invest and mentor blockchain and cryptocurrency seed stage startups. Just like *Shark Tank*, the competition is fierce because they only invest in five to ten companies a year. The lead investors have deep experience in the space, including Jed McCaleb, co-founder of Ripple and Stellar; Haris Doumanidis, former professor at MIT; and Raj Chowdhury, CEO of HashCash.[57]

Once a startup has launched and made progress, they may seek a large cash infusion from venture capitalists.

Venture capitalists. With a venture capital deal, private investors pool their money and have a professional venture capital (VC) firm invest the money in later-stage startups. VCs look for high-growth potential startups that have gone to market but need a large cash infusion to further scale operations. VC firms typically seek 20 to 30 percent equity in exchange for the cash. Some of the top US-based VCs investing in blockchains and crypto companies are Andreesen Horowitz; Blockchain Capital; Coinbase Ventures; Digital Currency Group; Lightspeed Venture Partners; Pantera Capital; Paradigm; Plug and Play; Ribbit Capital; and Sequoia Capital.[58]

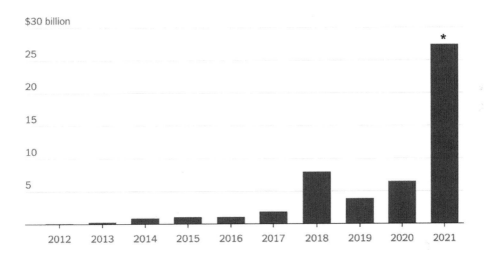

Figure 4.9: Worldwide venture capital funding in blockchain startups (up to November 2021)

Source: h ttps://specials-images.forbesimg.com/imageserve/61c8648aa068769c5d55465f/Global-venture-capital-investment-in-cryptocurrency-and-blockchain-companies/960x0.jpg?fit=scale

Figure 4.9 show the global VC investment in blockchain startups from 2012 to November of 2021, according to Pitchbook.[59] 2021 was a big year for VC funding, reaching nearly $30 billion. Other sources report slightly lower or higher figures; CB Insights reported that VCs invested $25.2 billion and Galaxy Digital Research reported $32.8 billion in crypto and blockchain startups in 2021.[60] No matter who's calculating the numbers, the trend is undeniable: VC investment in blockchains and crypto increased dramatically in 2021. What exactly are these VCs investing in? According to Galaxy Digital Research, *"About 43 percent of crypto funding went into companies involved in trading, exchange services, investing, and lending of crypto assets, while 17 percent was directed toward startups in NFTs (non-fungible tokens), DAOs (decentralized autonomous organizations),*

175

Web3 (a decentralized online ecosystem based on the blockchain), and the Metaverse (a network of 3D virtual worlds). Other categories that drew significant VC interest include custody, infrastructure, and decentralized finance."[61]

Top venture capital deals. When startups want to attract a large amount of cash, they often do a funding round that invites multiple VCs to invest. Some of the top VC deals are listed in Table 4.1. It's interesting that nine of the top deals occurred in 2021...who says crypto is a fad?

Top blockchain native companies. A blockchain native company is a company that started out in the blockchain/crypto space. Among the tens of thousands of 'blockchain/crypto' native companies, a few have achieved impressive growth. Table 4.2 lists the top revenue generators as of December 2021, according to Investopedia. The winners primarily serve two markets. Coinbase, Monex, Voyager, SOS, and Silvergate provide exchange, brokerage, and other financial services. BIT Mining, Canaan, HIVE, Riot, and Bitfarms make hardware, like computer chips and mining equipment, and also run large crypto-mining operations. One sees the dominance of Asia and North America among these winners.

Top traditional enterprises active in blockchains and crypto. A number of surveys report a steady march of adoption of blockchain technologies by traditional enterprises. Forbes, for example, runs an annual list of 50 largest companies with revenues over $1 billion that are most active in blockchains/crypto (see Figure 4.10). You will likely recognize many of these companies.

Financial services firms were the first to recognize Bitcoin as a potential threat or opportunity.[62] Financial services firms are seeking to lower transaction costs and to speed settlement times for remittances; cross-border payments; bond issuances and settlements; derivatives; equities; and trade finance. We've already mentioned Binance, Coinbase, and JPMorgan as blockchain adopters. Many companies are using blockchains in their supply chains to prevent counterfeit products and to monitor the condition and location of products as they move across supply chains. In this book, we cover supply chain

Number of VC Investor(s)	Investment in	Product/service	Amount Raised	Year
Not available	Bitmain	Crypto-mining hardware	$1 billion	2018
9 investors	NYDIG	Institutional digital asset brokerage & services	$1 billion	2021
23 investors	FTX Exchange	Cryptocurrency exchange	$900 million	2021
1 investor	Celsius Network	DeFi	$750 million	2021
14 investors	Forte Labs	NFTs and token-based games	$725 million	2021
14 investors	Solare	NFT football game	$680 million	2021
6 investors	Moonpay	Crypto payments infrastructure	$555 million	2021
2 investors	Circle	Crypto payments infrastructure	$440 million	2021
8 investors	Genesis Digital Assets	Crypto-mining	$431 million	2021
7 investors	Bitmain	Crypto-mining hardware	$422 million	2021
10 investors	FTX Exchange	Cryptocurrency exchange	$420 million	2021

Table 4.1: Ten largest VC deals in blockchain/crypto

Source: Blockdata[63]

uses at Maersk, Walmart, Cargill, and Carrefour. Many software, social media and tech services companies are helping themselves and their clients to build, develop, and host blockchain-based services. These companies help their clients explore blockchain technologies by offering strategy, opportunity analysis, development, and implementation services. For example, IBM was the tech partner for the Maersk's TradeLens platform and for the Food Trust used by Walmart and Carrefour.

Company	Founded[64]	Business	Headquarters	Trailing 12 month revenue[65]
Coinbase Global	2012 by Brian Armstrong and Fred Ehrsam	Crypto financial infrastructure	No physical HQ (fully remote), but based in United States	$5,900 million
Monex Group	1999 by Oki Matsumoto	Crypto Financial services	Tokyo, Japan	$937 million
BIT Mining	2001 by Zhaoxing Luo	Crypto mining	Hong Kong, China	$450 million
Canaan	2013 by N.G. Zhang	Application-specific, integrated circuits (ASIC)	Hangzhou, China	$438 million
Voyager	2017 by Gaspard de Dreuzy, Oscar Salazar, Philip Eytan, Serge Kreiker, Stephen Ehrlich	Crypto asset brokerage	Jersey City, United States	$254 million
SOS	2001 by Zheng Yu Wang and Andrew Mason	AI blockchain	Qingdao, China	$225 million
HIVE Blockchain Technologies	2013 by Harry Pokrandt, Marco Streng, Olivier Roussy Newton	Crypto mining	Vancouver, Canada	$195 million
Silvergate Capital	Sub-organization of Silvergate Bank, founded in 1988	Crypto financial infrastructure	La Jolla, United States	$149 million
Riot Blockchain	2000 by Pierre Rochard	Crypto mining	Castle Rock, United States	$128 million
Bitfarms	2017 by Emiliano Grodzki, Pierre-Luc Quimper, Roy Sebag	Crypto mining	Brossard, Canada	$121 million

Table 4.2: Ten largest blockchain companies in 2021

Sources: Crunchbase[66], Investopedia[67], and Wikipedia

Figure 4.10: Forbes Blockchain 50 2021 list

In 2021, Blockdata did an extensive study of blockchain adoption by the world's top 100 public companies. One of their analyses focused on the code bases used by these companies (see Figure 4.11). Enterprises most frequently adopted private-permissioned blockchains including those built on Fabric, Quorum, Corda, MedliLedger, and Data Gumbo. Private-permissioned blockchains require additional investments, such as running a node. Enterprises also build and use apps on public blockchains, most commonly Ethereum.[68] Enterprise adoption of public blockchains will likely increase as new protocols (like the Baseline Protocol) and layer 2 solutions that ride on top of public blockchains mature. These innovations allow enterprises to maintain data confidentiality while still taking advantage of the public networks for settlement.

So far, we've covered the major crypto markets and the major investors and adopters of crypto/blockchains. Next, we tour the major enablers.

179

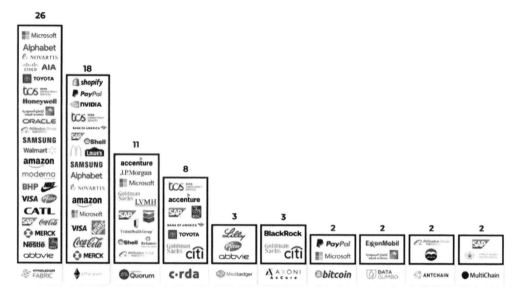

Figure 4.11: Top blockchain technologies used by top 100 companies
(Fabric, Ethereum, Quorum, Corda, MediLedger, Axoni, Bitcoin,
Data Gumbo, AntChain, MultiChain)

Source: https://forkast.news/wp-content/uploads/2021/09/Blockchain-technologies-1260x779.jpeg

4.4. Enablers

The global blockchain landscape includes important groups of enablers. Here we cover three: working groups/consortia, standards organizations, and legislators/regulators.

4.4.1. Blockchain working groups/consortia

Blockchains are meant to be shared among trading partners. This means that companies, often within the same industry, must work together to plan for solutions that meet the needs of all. To comply with anti-trust laws, companies can join a working group/consortium, which is an association of companies formed for a common purpose, but with clear rules to comply with anti-trust laws. Working groups/consortia are associations with 'lightweight' legal rules, often formed with a simple Memorandum of Understanding (MoU) that outlines terms such as not discussing pricing strategies (which would violate anti-trust) and the intellectual property (IP) rights of the IP created by the group. Since members are free to exit, companies only stay engaged if they perceive the group is making progress.

According to a survey by Deloitte, companies join consortia to achieve cost savings; to accelerate learning; to share risks; to build a critical mass of adoption; to maintain relevance; and to influence standards.[69] By 2020, there were over 220 major blockchain consortia. Consortia are helpful for exploring use cases and building proof-of-concepts, which are test systems that do not serve as official records, but fewer than five percent of consortia ever implemented a production application.[70] Many consortia disbanded due to the lack of a compelling business case, a misalignment of incentives, and other competing priorities, like dealing with crises prompted by the COVID-19 pandemic.[71] Shared governance challenges also were a major obstacle, discussed in Chapter 2. The ones that make it are usually operated by a neutral facilitator/benevolent dictator. Blockdata found that 53 consortia were still active in 2021 (see Figure 4.12).

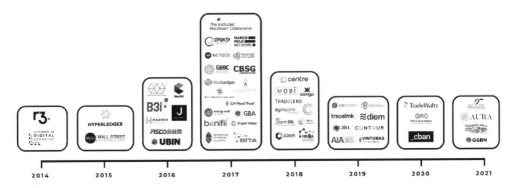

Figure 4.12: Active blockchain consortia in 2021

Source: Blockdata, https://images.blockdata.tech/blog-posts/post-images/6182ab9c93b5aa0012c3243
a/2a3fdd82-e5a9-45d3-b997-70c8b7461664/2021-11-3-1635953565560/timeline-of-active-blockchain-
consortiums.jpeg

Here we cover some sample of consortia, including R3; Hyperledger Foundation; B3i; Enterprise Ethereum Alliance; The Global Blockchain Business Council (GBBC); Blockchain in Transportation Alliance (BiTA); and the Blockchain for Energy Consortium. While members come and go, these consortia have sustained enough dedicated members to remain relevant as of 2022.

R3. Founded in 2014 by David Rutter in New York City, R3 is one of the first consortia of significance. R3 was launched with nine large banks: Barclays; BBVA Francés; State Street; JPMorgan; Commonwealth Bank of Australia; Goldman Sachs; Royal Bank of Scotland; Credit Suisse; and UBS. R3 swiftly grew to 60 members. In 2017, R3 released Corda. As we learned in the last chapter, Corda is a code base for launching private, permission blockchain applications. Corda is designed to increase privacy, reduce data redundancy (not everyone needs to see a transaction), and scalability (see Glossary for more on Corda).[72] Corda is used world-wide, primarily by large financial services companies, including CitiBank, MetLife, BNP Paribas, and Banco Bradesco.[73] R3 released Conclave in February of 2021, which allows multiple parties to submit data for analysis without revealing the actual data to anyone.[74] Because R2 is private, it's difficult to identify the number of members and the extent to which they are actually using the products. R3's website features sixteen case studies, including B3i's Fluidity Platform and VaultChain for precious metal market.[75]

Hyperledger Foundation. The Linux Foundation launched this non-profit organization with 30 corporate founders in December of 2015. Brian Behlendorf, the developer of the Apache Web server, served as Executive Director until 2021 when Daniela Barbosa took over. As of January 2022, 172 corporate members are listed on its website, of which seven are premier members: Accenture, ConsenSys, DTCC, Fujitsu, Hitachi, IBM, and JPMorgan. It aims to advance the application of enterprise-grade blockchains across industries.[76] Its four-part mission is to:

1. *"foster and coordinate the premier community of software developers building enterprise grade open-source software, in the form of platforms, libraries, tools*

and solutions, for multiparty systems using blockchain, distributed ledger, and related technologies;

2. *host the technical infrastructure for the Foundation, establishing a neutral home for community infrastructure, meetings, events, and collaborative discussions;*

3. *drive broad adoption of the technology by building a substantial and diverse ecosystem of solution providers delivering production solutions and networks, and organizing industry end-users; and*

4. *advocate for the use and adoption of enterprise multiparty systems technologies through marketing, education and outreach; and work with other aligned organizations to accelerate implementation and public acceptance."*[77]

The Hyperledger Foundation manages the community's projects from proposal to end-of-life (see left side of Figure 4.13). Many proposals come from companies who wished to donate their programming code and other intellectual property. Why would a company give away its technology? If a company can get enough interest in their donated open-source software, it is more likely to be widely adopted. Their customers prefer open-source software to avoid vendor lock-in, so companies that give away their code can differentiate themselves based on services that use the codebase, but not on the codebase itself.

As of 2022, the Hyperledger Foundation has 15 active projects of which six projects have achieved 'graduated' status (see right side of Figure 4.13). Graduated projects have passed several milestones, including meeting the legal requirements, having a diverse and dedicated community support, and is being used in real world applications.[78] Among the graduated projects, the 2021 study by Blockdata found Fabric to be the most used codebase by enterprises. Much of the original Fabric code was donated by IBM. Intel donated Sawtooth, an enterprise-as-a-service platform; it can set authorizations for both permissioned and permissionless applications. ConsenSys donated Besu, an Ethereum client for enterprise blockchains and the first project in the foundation focused on public blockchains. Soramitsu donated Iroha, a permissioned blockchain platform that enables multi-signature features on several platforms, including mobile applications. Aries and

Indy are sister projects. Together, they provide a toolkit for self-sovereign identity (SSI) and verifiable credentials for client-side components (wallets, agents) as well as for the distributed ledger-side. The Sovrin Foundation donated the code, which was initially built by Evernym. (Evernym was bought by Avast in 2021). We'll see these projects in use in the SSI chapter.

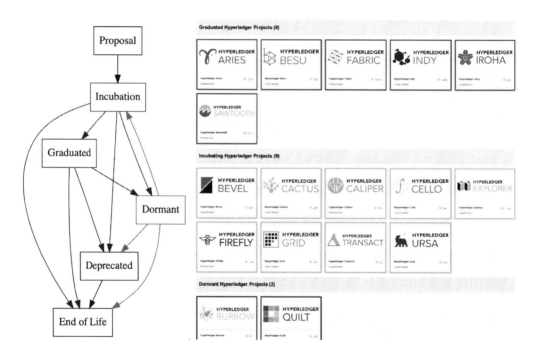

Figure 4:13 Hyperledger's project life cycle and projects as of 2022

Source: Left: https://tsc.hyperledger.org/project-lifecycle.html; Right: https://www.hyperledger.org/

Blockchain Insurance Industry Initiative (B3i). B3i was founded in October 2016 in Zurich Switzerland to focus on blockchain standards for the insurance sector. Its mission is *"better insurance enabled by frictionless risk transfer"*. By 2021, it had 21 major insurers as co-owners and more than 40 community members.[79] B3i's first major product is B3i RE, a distributed ledger application for automating reinsurance administration.[vi] Ongoing projects include applications for Managing General Agent (MGA), international premium payments tracking, and climate risk models.[80]

Enterprise Ethereum Alliance (EEA). Many companies want an enterprise-grade blockchain based on the Ethereum protocol. To help make that a reality, Microsoft; Accenture; JPMorgan; BNY Mellon; CME Group; MasterCard; Santander; Wipro; and 26 other enterprises founded the Enterprise Ethereum Alliance in February 2017.[81] Its mission is to *"Enable organizations to adopt and use Ethereum technology in their day-to-day business operations."* As of 2022, the EEA has 102 members listed on its website. To help make progress given the size of the alliance, working groups focus on areas. There are EEA community projects, interest groups and working groups. EEA community projects focus on open-source standards, including the Baseline Protocol, which enables confidential transaction on Ethereum. EEA interest groups include DeFi, Eth2 for Enterprise, Ethereum mainnet, financial services, supply chain, and tokenization. EEA working groups are more technically oriented, focusing on topics such as cross-chain interoperability. [82]

The Global Blockchain Business Council (GBBC) was launched in 2017 in Davos Switzerland. The GBBC is a non-profit that is *"dedicated to furthering adoption of blockchain through engaging regulators, business leaders, and global changemakers on how to harness this ground-breaking technology to create more secure, equitable, and functional societies."[83]* By 2022, GBBC had 350 institutional members from across the globe. Sandra Ro serves as CEO. The GBBC publishes leading edge research and white papers and hosts a number of initiatives focused on specific issues. For example, its legal and regulatory group informs regulators from around the world and publishes the International Journal of Blockchain Law.[84]

---

vi Reinsurance is when one insurance company sells some of its liability to another insurance company to mitigate the risk of catastrophic losses from major claims events, such as major hurricanes, floods, earthquakes, and wildfires.

The Blockchain in Transportation Alliance (BiTA) was launched in 2017 to develop data standards for the entire transportation industry. The BiTA Standards Council, a separate not-for-profit organization, is chaired by Dale Chrystie, a business fellow and blockchain strategist at *FedEx*. So far, standards for tracking data and location components have been released.[85] The standard is designed to answer the question, *"Where is my shipment?"*

The Oil & Gas Blockchain Consortium (OOC) launched in 2019 in Houston Texas with ten founding members. The OOC changed its name to **Blockchain for Energy** in 2020 and has eight members: Chevron; ConocoPhillips; ExxonMobile; Hess; Pioneer; Repsol; WesternGeco; and Worley. Members collaborate on use cases pertaining to trucking; joint operating agreements; and seismic data management.[86] As of 2022, two applications have been built and are ready for use, namely, water haulage and chemical haulage apps built by Data Gumbo.

While our coverage is far from exhaustive, it underscores the point that people are taking blockchains for business seriously across sectors and across the globe.

4.4.2. Standards organizations

"The nice thing about standards is that you have so many to choose from."

Andrew S. Tanenbaum and David Wetherall (1981), p. 702[87]

Standards are common technical blueprints to help interoperability, compatibility, safety, repeatability, and quality. Think about some of the standards that ease our everyday lives. Standard units for time (years, months, days, hours, minutes, seconds) and time zones help us to coordinate events worldwide. Standard units for measurement allow us to follow cooking recipes and to buy clothes and shoes that fit. Standards for traffic rules and signs allow us to safely drive, fly, and sail. Standards for the Internet, particularly TCP/IP, allow our machines to find each other and exchange messages online. Ever wonder where these standards come from? Here we examine two types of standards, namely, de facto and de jure standards.

De facto standards are standards that have achieved wide-spread adoption in practice but were not officially established by a recognized standards-making body. Look at your computer's keyboard. You are likely using a QWERTY keyboard, which was developed in the 1870s. It's a highly inefficient design because the most used letters are not positioned by our index fingers. Other keyboards were designed to minimize finger motions, such as the Dvorak keyboard. Despite its inferior design, the QWERTY layout remains the dominant keyboard design, serving as an example of a de facto standard. Why do you think this is?

Ethereum's token standards are examples of de facto standards in the blockchain space.[88] Recall from Chapter 2 that Ethereum Improvement Proposals (EIPs) are the primary conduit for changes to Ethereum. Some of the EIPs have become de facto standards (see Table 4.3). The public Ethereum has two token standards that are widely used, the ERC-20 Token Standard for fungible tokens and the ERC-721 Token Standard for non-fungible tokens. In June of 2019, the ERC-1155 Token Standard was issued that allows for the creation of both fungible and non-fungible tokens within a single smart contract.[89] It too will likely become a de facto standard.

EIP number	Title	Website
ERC-20	Token standard for fungible tokens	https://eips.ethereum.org/EIPS/eip-20
ERC-721	Token standard for non-fungible tokens	https://eips.ethereum.org/EIPS/eip-721
ERC-1155	Standard interface to allow a smart contract to manage multiple token types	https://eips.ethereum.org/EIPS/eip-1155

Table 4.3: Examples of token standards by the Ethereum community

De jure standards are standards that are endorsed by official standards organizations. For example, look at the back cover of this book. You will see a bar code that is part of the UPS barcode standard that was initially developed in 1973 by the Universal Product Code Council, which is now called GS1. GS1 still serves as the organization that oversees bar code standards. GS1 has been working with enterprises to consider enhancements to its existing standards for blockchain applications. For example, GS1 worked with the IBM Food Trust and TradeLens during their development.[90] Many other traditional standards organizations are tackling blockchain extensions and adaptations (see Table 4.4). These include IEEE, ISO, and NIST.

Standards organizations	Reference sites to blockchain projects
GS1	https://www.gs1.org/standards/blockchain
IEEE Blockchain Initiative (BCI)	https://blockchain.ieee.org/standards
International Organization for Standards (ISO) TC 307	https://www.iso.org/committee/6266604.html
National Institute of Standards & Technology (NIST)	https://www.nist.gov/blockchain

Table 4.4: Blockchain standards' initiatives by standards organizations

- *The IEEE*—a globally recognized standards-setting body—started a blockchain group (BCI) in January of 2018. As of 2022, the IEEE BCI has published six blockchain standards for cryptocurrency exchanges; custodian framework for crypto exchanges; e-invoices; cryptocurrency payments; blockchain IoT; and blockchain systems. IEEE has another 50 blockchain standards under development.[91]

188

- The *International Organization for Standards (ISO)* launched the Technical Committee (TC) 307 on blockchains and distributed ledgers in 2016. Representatives from 44 countries are participating, including the *American National Standards Institute (ANSI)* and the *British Standards Institution (BSI)*. As of 2022, it has published six blockchain standards and 11 are under development. The ISO published standards on a vocabulary of terms, privacy and personally identifiable information protection, blockchain reference architecture, a taxonomy and ontology, smart contracts, and security of digital assets.[92]

- The *National Institute of Standards and Technology (NIST)* is looking into blockchains and published a primer in 2018. As of 2022, NIST researchers are investigating blockchain use cases, protocols, security guarantees, and cryptographic mechanisms. Research outcomes include scientific papers and the production of software for experimentation as well as providing direction for other NIST endeavors in this space.[93]

Standards-making bodies typically need about three years from the time proposals are announced until standards are published.[94] The time is needed to ensure broad stakeholder input and review.

4.4.3. Legislators and regulators

"Regulators are still trying to manage this machine with rules devised for the industrial age."

Don and Alex Tapscott, authors of *Blockchain Revolution*[95]

It's time to revisit your high school civics class. What is the difference between a legislator and a regulator? How are laws and regulations made? For the sake of this discussion, we'll start with the federal government of United States, but the answers will differ by country. The US Federal legislative branch, called the US Congress, comprises the House of Representatives (currently 435 representatives) and the Senate (two senators per US state). Only a representative can propose a new law, which is

189

called a 'bill'. When the representative gets enough support, the bill is read to the House of Representatives, and the speaker of the House sends the bill to one of the standing committees. The standing committee reviews, seeks expert opinions, debates, and revises the bill. Once the standing committee approves the bill, it goes back to the House of Representatives for debate and proposed changes. The House votes upon it. If the majority vote yes, the bill passes to the Senate for the same process (committees, debates, and changes). If the majority of the senators vote yes, the bill is passed to the US President. If the President signs the bill, it becomes a law. If the President vetoes the bill, it goes back to Congress where it can still become a law if 2/3 of the representatives and 2/3 of the senators vote in favor of it.[96] Very few bills make it pass the first step, let alone becoming a law. The legislative process is slow in a democracy, which is one of the reasons why laws lag technical innovations. This means that technical innovators need to make sure their inventions comply with existing laws, or they will need to invest in lobby activities to try to change them.

US Federal banking laws. Some of the existing US federal laws that are most relevant to the crypto space are the Bank Secrecy and Money Laundering Control acts. The **Bank Secrecy Act (BSA)** of 1970 requires financial institutions—including banks, credit card companies, life insurers, money service businesses and broker-dealers—to report cash transactions over $10,000 to the US Department of the Treasury. Financial intuitions must also identify the individual making the transaction ('know your customer') as well as the source of the cash. The **Money Laundering Control Act of 1986** makes it illegal to pass money from one person to another with the intent to disguise the source, ownership, location or control of the money. Think about a Bitcoin transaction. Nakamoto's whole intent was to bypass financial institutions, so how do these laws apply? In general, cryptocurrency exchanges fall under the laws, which is why they now require customers to submit legal forms of identification to comply with 'know your customer' and why they submit reports to the US government. If the Bitcoin miners are ever considered to be financial institutions, that would seriously jeopardize the future of crypto since there is no way for a Bitcoin miner to know the individual's submitting transactions.

US State laws. Besides US federal law, US States also have the right to make State laws, under the processes defined by the State's constitution. By 2021, 33 US States had introduced legislation related to crypto/blockchain according to the National Conference of State Legislatures.[97]

Some US State laws are quite controversial. One notable example was a regulation published in June of 2015 by the Department of Financial Services (DFS) for New York State that required companies to get a BitLicense for virtual currencies. Many small firms found compliance to be too expensive (or too invasive) and stopped operating in the state. A further controversy happened when the chief architect of the regulation, Benjamin Lawsky, left the DFS to start his own consulting process to help clients maneuver through the onerous process he helped to create to obtain a BitLicense.[98] The BitLicense requires companies to store transaction receipts; disclose risks; publish a customer complaint policy; maintain a cybersecurity program; hire a compliance officer; and abide by anti-money-laundering rules.[99] For startups, complying with such regulations can cost hundreds of thousands of dollars, prompting them to establish their businesses in other US states with more welcoming regulations, like Wyoming.

The State of Wyoming. Wyoming is America's least populated state with 579,000 residents, but it is the nineth largest state by landmass. Wyoming's motto is *"equal rights"*, as it was the first US State to give equal voting rights to women in 1869. In that context, it is not surprising that Wyoming is leading in pro-crypto laws. From 2017 to 2021, Wyoming passed 24 ground-breaking laws.

The first law aimed to fix an antiquated money transmitter law. Under the old law, exchanges were disincentivized to service the citizens of Wyoming because of a law that required 100 percent cash reserves for all transactions. Under the new law, passed in 2017, they can. Once that law was passed, Wyoming legislators realized that the new world of crypto and blockchains could help to diverse their economy beyond energy (coal, oil, gas, and minerals) and ranching. The legislators aimed to make Wyoming an attractive place to build new businesses based on crypto and blockchains.

Wyoming passed the world's first token taxonomy act in 2019. The law recognizes three types of tokens: cryptocurrencies (like Bitcoin), security tokens (investment tokens that fall under the regulations of the SEC), and a third new type, defined as a 'utility' or 'consumer' token, used exclusively for the purpose of consumption. In the non-digital world, consumer tokens are commonly used at arcades, theme parks, and other entertainment venues. One token, such as a metal coin or printed ticket, always has the same consumptive value, such as one token allows the holder to play one game, to ride one ride, or to redeem one drink. The Wyoming law allows for digital utility tokens. As an example of a digital utility token, consumers might buy tokens to raise money for a startup that could later be redeemed to access the startup's services. A utility token is not considered a security token under Wyoming law provided that the coin will have the same expected value in the future.

Wyoming was the first state to map digital assets to the **Uniform Commercial Code (UCC)** law. The UCC is NOT a federal law, but rather a uniformly adopted state law. The point of the UCC is to allow a business to operate legally in many states under the same rule of law. The UCC adopted Wyoming's proposal, which will be debated and considered for UCC adoption sometime after 2023.

Wyoming created a **FinTech Sandbox** law in 2019 to welcome entrepreneurs and to allow experimentation on new business models that are not currently covered under regulation. The FinTech Sandbox allows enterprises to operate for two years—extendable to a third year—giving the legislators time to pass sound regulations around these new markets.

One of Wyoming's most innovative laws created an entirely new type of financial institution, called a **Special Purpose Depository Institution (SPDI)**. The law passed in 2019. A SPDI is a fully-reserved, Wyoming State chartered fiat bank that can also custody crypto assets.[100] A SPDI bank is not allowed to have fractional reserves, meaning that the customers' deposits must remain at the SPDI bank. Given this stipulation, SPDIs are not required to obtain insurance from the Federal Deposit Insurance Corporation (FDIC)—though they may do so. SPDI banks can take custody (but not ownership) of digital assets. SPDI banks charge fees for services, such as keeping the digital assets safe and executing and settling transactions, but they are not allowed to offer loans.[101] The crypto exchange Kraken was the first chartered SPDI bank, called Kraken Bank, granted in 2020.[102] Custodia Bank, founded by Caitlin Long, was the second chartered SPDI bank, also in 2020.[103] Kraken Bank and Custodia Bank applied to obtain a master account from the US Federal Reserve, which provides a bank routing number needed for transactions. Additionally, a master account would allow SPDI banks to interact with the Federal Reserve rather than depend on other banks. Customarily, a Fed master account requires FDIC insurance, but SPDI banks do not need insurance since they keep 100 percent of deposits in reserve. The Fed was slow to decide on the requests. Both SPDI banks were awaiting the Fed's responses in 2021. In December of 2021, Wyoming's Senator, Cynthia Lummis, accused the Federal Reserve of illegally delaying master bank applications.[104]

Wyoming also passed a law that would allow Decentralized Autonomous Organizations (DAOs) to incorporate. Recall from Chapter 3 that a DAO is an organization with investors, but without managers or employees. The investors govern the organization with governance tokens, allowing them to vote on decisions, thus serving the same functions as a Board of Directors. The question the Wyoming law addressed is: how can a DAO incorporate to become a legally recognized company? Normally, a startup needs to provide articles of registration and a list of company officers to incorporate. But DAOs do not have officers, so how can they incorporate? The 2021 Wyoming law allows DAOs to register as companies without listing officers!

So we've covered a bit about existing laws and new laws that apply to the crypto space. Now let's turn our attention to the regulators.

US Regulators. A regulatory agency is an official government organization responsible for rulemaking and for making sure that citizens and businesses comply with the rules.[105] US Professor Carol Goforth, author of *Regulation of Cryptotransactions*, writes, *"The ability of administrative agencies to fill in legislative gaps through the process of* *informal rulemaking has been heralded as one of the great innovations in modern law… There are estimates that more than ninety percent of modern American laws are rules adopted by agencies rather than statutes imposed by legislators.*"[106] When regulations are confusing or silent on new ways to transact, innovation adoption slows. Deloitte's 2021 survey of 1,280 senior executives in ten countries reported that sixty percent of respondents identified regulatory barriers as the biggest obstacle to the use of digital assets.[107]

In the US Federal government, there are over 100 regulatory agencies. Given that financial services are one of the most heavily regulated industries, it's apt to focus upon it. A complex web of federal and state regulators oversees financial services in the United States (see Figure 4.14). The agencies that are most relevant to our context of crypto and blockchains include the Internal Revenue Service (IRS), Securities and Exchange Commission (SEC), and the Commodity Futures Trading Commission (CFTC). The IRS views crypto as property; the SEC views most crypto as securities; and the CFTC views crypto as commodities. Yes, it is confusing. The US regulatory framework for crypto is often described as a 'patchwork' of guidance.[108]

At the Federal level, the US Treasury Department was one of the first regulators to enact a cryptocurrency policy. In 2013, it classified Bitcoin as a convertible, decentralized, virtual currency, and therefore subject to property taxes. Subsequently, the Internal Revenue Service (IRS) treats cryptocurrencies as property for Federal income tax purposes. People must report gains or losses on their US tax returns.[109]

The ***Securities and Exchange Commission (SEC)*** was established to protect investors who buy stocks and bonds. Federal laws require companies that plan to raise money by selling their own securities to file reports about their operations with the SEC, so that investors have access to all material information. The commission has powers to prevent or punish fraud in the sale of securities and is authorized to regulate stock exchanges. The SEC views many digital token sales as investment contracts, and thus subject to SEC regulations. It's useful to understand how the SEC guides its rulings. The SEC applies the '*Howey Test*' to determine whether an investment is considered a security and thus subject to SEC regulations. The 'Howey Test' comes from a 1946 Supreme Court case where the SEC sued the Howey Company of Florida. The Howey Company was a citrus farm that leased land to raise investment funds but it did not register transactions with the SEC. The Supreme Court deemed that the transactions were indeed securities based on a four-part test. A transaction is considered a security investment if (1) it includes an investment of money (2) in a common enterprise (3) with an expectation of profit (4) based solely on the efforts of a promoter or third party. Based on this test, mostly all new investments in cryptocurrencies are now viewed as securities.[110] However, the SEC deemed that Bitcoin is NOT a security; by the time the SEC examined Bitcoin, the governance was so decentralized that the SEC could not find an identifiable promoter or third party.[111]

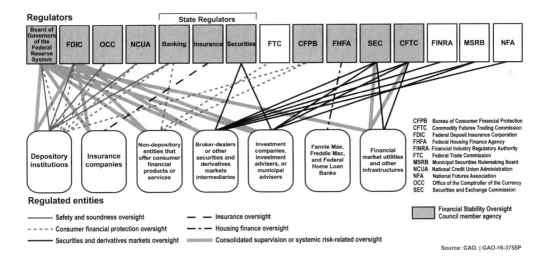

Figure 4.14: US GAO map of US regulatory environment[112]

Source: http://www.gao.gov/modules/ereport/handler.php?1=1&path=/ereport/GAO-16-375SP/data_center/General_government/5._Financial_Regulatory_Structure

The **Commodity Futures Trading Commission (CFTC)** regulates commodity futures and option markets in the United States. The agency protects market participants against manipulation, abusive trade practices, and fraud. Through oversight and regulation, the CFTC enables the markets to serve better their important functions in the US economy, providing a mechanism for price discovery and a means of offsetting price risk. The CFTC views crypto as a commodity. The CFTC regulates fraud in the spot markets for crypto and it also regulates derivatives trading.[113]

Global crypto laws and regulations. Governments all over the world are examining the blockchain space. The US Library of Congress publishes an annual report of global cryptocurrency regulations. For each country, it looks at whether there is an absolute or explicit ban on cryptocurrencies. The countries with absolute bans are Algeria; Bangladesh; Bolivia; China; Ecuador; Egypt; Guyana; Iraq; Kyrgyzstan, Morocco; Nepal; Oman, and Tunisia (see Figure 4.15).[114]

China was one of the first countries to ban financial institutions from accepting, using, or selling virtual currencies in 2013. A year later, China required financial institutions to close bitcoin trading accounts. By July of 2018, China forced the closure of 173 cryptocurrency exchanges and many bitcoin mining operations.[115] When China's President Xi Jinping announced strong support for blockchain technologies in October of 2018, it was clear that China's government wanted control over the space; China will likely issue a tokenized Chinese yuan by the time this book is in print, becoming the first country with a **Central Bank Digital Currency (CBDC).**[116] A CBDC is digital version of fiat currency, completely controlled by the country's government. China's CBDC is called the digital yuan, or e-CNY. Many see China's move as an attempt to usurp the US Dollar as the world's dominant currency.[117]

In addition to China, nine countries have live pilot programs on Central Bank Digital Currencies (CBDCs) as of February 2022. The Bahamas; Antigua and Barbuda; St. Kitts and Nevis; Monserrat; Dominica; Saint Lucia; St Vincent and The Grenadines; Grenada; and Nigeria.[118]

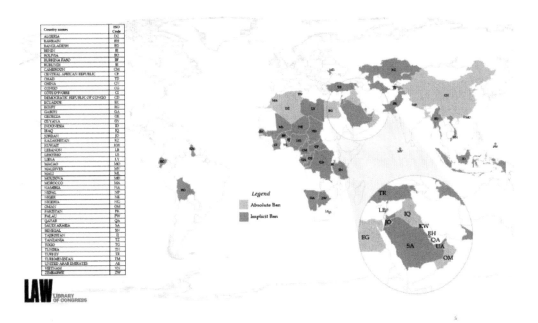

Figure 4.15: 2021 legal status of cryptocurrencies

Source: Library of Congress (2021).[119]

Some governments like Cyprus, El Salvador, Estonia, Malta, Singapore, Switzerland, and Gibraltar are supportive.[120] El Salvador, for example, was the first country to make Bitcoin legal tender in 2021. El Savador's president, Nayib Bukele, said that legalizing Bitcoin would stimulate investment in his country and would help the 70 percent of Salvadorans who don't have access to traditional financial services.[121] The law means that businesses must accept bitcoin for payments. To incentivize adoption, the government announced that it would launch a digital wallet, preloaded with $30 worth of bitcoin, for citizens to download for free. While the Bitcoin community cheered the announcement, the World Bank and the International Monetary Fund said that adopting bitcoin could leave the country open to money laundering and other illicit financial activity.[122]

United Kingdom (UK). In 2017, the UK government treated bitcoin as foreign currency for the purposes of taxation. No value-added tax (VAT) is due when exchanging bitcoin for other currencies, but profits and losses are subject to capital gains tax. Cryptocurrency mining and getting paid in cryptocurrencies may be subject to income tax and national insurance contributions.[123] Beyond taxation, Naseem Naqvi, President of the British Blockchain Association, points out that the UK is a pioneer in the blockchain landscape. He notes that the UK government was among the first to create a national roadmap for distributed ledgers, back in 2015.[124]

Estonia. Estonia is one of the more forward-thinking countries when it comes to cryptocurrencies and blockchain technologies.[125] Bitcoin is legal, provided the trader identifies the buyer for any transaction over 1,000 euros.[126] Although Estonia does not recognize cryptocurrencies as a legal tender within the country, Estonia remains open and innovative to the idea by recognizing cryptocurrency as *"value represented in digital form"*. In June 2018, Estonia attempted to introduce a national cryptocurrency known as 'estcoin' through a government plan but the plan was ultimately criticized by the European Union (EU), sending the Estonia government back to the drawing board.[127]

For updates on specific regulations by country, the US Library of Congress maintains a list of cryptocurrency regulations around the world.[128]

4.5. Blockchain's maturity

Taking the entire blockchain landscape into consideration, how mature is the blockchain market as we enter 2022? To answer this question, we'll look at Gartner's assessment of where blockchains are placed on its well-known hype cycle. Gartner's technology hype cycle comprises five phases that map the level of expectations about the innovation over time (see Figure 4.16). During the **technology trigger phase**, early proof-of-concepts capture media attention and interest, but there are no real applications. During the **peak of inflated expectations phase**, a few early successes garner even more attention. Senior executives start to take notice, new entrants jump into the market, and the technology may be viewed as a silver bullet, i.e., something that promises to instantly solve a long-standing problem. Many organizations start testing the technology, but enter the **trough of disillusionment phase** when instant success is not achieved. Organizations regroup. They learn to apply sound project management, change management, and what we call 'action principles' to deliver successful applications. In other words, it's hard work to get value from a new innovation. As time passes, upgraded versions of the technology are released, the market producers consolidate, and organizational consumers learn how to gain value from the innovations. Gartner calls this the **slope of enlightenment phase**. The last phase, called the **plateau of productivity phase**, sees market maturity, wide-spread adoption, and integration into the enterprises' standard technology portfolios.

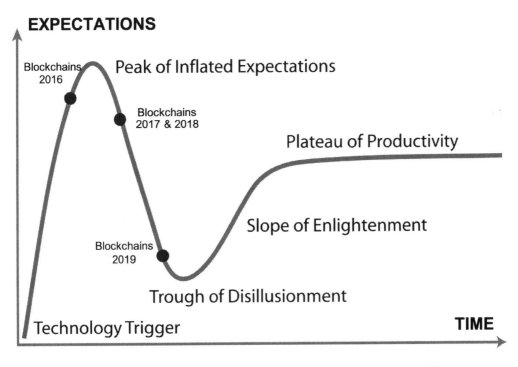

Figure 4.16: Gartner's mapping of blockchains 2016-2019[129]

Every year, Gartner updates its map of current emerging technologies through the five phases. In 2015, blockchains were not yet on Gartner's map. However, by July of 2016, Gartner placed blockchains as past the 'technology trigger phase' and was indeed approaching the apex of the 'peak of inflated expectations phase'. A year later in July 2017, Gartner placed blockchains as nearly finished with that phase; blockchains were headed for the 'trough of disillusionment'. A year later, the market hadn't budged. Finally, by September of 2019, Gartner placed blockchain technologies as near the bottom of the trough. In 2019, Gartner estimated that more than 90 percent of enterprise blockchain platform implementations will fail or will need to be replaced. This is due to a fragmented blockchain market and unrealistic expectations.[130]

After 2019, Gartner started de-composing the blockchain market into 22 different components and placed these on the hype cycle[vii]. At the time of this writing, their 2021 hype cycle for blockchains was released. Figure 4.17 shows where Gartner placed decentralized exchanges (DEX), NFTs, DeFi, smart contracts, blockchain platforms, consensus mechanisms, blockchain wallets, and cryptocurrencies on the maturity curve.

We make two points about the hype cycle. First, it is a useful tool for discussing overall global trends, but industries and specific organizations within industries adopt technologies at different rates. For example, companies like EY, IBM, Microsoft, and Walmart had already reached the slope of enlightenment by 2019. Second, the pace of adoption is not deterministic; individuals and organizations do not just sit around and wait for the future, they actively create it.

4.6. Conclusion: The landscape shifts rapidly

The global blockchain landscape shifts rapidly and unpredictably—there will be big winners and big losers that we cannot foresee today. This chapter has been tempered with phrases such as 'as of the beginning of 2022' and 'so far' to reflect that fact. We

---

vii The link to view Gartner's 2019 Hype Cycle for Blockchain Business is here: https://www.gartner.com/en/newsroom/press-releases/2019-09-12-gartner-2019-hype-cycle-for-blockchain-business-shows

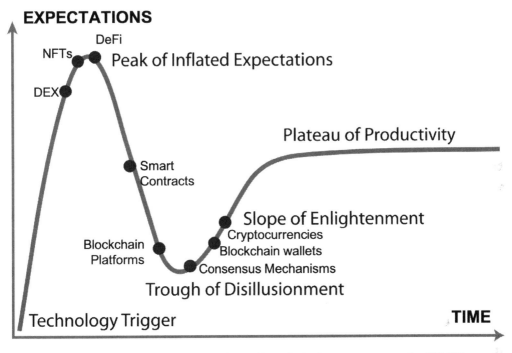

Figure 4.17: Gartner's mapping of blockchain components in 2021[131]

encourage readers to investigate how the landscape has shifted since this writing. While the value of markets will fluctuate widely and individual players will come and go, the ***categories*** of key players will remain relevant. Investors, startups, traditional enterprises, blockchain working groups/consortia, standard-making bodies, legislators, and regulators will continue to shape and transform the global blockchain landscape.

With the close of Chapter 4, we have concluded the foundational chapters. By now, readers should have a solid grasp of the aims of blockchains to decentralize the World Wide Web; the myriad of ways blockchain networks are governed; how the component parts of a blockchain application function as an integrated whole; and the major markets and players in the global blockchain landscape. The next set of chapters takes us on a tour of blockchain applications for finance, supply chains, the media, and credentials.

Citations

[1] Vigna, P. (November 4, 2019). Large Bitcoin Player Manipulated Price Sharply Higher, Study Says, *The Wall Street Journal*, https://www.wsj.com/articles/large-bitcoin-player-manipulated-price-sharply-higher-study-says-11572863400

[2] Griffin, J. and Shams, A. (2019). Is Bitcoin Really Un-tethered?, https://ssrn.com/abstract=3195066 or http://dx.doi.org/10.2139/ssrn.3195066

[3] Willams-Grut, O. (Jan 17, 2018). Here are all the theories explaining the crpto market crash," https://www.insider.com/bitcoin-cryptocurrency-market-crash-explained-causes-2018-1

[4] Brookes, M. (January 24, 2022). Will crypto recover? When cryptocurrency market and price of Bitcoin could bounce back – 2022 crash explained, NationalWorold, retrieved January 31, 2022 from https://www.nationalworld.com/lifestyle/money/will-crypto-recover-when-cryptocurrency-market-and-price-of-bitcoin-could-bounce-back-2022-crash-explained-3243971.

[5] Sergeenkov, A. (September 29, 2021). China Crypto Bans: A Complete History. Coindesk, Retrieved January 31, 2022 from https://www.coindesk.com/learn/china-crypto-bans-a-complete-history/.

[6] Lau, Y. (November 9, 2021). Cryptocurrencies hit market cap of $3 trillion for the first time as Bitcoin and Ether reach record highs, Retrieved February 5, 2022 from Cryptocurrencies hit market cap of $3 trillion for the first time as Bitcoin and Ether reach record highs.

[7] Morris, C. (January 21, 2022). Fortune. Cryptocurrencies lose $205 billion in 24 hours, retrieved February 5, 2022 from https://fortune.com/2022/01/21/cryptocurrency-crash-bitcoin-ether-cardano-doge-205-billion-loss/

Chambers, C. (January 24, 2022) Bitcoin Crash of 2022. Firbes. Retrieved February 5, 2022 from https://www.forbes.com/sites/investor/2022/01/24/bitcoin-crash-of-2022/?sh=13d949a110e8

[8] This website tracks the trading price of cryptocurrencies in $US dollars and the total number of coins in circulation to calculate a market cap: https://coinmarketcap.com/all/views/all/

[9] Chaum, D. (1982). *Computer Systems Established, Maintained and Trusted by Mutually Suspicious Groups*, University of California, Berkeley.

[10] Popper, N. (2015). *Digital Gold: Bitcoin and the Inside History of the Misfits and Millionaires Trying to Reinvent Money*, Harper, New York.

[11] Burniske, C. and Tatar, J. (2017). *Cryptoassets: The Innovative Investor's Guide to Bitcoin and Beyond,* McGraw Hill, United States.

[12] Sielski, M. (2020). Namecoin: A cryptocurrency supported by Satoshi Nakamoto. Retrieved February 2, 2022 from https://forexclub.pl/en/namecoin-nmc-kryptowaluta-ktora-poparl-satoshi-nakamoto/

[13] https://en.bitcoinwiki.org/wiki/Namecoin; https://en.bitcoinwiki.org/wiki/Litecoin

[14] Browne, R. (December 20, 2017). Litecoin founder Charlie Lee says he's sold all his holdings in the cryptocurrency. Retrieved February 2, 2022 from https://www.cnbc.com/2017/12/20/litecoin-founder-charlie-lee-sells-his-holdings-in-the-cryptocurrency.html

[15] https://en.wikipedia.org/wiki/Dogecoin

[16] Pound, J. (May 4, 2021). "Dogecoin surges 30% to a record above 50 cents as speculative crypto trading continues". CNBC, retrieved February 1, 2022 from https://www.cnbc.com/2021/05/04/dogecoin-surges-above-50-cents-to-record-as-speculative-crypto-trading-continues.html

[17] Dog Products (July 4, 2021). 13 Popular Dog-Themed Cryptocurrencies. Retrieved February 3, 2022 from https://dogendorsed.com/popular-dog-themed-cryptocurrencies/

[18] Whittemore, N., and Collins, C. (2019), "A History of Crypto Exchanges," *Nomics*, https://blog.nomics.com/essays/crypto-exchanges-history/

[19] Popper, N. (2015). Digital Gold: Bitcoin and the inside story of the misfits and millionaires trying to reinvent money. Haper, New York.

[20] *Mt. Gox CEO Mark Karpeles pleads not guilty to embezzlement*, July 11th 2015, http://www.aljazeera.com/news/2015/08/japan-arrests-mtgox-bitcoin-head-missing-387m-150801054245349.html

[21] Coinmarket tracks cryptocurrency exchanges on its website at https://coin.market/exchanges

[22] https://en.wikipedia.org/wiki/Kraken_(company)

[23] Prathap, M. (December 24, 2021). Top 6 stablecoins in the crypto market — what are they, how they work and why they have governments worried. https://www.businessinsider.in/investment/news/top-6-stablecoins-in-the-crypto-market-what-are-they-how-to-they-work-and-why-they-have-governments-worried/articleshow/87667452.cms

[24] Prathap, M. (December 24, 2021). Top 6 stablecoins in the crypto market — what are they, how they work and why they have governments worried. https://www.businessinsider.in/investment/

news/top-6-stablecoins-in-the-crypto-market-what-are-they-how-to-they-work-and-why-they-have-governments-worried/articleshow/87667452.cms

[25] Cuen, L. (August 30, 2019). Why Tether volume is at all-time highs. https://www.coindesk.com/why-tether-volume-surged-to-all-time-highs-in-august

[26] Diem Association press release (January 31, 2022). Statement by Diem CEO Start Levey. Retrieved February 1, 2022 from

https://www.prnewswire.com/news-releases/statement-by-diem-ceo-stuart-levey-on-the-sale-of-the-diem-groups-assets-to-silvergate-301471997.html

[27] USD Coin. https://www.coinbase.com/usdc

[28] Gemini Coin https://gemini.com/

[29] JP Morgan Press Release (February 14 2019). JP Morgan Creates Digital Coin for Payments. https://www.jpmorgan.com/global/news/digital-coin-payments

[30] Perez, E. (October 2, 2019). Stablecoins Backed by Precious Metals, *CoinTelegraph*. https://cointelegraph.com/news/stablecoins-backed-by-precious-metals-how-do-they-work

[31] Petro news (2020). *CoinTelegraph*, https://cointelegraph.com/tags/petro

[32] Makerdao. A better money. https://makerdao.com/en/

[33] Ikeda, S. (2020). The controversy surrounding privacy coins. CPO Magazine, retrieved February 1, 2022 from

https://www.cpomagazine.com/data-privacy/south-koreas-new-crypto-aml-law-bans-trading-of-privacy-coins-monero-zcash/

[34] Bitcoin Forum (April 2, 2020). Nicolas van Saberhagen = Satoshi? Retrieved February 3, 2022 from https://bitcointalk.org/index.php?topic=5237406.0

[35] Monero uses the CryptoNote protocol developed by Nicolas van Saberhagen, that defined an algorithm with increased data obfuscation compared to Bitcoin. With Monero, a recipient's address is only used once, so that the sender cannot trace subsequent transactions on the ledger. When the recipient spends money out of that address (thus becoming a "sender" address in a subsequent transaction), the address gets hidden within a group signature https://cryptonote.org/whitepaper.pdf; https://en.wikipedia.org/wiki/Monero_(cryptocurrency).

[36] https://z.cash/technology/

[37] https://oasisprotocol.org/

[38] https://messari.io/asset/oasis-labs/

[39] https://www.anjuna.io/what-is-a-secure-enclave

[40] G. Zyskind, O. Nathan and A. Pentland, "Decentralizing Privacy: Using Blockchain to Protect Personal Data," *2015 IEEE Security and Privacy Workshops*, 2015, pp. 180-184, doi: 10.1109/SPW.2015.27.

[41] The Secret Network Primer. Retrieved February 5, 2022 from https://republic.com/blog/crypto/secret-network-primer#:~:text=Secret%20Network%20is%20designed%20to,for%20hosting%20private%20decentralized%20applications.

[42] https://messari.io/asset/secret-network/profile/regulation

[43] Versprille, A. (January 6, 2021). NFT Market Surpassed $40 Billion in 2021, New Estimate Shows. Retrieved February 3, 2022 from https://www.bloomberg.com/news/articles/2022-01-06/nft-market-surpassed-40-billion-in-2021-new-estimate-shows

[44] Paul, T. (February 2, 2022). The most popular NFT marketplaces you should know about. Retrieved February 3, 2022 from https://www.prestigeonline.com/sg/pursuits/tech/top-nft-marketplaces/

[45] BBC News (December 5th 2017), *CryptoKitties craze slows down transactions on Ethereum*, retrieved February 3, 2022 from http:/ www.bbc.com/news/technology-42237162

Wong (December 4th 2017), *The Ethereum network is getting jammed up because people are rushing to buy cartoon cats on its blockchain*, retrieved February 3, 2022   https://qz.com/1145833/cryptokitties-is-causing-ethereum-network- congestion/

[46] Locke, T. (March 22, 2021). Jack Dorsey sells his first tweet ever as an NFT for over $2.9 million. Retrieved February 3, 2022 from https://www.cnbc.com/2021/03/22/jack-dorsey-sells-his-first-tweet-ever-as-an-nft-for-over-2point9-million.html

[47] Kastrenakes, J. (2021). Beeple sold an NFT for $69 million through a first-of-its-kind auction at Christie's, the Verge, retrieved August 2, 2021 from https://www.theverge.com/2021/3/11/22325054/beeple-christies-nft-sale-cost-everydays-69-million

[48] To buy a Beeble: https://www.masterworks.io/insights/beeple-digital-art-distruptor/?utm_source=google+sem&utm_medium=platform&utm_campaign=art_nfts_artists_beeple&gclid=CjwKCAiAl-6PBhBCEiwAc2GOVCaHEFO80VnPx2vHLesL3ND8eoDkZtbK4agPsrqgYpHObvE30tj1fhoC_TcQAvD_BwE&gclsrc=aw.ds

[49] Aird & McBurney LP (July 29, 2021). Bought an NBA Top Shot NFT? What Did You Actually Buy? Retrieved February 3, 2022 from https://www.lexology.com/library/detail.aspx?g=6d4d1894-f8cb-4640-b764-b7771a8b77cb

[50] Wall Street Journal (March 11, 2021). NFTs Are Fueling a Boom in Digital Art. Here's How They Work. Retrieved February 3, 2022, from https://www.wsj.com/video/series/wsj-glossary/nfts-are-fueling-a-boom-in-digital-art-heres-how-they-work/F5BA93AD-3DCD-4EFA-B064-C9143C81CB88

[51] JDSupra (March 11. 2021). NBA Top Shot Moments – What Are You Actually Buying? Retrieved February 3, 2022 from https://www.jdsupra.com/legalnews/nba-top-shot-moments-what-are-you-3632095/

[52] Hissong, S. (January 24, 2022). NFT Scams Are Everywhere. Here's How to Avoid Them, RollingStone, retrieved February 6, 2022 from https://www.rollingstone.com/culture/culture-features/nft-crypto-scams-how-to-not-get-scammed-1286614/

[53] Servantes, I. (February 4th 2022). Nike sues StockX for turning its sneakers into NFTs. Retrieved February 6, 2022 from https://www.inputmag.com/style/nike-stockx-nft-nfts-lawsuit-virtual-sneakers-shoes-metaverse

[54] Jenna Pilgrim talks about Intellectual Property and NFTs (2022). Retrieved February 18, 2022 from https://youtu.be/d6YzEJv_Qo4

[55] https://en.wikipedia.org/wiki/Shark_Tank

[56] https://www.fundwisdom.com/article/brian-thopsey/list-blockchain-angel-investors-and-venture-fund-managers

[57] https://satoshiangels.com/

[58] Pitchbook (August 27, 2021). 6 VC firms investing in blockchain and cryptocurrency, Retrieved February 3, 2022, from https://pitchbook.com/blog/vc-firms-investing-in-blockchain-and-cryptocurrency

The Coin News (January 2, 2022). An Overview Of Web3 Venture Capital Activity In 2021. Retrieved February 4, 2022 from https://thecoin.news/post/59969

[59] The Coin News (January 2, 2022). An Overview Of Web3 Venture Capital Activity In 2021. Retrieved February 4, 2022 from https://thecoin.news/post/59969

[60] CB Insights (2022). State Of Venture 2021 Report. Retrieved February 3, 2022 from https://www.cbinsights.com/research/report/venture-trends-2021/

[61] Zhang, H. (January 7, 2022). Where Did VC Money Go in 2021? Crypto Startups. Retrieved February 4, 2022 from https://www.institutionalinvestor.com/article/b1w6r1v3pjg15s/Where-Did-VC-Money-Go-

in-2021-Crypto-Startups

[62] Marr, B. (January 22, 2020). The 5 Biggest Blockchain And Distributed Ledger Trends Everyone Should Be Watching In 2020, *Forbes,* https://www.forbes.com/sites/bernardmarr/2020/01/22/the-5-biggest-blockchain-and-distributed-ledger-trends-everyone-should-be-watching-in-2020/#17056e9d56f0

[63] https://www.blockdata.tech/blog/general/top-10-funding-rounds-in-blockchain-crypto

[64] https://www.crunchbase.com/

[65] Johnston, M. (December 21, 2021). 10 Biggest Blockchain Companies, Investopedia, https://www.investopedia.com/10-biggest-blockchain-companies-5213784.

[66] https://www.crunchbase.com/

[67] Johnston, M. (December 21, 2021). 10 Biggest Blockchain Companies. Retrieved February 3, 2022 from https://www.investopedia.com/10-biggest-blockchain-companies-5213784

[68] Lim, M. (September 24, 2021). 81 of top 100 companies use blockchain technology, Blockdata research shows, Retrieved February 9, 2022 from https://forkast.news/81-of-top-100-companies-use-blockchain-technology-blockdata/

[69] Deloitte (2019). Deloitte's 2019 Global Blockchain Survey: Blockchains get down to business.

[70] ESI Intelligence (2019). https://esg-intelligence.com/blockchain-articles/2019/06/19/top-four-enterprise-blockchain-consortia-trends-2019/

ESL Intelligence (2020), List of all Blockchain Consortia, https://esg-intelligence.com/access-enterprise-blockchain-intelligence/list-of-all-blockchain-consortia/

[71] Van Niekerk, M. (August 16, 2020). Top Three Reasons Why Enterprise Blockchain Projects Fail. Retrieved February 6, 2022 from https://cointelegraph.com/news/top-three-reasons-why-enterprise-blockchain-projects-fail

[72] https://www.r3.com/

[73] Apps Run the World (2021). List of Corda Blockchain Platform Customers. Retrieved February 6, 2022 from https://www.appsruntheworld.com/customers-database/products/view/corda-blockchain-platform

[74] R3 (December 8, 2021). Introducing Conclave 1.2. Retrieved February 6, 2022 from https://medium.com/conclave-platform/introducing-conclave-1-2-7f3256bc0bd2

[75] https://www.r3.com/case-studies/

[76] The Linux Foundation (January 22nd 2016). The Hyperledger Project Charter, available at https://www.hyperledger.org/about/charter

[77] Hyperledger Project Charter. Retrieved February 9, 2022 from https://www.hyperledger.org/about/charter

[78] Hyperledger Foundation (2022). Project Incubation Exit Criteria, Retrieved February 9, 2022 from https://tsc.hyperledger.org/project-incubation-exit.html

[79] Crowell (January 28, 2021). Insurers and Industry Groups Launch New and Innovative Blockchain Initiatives. Retrieved February 10, 2022 from https://www.crowell.com/NewsEvents/AlertsNewsletters/all/Insurers-and-Industry-Groups-Launch-New-and-Innovative-Blockchain-Initiatives.

[80] B3i homepage: https://b3i.tech/

[81] *Enterprise Ethereum Alliance Becomes World's Largest Open-source Blockchain Initiative*, posted July 17th 2017 on https://entethalliance.org/enterprise-ethereum-alliance-becomes-worlds-largest-open-source-blockchain-initiative/

[82] https://entethalliance.org/eea-members/

[83] https://gbbcouncil.org/about/

[84] https://gbbcouncil.org/initiatives/legal-regulatory-group/

[85] BiTA Std 120-2019: LOCATION COMPONENT SPECIFICATIONhttps://static1.squarespace.com/static/5aa97ac8372b96325bb9ad66/t/5c7e8882f9619a98a55ec24d/1551796355748/BiTAS+Location+Component+Specification+v4.pdf

[86] https://www.oocblockchain.com/use-cases

[87] Lucasxhy (September 11, 2018). *Cross-Chain-Interoperability*, https://medium.com/@lucx946/cross-chain- interoperability-3566695a1a72

[88] Haimov, G. (2019) How to Create an ERC20 Token the Simple Way. Retrieved February 20, 2022 from https://www.toptal.com/ethereum/create-erc20-token-tutorial#:~:text=In%20recent%20years%2C%20the%20ERC20,defacto%20standard%20for%20Ethereum%20tokens.&text=It%20was%20the%20first%20popular%20specification%20to%20offer%20Ethereum%20token%20standardization.

[89] The Ethereum token standards are available on Github:

https://github.com/ethereum/EIPs/blob/master/EIPS/eip-20.md
https://github.com/ethereum/EIPs/blob/master/EIPS/eip-721.md
https://github.com/ethereum/EIPs/blob/master/EIPS/eip-1155.md

[90] GS1 (2018). Bridging Blockchains Interoperability is essential to the future of data sharing. https://www.gs1.org/sites/default/files/bridging_blockchains_-_interoperability_is_essential_to_the_future_of_da.pdf

[91] https://blockchain.ieee.org/

[92] https://www.iso.org/committee/6266604/x/catalogue/p/1/u/0/w/0/d/0

[93] https://www.nist.gov/blockchain

[94] https://www.iso.org/stages-and-resources-for-standards-development.html

[95] Tapscott, D., and Tapscott,A. (2016). *Blockchain Revolution*, Penguin Random House, NYC, 56.

[96] https://www.usa.gov/how-laws-are-made

[97] National Conference of State Legistaltors (July 23 2019). Blockchain 2019 Legislation, https://www.ncsl.org/research/financial-services-and-commerce/blockchain-2019-legislation.aspx

[98] *Banking on Bitcoin*. Movie directed by Christopher Cannucciari, released November 22nd 2016.

[99] https://en.wikipedia.org/wiki/Legality_of_bitcoin_by_country

[100] Allison, I. (November 14 2019). Wyoming's New Crypto Banking Law Could Defang New York's BitLicense, Coindesk, https://www.coindesk.com/wyomings-new-crypto-banking-law-could-defang-new-yorks-bitlicense

[101] The State of Wyoming. Special Purpose Depository Institutions, retrieved February 14, 2022 from https://wyomingbankingdivision.wyo.gov/banks-and-trust-companies/special-purpose-depository-institutions

[102] Kraken (2020). SPDI: Special Purpose Depository Institution Bank Charter, retrieved February 14, 2022 from https://www.kraken.com/en-us/learn/finance/spdi-bank-charter

[103] del Castillo, M. (October 28, 2020). Avanti Unanimously Wins Bitcoin Banking Charter, retrieved February 14, 2022 from https://www.forbes.com/sites/michaeldelcastillo/2020/10/28/avanti-unanimously-wins-bitcoin-banking-charter/?sh=28de79aa16aa

[104] Protos (December 3, 2021). "Federal Reserve 'illegally' delaying Kraken's master bank account, says Senator", retrieved February 14, 2022 from https://protos.com/federal-reserve-illegal-delay-master-bank-kraken-avanti-cynthia-lummis/

[105] https://en.wikipedia.org/wiki/Independent_agencies_of_the_United_States_government

[106] Goforth, C. (2020). Regulation of Cryptotransactions, West Academic Publishing, St. Paul, p. 11.

[107] Deloitte (2021). 2021 Global Blockchain Survey. Retrieved February 7, 2022 from https://www2.deloitte.com/content/dam/insights/articles/US144337_Blockchain-survey/DI_Blockchain-survey.pdf

[108] Deloitte (2021). 2021 Global Blockchain Survey. Retrieved February 7, 2022 from https://www2.deloitte.com/content/dam/insights/articles/US144337_Blockchain-survey/DI_Blockchain-survey.pdf

[109] IRS (2019). Frequently Asked Questions on Virtual Currency Transactions. https://www.irs.gov/individuals/international-taxpayers/frequently-asked-questions-on-virtual-currency-transactions

[110] SEC (May 9, 2019). How we Howey. https://www.sec.gov/news/speech/peirce-how-we-howey-050919

[111] Mark Vilardo, special counsel, Office of Chief Counsel, Division of Corporation Finance, United States Securities and Exchange Commission discussed rulings during the Evolving Regulation of Crypto, October 25, 2019, School of Law, University of Arkansas.

[112] Source: http://www.gao.gov/modules/ereport/handler.php?1=1&path=/ereport/GAO-16-375SP/data_center/General_government/5._Financial_Regulatory_Structure

[113] Goforth, C. (2020). Regulation of Cryptotransactions, West Academic Publishing, St. Paul, p. 11.

[114] US Library of Congress (November 2021). Regulation of Cryptocurrency Around the World: November 2021 Update. Retrieved February 20, 2022 from https://tile.loc.gov/storage-services/service/ll/llglrd/2021687419/2021687419.pdf

[115] https://en.wikipedia.org/wiki/Legality_of_bitcoin_by_country_or_territory

[116] China 'Blockchain Day' could become reality after Xi Jinping's endorsement of technology https://www.scmp.com/economy/china-economy/article/3035368/china-blockchain-day-could-become-reality-after-xi-jinpings

[117] Horsley, S. (January 13, 2020). China To Test Digital Currency. Could It End Up Challenging The Dollar Globally? National Public Radio (NPR), https://www.npr.org/2020/01/13/795988512/china-to-test-digital-currency-could-it-end-up-challenging-the-dollar-globally

[118] Seth, S. (Febraury 9, 2022). Central Bank Digital Currency (CBDC). Retrieved February 20, 2022 from https://www.investopedia.com/terms/c/central-bank-digital-currency-cbdc.asp

[119] US Library of Congress (November 2021). Regulation of Cryptocurrency Around the World: November 2021 Update. Retrieved February 20, 2022 from https://tile.loc.gov/storage-services/service/ll/llglrd/2021687419/2021687419.pdf

[120] Gautam, A. (March 5th, 2019). Which Countries Have the Best Cryptocurrency Regulations? https://hackernoon.com/which-countries-have-the-best-cryptocurrency-regulations-f3a45341b34

[121] Hernandez, J. (2021). El Salvador just became the first country to accept Bitcoin as legal tender. National Public Radio, retrieved February 14, 2022 from https://www.npr.org/2021/09/07/1034838909/bitcoin-el-salvador-legal-tender-official-currencycryptocurrency#:~:text=El%20Salvador%20has%20become%20the,effect%20Tuesday%20morning%20was%20historic

[122] Lopex, O. and Livni, E. (October 7, 2001). In Global First, El Salvador Adopts Bitcoin as Currency, New York Times, retrieved February 14, 2022 from https://www.nytimes.com/2021/09/07/world/americas/el-salvador-bitcoin.html

[123] Gov.uk (December 19 2018). Check if you need to pay tax when you receive cryptoassets, https://www.gov.uk/guidance/check-if-you-need-to-pay-tax-when-you-receive-cryptoassets

Gov.uk (December 19 2018). Check if you need to pay tax when you sell cryptoassets, https://www.gov.uk/guidance/check-if-you-need-to-pay-tax-when-you-sell-cryptoassets

[124] Government Office for Science. (2015). Distributed Ledger Technology: beyond block chain, https://assets.publishing.service.gov.uk/government/uploads/system/uploads/attachment_data/file/492972/gs-16-1-distributed-ledger-technology.pdf

Naqvi, N. (2020). National Blockchain Roadmap. https://www.linkedin.com/posts/britishblockchain_uk-policymakers-government-activity-6634732895456100352-rq-q

[125] Global Regulations on Cryptocurrencies (August-September 2017), available at https://www.cyberius.com/global-regulations-on-cryptocurrencies-aug-sep-2017/

[126] Majandus (in Estonian) (July 25, 2016). There are no intrinsic barriers to legitimizing the use of Bitcoin. Retrieved 15 March 2017. https://majandus24.postimees.ee/3776225/analuus-olemuslikke-takistusi-bitcoini-kasutamise-seadustamiseks-pole

127 Ummelas, O. (June 1, 2018). "Estonia Scales Down Plan to Create National Cryptocurrency". Bloomberg. Retrieved 7 October 2018.

Comply Advantage, https://complyadvantage.com/knowledgebase/crypto-regulations/cryptocurrency-regulations-estonia/

128 US Library of Congress. Regulation of Cryptocurrency Around the World https://www.loc.gov/law/help/cryptocurrency/world-survey.php. This website tracks major bitcoin regulations by jurisdiction: https://en.wikipedia.org/wiki/Legality_of_bitcoin_by_country_or_territory

129 Figure was created from Gartner's generic hype cycle and 2015, 2016, and 2017 versions:

https://upload.wikimedia.org/wikipedia/commons/thumb/9/94/Gartner_Hype_Cycle.svg/1200px-Gartner_Hype_Cycle.svg.png
http://na2.www.gartner.com/imagesrv/newsroom/images/emerging-tech-hc-2016.png;
https://blogs.gartner.com/smarterwithgartner/files/2017/08/Emerging-Technology-Hype-Cycle-for-2017_Infographic_R6A.jpg

130 De Meijer (September 27, 2019). Gartner and Blockchain: The Good and the bad, https://www.finextra.com/blogposting/17938/gartner-and-blockchain-the-good-the-bad-and-the-

131 https://blogs.gartner.com/avivah-litan/files/2021/07/Downloadable_graphic_Hype_Cycle_for_Blockchain_2021-1.png

PART II

Business Application Examples

Chapter 5

Business Applications for Financial Services–Part 1

What's inside: Bitcoin was the first blockchain-enabled application for one type of financial service, peer-to-peer payments. In this chapter, we examine three other blockchain-enabled applications for financial services. Ripple and Stellar are platforms for global payments and currency exchanges that help move fiat currencies around the world by using cryptocurrencies as bridges. Aave allows individuals to loan and borrow cryptocurrencies. We tell the stories of how these applications were founded and where they are today. Taking a deep dive into three applications allows readers to apply lessons from prior chapters on governance and on how blockchains work. Like any software application, Ripple, Stellar, and Aave have governance processes for improving their code bases. We map their services, distributed ledgers, digital assets, consensus mechanisms, smart contracts, code bases, and interfaces to the Blockchain Application Framework.

Learning objectives:

- Contrast global payments and currency exchange transactions before and after blockchains.
- Contrast lending and borrowing before and after DeFi.
- Map Ripple, Stellar, and Aave to the Blockchain Application Framework.
- Describe the governance process to improve Ripple, Stellar, and Aave.

5.1. Overview of the cases

Although blockchains are being used across all industries, financial services were the first blockchain applications. We've learned about many blockchain innovations in financial services already. We've celebrated Bitcoin as the first blockchain application—it is a financial services application for peer-to-peer payments. It moves bitcoins from senders' addresses to receivers' addresses. In the last chapter, we covered centralized cryptocurrency exchanges, which facilitate the buying and selling of cryptocurrencies, but which also introduce trusted third parties.

In Chapter 2, we explored new financing models, including Initial Coin Offerings (ICOs), Security Token Offerings (STOs), Initial Exchange Offerings (IEOs), and Initial DEX Offering (IDOs). We cannot overstate the impact of these new ways to raise funds for new ventures. Not only do they provide startups with new channels for funding, but they also offer more inclusivity. Before these models, average investors could not buy stock until the Initial Public Offering, long after the qualified investors had already taken the lion's share of opportunities.

In this chapter and the next, we explore other important examples of blockchain-enabled applications for financial services. In this chapter, we explore global payments/remittances, fiat currency exchanges facilitated by cryptocurrency bridges, and lending/borrowing. Ripple, Stellar, and Aave are the specific blockchain applications covered in detail (see Table 5.1).

Ripple and Stellar are examples of financial services applications for global payments and currency exchanges that run on their own networks. Both are US-based startups. Ripple and Stellar each operate as public-permissioned blockchain networks, meaning that anyone is allowed to transact in the networks, but adopters can select which validator nodes they accept to perform validations. Ripple and Stellar do have native digital assets, which grab much of the attention because both cryptocurrencies are typically among the top thirty cryptocurrencies by market capitalization, but our focus is on their services.

Enterprise	Enterprise Type	Blockchain Application	Status as of 2022
Ripple	Private startup	Global payments and currency exchange; targets institutions	Ripple provides an open-sourced network that enterprise adopters access through gateways. The network has been running since 2014.
Stellar	Non-profit	Global payments and currency exchange; targets the underserved	Stellar provides an open-sourced network upon which enterprise adopters build applications. The network has been running since 2015.
Aave	Private startup	DeFi lending/borrowing	Aave has been running on Ethereum since 2017 and on Polygon and Avalanche since 2021. By February 2022, Aave's smart contracts across five markets managed a liquidity pool worth $18.6 billion.

Table 5.1: Blockchain application examples for financial services

While Ripple and Stellar transactions can send/receive cryptocurrencies, the main value is streamlining fiat currency global payments and fiat exchanges using cryptocurrency bridges.

Aave is an example of pure DeFi—it is a completely decentralized set of smart contracts that deals only in cryptocurrencies. The dApps allow lenders to earn interest on their cryptocurrency deposits and allows borrowers to take out cryptocurrency loans. Aave, originally called ETHLend, launched in 2017. The Aave company is based in London, England.

Before exploring the case studies, we need to understand better the pain points in today's financial services to appreciate the aims of these blockchain applications.

5.2. Global payments, currency exchange, and lending before blockchains

Global finance comprises markets worth hundreds of trillions of dollars each year. Here, we focus on three aspects of global finance: global payments, currency exchange, and lending/borrowing (see Table 5.2). Global payments, also called remittances, are payments made from a sender in one country to a receiver in another country. They typically require exchanging the sender's fiat currency to the receiver's fiat currency. People also exchange fiat currencies for investment reasons. The lending industry provides loans to borrowers.

Global Market	Definition	Global Market Size
Global payments	Global payments are payments made from a sender in one country to a receiver in another country.	US$135 trillion per year
Currency exchange	Currency exchange is a swap of one currency for another.	US$2,409 trillion per year
Lending/Borrowing	Lenders loan money to borrowers for a certain period under an agreement. The borrower pays the lender back more money than the loan amount.	US$226 trillion per year

Table 5.2: Global markets for financial services

5.2.1. Global payments/remittances

According to McKinsey, the world sends more than $135 trillion dollars across borders each year.[1] Intermediaries collect about $2.2 trillion in revenue to facilitate these transactions. Money may move around the world in several ways using a variety of services, but we'll focus on a simplified version of the process. In today's global financial systems, each country has its own national payment system and uses its own sovereign currency.[2] A bank must be licensed to use its country's national payment system. International transactions often rely on the cooperation between banks in different countries, creating a messy web of correspondent bank relationships (see Figure 5.1 for a simplified depiction).[3] With a cross-border payment in today's global financial system, the sending and receiving parties' financial institutions, national payment systems, and corresponding banks process the transaction. Parties to an exchange have no access to the status of the transaction or even which institution controls a transaction as it works its way through the system. Fees accumulate with each step in the process. Trading partners do not always know the fees in advance, which can become quite substantial. Sending remittances costs an average of 6.8 percent of the amount sent and takes several business days to settle.[4,5] The costs for sending money to sub-Saharan Africa are even higher, with an average cost of nine percent for remittances.[6] Global payments usually involve exchanging currencies.

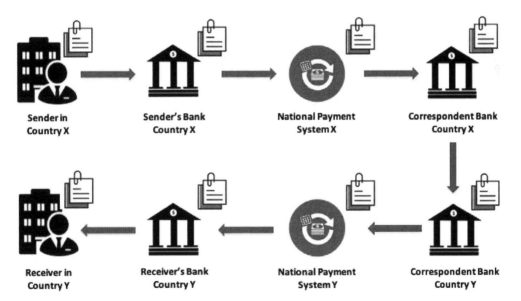

**Figure 5.1: A simplified example of cross-border payments
before blockchains**

5.2.2. Currency exchanges

Currency exchange is a swap of one currency for another. In the world of fiat currencies, on average, $6.6 trillion dollars are exchanged every day on the foreign exchange markets.[7] Annually, that's $2,409 trillion worth of currencies exchanged each year! Most foreign exchange dealers are large banks, central banks, hedge fund managers, and investment management firms. The fiat currency exchange rate is determined by the open foreign exchange markets, with rates determined by supply and demand. Exchange rates fluctuate daily.

Exchange rates are always listed as a pair: the base currency and the quote currency. The base currency is the currency you want to buy or sell, followed by the quote currency, which is the price you will accept or pay for one unit of the base currency. Figure 5.2 provides an example of the exchange rates from the Board of Governors of the US Federal Reserve System, posted on February 22, 2022.[8]

Buyers and sellers are matched through electronic order books. Order books post buy orders (including buyer information, volume, and price), sell orders (including seller information, volume, and price), and order history. Until the offer is taken, the order maker may remove or update the offer. While there are open foreign exchanges, there are also 'dark pools' where orders are taken anonymously on a private exchange to protect the identities of the parties. 'Whales'—investors with enough money to influence the market but who don't want the public to know what they are doing before the order is executed—often use dark pools. They are legal in most countries. The US SEC regulates the US dark pools.[9]

So what are the major problems with currency exchanges? Currency exchange is expensive, slow, and opaque to the average person. Perhaps you've traveled abroad and used your credit card to pay your expenses. Perhaps you bought something on Amazon from a foreign merchant. When you do, your credit card bill will show fees of one to three percent of the value of the transaction for purchases that pass through a foreign

Foreign Exchange Rates -- H.10 Weekly

(Rates in currency units per U.S. dollar except as noted)

COUNTRY	CURRENCY	Feb. 14	Feb. 15	Feb. 16	Feb. 17	Feb. 18
*AUSTRALIA	DOLLAR	0.7127	0.7152	0.7183	0.7195	0.7174
BRAZIL	REAL	5.2153	5.1807	5.1584	5.1599	5.1219
CANADA	DOLLAR	1.2732	1.2742	1.2687	1.2698	1.2748
CHINA, P.R.	YUAN	6.3567	6.3385	6.3366	6.3381	6.3251
DENMARK	KRONE	6.5826	6.5505	6.5366	6.5461	6.5666
*EMU MEMBERS	EURO	1.1306	1.1363	1.1381	1.1364	1.1327
HONG KONG	DOLLAR	7.8025	7.8014	7.8011	7.7997	7.8004
INDIA	RUPEE	75.6300	75.2000	75.0300	75.0200	74.6300
JAPAN	YEN	115.7200	115.6400	115.4100	115.0300	115.0800
MALAYSIA	RINGGIT	4.1900	4.1848	4.1834	4.1870	4.1852
MEXICO	PESO	20.4020	20.3630	20.3120	20.2850	20.2990
*NEW ZEALAND	DOLLAR	0.6613	0.6642	0.6670	0.6699	0.6694
NORWAY	KRONE	8.8883	8.8919	8.8719	8.9161	8.9953
SINGAPORE	DOLLAR	1.3475	1.3445	1.3434	1.3430	1.3458
SOUTH AFRICA	RAND	15.1075	15.0750	15.0600	14.9700	15.1175
SOUTH KOREA	WON	1196.2100	1199.7800	1197.5100	1197.3900	1195.4000
SRI LANKA	RUPEE	202.0000	202.0000	200.8900	202.5000	202.0000
SWEDEN	KRONA	9.3785	9.2674	9.2740	9.3300	9.3911
SWITZERLAND	FRANC	0.9265	0.9258	0.9219	0.9202	0.9210
TAIWAN	DOLLAR	27.8900	27.8700	27.8400	27.8600	27.8500
THAILAND	BAHT	32.4500	32.3900	32.2800	32.1000	32.1700
*UNITED KINGDOM	POUND	1.3516	1.3539	1.3585	1.3624	1.3585
VENEZUELA	BOLIVAR	4.4525	4.4299	4.4301	4.4258	4.3922

Figure 5.2: US Fed's exchange rates posted in February 2022

Source: https://www.federalreserve.gov/releases/h10/current/default.htm

bank or require a currency exchange. You had no choice in the matter and no idea which institutions were involved in your transactions.

Besides the transaction costs, there are other pain points to currency exchange. Sometimes there is no direct market between two currencies. If someone from Thailand wants to send Thai bahts (THB) to a person in Brazil, it needs to be exchanged to the Brazilian real (BRL). There may not be a direct market, so multiple exchanges would need to occur, which escalates fees.

Next, we look at lending and borrowing.

5.2.3. Lending and borrowing

Lending involves loaning money to someone with the expectation that the borrower will pay back more money than the original amount in the form of interest payments. The lending market is racking up unprecedented levels of global debt. According to the International Monetary Fund (IMF)—an organization comprising 190 countries—global debt rose to \$226 trillion in 2020.[10] This includes borrowing by governments (public debt), intuitions, and consumers. Over the past fifty years, the world increasingly borrows more money than it generates in value, as measured by Gross Domestic Product (GDP) (see Figure 5.3). While the entire global financial system can absorb some losses, if a large proportion of borrowers default, we end up with collapses like the 2008 Global Financial Crisis.

The loaning of money involves considerable counter-party risks. How can the lender be confident that the borrower will pay them back as agreed? Loans typically require collateral, meaning that the borrower has to stake something of value to give the lender if the borrower defaults. Enter the banks and other financial institutions to mitigate counter-party risks. Additionally, governments and regulators provide deposit insurance and enforce rules to reduce the risks of losses to depositors and to reduce the amount of debt an individual can incur based on their ability to pay back a loan.

Here's an overview of lending and borrowing using a bank: Lenders deposit money in a bank in return for earning interest, but the interest rates they earn on deposits are paltry. In February of 2022, the US national bank average for interest payments on savings accounts was only .06 percent. If you deposit \$1,000 in a savings account, after a year, you will only earn 60 cents in interest![i] So why do it? Some depositors like to keep cash on hand in case of emergencies, and a bank is a relatively safe bet. In the US, banks must be insured from the Federal Deposit Insurance Corporation (FDIC) to get a bank

---

i This calculation assumes a fixed term, compounded annually fixed rate. To calculate interest rates, see: https://www.calculator.net/interest-calculator.html? To calculate loan payments, see: https://www.calculator.net/payment-calculator.html

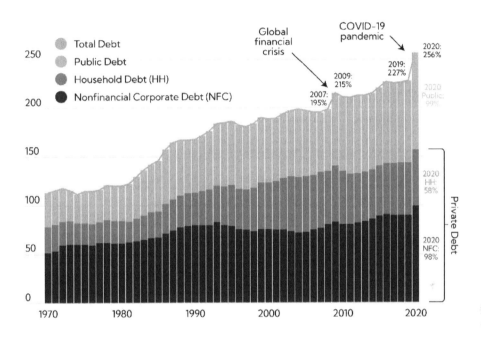

Figure 5.3: Global debt as a percentage of GDP 1970 to 2020

Source: https://blogs.imf.org/wp-content/uploads/2021/12/FINAL-eng-global-debt-blog-dec-8-chart-127.jpg

charter. (Although in the last chapter, we learned that SPDI banks argue that they should not be required to obtain FDIC insurance since they hold all deposits in reserve.) The FDIC insures an account holder up to $250,000 per insured bank.

So, from a lender's perspective, traditional banking services offers a relatively safe place to deposit money, but the financial returns are small. Their deposits are used to loan money to borrowers. Borrowers, on the other hand, pay relatively high interest rates to the bank. On February 27, 2022, the average fixed-mortgage rate was 4.25 percent. If a borrower borrows $1,000 for one year, the borrower will pay the bank $23.17 in interest. The difference between what the bank pays to depositors and receives from borrowers is called the spread. In our little scenario of depositing and borrowing $1,000, the spread is huge; it's 70 times greater for borrowers than for depositors!

Banks loan out more money to borrowers than they retain in deposits. It's called fractional reserve banking and it is allowed because it helps to expand the economy. But there are risks! If a large portion of depositors suddenly demand their money back in cash, the bank could go bankrupt. It's called a run on the bank, and the history of banking is littered with them. Therefore US banks need FDIC insurance to help protect depositors. Additionally, borrowers may default on their loans, which happened in droves during the 2008 Global Financial Crisis. Recall the quote from Satoshi Nakamoto, *"Banks must be trusted to hold our money and transfer it electronically, but they lend it out in waves of credit bubbles with barely a fraction in reserve."*[11]

So far, we've provided an overview of global payments, currency exchange, and lending. The flaws in these markets lead to financial exclusion, high transaction costs, and slow settlement times.

5.2.4. Financial exclusion, high transaction costs, slow settlement times

By now, you can see the pain points for the average individual. Financial services—if you are lucky enough to have access to them—are expensive, slow, and opaque. Many people are not so lucky. According to the President of the World Bank, "Around 2 billion people don't use formal financial services and more than 50% of adults in the poorest households are unbanked. Financial inclusion is a key enabler to reducing poverty and boosting prosperity."[12] Why are so many people excluded?

Because of the high transaction costs, financial intuitions cannot offer reasonably priced services for low-income people. On average, American banks incur costs of $349 a year per checking account and recover only $268 in transaction fees.[13] In short, banks lose money on checking accounts, so they have few financial incentives to service low-income people. Another problem is 1 billion people cannot establish their national identities, which also excludes them from accessing financial services.[14] Without access to traditional financial services, people cannot establish credit for borrowing. Consequently, up to a quarter of the world's population doesn't have access to financial services—they rely solely on cash.

According to research by McKinsey, everyone will benefit from larger financial inclusion.[15] If 1.6 billion more people are included, McKinsey estimated they would generate:

- $3.7 trillion to GDP by 2025
- $2.1 trillion in new credit
- $4.2 trillion in new deposits
- 95 million new jobs

Experts generally agree that banks and governments need to be part of the solution.[16] Individuals cannot simply adopt cryptocurrencies to solve all of their financial needs. They need access to fiat currencies for credit and payments. The Financial Services for the Poor Program, funded by the Bill & Melinda Gates Foundation, defined the minimum requirements for a globally inclusive mobile payments platform: The platform must run on inexpensive mobiles phones;[17] it must support national currencies; governments must set regulations to deter fraud, money laundering and cyberterrorism; transactions must settle quickly for small merchants, and it must be interoperable with other systems.[18] So far, there are about 150 mobile payment platforms, such as Apple Pay, Google Pay, PayPal, Venmo, AliPay, WeChat Pay, and Wise, but they operate in islands and are controlled by corporations. So how might blockchains help?

Alin Dragos, a member of the MIT Digital Currency Initiative, believes banks can increase financial inclusion if they adopt blockchains to radically reduce their back office costs. He estimates banks could get their average costs per account down to $100 per year. A more ambitious bank might build a blockchain centric bank, which might reduce costs to $50 a year.[19] Additionally, blockchains for identities could help the more than 230 million undocumented migrants worldwide gain access to financial services and employment.[20]

So, there are plenty of problems to tackle in the global payments, currency exchanges, and lending/borrowing markets. Many people recognized that blockchain applications could alleviate many of the pain points.[21] We'll examine three specific applications. Ripple and Stellar each built global payments and currency exchange applications with transparent order books, rapid settlement times and low transaction costs. Stellar added automatic market makers (AMM) functionality in 2021. Ripple and Stellar also solve the problem of exchanging currencies when no direct markets exist (like our Thai baht to Brazilian real example) by using their native digital assets as bridge currencies. In Ripple, for example, the sender's fiat currency can be exchanged for Ripple's XRP and the receiver of the XRP can convert it to a different fiat currency from the sender's fiat currency. Ripple and Stellar are very similar applications; both applications were co-founded by Jed McCaleb and have similar protocols. They have different target markets. Ripple primarily targets institutional customers; Stellar aims to expand access to financial services for those excluded today. Aave is a decentralized application for lending and borrowing, with lower transaction fees, faster settlement times, and smaller spreads than traditional financial institutions. This application allows people to lend and borrow cryptocurrencies with no financial intermediaries.

5.3. Ripple

"Digital currencies were born out of the necessity for a monetary form that was not controlled by a central bank and cannot be manipulated by politics... Ripple is the first currency exchange that allows trading in all currencies or any unit that has value like frequent flier miles, virtual currencies, and mobile minutes."

Elliott Branson, author of *Ripple: The Ultimate Guide to Understanding Ripple Currency* [22]

Ripple was founded by Chris Larsen and Jeb McCaleb in 2012 to build upon Ryan Fugger's idea for a decentralized, real-time settlement system. Headquartered in San Francisco, Brad Garlinghouse is its current CEO.[23] Ripple received angel funding in 2013, Series A funding in 2015, Series B funding in 2016, and Series C funding in 2019. Investors include Azure Ventures Group; Accenture; Andreessen Horowitz; CME Ventures; Google Ventures; SBI Group; Santander InnoVentures; Route 66 Ventures, Standard Chartered; and Tetagon.[24] By 2022, Ripple employed over 500 people and over 300 financial institutions had joined RippleNet, but 95 percent of customers are based outside of the US. As we will explain, adoption in the US is low because of the US Securities and Exchange Commission's (SEC) ongoing issues with Ripple's native digital asset, XRP. [25]

Ripple aimed to overcome Bitcoin's relatively slow settlement times, inability to trade other currencies, and massive electricity consumption, while still being inexpensive, transparent, private, and secure. According to Ripple's website, its network handles 1,500 transactions per second (TPS), settles payments in four seconds, operates 24x7, and can scale to 50,000 TPS. The average transaction fee is less than a cent. It also claims a seven-year track record of its distributed ledger closing without incident.[26] (The ledger halted for 15 minutes on November 3, 2021 in response to several validators experiencing issues, but it recovered automatically and without human intervention.[27])

Ripple's target customers are primarily institutional enterprises like banks, corporates, payment providers and exchanges. For banking customers, Ripple envisions that banks will capture new revenue by booking new corporate and consumer clients, reduce their transaction costs, and provide one integration point and a consistent experience for rules, standards and governance.[28] For corporates, Ripple promises on-demand payment with tracking and delivery confirmation and richer data transfers such as appending invoices to payment transfers.[29]

By 2018, Ripple offered three integrated services: xCurrent to process payments, xRapid to source liquidity, and xVia to send payments. In 2019, Ripple dropped the separate naming of services and now just calls the service 'RippleNet'. In November of 2021, Ripple announced that it would launch a new product called 'Liquidity Hub'. Liquidity Hub will allow traditional financial services firms to offer their customers the ability to buy and sell cryptocurrencies.[30] Ripple X, Ripple's open developer platform, also announced in November of 2021 the launch of non-fungible token (NFT) functionality.[31]

Institutional customers use an API to connect to the Ripple network via a Ripple Gateway (see Figure 5.4). Gateways can establish trust lines up to certain amounts with other gateways. Two gateways that trust each other can transact directly. However, if the sending gateway does not have a direct trust line with the receiving gateway, the network protocol will find a path of trust, thus transactions will 'ripple' through the network. One may think of this path as appropriating other people's trust. If Sally wants to send money to Sam without really trusting Sam, Sally could send money to someone she trusts, say John; John then sends the money to someone he trusts, say Sue; Sue sends the money to Sam, whom she trusts. If no path of trust can be found, the value can be transferred using Ripple's native digital asset called 'Ripple' (symbol XRP). In this way, XRP can be used as a bridge currency if no paths of trust exist between trading partners. The protocol searches for the best possible exchange rates and makes the currency exchanges in seconds, costing just a few cents worth of fees.[32]

Here's how Ripple transactions work:

"When a customer sends money into the XRP Ledger, a gateway takes custody of those assets outside of Ripple and sends issuances in the XRP Ledger to the customer's address. When a customer sends money out of the XRP Ledger, she makes an XRP Ledger payment to the gateway, and the gateway credits the customer in its own system of record, or in some other account. Like issuances, XRP can be freely sent and exchanged among XRP Ledger addresses. Unlike issuances, however, XRP is not tied to an accounting relationship—XRP can be sent directly from any XRP Ledger address to any other, without going through a gateway or liquidity provider."[33]

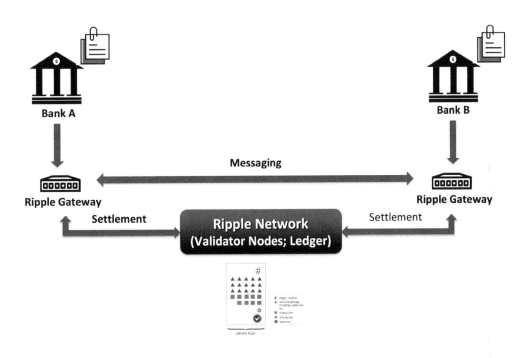

Figure 5.4: A high-level depiction of two banks using Ripple

Compared to Bitcoin which only has two transaction types (Pay-to-PubkeyHash and Pay-to-Script-Hash)[34], Ripple has 24 transaction types as of 2022. They are associated with setting up accounts and trust lines, payments (e.g., Payment, PaymentChannelCreate, PaymentChannelFund; PaymentChannelClaim), offers (e.g., OfferCreate, OfferCancel); escrows (EscrowCreate; EscrowFinish; EscrowCancel); and NFTs (NFTTokenMint; NFTTokenCreateOffer; NFTTokenAcceptOffer; NFTTokenBurn.)[35]

As of 2022, Ripple's customers include such powerhouses as American Express, MoneyGram, Santander, and SBI.[36] Typically, Ripple's customers market the Ripple applications under their own brands. For example, Santander launched a service called One Pay FX in 2018. The app runs on a version of Ripple and services customers in six countries: Brazil, Chile, Poland, Portugal, Spain, and the United Kingdom.[37] With an app, customers can send global remittances with four or five clicks.[38] By 2022, One Pay FX was handling 50 percent of Santander's international payments in these countries.[39]

Another corporate customer, SBI Remit, enables Thai nationals living in Japan to send money directly to their Siam Commercial Bank (SCB) accounts in Thailand. Prior to this service, Thai nationals living in Japan had to hire agents and use cash for transfers. After the service, which took just three months to deploy, transfers settle in three seconds.[40] By 2022, SCB was processing, on average, 80,000 transactions per month, worth $400 million in monthly person-to-person remittances.[41]

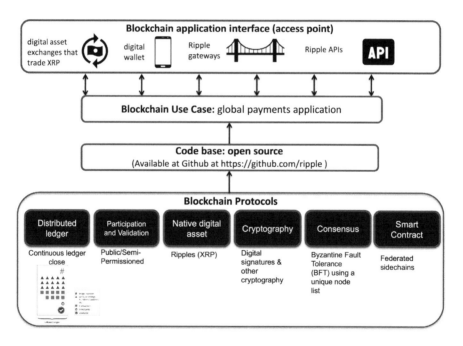

Figure 5.5: Ripple mapped to the Blockchain Application Framework

Figure 5.5 maps Ripple to the Blockchain Application Framework developed in Chapter 3. Beginning with the protocols, Ripple defined a new distributed ledger protocol, called the Ripple Transaction Protocol (RTXP).[42] The protocol is sometimes referred to as 'semi-permissioned' in that XRPs can be sent to anyone (permissionless), but also features trust lines where transactions can only ripple through the network on approved paths.

Distributed ledger. Ripple does not structure transactions as a chain of blocks. It structures the ledger as a long list of sequenced transactions and account settings/balances that gets closed every few seconds.[43] The ledger, which is called XRPL, stores all transactions such as offers, payments, and cancel orders. The ledger also stores authorized trust lines, which allows wallet holders to specify which types of cryptocurrencies they will accept and up to what amount. This prevents people from airdropping unwanted assets into the wallet. Every version of the ledger has a unique ID and time stamp. Like Bitcoin, Ripple transactions are permanently stored on Ripple's distributed ledger and are irreversible. On February 23, 2022, Ripple was on the 69,885,079th version of the ledger (Figure 5.6).

**Figure 5.6: A small snapshot of Ripple's ledger
on February 23, 2022 at 3:21 PM UTC**

Source: https://xrpscan.com/ledger/69885079

Native cryptocurrency. Ripple's native cryptocurrency, called 'ripples' (XRP), serves several purposes. As noted above, XRP can be used as a bridge currency if no path of trust can be found between trading partners. XRP is also a way to pay gateways, as each may establish fees in the form of XRP for using the gateway. If trading partners transact directly without using gateways, senders of ripple transactions pay a small amount of ripples so that attackers won't spam the system with millions of transactions, as the attackers would run out of XRP.[44] Designed to be a scarce asset, the XRP money supply is exactly 100 billion ripples and was issued at the launch of the protocol, rather than released through the process of mining as Bitcoin does.[45] Ripple is a deflationary currency—once ripples have been used to pay for transactions, they are destroyed. Participants are not required to use ripples; they can transact directly with other currencies.[46]

Consensus protocol. Ripple uses a Byzantine Fault Tolerance (BFT) consensus protocol. In this consensus system, transactions for which the majority of nodes on the network agree upon get recorded in the ledger.[47] (See Chapter 3 for a longer explanation). A Ripple transaction is considered 'safe' after it has been validated by 80 percent of the nodes.[48]

When institutions join the ripple network, they can select which nodes they want to perform validation checks from among the 147 mainnet nodes registered (as of March 2022) or they can accept the default list of about 33 nodes maintained by Ripple, which is called a Unique Node List (UNL) (see https://xrpscan.com/validators for a list of registered nodes). Ripple advises users to pick validator nodes across continents and across industries where collusion is unlikely, such as selecting merchants; financial firms; non-profits; political parties; and religious groups from North America, Europe, Asia, and Australia (see Figure 5.7).[49] In practice, network participants typically accept Ripple's default list of nodes rather than pick their own nodes. David Mazières of the Stellar Foundation wrote that this behavior centralizes power:

"Generally, membership in Byzantine agreement systems is set by a central authority or closed negotiation. Prior attempts to decentralize admission have given up some of the benefits. One approach, taken by Ripple, is to publish a 'starter' membership list that participants can edit for themselves, hoping people's edits are either inconsequential or reproduced by an overwhelming fraction of participants. Unfortunately, because divergent lists invalidate safety guarantees, users are reluctant to edit the list in practice and a great deal of power ends up concentrated in the maintainer of the starter list." [50]

Figure 5.7: Live Ripple network topology on February 23, 2022

Source: The location of Ripple Nodes can be viewed on https://livenet.xrpl.org/network/nodes

Without the incentives of mining, Ripple asks intuitions to run a validator node when they join the system to help secure the network. The costs of performing the validator role are near zero dollars.[51] It only takes a few seconds for transactions to settle and it uses much less electricity than Bitcoin—about as much electricity as it costs to run an email server. [52]

Smart contracts. Ripple was initially launched without smart contract capabilities. In July 2014, Ripple Labs proposed a project to add smart contracts to Ripple. Just a year later, Ripple abandoned the project, saying it was not needed.[53] Then, in 2021, RippleX announced that it will introduce 'federated sidechains' to meet user demand for smart contracts while still keeping the ledger lean. Each sidechain would work as its own blockchain with its own ledger but allows XRP and issued tokens to migrate between chains.[54] As of March 2022, federated sidechains are available to the public for testing.[55]

Code base. Ripple's code base is open source and may be downloaded from Github, at https://github.com/ripple.[56]

Application interfaces. Users may transact directly with the Ripple network using a Ripple wallet, but it requires a minimum balance of 20 XRPs.[57] Most customers use Ripple gateways operated by cryptocurrency exchanges or financial intuitions.[58] Ripple has bridge protocols that allow payments to and from external networks. For example, Ripple has a Bitcoin bridge protocol that allows users to send ripples to bitcoin addresses.[59]

Governance. Ripple Labs holds a lot of power over Ripple due to its large XRP holdings (60 billion XRP).[60] Xrlp.org manages proposed changes to the XRP Ledger using an 'amendment' process. [61] Any proposed changes require 80 percent of the registered nodes to indicate support for a period of two weeks.[62] Since Ripple's launch in 2014, 32 amendments have been enabled, most of which were presumably proposed by Ripple Labs. (The proposals' authors are not visible on the website to confirm this assertion). Voting can be viewed on https://xrpscan.com/amendments.

Legal issues with Ripple. In 2015, Ripple was fined $700,000 by the US Department of the Treasury for violating the Bank Secrecy Act of 1970, specifically charging that Ripple willfully failed to implement an anti-money laundering (AML) program and failed to report suspicious activity.[63] Ripple agreed to enhance its protocol to meet current banking regulations.[64] In 2018, investors launched a class action lawsuit against

Ripple, claiming that Ripple illegally sold them unregistered securities. In 2020, the SEC filed legal proceedings against Brad Garlinghouse (CEO) and Chris Larsen (co-founder) for selling unregistered securities. Specifically, the SEC found that XRP is a security under the Howey Test because Ripple Labs distributed XRP in a centralized fashion. In pre-trial discovery hearings, the court ruled in favor of Garlinghouse and Larsen. They asked the court to require the SEC to release its 2012 documents on XRP, which allegedly shows that the SEC did not view XRP as a security. As of this writing in 2022, the case is still in court.[65]

In summary, Ripple is an important blockchain application—it's running, it's working, and its adoption rate by institutional customers is increasing, at least outside of the US.

5.4. Stellar

> *"Stellar Development Foundation and Stellar seek to unlock the world's economic potential by making money more fluid, markets more open, and people more empowered."*

Stellar Development Foundation[66]

> *"Our goal is to make global payments as open as the Internet, so that anyone can send money around the world easily, regardless of what financial institutions they are using. Payments should move like email and should all be interoperable."*

Jed McCaleb, Cofounder and CTO of Stellar Development Foundation[67]

Jed McCaleb co-founded Ripple in 2012, but he soon left Ripple over disagreements with fellow founders.[68] He next launched a similar solution, but for a different target audience. Jed McCaleb and Joyce Kim co-founded the Stellar Development Foundation (SDF)—a US-based, non-profit organization—in 2014. Stellar's mission is to expand financial access and literacy worldwide.[69] The white paper for the Stellar protocol was released in April of 2015 and the network went live in November of that year.[70,71]

By the end of 2017, SDF had secured $3 million in funding from Stripe.[72] As of March 2022, SDF has about 50 employees based in eight countries.[73]

Stellar enables the creation and trade of all forms of digital assets, including currencies, cryptocurrencies, commodities, stocks, and bonds.[74] Stellar's network for global payments settles transactions in three to five seconds at a very low transaction fee of one lumen (Stellar's native digital asset) for 100,000 transactions. On February 23, 2022 one lumen cost just $.18 (eighteen cents)! Stellar can process over 1,000 operations per second.

SDF does not have direct contact with users. Instead, SDF aims to have other institutions develop business models and use the Stellar code base to develop applications for services such as remittances, micropayments, mobile branches, mobile money, and other services for the under-banked. Stellar does not charge institutions or individuals any fees to use the Stellar network, beyond the modest per-transaction fee. Its network is based on open source code that is supported by the foundation, but adopters are free to develop commercial applications, modify or distribute the source code.

Stellar use cases. Institutional users that connect to the Stellar network as anchors, are responsible for being licensed and for complying with regulations.[75] Jed McCaleb explained, *"The Stellar foundation is never in the flow of funds; we don't have customers. We provide the software and financial institutions deploy it. The burden of regulatory compliance lays on the anchor—the financial institutions—using the network because they still have the relationship with the person who's sending the money and the person who's receiving the money."*[76]

One of its first adopters was the Parkway Project. Oradian, an Africa-focused FinTech, led the project. It aims to bring financial services to 300,000 unbanked people in rural Nigeria, 90 percent of whom are women.[77] The project was halted for a while when the Nigerian Central Bank stopped all remittance companies from operating in Nigeria except Western Union and MoneyGram. Eventually, Cowrie, a FinTech focused on Pan African cross borders payments was successful in developing a service on the Stellar network in Nigera. The **Cowrie Exchange** is anchored to the Nigeria Inter-Bank Settlement System Plc (NIBSS). Cowrie serves as the issuer of the stable coin, NGNT, that is pegged to Nigeria's fiat currency, Nigeria Naira, allowing people to send payments to and from Nigeria and the European Union.[78] Its customers include Tempo, SatoshiPay, and Coinqvest, which also have their own services built on the Stellar Network.[79]

Tempo adopted Stellar for cross-border payments for customers to pay utility bills.[80] As of 2018, Tempo has helped customers from Europe—mostly based in France and Germany—to transfer payments to Coins.ph, their company based in the Philippines.[81] Jed McCaleb said: *"Tempo is pretty awesome; there's real money flowing across the live network."*[82]

SatoshiPay allows web publishers to charge viewers a very small amount of crypto. A publisher posts the Stellar Wallet widget as a payment option on their website, and users just click on it and the micropayment gets processed and settled on the Stellar ledger.[83] Its other services include Dtransfer for cross-border payments, Pendulum to connect fiat to DeFi ecosystems, and Solar Wallet to buy, sell, and withdraw digital assets.[84]

Coinqvest has an application for customers to pay merchants using digital currencies (Euros, Naira, and US Dollars) or cryptocurrencies (lumens, bitcoins, ether, litecoins, or ripples).[85]

Saldo is another adopter. It uses the Stellar Network to help US migrant workers to pay utility bills for their families in Mexico. The application serves a vital need because utility providers require monthly payments, but a typical utility bill is less money than the transaction fee to send the payment across borders.[86]

Litemint allows users to mint, buy, and sell NFTs on their marketplace for very little cost. According to its website, *"By building our marketplace on Stellar we opened up the world of NFT to everyone. Low, flat fees allow anyone to mint NFT and collectibles* *and list them at any price and in any currency that fit your business requirements, even sub-dollar items can be minted efficiently!"*[87]

IBM. In October of 2017, IBM and KlickEx—a Polynesian-based payments system for low value electronic foreign exchange—announced it would use Stellar for cross-border payments. Jed McCaleb said: *"IBM is using Hyperledger Fabric for some parts of the project, and they're using Stellar to do the cross-border payments."*[88] The offering was called **IBM World Wire,** and it allowed existing financial institutions to connect to the network using World Wire API, send a payment through a Stellar anchor, and settle the transaction on the Stellar network.[89] According to Jesse Lund, Vice President of IBM at the time, *"Stellar provides a bridge for us from these purely private network and this completely open wild west network."*[90] IBM essentially built a sub-network to enforce rules, but used the Stellar network to provide an open audit trail. In October of 2021, IBM decided to shift its focus away from operating the IBM World Wire Network and donated the code base to the open-source community.[91]

As far as network statistics, the Stellar Network had 6.6 million accounts; over 40,000 accounts were active daily, and the ledger was closing every 6.2 seconds on February 27, 2022.[92]

Here's how Stellar transactions work: A user creates a transaction by specifying the source account, list of operations, and other parameters. A Stellar transaction may have up to 23 operations: Create Account; Payment; Path Payment Strict Send; Path Payment Strict Receive; Manage Buy Offer; Manage Sell Offer; Create Passive Sell Offer; Set Options; Change Trust; Allow Trust; Account Merge; Manage Data; Bump Sequence; Create Claimable Balance; Claim Claimable Balance; Begin Sponsoring Future Reserves; End Sponsoring Future Reserves; Revoke Sponsorship; Clawback; Clawback Claimable Balance; Set Trustline Flags; Liquidity Pool Deposit; and Liquidity Pool Withdraw.[93] The transaction is digitally signed by the sender, submitted to the Stellar network, and validated by the Stellar Core. Validated transactions are propagated to the entire Stellar network. Validator nodes collect recently approved transactions into a proposed transaction set and share it with the network. The Stellar Consensus Protocol selects one of the proposed transactions sets, creates a new version of the ledger, and propagates it to the network.[94]

Figure 5.8 maps Stellar to the Blockchain Application Framework developed in Chapter 3. As noted above, McCaleb was also cofounder of Ripple, which he left to start Stellar.[95] Due to the common history, Stellar's protocol was based on the Ripple protocol, so they are similar in terms of its distributed ledger process. Both networks also make use of APIs to connect organizations to the networks, but Stellar uses the term 'anchors' whereas Ripple calls them trust lines between 'gateways'. Stellar, as we shall see, uses a different consensus algorithm than Ripple and aims to be more decentralized.

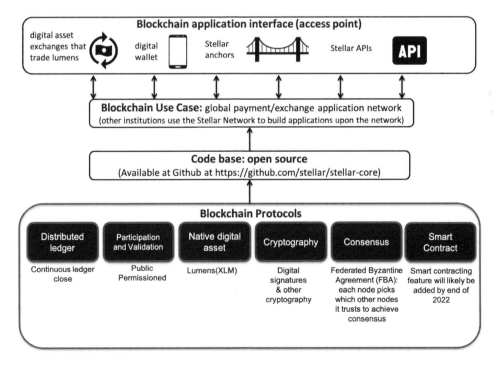

Figure 5.8: Stellar mapped to the Blockchain Application Framework

Distributed ledger. Like Ripple, Stellar structures the ledger as a long list of sequenced transactions and account balances that get closed every few seconds. The ledger also stores the current order books, which records the buy and sell offers for different currencies. Stellar's transactions are permanently stored on the distributed ledger and are irreversible. On February 27, 2022, Stellar was on its 39,812,979th ledger version (see Figure 5.9).

Ledger 28825068

Summary

Closed at: 23 Mar 2020 16:39:13 UTC
Ledger hash: 0f950f666a41c67a684...
Transactions: 39 (113 operations)
Failed transactions: 6

Total Existing XLM: 105,443,902,087.34729 XLM
Base Fee: 0.00001 XLM
Fee Pool: 1,809,798.7684961 XLM
Protocol version: 12

Ledger Transactions

Transaction 989f4924039027f10948b3852f33a6a64d32406288b8f1dd9acd3a4dd88027ce

Source account: GDDVPI...CGPI45
Ledger: 28825068
Fee paid: 0 XLM
Hide operations ∧

Created at: 23 Mar 2020 16:39:13 UTC
Operations: 1
Sequence number: 123802724364980224

Operation 123802724364980225 - Manage Sell Offer
GDDV...PI45 updated offer 182864614 – sell 118,525.8066206 SHX for XLM at 0.0044798 XLM/SHX. ∨

Transaction 600bcb120eb5affbe165aea357fbc36cb212efb18910bf776908c1a0b7080325

Source account: GCWRLP...ZWBXSH
Ledger: 28825068
Fee paid: 0 XLM
Hide operations ∧

Created at: 23 Mar 2020 16:39:13 UTC
Operations: 2
Sequence number: 123802724364984320

Operation 123802724364984321 - Manage Buy Offer
GCWR...BXSH cancelled offer 182870651. ∨

Operation 123802724364984322 - Manage Sell Offer
GCWR...BXSH placed new offer – sell 430.5384764 XLM for XCN at 0.3099996 XCN/XLM. ∨

Figure 5.9: A snapshot of Stellar's ledger, showing the header and the first two transactions

Source: https://stellar.expert/explorer/public/ledger/28825068

Native cryptocurrency. Stellar's native digital asset, lumens (XLM), serves several purposes. First, lumens are used to fund the operations of the SDF. Stellar released 100 billion lumens in 2014, retaining five percent for the foundation to operate, and holding the rest in reserve. XLM is an inflationary currency—new lumens are added to the network at the rate of one percent of the money supply each year.[96] The foundation aimed to distribute lumens to a broad range of individuals and organizations, including 50 percent to individuals, 25 percent for non-profits aiming to reach underserved populations, and 20 percent to bitcoin holders.[97] To reach individuals, the foundation releases lumens for auctions on exchanges like Kraken. People and institutions may also apply to the SDF for lumens to fund projects. In order to provide additional stability to the system, employees of the foundation are not allowed to buy lumens at auctions, and Stellar's owners agreed not sell any of the lumens for at least five years.[98,99] In November of 2019, the SDF decided to burn 50 billion lumen that were in reserve because it was having a hard time getting them distributed into the market.[100] As of March 2022, the total money supply was 50 billion lumens, of which over 25 billion lumens had been distributed, and SDF retains 25 billion lumens.[101]

Second, lumens can be used as a bridge currency within the Stellar network if no direct markets exist between trading partners. Jed McCaleb offered this example:

> *"If you imagine somebody wants to send money from Thailand to Brazil, there's probably not a good liquid market between those two currencies. So you would go to some bridge currency in the middle. Maybe you would go Thai baht to US dollars, US dollars to Brazilian real. But you could also go to the lumens in the middle, or bitcoins. You can go through multiple hops to get the best rates."* [102]

Finally, lumens are used to prevent Denial of Service (DoS) attacks. Each Stellar transaction requires a minor fee of 0.00001 lumens. *"This fee prevents users with malicious intentions from flooding the network (otherwise known as a DoS attack). Lumens work as a security token, mitigating DoS attacks that attempt to generate large numbers of transactions or consume large amounts of space in the ledger."* [103]

Consensus protocol. Stellar's protocol is called the Stellar Consensus Protocol (SCP).[104] Its main distinction from Ripple is a new model for consensus called Federated Byzantine Agreement (FBA). FBA distinguishes between a network-level *quorum* of nodes that need to agree, and a *quorum slice* that a particular node chooses to rely upon to validate transactions. Figure 5.10 shows which nodes SDF 1 includes in its quorum slice. This protocol ensures that the Stellar network remains permissionless in that anyone may join but empowers each participant operating a node to decide which other nodes it will trust to validate transactions.[105]

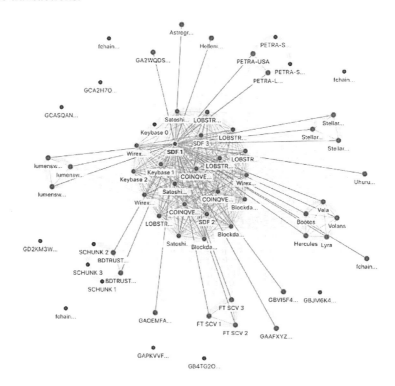

Figure 5.10: Quorum slice for SDF 1 node

Source:https://stellarbeat.io/nodes/GCGB2S2KGYARPVIA37HYZXVRM2YZUEXA6S33ZU5BUDC6THSB 62LZSTYH?center=0&no-scroll=1

As of February 2022, the Stellar network had 36 full validator nodes, operated by the SDF, Franklin Templeton (global fund manager based in US), Coinqvest (based in Estonia), Lobstr (wallet company based in Belarus) and many others.[106, 107] Nodes are distributed globally, in such countries as the US, United Kingdom, Germany, and Singapore.[108] When asked how quorum slice selection works in practice, Jed McCaleb explained that people select a diverse set of nodes where collusion behind the scenes would be highly unlikely. He said: *"Nodes are advertised on each company's website. It would be very unlikely for a company and a university to collude, so while there is no magical answer, people can make sound judgments."*

Smart contract. Stellar did not launch with a Turing complete smart contracting feature.[109] However, in January 25, of 2022, Tomer Weller, VP of Technological Strategy for the Stellar Development Foundation announced on Twitter the integration of smart contracts on Stellar, with an expected deployment date by the end of 2022.[110]

Code base. Stellar's code base is open source and may be downloaded from Github, (https://github.com/stellar/stellar-core).

Application interface. Users may transact directly with the Stellar network using a digital wallet, but it requires a minimum balance of 20 XLMs to ensure that accounts are authentic.[111] Stellar does not own or operate any digital wallets, but maintains a list of organizations that do (see https://www.stellar.org/lumens/wallets/). Users may also access the Stellar network through anchor institutions who built services on top of the network. Anchors take deposits from their customers and issue credits to addresses stored on the distributed ledger.

Governance. SDF is the primary source of changes to the Stellar code base and ecosystem, but as an open-source community, anyone is welcome to submit improvement proposals.[112] Stellar has two types of proposals: Core Advancement Proposals (CAPs) and Stellar Ecosystem Proposals (SEPs). Both are managed on Github. CAPs are proposals for changes to the Stellar code base and require the majority of node validators to implement the change to be considered final. As of March 2022, 22 CAPs have been finalized. Of these 22, Jonathan Jove, a software engineer at SDF authored eight; Nicolas Barry, CTO of SDF, authored three, and Jed McCaleb authored one. [113] SEPs are proposed changes to interfacing with Stellar, often in the form of a new API. So far, six SEPs have been finalized and were authored by SDF or Inter/stellar, a company co-founded by Mike Kennedy and Jed McCaleb.

According to McCaleb, SDF's goals for 2020 were: *"We are still super focused on making the network useful for people. We are not just building this for the technology; we want Stellar to materially improve people's lives. We are releasing a Latin American-focused consumer wallet this spring and we are going to do a lot to grow its adoption and usefulness."* [114]

In summary, Stellar is an important blockchain network—it's running, it's working, and its adoption rate is increasing. The next case provides a DeFi example of lending and borrowing.

5.5. Aave

Based on his background in FinTech and law, Finnish entrepreneur Stanti Kulechov was fascinated by using smart contracts for automatic execution. He saw DeFi as a more inclusive way to allow everyone to lend and borrow money. In 2017, he founded ETHLend and raised $16.2 million in funds through an ICO. He changed the name to 'Aave' in 2018, which is the Finnish word for 'ghost'.

Aave is a non-custodial liquidity application that allows participants to earn interest on deposits (lenders), to borrow crypto-assets, or to serve as liquidators.[115] 'Non-custodial' means that only the users can move funds, i.e., there is no central company or government that can lock users out or deny them access to their assets. Cryptocurrency holders deposit cryptoassets into liquidity pools to earn interest in the form of Aave's native digital token, aToken. They are called 'liquidity' pools because depositors can get their cryptocurrency deposits back easily, quickly, and without affecting its price. As of February 28, 2022, Aave runs five markets: Aave V1, Aave V2, AMM Market,

Aave Market Polygon, and Aave Market Avalanche. The total liquidity pool, i.e., the total deposits, across these five markets was $18.3 billion dollars on this day (Table 5.3).

Market	Launch Date	Smart contracts deployment platform	Liquidity pool
Aave V1	November, 2017	Ethereum	$128 million
Aave V2	December, 2020	Ethereum	$11 billion
AMM Market	March, 2021	Ethereum	$12 million
Aave Market Polygon	April, 2021	Polygon	$1.7 billion
Aave Market Avalanche	October, 2021	Avalanche	$5.9 billion

Table 5.3: Aave's five markets on February 28, 2022

Aave V1 and Aave V2 are the first and second versions of Aave; both versions run on Ethereum, and therefore incur the relatively high transaction fees of Ethereum. Aave V1 is being slowly phased out, and it is reflected in its lower-valued liquidity pools compared to AaveV2. On this day in February 2022, V1's total market size was just $128 million, while V2's total market size was about $11 billion. The AMM Market was launched in March 2021. It is an automatic market maker (AMM) linked to Uniswap, which also runs on Ethereum. The AMM Market allows users who deposit tokens in Uniswap to use those tokens as collateral in the Aave market. It's primarily used for flash loans.[ii] Its market value was $12 million on this day. To lower transaction fees, users can use the market that runs on Polygon, a layer 2 solution that rides atop of Ethereum. Aave Market Polygon had $1.7 billion in liquidity on this day. Aave was launched on Avalanche, another blockchain network, in October of 2021. Within a few hours of launch, the lending pool exceeded $1 billion worth of cryptocurrencies![116] A few months later, the Aave Market Avalanche had a liquidity pool worth nearly $6 billion.

---

ii A flash loan allows a DeFi borrower to borrow cryptocurrency without requiring collateral. The temporary loan is managed by a smart contract that calls on other smart contracts, primarily to take advantage of price arbitrage across different DeFi markets. The loan is borrowed at the beginning of the transaction and paid back at the end of the transaction…it all happens 'in a flash'.

Focusing on the Aave V2 market, Figure 5.11 shows the six largest liquidity pools on February 28, 2022 (there are 32 pools in all). Ethereum's liquidity pool shows $4.08 billion worth of ETH deposits and $172 million worth of ETH out on loans to borrowers. Three rates are quoted: the annual percentage yield (APY) earned for depositing ETH into the liquidity pool and two APY rates for borrowing ETH. Users may borrow at a variable rate or stable rate. Variable rates fluctuate with market factors; the stable rate is constant for the duration of the loan. Stable rates are typically higher than variable rates, but some borrowers prefer to definitively know their expenses. Some of the rates also have additional incentives to use the Aave Market Polygon, showing that depositors will get a bonus in Polygon's native digital currency, MATIC, if they use the Polygon market instead of the Aave V2 market. As with traditional financial services, there is a spread between interest earned and interest paid, but the spreads are much narrower in DeFi.

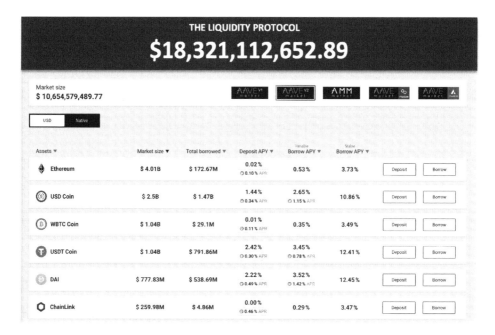

Figure 5.11: Aave homepage on February 28, 2022

Source: https://aave.com/

Figure 5.12 maps Aave V2 to the Blockchain Application Framework developed in Chapter 3.

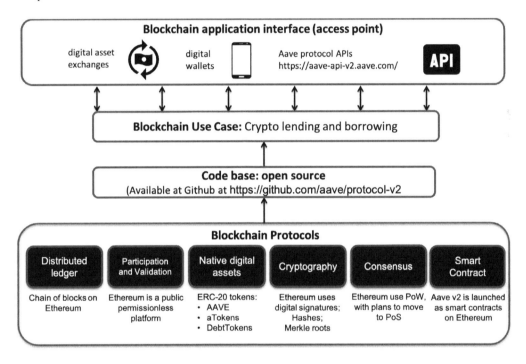

Figure 5.12: Aave V2 mapped to the Blockchain Application Framework

Distributed ledger. Aave V2 runs on Ethereum, so its smart contracts and transactions are stored on the Ethereum ledger, structured as a chain of blocks.

Participation and validation. Ethereum and Aave are open to all. Ethereum is a public permissionless blockchain platform.

Native digital assets. Aave V1 has several native digital assets, including AAVE governance tokens, aTokens (for lenders), and DebtTokens (for borrowers). These are ERC-20 coins (see Chapter 4).

The AAVE token is its governance token, with a total money supply of 16 million AAVE. AAVE governance tokens are used to govern the ecosystem reserve, Aave markets, and safety module (see Figure 5.13). Holders of AAVE may vote upon Aave Improvement Protocols (AIPs). The AIP process begins with an Aave Request for Comment (ARC). After open feedback has been provided, the ARC moves to a 'snapshot pool' vote to gauge its viability. If the ARC is deemed viable, it becomes a formal AIP to be voted upon using the AAVE tokens. AIPs are published on GitHub (https://github.com/aave/aip). AAVE tokens can also be staked to the safety module to provide a type of deposit insurance. AAVE stakers earn rewards and fees for their stakes.

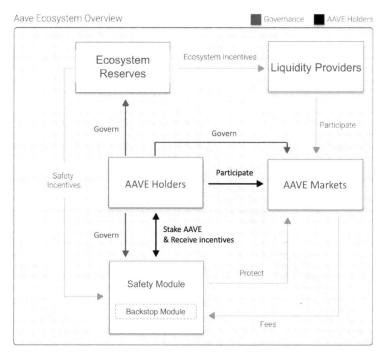

Figure 5.13: Aave governance tokens govern the ecosystem reserve, Aave markets, and safety module

Source: https://docs.aave.com/aavenomics/ecosystem-overview

248

The aTokens are Aave's interest bearing tokens. aTokens are stable coins that are pegged 1:1 to the deposited crypto asset. aTokens are created, i.e., 'minted', when deposits are made to a liquidity pool and destroyed, i.e., 'burned', when they are withdrawn. For example, if a person deposits five bitcoins to an Aave liquidity pool, the Aave dApp mints 5 aBitcoins. The person's digital wallet will show the balance in aBitcoins. The wallet will accrue interest in aBitcoins. When the person wants to withdraw from the liquidity pool, the Aave dApp burns the aBitcoins and sends bitcoins back to the person's wallet.

One special type of aToken is used to delegate voting rights to someone else. AAVE holders can delegate their votes to a representative by sending a special type of token, called a DelegationAwareAToken to the delegatee's address. This is a 1:1 peg to the AAVE governance token, and it can be rescinded at any time.

Aave's DebtTokens are used for borrowing. Like the aTokens, DebtTokens are pegged 1:1 to the borrowed asset, but unlike aTokens, DebtTokens are non-transferable, meaning that a borrower cannot sell their debt to someone else. There are two types of DebtTokens, one for loans with a stable interest rate and one with a variable interest rate.

Smart contracts. Aave was implemented as a series of smart contracts deployed on Ethereum, including smart contracts for tokenization, lendingpools, flashloans, and fee algorithms.[117] They are published on Github. According to Stanti Kulechov, Aave has five independent audits of any smart contract before deployment.

Code Base. The Aave V2 code base can be found at https://github.com/aave/protocol-v2

Application interface. Users can access Aave V2 via an Ethereum wallet such as MetaMask. Developers can access Aave V2 via its APIs, https://aave-api-v2.aave.com/

Governance. Aave is governed on-chain by the AAVE governance token discussed above. Of the 16 million AAVE governance tokens, only 3 million are owned by Aave's founders. This percentage of ownership is a considerably smaller portion compared to Ripple Labs, the Stellar Development Foundation's reserve, and other DeFi applications.

The founders of the Defi application Compound, for example, own fifty percent of the Compound's governance tokens.[118]

Aave is just one of many DeFi applications. Readers are also encouraged to investigate Uniswap, Chainlink, Wrapped Bitcoin, Terra, Pancake Swap, and Maker. On this day, March 14, 2022, the total DeFi market was worth $126 billion![119]

5.6. Conclusion

The founders of Ripple, Stellar, and Aave all created 'native blockchain' businesses. By taking a deep dive into each, we can appreciate the importance of governance discussed in Chapter 2 and how to map blockchains to the Blockchain Application Framework in Chapter 3. On governance, Ripple is the most centrally controlled due to Ripple Labs' large XRP holdings, but anyone can propose amendments. Stellar's improvements are largely influenced by the SDF, but anyone may make proposals. Aave is an example of on-chain governance, with the use of governance tokens to make decisions about the Aave networks—it's exciting to think about this new on-chain governance model for organizing human activity. On the Blockchain Application Framework, Ripple, Stellar, and Aave have made their code bases available for all to see. This transparency gives the public more confidence that the applications function as claimed.

In the next chapter, we'll explore blockchains applications for financial services by 'non-blockchain native' companies. These traditional enterprises decided to adopt some blockchain-enabled solutions to enhance their financial services offerings.

Citations

[1] McKinsey (2016), *Global Payments 2016: Strong Fundamentals Despite Uncertain Times*, https://www.mckinsey.com/~/media/McKinsey/Industries/Financial Services/Our Insights/A mixed 2015 for the global payments industry/Global-Payments-2016.ashx

[2] Again, the actual process depends on which services are used. Many banks use SWIFT (Society for the Worldwide Interbank Financial Telecommunication), an international payment network; members of the European Union might use SEPA (Single Euro Payments Area) to manage bank transfers of money. SEPA *"enables customers to make cashless euro payments to anyone located anywhere in the area, using a single bank account and a single set of payment instruments; SEPA guarantees that euro payments are received within a guaranteed time, and banks are not allowed to make any deductions of the amount transferred."* SEPA is also used by Iceland, Liechtenstein, Norway, Switzerland, Monaco and San Marino. https://en.wikipedia.org/wiki/Single_Euro_Payments_Area

[3] http://paymentsviews.com/2014/05/15/there-is-no-such-thing-as-an-international-wire/

[4] *Navigating the world of cross-border payments*, http://www.iqpc.com/media/1003982/57107.pdf

[5] McKinsey (2015), *Global Payments 2015: A Healthy Industry Confront Disruption*, http://www.mckinsey.com/~/media/mckinsey/dotcom/client_service/financial services/latest thinking/payments/global_payments_2015_a_healthy_industry_confronts_disruption.ashx

[6] International Monetary Fund (2021). No Easy Solution: A Smorgasbord of Factors Drive Remittance Costs. Retrieved February 22, 2022 ,from https://www.elibrary.imf.org/downloadpdf/journals/001/2021/199/001.2021.issue-199-en.xml

[7] Segal, T. (August 18, 2021). Forex Market: Who Trades Currencies and Why. Retrieved February 25, 2022, from https://www.investopedia.com/articles/forex/11/who-trades-forex-and-why.asp#:~:text=The%20foreign%20exchange%20or%20forex,FX%20and%20OTC%20derivatives%20markets.

[8] https://www.federalreserve.gov/releases/h10/current/

[9] Ponciano, J. (August 4, 2021). SEC 'Looking Closely' At 'Dark Pools'—Here's What They Are And Why Reddit Traders Are Rallying. Retrieved February 26, 2022 from https://www.forbes.com/sites/jonathanponciano/2021/08/04/sec-looking-closely-at-dark-pools-heres-what-they-are-and-why-reddit-traders-are-rallying/?sh=25bcce802e42

[10] Gaspar, V., Medas, P., and Perrelli, R. (December 15, 2021). Global Debt Reaches a Record $226 Trillion. Retrieved March 1, 2022 from https://blogs.imf.org/2021/12/15/global-debt-reaches-a-record-226-trillion/

[11] Nakamoto, S. (February 9, 2009). Bitcoin open source implementation of P2P currency. Retrieved February 26, 2022 from http://p2pfoundation.ning.com/forum/topics/bitcoin-open-source?id=2003008%3 ATopic%3A9402&page=1

[12] The World Bank, *Financial Inclusion*, posted on http://www.worldbank.org/en/topic/financialinclusion/ overview

[13] American Bankers Association (2016), *Fees and Pricing of Banking Products*, http://www. texasbankers.com/docs/FeesandPricingofBankingProducts.pdf

[14] World Economic Forum (November 20, 2020). A billion people have no legal identity - but a new app plans to change that. Retrieved March 1, 2022 from https://www.weforum.org/agenda/2020/11/legal-identity-id-app-aid-tech/#:~:text=The%20latest%20data%20from%20the,men%20lack%20a%20legal%20 ID.

[15] McKinsey (2016), *Digital Finance for All*, http://www.mckinsey.com/~/media/McKinsey/Global Themes/Employment and Growth/How digital finance could boost growth in emerging economies/MG-Digital-Finance-For-All-Full-report-September-2016.ashx

[16] Peric, K. (April 18th 2017), *Fighting Poverty with Digital Payments*, presented at MIT Blockchain for Business Conference. http://events.technologyreview.com/video/watch/kosta-peric-bill-and-melinda-gates-foundation-fighting-poverty/

[17] Most of the 150 person-to-person, mobile payment platforms in Africa and Asia can operate on a $5 phone and only need a basic 2G calls and SMS. Source: Peric, K. (April 18th 2017), *Fighting Poverty with Digital Payments*, presented at MIT Blockchain for Business Conference. http://events.technologyreview. com/video/watch/kosta-peric-bill-and-melinda-gates-foundation-fighting-poverty/

[18] Peric, K. (April 18th 2017), *Fighting Poverty with Digital Payments*, presented at MIT Blockchain for Business Conference. http://events.technologyreview.com/video/watch/kosta-peric-bill-and-melinda-gates-foundation-fighting-poverty/

[19] Dragos, A. (June 27th 2017), *Blockchain technology promises to drastically reduce the costs to offer a checking account*, https://medium.com/mit-media-lab-digital-currency-initiative/blockchains-and-financial-inclusion-f767a2347e3d

[20] *Blockchain and Financial Inclusion for Citizens in Poverty*, July 11th 2016, https://letstalkpayments. com/blockchain-and-financial-inclusion-for-citizens-in-poverty/

[21] Arshadi, N. (2017), *Application of Blockchain to the Payment System: A Less Costly and More Secure Alternative to ACH*, working paper.

[22] Branson, R. (2015), *Ripple: The Ultimate Guide to Understanding Ripple Currency,* Elliot Branson Publications.

[23] https://ripple.com/

[24] https://ripple.com/

[25] Partz, H. (December 3, 2020). 95% of Ripple's customers are not from the US, CEO Garlinghouse says. Cointelegraph. Retrieved February 22, 2022 from https://cointelegraph.com/news/95-of-ripple-s-customers-are-not-from-the-us-ceo-garglinghouse-says

[26] https://ripple.com/xrp/

[27] Ripple (January 28, 2022). Q4 2021 XRP Markets Report. Retrieved March 3, 2022 from https://ripple.com/insights/q4-2021-xrp-markets-report/

[28] https://ripple.com/use-cases/

[29] https://ripple.com/use-cases/corporates/

[30] Browne, R. (November 9, 2022). Ripple to launch crypto service for financial companies amid legal battle with the SEC. Retrieved February 27, 2022 from https://www.cnbc.com/2021/11/09/ripple-launches-enterprise-crypto-feature-amid-legal-battle-with-sec.html

[31] Mouyya, E. (November 21, 2021). XRP Ledger reveals plan to power the development of NFTs. Retrieved February 27, 2022 from https://www.fxstreet.com/cryptocurrencies/news/xrp-ledger-reveals-plan-to-power-the-development-of-nfts-202111211311

[32] Branson, R. (2015), *Ripple: The Ultimate Guide to Understanding Ripple Currency,* Elliot Branson Publications

[33] Retrieved March 30, 2020 from https://ripple.com/build/gateway-guide/

[34] https://en.bitcoin.it/wiki/Transaction

[35] Bitcoin's two transaction types are described here: https://en.bitcoin.it/wiki/Transaction; For a list of Ripple transactions, see: https://xrpl.org/transaction-types.html

[36] https://ripple.com/network/financial-institutions/

[37] Santander website, One Pay FX: blockchain for streamlining international transfers, https://www.santander.com/en/stories/one-pay-fx-blockchain-for-streamlining-international-transfers

[38] Ripple Case study (October 1, 2018).: Swell 2018: How Banco Santander Launched a Payment App for Millions, https://ripple.com/insights/swell-2018-how-banco-santander-launched-a-payment-app-for-millions/

[39] https://ripple.com/customer-case-study/santander/

[40] Ripple case study: https://ripple.com/customer-case-study/sbi-remit/

[41] https://ripple.com/customer-case-study/scb/

[42] Schwartz, D., Youngs, N., and Britto, A. (2014), *The Ripple Protocol Consensus Algorithm*, https://ripple.com/files/ripple_consensus_whitepaper.pdf

[43] https://ripple.com/build/ledger-format/

[44] Branson, R. (2015), *Ripple: The Ultimate Guide to Understanding Ripple Currency,* Elliot Branson Publications.

[45] Branson, R. (2015), *Ripple: The Ultimate Guide to Understanding Ripple Currency,* Elliot Branson Publications.

[46] *Technical FAQ: Ripple Consensus Ledger*, https://ripple.com/technical-faq-ripple-consensus-ledger/

[47] *Ripple Review*, http://www.toptenreviews.com/money/investing/best-cryptocurrencies/ripple-review/

[48] Bob Way at Ripple.com, as reported in Seibold, S., and Samman, G. (2016), *Consensus: Immutable Agreement for the Internet of Value*, KPMG White paper.

[49] *Selecting Validators*, https://wiki.ripple.com/Consensus

[50] Maziières, D. (2016), *The Stellar Consensus Protocol: A Federated Model for Internet-level Consensus*, White Paper, https://www.stellar.org/papers/stellar-consensus-protocol.pdf

[51] *Technical FAQ: Ripple Consensus Ledger*, https://ripple.com/technical-faq-ripple-consensus-ledger/

[52] *Technical FAQ: Ripple Consensus Ledger*, https://ripple.com/technical-faq-ripple-consensus-ledger/

[53] Maxim, J. (June 24th 2015), *Ripple Discontinues Smart Contract Platform Codius, Citing Small Market*, https://bitcoinmagazine.com/articles/ripple-discontinues-smart-contract-platform-codius-citing-small-market-1435182153/

[54] PYMNTS (June 8, 2021). Ripple Proposes New XRP Ledger Tools For Smart Contracts. Retrieved February 24, 2022 from https://www.pymnts.com/blockchain/2021/ripple-proposes-new-xrp-ledger-tools-for-smart-contracts/

[55] https://xrpl.org/federated-sidechains.html

[56] https://github.com/ripple

[57] Agarwal, H. (December 31st 2017), *Ripple (XRP) Wallet—Best Wallets For Ripple*, https://coinsutra.com/best-ripple-xrp-wallets/

[58] https://ripple.com/build/gateway-guide/

[59] Branson, R. (2015), *Ripple: The Ultimate Guide to Understanding Ripple Currency,* Elliot Branson Publications.

[60] Mapperson, J. (December 4, 2020). Ripple CTO says community could force the company to burn 48 billion XRP, CoinTelegraph, retrieved March 14, 2022 from https://cointelegraph.com/news/ripple-cto-says-community-could-force-the-company-to-burn-48-billion-xrp

[61] https://xrpl.org/known-amendments.html

[62] https://xrpl.org/amendments.html

[63] Press release by the United States Department of the Treasury on May 5th 2016: https://www.fincen.gov/sites/default/files/shared/20150505.pdf

[64] Todd, S. and McKendry, I. (2015), What Ripple's Fincen Fine Means for the Digital Currency Industry, *American Banker*, https://www.americanbanker.com/news/what-ripples-fincen-fine-means-for-the-digital-currency-industry

[65] Jain, A. (Febriary 23. 2022). RIPPLE XRP Lawsuit: 'There's a pretty good chance SEC will lose all merits'. Retrieved February 22, 2022 from https://ambcrypto.com/xrp-lawsuit-theres-a-pretty-good-chance-sec-will-lose-all-merits/

[66] https://www.stellar.org/foundation

[67] Personal interview with Mary Lacity in 2017

[68] Forbes Profile on Jed McCaleb, retrieved February 27, 2022 from https://www.forbes.com/profile/jed-mccaleb/?sh=356083a876bf

[69] https://www.stellar.org/about/mandate/

[70] Maziières, D. (2016), *The Stellar Consensus Protocol: A Federated Model for Internet-level Consensus*, White Paper, https://www.stellar.org/papers/stellar-consensus-protocol.pdf

[71] https://en.wikipedia.org/wiki/Stellar_(payment_network)

[72] Stellar Funding, https://www.crunchbase.com/organization/stellar

[73] Email exchange with Jed McCaleb, March 25, 2020.

[74] Stellar Develop Foundation (2020), Cowrie's cross-border payment services for Nigeria powered by Stellar, https://www.youtube.com/watch?v=sDj8THW1UWg&feature=youtu.be

[75] https://www.stellar.org/how-it-works/stellar-basics/

[76] Personal interview with Mary Lacity

[77] ShapShak, T. (2016), Instant Money Transfer Service Stellar Launches for Nigeria's Rural Women, *Forbes Magazine*, https://www.forbes.com/sites/tobyshapshak/2016/02/02/stellar-launches-mobile-money-service-for-nigerias-rural-woman/ - 5240e9c97183

[78] Stellar Develop Foundation (2020), Cowrie's cross-border payment services for Nigeria powered by Stellar, https://www.youtube.com/watch?v=sDj8THW1UWg&feature=youtu.be

[79] Cowrie Exchange case study: https://stellar.org/case-studies/how-tempo-and-cowrie-are-building-on-stellar

[80] *Business Solutions Powered by Stellar*, https://www.stellar.org/how-it-works/powered-by-stellar

[81] https://coins.ph/blog/conveniently-send-money-from-europe-to-the-philippines-with-tempo/

[82] Personal interview with Mary Lacity

[83] SatoshiPay case study: https://www.stellar.org/case-studies/satoshipay

[84] https://satoshipay.io/

[85] https://www.coinqvest.com/en/integrations

[86] Stellar Case Study. Saldo. https://www.stellar.org/case-studies/saldo Saldo's home page: https://saldo.mx/index.html

[87] https://litemint.com/about

[88] Personal interview with Mary Lacity

[89] https://www.ibm.com/downloads/cas/YW3W2JPZ

[90] Stellar Case Study. IBM World Wire, https://youtu.be/GtQY8Jfa4NA

[91] Rugg, R. and Gauer, N. (October 21, 2021). Fueling the financial industry with open source cross-border payments, IBM blog, retrieved February 27, 2022 from https://www.ibm.com/blogs/blockchain/2021/10/fueling-the-financial-industry-with-open-source-cross-border-payments/

[92] https://stellar.expert/explorer/public/network-activity

https://stellar.expert/explorer/public/ledger/28825068

[93] List of Stellar operations: https://developers.stellar.org/docs/start/list-of-operations/

[94] For more details on Stellar transactions, see https://developers.stellar.org/docs/glossary/transactions/

[95] Bello, K. (May 2016), *Ripple vs Stellar Lumens*, https://www.youtube.com/watch?v=aeONeHlF9y4

[96] *Difference between Ripple and Stellar*, https://galactictalk.org/d/242-difference-between-ripple-and-stellar

[97] https://www.stellar.org/lumens/

[98] https://www.stellar.org/about/mandate/

[99] https://www.stellar.org/lumens/

[100] Dale, B. (November 5th, 2019). Stellar's Foundation Just Destroyed Half the Supply of Its Lumens Cryptocurrency, Coindesk, https://www.coindesk.com/stellars-foundation-just-destroyed-half-the-supply-of-its-lumens-cryptocurrency

[101] See https://dashboard.stellar.org/ for current distribution numbers

[102] Personal interview with Mary Lacity

[103] https://www.stellar.org/lumens/

[104] Maziières, D. (2016), *The Stellar Consensus Protocol: A Federated Model for Internet-level Consensus*, White Paper, https://www.stellar.org/papers/stellar-consensus-protocol.pdf

[105] https://medium.com/a-stellar-journey/on-worldwide-consensus-359e9eb3e949

[106] https://stellarbeat.io/nodes

[107] To view organizations operating nodes, see https://stellarbeat.io/organizations

[108] To view live nodes, see https://dashboard.stellar.org/

[109] Benoliel, M. (December 4th 2017), *Why Stellar could be the next big ICO platform*, https://hackernoon.com/why-stellar-could-be-the-next-big-ico-platform-f48fc3cb9a6c

[110] https://twitter.com/tomerweller/status/1486127042089283585?ref_src=twsrc%5Etfw

[111] https://www.stellar.org/lumens/

[112] Kolton (2019). How Changes are Made to the Stellar Network. Retrieved March 14, 2022 from https://medium.com/stellar-community/how-changes-are-made-to-the-stellar-network-760abbb8d127

[113] Stellar core advancement proposals: https://github.com/stellar/stellar-protocol/blob/master/core/README.md

[114] Email exchange with Jed McCaleb, March 25, 2020.

[115] Rosenblatt Securities. Stani Kulechov, CEO, Aave. Retrieved February 24, 2022 from https://www.rblt.com/fintech-summit-biography/stani-kulechov

[116] Grabundzija, A. (October 6, 2021). Aave on Avalanche (AVAX) just touched $1 billion. Here's why. Retrieved February 28, 2022 from https://cryptoslate.com/aave-on-avalanche-avax-just-touched-1-billion-heres-why/

[117] Aave's smart contracts can be viewed here on Github: https://github.com/aave/aave-protocol/tree/master/contracts

[118] Clear Chain Capital. (April 18, 2021). A Detailed Study of the $AAVE Platform and Token, retrieved March 14, 2022 from https://medium.com/coinmonks/a-detailed-study-of-the-aave-platform-and-token-1310908b8a08#:~:text=There%20are%20a%20total%20of,the%20founding%20team%20and%20investors.

[119] Track the Defi market here: https://www.tradingview.com/chart/?symbol=CRYPTOCAP%3ATOTAL DEFI

Chapter 6

Business Applications for Financial Services–Part 2

What's inside: This chapter provides three examples of non-blockchain native companies that chose blockchain solutions. Santander is a large global bank that has been a leader in exploring blockchain-related innovations. Here, we focus on Santander's digital bond issuance on Ethereum because it proved that public blockchains can comply with existing regulatory frameworks. we.trade is a joint venture by 12 European banks to help their banking customers with trade finance. KoreConX is a company that provides all-in-one financing and compliance services for private companies. KoreConX and we.trade are both built on Hyperledger Fabric, a private permissioned blockchain code base.

Learning objectives:

- Map Santander's bond issuance to the Blockchain Application Framework.
- Explain the difference between a consortium and a joint venture.
- Explain why KoreConX and we.trade chose private permissioned blockchains.

6.1. Overview of the cases

In this chapter, we explore blockchains applications for financial services by non-blockchain native companies, including Santander, we.trade, and KoreConX (see Table

6.1). These traditional enterprises decided to adopt blockchain-enabled solutions to enhance their financial services offerings.

Enterprise	Enterprise Type	Blockchain Application	Status
Santander	Public company	Santander is involved in many blockchain-enabled financial services, but we highlight its bond issuance and settlement	Santander issued a one year, $20 million bond on Ethereum in 2019 and a €100 million bond in 2021.
we.trade	First a consortium, then a joint venture	Trade finance	we.trade launched in 2017 and reached full operations by July 2018; by 2020, 17 European banks had used it; by June 2022, its future is uncertain.[i]
KoreConX	Private company	All in one platform for fund raising and compliance.	KoreConX has 75,000 private companies on the platform, 1.2 billion shares, 32 million options, and 1.2 million warrants. KoreChain was launched in October 2019.

Table 6.1: Blockchain application examples for financial services

The global bank, Santander, is involved in many blockchain-enabled financial services, but we highlight its bond issuance and settlement on a public blockchain in this

i Ledger Insights (June 6, 2022). HSBC, SocGen, IBM backed blockchain company we.trade starts insolvency procedure. Retrieved June 6, 2022 from https://www.ledgerinsights.com/hsbc-socgen-ibm-backed-blockchain-company-we-trade-starts-insolvency-procedure/

chapter. we.trade was founded by a consortium of banks that pooled money to develop a blockchain platform to automate trade finance services, primarily for small-to-mid-sized customers, and then a joint venture to launch the service into production in 2018. KoreConX was founded by Oscar Jofre and Jason Futko in 2016 to empower private markets with better tools for managing a compliant business, accessing financing, and providing liquidity to investors. Santander, we.trade, and KoreConX are examples of traditional enterprises coming together to uplift all parties rather than to eliminate any one of them. No parties were threatened with disintermediation.

6.2. Santander

"Banco Santander was one of the first global financial institutions that really wanted to understand the implications of blockchain technologies on the financial industry. We were one of the first banks to take the concept seriously and allocate resources to figure it out."

John Whelan, Managing Director, Digital Investment Bank, Santander[1]

Santander is a wholly owned subsidiary of the Spanish conglomerate, Santander Group. Santander has a long history stretching back to 1857, when it was founded in Spain.[2] Like many global banks, Santander aggressively explores emerging technologies to help achieve its mission *"to provide easy-to-use banking products and services"*.[3] Santander was one of the first major banks to recognize the potential impact of Bitcoin to the financial services industry. It's been active in the space since 2014. So far, Santander's major blockchain explorations include:

- **Impact Studies.** In 2014, Santander was one of the first banks to commission a study of Bitcoin and its potential uses in the financial industry.[4]

- **Blockchain Lab.** In 2016, Santander was also one of the first banks to create a Blockchain Lab to experiment with blockchain technologies. Santander explores use cases based on three questions: Is the current process slow?

Costly? Error-prone? In the blockchain space, the bank is primarily exploring private networks that are operated by an organization or consortium, but it has also experimented with public blockchains.[5]

- **Venture capital investments.** Santander's UK-based venture capital arm, initially called Santander InnoVentures, provided funding for Ripple. It's also provided funding for Digital Asset Holdings, the private blockchain platform that was founded by Blythe Masters, the inventor of the credit default swap; Elliptic, a startup aiming to establish a global standard for blockchain monitoring; and Securitize, a platform for security token issuance and life cycle management.[6] In 2020, Innoventures was renamed Mouro Capital.[7]

- **Santander One Pay FX.** In 2018, Santander used a Ripple-enabled mobile app for cross border payments between Spain, United Kingdom, Brazil, and Poland for its retail customers.[8] One Pay FX does not use the public Ripple network or XRP, rather, it uses a new enterprise platform that applied Ripple's technology.

- **we.trade**. In 2018, Santander, as noted below, became a founding member of we.trade.[9]

- **Enterprise Ethereum Alliance** (EEA). Santander is a member of the EEA. In 2018, Julio Faura, chairman of the EEA, and founding EEA member from Santander Bank, said, *"The Alliance's mission from day one has been to build the framework that could be used to meet all the needs of its members. The public release of the Enterprise Ethereum Architecture Stack enables enterprise members to collaborate and collectively contribute to, and benefit from, the global Ethereum effort and the EEA's forthcoming specification."*[10]

- **Hyperledger Foundation.** Santander worked on Hyperledger Avalon, a trusted compute service framework which aimed to make sure computations are done correctly and secretly by using zero-knowledge proofs, multi-party compute, and trusted execution environments.[11] Avalon has since reached end of life, meaning that it is no longer actively developed or maintained.[12]

- **Smart Payments.** In 2019, Santander and other Spanish banks (Bankia, BBVA and CaixaBank) and Iberpay, which manages Spain's national payment system, began a six-month POC to test smart payments on a private blockchain. Grant Thornton's Blockchain Lab served as the technology partner. Each partner operates a node.[13]

- **Fnality International.** Santander and 13 other major banks (The Bank of New York Mellon; Barclays; Canadian Imperial Bank of Commerce; Commerzbank; Credit Suisse; ING Group; KBC Bank; Lloyds Banking Group; Mitsubishi UFJ Financial Group; Nasdaq; Sumitomo Mitsui Banking Corporation; State Street Corporation and UBS) had been working quietly on the issuance of blockchain-based currencies in the commercial and central banking sector worldwide for several years. On June 3, 2019, the banks publicly announced the project when they created a new company, called Fnality International. Fnality is headquartered in London; it raised $63.2 million in funding from participating banks. It aims to create tokens that would be fully backed and guaranteed at all times by a central bank's national fiat currency.[14] Fnality plans to begin with the tokenization of the Euro, US dollar, British pound, Canadian dollar, and the Japanese yen.[15] Within each jurisdiction, settlement will be achieved in compliance with local settlement finality laws and regulations.[16] *Clearmatics*, Fnality's technology partner, is building a solution on a private version of Ethereum called Autonity.[17] The project has been built and tested, but implementation still requires approvals from regulators.[18]

- **Digital Bond Issuance.** In 2019, Santander completed a complete end-to-end bond issuance on the public Ethereum blockchain network.[19] We'll take a closer look at this unique and important application.

263

The context. Santander wanted to learn what it takes to launch a real financial instrument on a public blockchain. For Santander, a pilot is a significant undertaking because it involves real money, meaning that the solution must comply with all internal security requirements and with all regulations and it must be approved by the new products committee. It selected a bond issuance because it's a low volume financial instrument with clearly defined rules. Santander could also use its separate legal entities to serve as the independent parties typically involved in a bond issuance and settlement.[20]

The solution. Santander's Digital Bond Issuance was for a standard, one-year $20 million bond that paid a 1.98 percent fixed rate, payable over four quarters. It was launched in September 2019 on Ethereum, the public blockchain, which was used as the register and clearing house.[21] Banco Santander S.A. served as the *issuer* of the bond; Santander Securities Services Treasury as the *investor*; Santander Corporate Investment Bank served as the *dealer* which connects issuers with investors; and Santander Securities served as the *custodian* bank.[22] Based on legal advice from the global law firm Allen & Overy, Santander issued the digital bond under English law because English law requires a register of record, but it does not specify the type of register.[23] Under English law, a register of record could be a piece of paper, a spreadsheet, a central securities depository, or, yes, even a blockchain. (Santander could not use Spanish law because it requires that the register of record is a central securities depository.)

In order to execute the digital bond, the issuer and investor had to be onboarded to the blockchain issuance platform to comply with KYC and AML. The blockchain issuance platform maintains a whitelist of trustworthy participants that also controls ownership limits. Bond tokens were created in the form of 100 units at $200,000 per unit.[24] Figure 6.1 depicts the workflow, which can be followed on etherscan.io.

- In step 1, the *investor* sent $20 million of real cash from their cash account to a custody account at the *custodian* bank.

- In step 2, the *custodian* verified that the real cash was in fact received and created digital cash tokens that the *custodian* then sent back to the *investor*.

(This was the tokenization step). The *investor* was then ready to invest their digital cash tokens in the bond.

- Steps 3 and 4 happen concurrently: the *investor* committed the 20 million digital cash tokens to be invested in the $20 million bond; the *issuer* authorized the transaction to proceed. An atomic swap was done where the bond was delivered to the *investor* and the *issuer* received the $20 million in digital cash tokens. Both the bond and the commitment are controlled by a smart contract running on Ethereum. Essentially, the smart contract serves as the escrow account. In the future, the *issuer* may have many investment options for these digital tokens, but in today's world, the *issuer* can't do much with them. So, at this stage in blockchain maturity, the *issuer* converted the tokens back to US dollars.

- In step 5, the *issuer* sent the digital cash tokens to the *custodian* bank.

- In step 6, the *custodian* destroyed the tokens (called de-tokenization) and wired $20 million in real cash to the *issuer's* account.

As far as quarterly payments from the issuer to the investor, steps 7 to 11 are controlled by the smart contract:

- In step 7, the *issuer* sends the quarterly payment in real cash from their cash account to a custody account at the *custodian*.

- In step 8, the *custodian* verifies that the real cash is in fact received, creates digital cash tokens, and sends the tokens back to the *issuer*.

- In step 9, the *issuer* sends the digital cash tokens to the smart contract, which distributes the token to the *investor*.

- In step 10, the *investor* sends the tokens to the *custodian* bank.

- In step 11, the *custodian* bank destroys the tokens and wires real cash to the *investor's* account.[25]

265

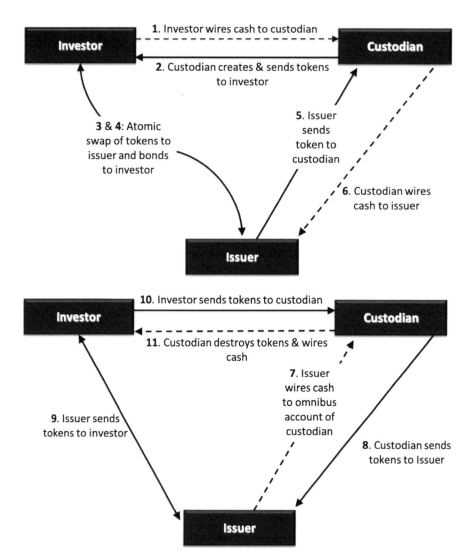

Figure 6.1: Digital blockchain issuance and settlement workflow

Cash flows are steps 1, 6, 7, and 11; tokens flows are in steps 2, 3, 5, 8, 9, and 10; bonds are step 4

Source: Santander, with permission

Proof of transactions are viewable on Ethereum (see Figure 6.2).[26] The bond issuance is mapped in to the Blockchain Application Framework in Figure 6.3.

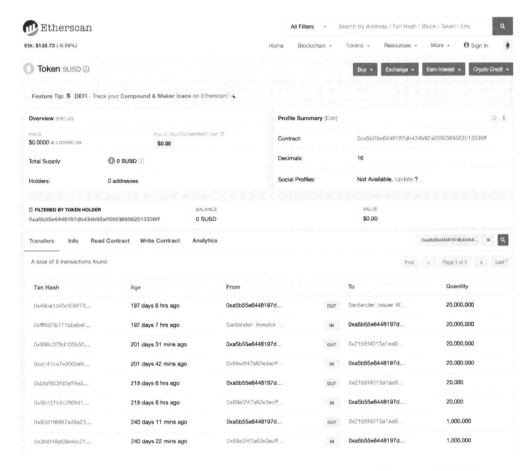

**Figure 6.2: Ethereum's records of Santander's ERC-20 token (SUSD)
as of March 30, 2022**

*Source: https://etherscan.io/token/0xa5b55e6448197db434b92a0595389562513336ff?a=
0xa5b55e6448197db434b92a0595389562513336ff*

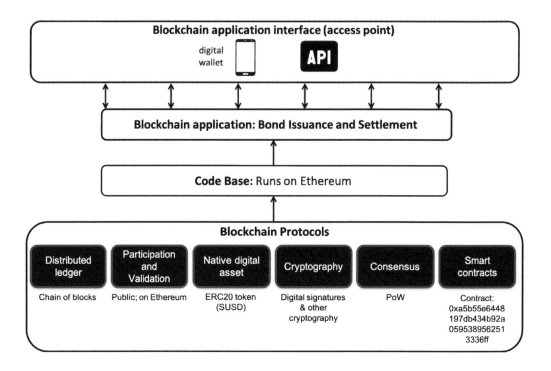

Figure 6.3: Santander bond mapped to the Blockchain Application Framework

Santander's 2019 bond issuance proved that bonds could be fully compliant on public blockchains. Other banks in Thailand and China followed its example. In April 2021, Santander, along with Goldman Sachs, Banco Santander SA and Societe Generale AG serve as joint managers for the European Union's €100 million ($121 million), two-year bond issuance on Ethereum.[27]

In reflecting upon all of Santander's blockchain initiatives, many of which potentially will disrupt the bank's traditional revenue streams, John Whelan, Managing Director, Digital Investment Bank said, *"My own sense is that we have no choice. The technology allows this to be built. If we do not build it, somebody else will. So, I think the banks realize that our competitors are not just other banks, but our competitors are also big tech, whether it's Facebook, Google, Alibaba or TenCent. In many respects, money and value are just ones and zeros in a machine and that's an engineering problem, not a financial problem."* [28]

6.3. we.trade

"Blockchain is not easy. You need many players progressing at the same pace and it's not just about the technology. The business side, sales and marketing, legal, compliance, and operations are all very important too. One of the key objectives is to get all the participants acting at the same pace on the network."

Ciaran McGowen, former CEO at we.trade [29]

we.trade is a trade finance platform that began development in 2017 and reached full operations by July 2018. The we.trade platform was developed first by a consortium of European banks and then formalized as a Dublin-based Joint Venture (JV) among CaixaBank; Deutsche Bank; Erste Group; HSBC; KBC; Natixis; Nordea; Rabobank; Santander; Société Générale; UBS; and UniCredit. [30] IBM Blockchain Services is the technology provider; IBM also became a shareholder in 2020. According to Crunchbase, we.trade has raised $6.6 million in total funding from Santander Bank, CRiF, HSBC, IBM, and Rabo Frontier Ventures. The largest round for €5,500,000 was debt financing in February of 2021. [31] (Debt financing raises money by selling debt to investors; its main advantage is that we.trade does not give up control of the business, as would have happened if it pursued equity financing.) By second quarter 2021, we.trade had processed 1500 transactions worth more than €120M with 400 SME and corporate clients. [32] As of March 2022, the platform is being used across trading partners in 17 banks. [33]

Let's first understand the pain points in trade financing before we.trade. Trade finance is a process which helps to reduce counter-party risks for the financing of trade between a buyer and a seller, often internationally. Exporters/sellers need to mitigate payment risks and want to get paid as early as possible by importers/purchasers. Importers/purchasers want to make sure goods were shipped and often want extended credit on their payment. Trusted third parties like banks step in to reduce the financial risks of exporters and importers. The exporter's bank may loan money to the exporter based on the contract. If exporters want to mitigate their risks further, they may even sell their receivables at a discount. The importer's bank may provide a letter of credit that will ensure the exporter of getting paid upon proof that the goods were shipped, such as a bill of lading. Setting up open accounts and lines of credit typically take seven days (see Figure 6.4). Moreover, many banks struggle with establishing trade finance services, particularly to scale. According to Roberto Mancone, a co-founder and first COO of we.trade, *"The traditional trade finance model run by banks had not evolved for decades. Both banks and companies were constrained. Banks were not able to scale their platform to make it available to all clients."*[34]

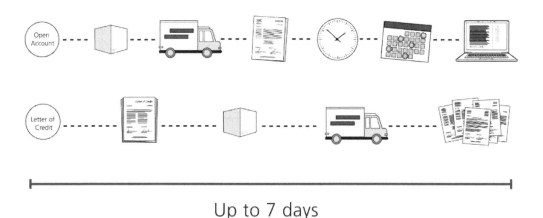

Up to 7 days

Figure 6.4: Trade finance process before we.trade

Source: we.trade explainer video[35]

Development of we.trade. we.trade, founded by seven European banks in March 2017, came together to reduce the pain points common to many banks. Initially, the seven banks formed a consortium, with each bank putting in about $200,000, an amount below capital investment levels that do not require layers of approvals. The banks did not merely want to do a POC—they were committed to developing a live platform in 12 months. To move things forward, they did not require unanimous decisions, but rather required a 51 percent or 67 percent majority depending on the complexity of the decision. To prevent anti-trust violations, the banks were prohibited from discussing go-to-market strategies. While the consortium was focused on the technical implementation, the partners also were working in parallel to develop a legal entity. The joint venture came in February of 2018, when all the consortium's intellectual property was transferred to it. The banks, which had now grown to 12 members, became shareholders in the JV, but each bank still needs a license to operate the software. Banks could also license the software without becoming investors. Roberto Mancone became the COO of the JV. He said, *"We needed a legal entity before the platform went live, one with a proper board, a clear strategy, and standard rules of governance."*[36]

While still a consortium, we.trade brought in IBM because it wanted to build a platform that would not only work for the initial participating banks, but for hundreds of banks.[37] we.trade is built on the IBM Blockchain Platform using HyperLedger Fabric, a permissioned blockchain. Each bank operates a node. Functionally, we.trade helps customers to find trusted trade partners, request financing, automate and secure payment, and track the trade journey end-to-end. The participating banks verify the buyers and sellers.

A typical process works as follows: Alice, the seller, wants to sell goods to Bob, the buyer. Provided that Alice's and Bob's banks are licensed to use we.trade, they can use the platform to facilitate the trade. Alice logs in to we.trade through her bank's portal, creates a trade proposal for Bob that specifies terms and conditions, such as payment schedules. Bob gets pinged to review the proposal. If the Bob agrees, Bob's bank then reviews the proposal. If Bob's bank agrees, the smart contract is launched. The entire process can be done in an hour (see Figure 6.5). Once Bob signals receipt of the goods, Bob's bank automatically pays Alice.

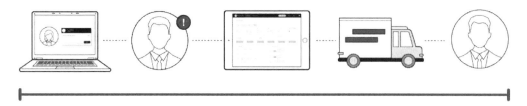

Done within 1 hour

**Figure 6.5: we.trade reduces the trade finance agreement process
from days to hours**

Source: we.trade explainer video[38]

Figure 6.6 provides an overview of we.trade's financial products, namely auto-settlement, bank payment undertaking (BPU), BPU financing, and invoice financing. By 2020, 55 percent of transactions were automatic payments, 27 percent were for bank payment undertaking (BPU), and 18 percent were for BPU financing. we.trade added additional products for insurance, logistics, and credit reporting.[39] we.trade also focuses on green trade finance. [40]

According to Mancone, the most difficult challenge in realizing we.trade was getting traditional competitors to agree on business rules and governance. The joint venture allowed the competitors to share the risks and rewards and to establish a set of rules as if they were one company. By 2019, transactions were growing by 38 percent per month.[41] Mancone left we.trade in April of 2019, in part, because the platform does not reinvent trade financing; it primarily automates and improves traditional processes. He said, *"We are building solutions that are perceived as valuable by the providers of the solutions, not the users."[42]* He viewed we.trade as an important and courageous first step, but ultimately concluded, *"I can see how this technology can change the business model, but to do that you need the stakeholders to come from different industries, not the same industry. That way it will be the final consumer (company or corporate) that reaps the rewards, rather than a group of incumbents."* [43]

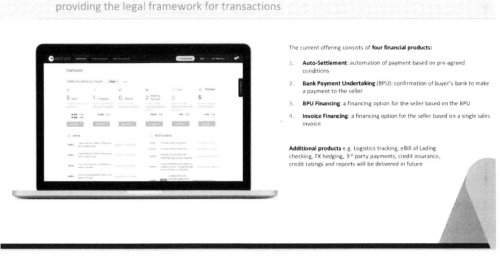

Figure 6.6: we.trade product overview

Source: Permission from we.trade

Ciaran McGowan, we.trade's next CEO, said that he was focusing on improving value for customers: *"The [client] feedback has been very positive, in that it's an innovative and intuitive solution. But it can be improved: our clients would like much more. For example, in terms of the efficiency of the end-user, they would like integration with their ERP system rather than having to duplicate entries. They are also very keen to have logistics services as part of the offering. The other feedback we're getting is the search facility for pairing companies—they want more customers on there in terms of opportunities. So that's driving our priority number one, which is expanding the we.trade network and going global." [44,45]*

By March 2020, banking customers from Austria; Belgium; Czech Republic; Denmark; Finland; Germany; Greece; Ireland; Italy; Liechtenstein; Luxembourg; Netherlands; Norway; Spain; Sweden; Switzerland; and the United Kingdom were participating.[46] Fees to use the platform for banks began at $55,000, largely to cover the cost of cloud hosting for the application.[47]

Customers are primarily small and medium-sized businesses (SMEs), which bear the brunt of late payments world-wide.[48] While adoption of the platform outside the initial investors has been slow, customers of the banks that use we.trade report business benefits. One client, for example, said the end-to-end trade process was reduced from 7 to 10 days to just a few hours.[49] Another client—a soft drink supplier—used we.trade's auto-settlement to have overseas suppliers pay their invoices on time. Before we.trade, 70 percent of invoices were late.[50]

we.trade's main challenge in scaling the network is that both the exporter and buyer need to bank with one of the licensed adopters.[51] It's essentially a 'four corner model' with the seller, seller's bank, buyer, and buyer's bank needing to be on the platform. After McGowan's departure, Mark Cudden—we.trade's Chief Technology Officer— became the senior most leader in we.trade. Cudden explained what we.trade has done to spur adoption and its strategy going forward. In 2021, the company worked to reduce the operating costs. we.trade has also brought on value-added services, such as CRIF SkyMinder, which allows customers to evaluate a company, potential counter-parties, and suppliers; avoid cyber risk and access best-in-market pricing.[52] To bring more customers to the network, we.trade was working on a 'three-corner model' that requires the seller, the seller's bank, and the buyer, but not necessarily the buyer's bank to be on the platform. It was also implementing numerous scaling strategies. When asked about competitors to we.trade, Cudden said, *"we.trade is the only platform that digitizes Open Account Trading from end-to-end. Other platforms digitize parts of the process,*

274

for example, Letters of Credits." Despite these efforts, we.trade was not able to scale fast enough, and was moving towards liquidation.

6.4. KoreConX

KoreConX is a platform that provides private companies access to global capital markets. KoreConX has been in live production since December 2016, and KoreConX's blockchain (KoreChain) was launched in October 2019.

Let's begin by understanding the problem KoreConX aimed to solve. More than 80,000 public companies have easy access to global investors who can use their cell phones to issue trades in seconds. In contrast, the 450 million private companies have very limited access to investors. Small, privately-owned companies rely on local dealers and brokers when trying to raise capital. Each deal is unique, and typically takes weeks for a private company to find a counterparty, negotiate an agreement, and gain approvals from their boards. Moreover, there is little automation; most private companies rely on local spreadsheets. The idea behind KoreConX is a platform *"to give small to medium-sized enterprises (SME) a single location to manage all of their corporate records, funding, investors and investment brokers so they could efficiently take advantage of innovative new capital-raising opportunities."*[53] Kiran Garimella, Chief Scientist and CTO for KoreConX, describes the platform as an *"infrastructure of trust that welcomes all regulated entities"*.[54] Besides running the platform, KoreConX is a transfer agent that also operates on the platform, but more than 600 KorePartners that include broker-dealers, securities lawyers, secondary market operators, and other service providers provide the bulk of the business operations on the platform. For example, providers ensure Know Your Customer (KYC), such as certifications for accredited investors that prove their net worth and income levels, and identity verification for non-accredited investors.

The platform provides an easy way to digitize digital securities, including equity, options, warrants, debentures, SAFE, bonds, convertible bonds, promissory notes, loans, or liens. KoreConX also digitizes intellectual property because IP is part of a company's valuation. However, issuing digital assets is a one-time event and represents a small portion of the transaction activity. The platform provides services for ongoing trades and corporate actions like shareholders meetings; pre-emptive rights; exercise of first rights of refusal; tag-along rights; drag-along rights; dividend distributions; exits; and mergers and acquisitions. The platform's features include portfolio management, CapTable management, minute books, deal rooms, investor relations, transfer agency, capital markets, secondary markets, and compliance (see Figure 6.7).

Basic services are free for everyone to use. Kore Plus+ features cost $150 per month, and include services like telephone support, investor relations dashboards, and shareholder reports. For KoreConX, it mainly earns revenues from its professional transfer agent services (prices vary). Numerous private issuers have chosen the KoreConX platform. Examples include BrewDog, LegionM, GoldenSeed, TastyEquity, Quadrant, Atomic Video, and S2A Modular.

KoreConX's KoreChain was built on Hyperledger Fabric, a private-permission-based blockchain (see Chapter 4 for more on Fabric). KoreConX chose blockchain because it's a secure multi-party transaction processing solution that is tamper-resistant and always available. It chose a **private** blockchain solution because financial transactions need to be confidential, with strict rules enforced on who is authorized to access data. Moreover, most countries require that investment data is stored within their own jurisdictions, which can only be guaranteed with a private blockchain. KoreConX chose Fabric because it was the most mature code base at the time of its evaluation in 2018. By Q1 2020, KoreConX's blockchain (KoreChain) was deployed in 23 countries, on five different cloud platforms (IBM, AWS, Azure, Google, Digital Ocean), and has the capacity to process 10 billion transactions per year (about 318 transactions per second).

The platform has been proven to be resilient. Garimella said, *"Blockchains by nature are resilient because they are distributed. When a node is unavailable for whatever reason and then reconnected to the network, the node automatically re-syncs with*

KoreConX delivers a complete, all-in-one solution.

Cap Table Management

Easily manage and update your cap table with detailed transactions, complete with documents linked to each shareholder's profile

For Companies

Portfolio Management

See a full view of all your investments in one centralized location, allowing you to access company information, investment details, documents and more.

For Companies

Shareholder Management

The all-in-one platform allows companies to easily manage shareholder communication, organize meetings, generate reports, news releases and more.

For Companies

Deal-Room Management

End-to-end management of capital raising activities for companies. Visibility on status of investors, creating deal rooms to share with groups for funding, mergers and acquisitions etc.

For Companies

BoardRoom Management

Efficiently manage your boardroom by tracking your minute book, corporate records, calendar of board events, documents, shareholder voting, and committees in a secure, centralized location

For Companies

Issuance platform

An end-to-end, private label solution for managing RegA+ and RegD type investments. Complete AML, KYC, ID verification, tracking of investors, and more with an all-in-one solution.

For Companies

Transfer Agent

SEC-registered* transfer agent service allows for share transfers to be managed and performed with ease and without the wait, risk, or cost.

For Companies

Broker-Dealer

An all-in-one solution for brokerdealers, enabling them to perform due diligence and maintain global compliance with confidence.

For Broker-Dealers

Compliance Management

Tools to empower broker-dealers and chief compliance officers to simplify compliance through the KYC and issuer verification processes

For Broker-Dealers

KorePartner Management

As a KorePartner, serve as a trusted advisor to companies in the global private capital market while accessing new opportunities.

For KorePartners

Infrastructure of Trust

The first fully permissioned, highly secure blockchain infrastructure for fully compliant, worldwide digital securities.

For Private Markets

Figure 6.7: KoreConX's services

Source: https://www.koreconx.com

t

277

the rest of the network. Node failures, therefore, don't affect the network as long as the minimum number of nodes for forming consensus are available. In our tests, when we brought down major areas of our global network and reconnected them, they 'heal' automatically. The process is totally hands-off."

KoreConX has 75,000 private companies on the platform, 1.2 billion shares, 32 million options, and 1.2 million warrants. As CTO, Garimella is enthusiastic about the technology, but he says that neither the investors nor the C-suite care about blockchains. Kiran Garimella, said, *"It's not blockchain alone that solves the problem. It's the application sitting on the blockchain that solves the problem."*

KoreChain aims to provide value for all the participants in the ecosystem. For the C-suite of private companies, the KoreConX offers guaranteed compliance, better issuance (multi-jurisdiction) and liquidity. For the C-suite of private equity investors, it offers access to global market opportunities, safety, protection, and due diligence. For broker-dealers, it improves deal flow, compliance, and syndication. For securities attorneys, it is about efficient compliance, more clients and business, managing regulatory and contract risks. For providers (transfer agents, KYC/AML, custodians), the main advantage is scalability.

Oscar A. Jofre, CEO of KoreConX said: *"In our daily conversations with companies (issuers), investors, broker-dealers, board members, and other stakeholders, we come across many examples of how efficient processes are valuable. Unlike in disconnected systems, when transactions on this platform are made efficient for one party, the benefits quickly spread to, and are shared by all the other parties involved in the transaction. Process efficiencies and reduced costs are the most obvious benefits, but the value goes beyond to improved user experience and stronger, sustained long-term relationships, and trust."* Table 6.2 highlights the improvements to transaction speeds.

Process	Old way	KoreConX way
Issuer due diligence	60-120 days	30 days or less
Verification	days to weeks	seconds
KYC	days to weeks	minutes
Capital raising round closing	weeks, months	minutes
Shareholder onboarding	months	seconds to minutes

Table 6.2: KoreConX transaction speed improvements

Source: KoreConX

6.5. Conclusion

Santander, we.trade, and KoreConX represent non-blockchain native organizations exploring blockchain applications to solve problems in today's financial systems. They are important examples of live production systems used by enterprises. Santander's bond issuance on a public blockchain is particularly forward-thinking. Public blockchains have the advantage of open networks and low investments in IT infrastructure. A 2022 study by HfS research on 1200 enterprise use cases found that enterprises were moving to public blockchains with greater frequency, particularly due to the advent of zero-knowledge proofs (discussed in Chapter 10) that allow private transactions on public networks.[55] In the next chapter, we'll explore blockchain applications in supply chains.

Citations

[1] Presentation by John Whelan, Managing Director, Digital Investment Bank, Santander, to the Blockchain Center of Excellence, University of Arkansas, December 3rd, 2019.

[2] https://en.wikipedia.org/wiki/Santander_Bank

[3] Santander website https://www.santanderbank.com/us/about/about-us/leadership

[4] Presentation by John Whelan, Managing Director, Digital Investment Bank, Santander, to the Blockchain Center of Excellence, University of Arkansas, December 3rd, 2019.

[5] Presentation by John Whelan, Managing Director, Digital Investment Bank, Santander, to the Blockchain Center of Excellence, University of Arkansas, December 3rd, 2019.

[6] https://santanderinnoventures.com/portfolio-companies/

[7] O'hear, S. (Sepetember 11, 2020. Santander spins out its $400M fintech venture capital arm, now called Mouro Capital. https://techcrunch.com/2020/09/11/mouro-capital/

[8] Delventhal, S. (April 13, 2018). Santander Launches Blockchain Payments Service, Investopedia, https://www.investopedia.com/news/santander-launches-blockchain-payments-service/

[9] https://we-trade.com/banking-partners

[10] Enterprise Ethereum Alliance Press Release (May 2, 2018). Enterprise Ethereum Alliance Advances Web 3.0 Era with Public Release of the Enterprise Ethereum Architecture Stack. https://entethalliance.org/enterprise-ethereum-alliance-advances-web-3-0-era-public-release-enterprise-ethereum-architecture-stack/

[11] HyperLedger Avalon (October 3, 2019). Introducing Hyperledger Avalon, https://www.hyperledger.org/blog/2019/10/03/introducing-hyperledger-avalon

[12] https://wiki.hyperledger.org/display/avalon#

[13] LedgerInsights (December 23rd, 2019). Santander, BBVA in Spanish blockchain smart payments trial, https://www.ledgerinsights.com/enterprise-blockchain-news-roundup-23dec/

[14] Huillet, M. (June 3, 2019). Major Utility Settlement Coin project raises $63 million for commercial realization, *CoinTelegraph*, https://cointelegraph.com/news/major-utility-settlement-coin-project-raises-63-mln-for-commercial-realization

[15] Allison, I. (June 13, 2019). 14 Banks, 5 Tokens: Inside Fnality's Expansive Vision for Interbank Blockchains, Coindesk, https://www.coindesk.com/fnality-utility-settlement-coin-central-bank-token-blockchain

[16] Huillet, M. (June 3, 2019). Major Utility Settlement Coin project raises $63 million for commercial realization, *CoinTelegraph,* https://cointelegraph.com/news/major-utility-settlement-coin-project-raises-63-mln-for-commercial-realization

[17] Allison, I. (June 13, 2019). 14 Banks, 5 Tokens: Inside Fnality's Expansive Vision for Interbank Blockchains, Coindesk, https://www.coindesk.com/fnality-utility-settlement-coin-central-bank-token-blockchain

[18] Molchan, Y/ (September 9, 2020). "Utility Settlement Coin" Backed by Top 13 Banks Unlikely to Launch This Year, Here's Why. https://u.today/utility-settlement-coin-backed-by-top-13-banks-unlikely-to-launch-this-year-heres-why

Sun, Z. (March 21, 2022). Euroclear invests in Fnality to advance digital ledger technology strategy. Retrieved April 4, 2022 from https://cointelegraph.com/news/euroclear-invests-in-fnality-to-advance-digital-ledger-technology-strategy

[19] Palmer, D. (December 10th, 2019). Santander Exec Claims Blockchain Success as Bank Redeems Ethereum-Issued Bond, Coindesk, https://www.coindesk.com/santander-exec-claims-blockchain-success-as-bank-redeems-ethereum-issued-bond

[20] Presentation by John Whelan, Managing Director, Digital Investment Bank, Santander, to the Blockchain Center of Excellence, University of Arkansas, December 3rd, 2019.

[21] Palmer, D. (December 10th, 2019). Santander Exec Claims Blockchain Success as Bank Redeems Ethereum-Issued Bond, Coindesk, https://www.coindesk.com/santander-exec-claims-blockchain-success-as-bank-redeems-ethereum-issued-bond

[22] Santander press release (September 12, 2019). Santander launches the first end-to-end blockchain bond, https://www.santander.com/en/press-room/press-releases/santander-launches-the-first-end-to-end-blockchain-bond%C2%A0

[23] Huillet, M. (September 12, 2019). https://cointelegraph.com/news/santander-issues-20-million-end-to-end-blockchain-bond-on-ethereum, CoinTelegraph, https://cointelegraph.com/news/santander-issues-20-million-end-to-end-blockchain-bond-on-ethereum

[24] Smart Contract viewable on Ethereum: https://etherscan.io/address/0xa5b55e6448197db434b92a0595389562513336ff

[25] Presentation by John Whelan, Managing Director, Digital Investment Bank, Santander, to the Blockchain Center of Excellence, University of Arkansas, December 3rd, 2019.

[26] Ethereum Transactions related to the digital bond are viewable:

Santander Issuer Waller: https://etherscan.io/address/0x12959b84d507df134ec59c1fc4044b03f33a9947#tokentxns.
Santander Investment Wallet: https://etherscan.io/address/0xe08193b5afcfea60fceb22f065e88e76718c6ee3
ERC20 Token (SUSD): https://etherscan.io/token/0xa5b55e6448197db434b92a0595389562513336ff?a=0xa5b55e6448197db434b92a0595389562513336ff

[27] Akhtar, T. (April 28, 2021). European Investment Bank Issues $121M Digital Notes Using Ethereum, retrieved April 4, 2022 from https://www.coindesk.com/markets/2021/04/28/european-investment-bank-issues-121m-digital-notes-using-ethereum/

[28] Presentation by John Whelan, Managing Director, Digital Investment Bank, Santander, to the Blockchain Center of Excellence, University of Arkansas, December 3rd, 2019.

[29] Email exchange with Mary Lacity

[30] IBM. Helping companies trade seamlessly with IBM Blockchain.

[31] we.trade finances. https://www.crunchbase.com/organization/we-trade/company_financials

[32] https://we-trade.com/commercialisation

[33] https://we-trade.com/banks

[34] IBM. Helping companies trade seamlessly with IBM Blockchain. https://www.ibm.com/blockchain/use-cases/success-stories/#section-7

[35] Video on we.trade:. https://vimeo.com/430330202

[36] Interview with Mary Lacity

[37] IBM Blockchain Video. Valuable Visionaries: Roberto Mancone, view-source:https://www.ibm.com/blockchain/use-cases/success-stories/#section-7

[38] Video on We.trade:. https://vimeo.com/430330202

[39] Blockchain Ireland Week (May 26, 2021). we.trade Virtual Roundtable Discussion, VIDEO available at https://we-trade.com/resources/videos

40 we.trade press release (November 25, 2021). we.trade accelerates digital green trade finance possibilities with EBRD partners QNB ALAHLI, Banca Comercială Română and UniCredit. https://we-trade.com/resources/we-trade-accelerates-digital-green-trade-finance-possibilities-with-ebrd-partners

41 we.trade Press Release (August 8th, 2020). we.trade transactions grow at 38% per month throughout 2019. https://cms.we-trade.com/app/uploads/we.trade_press_release_38percentgrowth_2019.08.08.pdf

42 Quote from PYMNTS (April 30, 2019). B2B PAYMENTSwe.trade Co-founder Quits, Reveals Blockchain Doubts, https://www.pymnts.com/news/b2b-payments/2019/wetrade-cofounder-quits-blockchain-doubt/

43 Quote from PYMNTS (April 30, 2019). B2B PAYMENTSwe.trade Co-founder Quits, Reveals Blockchain Doubts, https://www.pymnts.com/news/b2b-payments/2019/wetrade-cofounder-quits-blockchain-doubt/

44 Vanci, M. (December 17, 2019). Five Spanish banks will test payments with a private blockchain, *Criptonoticias,* https://www.criptonoticias.com/negocios/servicios-financieros/cinco-bancos-espanoles-probaran-pagos-blockchain-privada/

45 Quote from Was, S. (September 2019). Exclusive interview: New we.trade manager talks expansion plans, TradeLens partnership and platform roadmap, Global Trade Review. https://www.gtreview.com/news/fintech/exclusive-interview-new-we-trade-manager-talks-expansion-plans-tradelens-partnership-and-platform-roadmap/

46 we.trade website. Country pull down menu, https://we-trade.com/request-access

47 Morris, N. (2020). Automated trade payments prove popular for we.trade blockchain. Ledger Insights, https://www.ledgerinsights.com/wetrade-blockchain-trade-finance-automated-payments/

48 Morris, N. (2020). Automated trade payments prove popular for we.trade blockchain. Ledger Insights, https://www.ledgerinsights.com/wetrade-blockchain-trade-finance-automated-payments/

49 Blockchain Ireland Week (May 26, 2021). we.trade Virtual Roundtable Discussion, VIDEO available at https://we-trade.com/resources/videos

50 we.trade client case studies. Requires registering for access: https://we-trade.com/resources/case-studies

51 Morris, N. (2018). Trade finance blockchain race is about to start https://www.ledgerinsights.com/wetrade-trade-finance-blockchain-race/

52 https://we-trade.com/services/skyminder

[53] https://www.koreconx.com/about/

[54] Presentation by Kiran Garimella, Chief Scientist and CTO, presentation to the Blockchain Center of Excellence, University of Arkansas, December 3rd, 2019.

[55] Presentation by Saurabh Gupta, The Role of Enterprise Blockchain in Driving New Sources of Value. Presented to the Blockchain Center of Excellence, May 24, 2022.

Chapter 7

Business Applications for Supply Chains

What's inside: In this chapter, we examine blockchain-enabled applications to help supply chain partners—and often times end consumers—prove the authenticity and provenance of physical assets during their entire journeys from source to final destination. The specific solutions examined are IBM Food Trust to trace food from farm-to-fork and bait-to-plate; BeefChain to track beef and other meats; supply chain platforms by VeChain, Everledger, and EY OpsChain Traceability, to track food, diamonds, fine wines, fine beers, luxury items, and other high-valued goods; and DL Freight to process freight invoicing and payments. Lastly, we study VeriTX, which creates entirely new models for supply chains, such as pivoting from centralized to decentralized parts manufacturing by using 3D printing, AI and blockchains. The benefits from these solutions include more efficient supply changes, demonstration of ethical sourcing, fewer counterfeit products, fewer lost products, fewer disputes among trading partners, less waste, and better mission readiness rates.

Learning objectives:

- Describe the pain points in global supply chains and how blockchains aim to solve them.
- Identify ways that assets are represented on blockchain-enabled supply chain platforms.
- Debate the pros and cons of private, pubic, and hybrid blockchain-enabled supply chain platforms.

7.1. Overview of global supply chains

In the last two chapters we explored blockchain applications for global financial services. Global financial markets are inherently *digital*. Moving money around the world is about changing entries in *digital* ledgers. Given that financial assets are digital by nature, we did not have to worry about the things we will worry about in this chapter. Global supply chains are inherently about moving *physical* goods around the world and trying to keep track of the location, custodianship (i.e., the organization currently in charge of the goods), condition, and authenticity of the goods. Increasingly, global supply chains are also expected to capture data to make sure goods were produced with fair labor practices and with environmentally sustainable practices.

Consider the amount of data that is supposed to accompany the movement of physical goods. While manufacturers, exporters, couriers, freight forwarders, customs, inspectors, exporters, shippers, and importers are moving physical goods, they are also creating data about those movements with bills of lading; certifications; consignments; customs forms; inspections data; insurance forms; invoices; lines of credit; purchase orders; shipping manifestos; and receiving documents (see Figure 7.1). Figure 7.1 only shows the movement of goods across oceans, but there are complex domestic supply chains that connect to exports/imports. The exporting country has supply chains from raw material suppliers, farms, ranches, fisheries, manufacturers, warehousers, distributors, and transporters to the exporting port; the importing country has supply chains from the importing port to distributors, warehousers, transporters, wholesalers and retail stores. There's also the 'last mile' to include, such as home delivery services. As a consequence of so many players generating so much data, assets get lost or stolen, shipping containers get delayed in ports because of missing paperwork, inconsistent records across trading partners trigger disputes and counterfeit products slip through supply chains, to highlight some of the challenges.

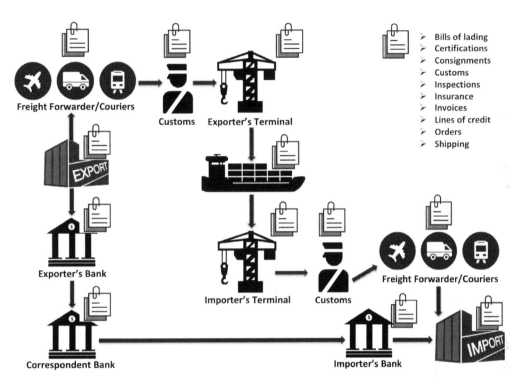

Figure 7.1: Global supply chains

While manufacturers; exporters; couriers; freight forwarders; customs; inspectors; exporters; shippers; and importers, move physical goods through the global supply chain, they are also creating data about those movements with bills of lading; certifications; consignments; customs forms; inspections data; insurance forms; invoices; lines of credit; purchase orders; shipping manifestos; and receiving documents.

Let's take a closer look at the specific challenges in global food supply chains. The food supply chain has been particularly challenging to coordinate because of its scale and perishability. The global food and grocery retail markets are a $12 trillion market.[1] While much of the world's food supply is safe, there is significant room for improvement. The World Health Organization reports that 600 million people get food poisoning and 420,000 die each year from consuming contaminated foods.[2] Besides food contamination, the world food supply suffers significant amounts of food waste, food mislabeling, and food fraud, such as claiming horse meat as lamb and claiming non-organically grown vegetables as organic.[3] Human rights and environmental problems, such as slave labor and unauthorized use of pesticides, remain grave concerns. For example, the International Labor Organization estimates that 3.5 million people are forced to work in agriculture, fishing, and forestry.[4] Each country has its share of food safety challenges, but next we focus on the US as the largest food producer.

The US food industry is a $6 trillion business.[5] The US Centers for Disease Control and Prevention (CDC) estimates that 48 million Americans get sick from food; 128,000 Americans are hospitalized; and 3,000 die of food-borne diseases each year.[6] The Food and Drug Administration (FDA) had 69 active food recalls from January 1 to March 22 in 2022, primarily for contaminated produce, dairy, and meat products.[7] Other recalls were prompted by mislabeling, some by circumventing import inspections, some by misbranding, and some because of undeclared allergens.[8] Food waste is also a large problem; $162 billion of food is wasted every year in the US, largely due to the inability to estimate demand and to track supplies.[9]

Some supply chain problems are a consequence of every organization in the supply chain creating and storing their own data in their own centralized systems. They share the data with the next partner in the supply chain. It's known as 'one step up, one step back' visibility. When a retailer must respond to a food recall, for example, it can take days or even weeks to trace the produce on its shelves to the farmers who grew it. Blockchain-enabled supply chains address many of the data challenges.

7.2. Overview of the cases

In Chapter 2, we introduced three supply chain solutions already in use: IBM Food Trust is a solution that tracks the location and condition of food; TradeLens tracks shipping containers; and MediLedger tracks and authenticates certain classes of pharmaceuticals.

Detailed case studies have been published for TradeLens and MediLedger (see endnotes).[10] In this chapter, we'll dig deeper into the IBM Food Trust and explore other blockchain solutions for food, luxury items, shipments, and parts (see Table 7.1).

Some of the supply chain cases we cover in this chapter were under development when public blockchains like Ethereum were barely a year old—like IBM Food Trust and Everledger—so a public blockchain was not a viable option. These first blockchain solutions are deployed on private-permissioned networks. Additionally, ecosystem partners selected private-permissioned blockchains because they were concerned that competitors could learn valuable information about their operations if they adopted a public blockchain solution. DL Freight chose a private-permissioned blockchain to ensure that transactions are confidential and only shared with authorized parties.

Some blockchain-enabled supply chain solutions are hybrid, with a private-permissioned blockchain to process transactions among trading partners and a public blockchain to allow consumers to authenticate a product by scanning a QR code. Examples include Walmart China's use of VeChain and EY's WineChain, which has since evolved into the OpsChain Traceability service.

Three solutions in this chapter, namely VeChain, BeefChain and VeriTX, use public blockchains. VeChain is a public permissioned blockchain like Ripple and Stellar; meaning that anyone can read the ledger, but only authorized nodes are allowed to validate transactions. BeefChain uses Bitcoin, Ethereum, and Cardano. VeriTX uses Algorand. Cardano and Algorand are public-permissionless blockchains that use Proof-of-Stake consensus.

In each case, make note of how the solutions bind the physical and digital worlds with technologies such as quick-response (QR) codes, machine vision, radio frequency identification (RFID) tags, near-field communication (NFC) chips, and Internet-of-Things (IoT) devices.

Enterprise(s)	Blockchain Application	Initial Developer(s)	Status
The IBM Food Trust	Food tracing from farm-to-fork and from bait-to-plate.	Walmart and IBM.	The IBM Food Trust processed 27 million transactions with 520 partners by 2022.
VeChain	Supply chain traceability, authenticity, and condition.	VeChain was founded in 2015 by the former CIO of Louis Vuitton China.	VeChain Thor's mainnet went live in 2018; It's now used by Walmart China, Bayer China, BMW China, LVMH Moët Hennessy Louis Vuitton, and others.
BeefChain	Meat quality and traceability.	Founded in 2018 in Wyoming.	Cattle are tagged and data is captured on Bitcoin, Ethereum, and Cardano. BeefChain and its partners, most notably with IOHK, continue to explore use cases and new business models.
Everledger	Diamonds, rare goods, and luxury goods tracking.	Everledger and IBM.	Everledger has tracked diamonds since 2017 and is now offering solutions for art, batteries, critical minerals, fashion, gemstones, insurance, luxury goods, and wines and spirits.
OpsChain Traceability	Authenticates and tracks consumer goods.	EY	15 million bottles were being tracked across 100 wineries; The solution is also used for beer and produce.
DL Freight	Freight invoicing and payments.	Walmart Canada and DLT Labs.	Launch in 2020; As of Summer 2021, DL Freight had processed 340,000 invoices worth $450 million. Disputes fell from 70 to less than two percent of invoices.
VeriTX	Trading platform for 3-D printed and traditionally manufactured parts.	Moog	Actively working with partners to move the platform to market in 2022.

Table 7.1: Blockchain application examples in supply chains

7.3. IBM Food Trust

IBM Food Trust aims to give customers increased supply chain efficiency, brand trust, food safety, sustainability, food freshness and reduced food fraud and waste.[11] While we've covered IBM Food Trust at a high level in Chapter 2, here we take a closer look at the solution. IBM and Walmart, the world's largest retailer which earns $573 billion in annual revenue, began conducting food traceability pilot programs for mangos and pork back in 2016. The solution, based on HyperLedger Fabric, reduced traceability for mangos from seven days to under three seconds.[12] In 2017, other supply chain partners joined the network, including Dole, McCormack, McLane, Driscoll's, Unilever, Golden State Foods, Nestle, and Kroger. By 2022, 520 members had joined.

To use the platform, products first must be registered using a unique product identifier, which will normally be a GS1 identifier such as GS1 Global Trade Item Number (GTIN). GTIN numbers are found on the labeling of many products, affixed as a machine-readable bar code. GTIN includes codes for company prefix and item reference. For example, the GTIN number 038900006198 maps to *"Dole Crushed Pineapple in Its Own Juice, 8 oz"* (see Figure 7.2).[13] You may look up GTIN numbers at https://gepir.gs1.org/index.php/search-by-gtin.

Figure 7.2: GS1 GTIN number for Dole Crushed Pineapple in Its Own Juice, 8 oz

Source: https://www.upcitemdb.com/upc/38900006198

If a product does not have a registered GS1 identifier, companies can create a unique IBM Food Trust Identifier—IBM has created 17 different types (see Figure 7.3).

Element	Syntax and Example
Product	urn:ibm:ift:product:class:<Company Prefix>.<Item Reference> urn:ibm:ift:product:class:1234567890123.product_123
Product with Lot #	urn:ibm:ift:product:lot:class:<Company Prefix>.<Item Reference>.<Lot Number> urn:ibm:ift:product:lot:class:1234567890123.product_123.lot4
Product with Serial #	urn:ibm:ift:product:serial:obj:<Company Prefix>.<Item Reference>.<Serial Number> urn:ibm:ift:product:serial:obj:1234567890123.product_123.serialnumber_4567
Location	urn:ibm:ift:location:loc:<Company Prefix>.<Location Reference> urn:ibm:ift:location:loc:1234567890123.store_123
Location with Extension	urn:ibm:ift:location:extension:loc:<Company Prefix>.<Location Reference>.<Extension> urn:ibm:ift:location:extension:loc:1234567890123.store_123.producedepartment
Public location type*	urn:ibm:ift:location:<TYPE>:loc:<ID> urn:ibm:ift:location:unlocode:loc:usnyc
Public location type with Extension*	urn:ibm:ift:location:<TYPE>:ext:loc:<ID>.<EXT> urn:ibm:ift:location:unlocode:ext:loc:usnyc.import
Logistic Unit	urn:ibm:ift:lpn:obj:<Company Prefix>.<Serial Reference> urn:ibm:ift:lpn:obj:1234567890123.pallet_12345678
Business Transaction identifier	urn:ibm:ift:bt:<Company Prefix>.<Location Reference>.<Transaction Id> urn:ibm:ift:bt:1234567890123.store_123.1234
Food Trust product identifier (FTPI)	urn:ibm:ift:product:class:<Company Prefix>.<Item Reference> urn:ibm:ift:product:class:1234567890123.product-123
Lot Food Trust product identifier (LFTPI)	urn:ibm:ift:product:lot:class:<Company Prefix>.<Item Reference>.<Lot Number> urn:ibm:ift:product:lot:class:1234567890123.product-123.lot4
Serial Food Trust product identifier (SFTPI)	urn:ibm:ift:product:serial:obj:<Company Prefix>.<Item Reference>.<Serial Number> urn:ibm:ift:product:serial:obj:1234567890123.product-123.serial-number-4567
Food Trust location identifier (FTLI)	urn:ibm:ift:location:loc:<Company Prefix>.<Location Reference> urn:ibm:ift:location:loc:1234567890123.store-123
Serial Food Trust location identifier (SFTLI)	urn:ibm:ift:location:extension:loc:<Company Prefix>.<Location Reference>.<Extension> urn:ibm:ift:location:extension:loc:1234567890123.store-123.toy-department
Food Trust license plate number (FTLPN)	urn:ibm:ift:lpn:obj:<Company Prefix>.<Serial Reference> urn:ibm:ift:lpn:obj:1234567890123.pallet-12345678
IFT_ENTITY	urn:ibm:ift:bt:<Company Prefix>.<Location Reference>.<Transaction Id> urn:ibm:ift:bt:1234567890123.store-123.1234
IFT_DISPOSITION	urn:ibm:ift:bv:disp:<Disposition> urn:ibm:ift:bv:disp:destroyed Valid Dispositions = active, container_closed, damaged, destroyed, dispensed, disposed, encoded, expired, in_progress, in_transit, inactive, no_pedigree_match, non_sellable_other, partially_dispensed, recalled, reserved, retail_sold, returned, sellable_accessible, sellable_not_accessible, stolen, unknown

Figure 7.3: IBM Food Trust Identifiers

Source: https://www.ibm.com/docs/en/food-trust?topic=reference-food-trust-identifiers

The GS1 or IBM Food Trust Identifiers become part of the product label in the form of bar codes, QR codes, RFID tags or other machine-readable labels. Once items are registered on the platform, IBM offers three services: Trace, Documents, and Fresh Insights. *Trace* helps participants follow food products through the supply chain by tracking location and status. Trace can also be used to follow how ingredients were transformed from raw materials to finished products (see Figure 7.4). *Documents* monitor current, expiring, and expired certificates of authenticity, quality, and other documents. *Insights* monitor at-risk inventory by tracking events such as time since harvest and dwell times at each location in the supply chain (see Figure 7.5). IBM has a tiered pricing model based on size of business, starting at $100 per month.

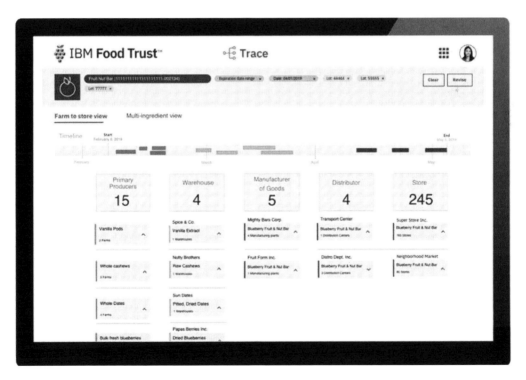

Figure 7.4: Screenshot of IBM Food Trust Trace solution

Source: https://1.cms.s81c.com/sites/default/files/2021-03-02/band_2cropped.jpg

293

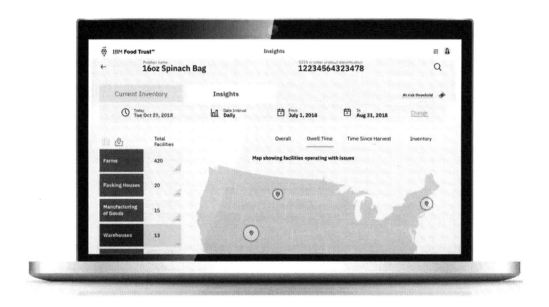

Figure 7.5: Screenshot of IBM Food Trust Insights solution

Source: https://1.cms.s81c.com/sites/default/files/2021-03-10/Customize_IBM_Food_Trust_insights.jpg

IBM runs the platform in its cloud, but it cannot interpret any of the data. IBM Food Trust platform relies on 'trust anchors' for validation using a Practical Byzantine Fault Tolerance (PBFT) consensus mechanism (see Chapter 3). Trust anchors receive a full copy of the encrypted ledger but can only view the hashes of the transaction if data owners grant access. Trust anchors are responsible for the following:[14]

- *"**Resource ownership**: Run accounts in tamper-resistant Z Secure Service Containers that ensure encryption of data, both in flight and at rest.*
- ***Verification**: Providing verification that events were submitted by an individual, with the corresponding hash.*
- ***Endorsement**: Trust Anchors can be added as endorsers to incoming transactions, providing an additional level of trust for the submitting company, such as private-label brands.*

- *Data extractions: In the event of an investigation, a member of the IBM Food Trust can use their decryption key and ask the Trust Anchors to extract the relevant data from the shared ledger and endorse its authenticity."[15]*

As the network grows, more participants will run trust nodes and possibly on other cloud environments.[16] By the third quarter of 2021, the platform has processed over 27 million transactions. The IBM Food Trust continues to expand both its network and services, particularly for cold chain and for consumer applications.

We noted that Walmart was the anchor tenet for the IBM Food Trust in the US, but it chose different partners for its China-based operations. In 2019, Walmart China launched the Walmart China Blockchain Traceability Platform, with the help of PwC and VeChain. By year end, it aimed to have over 100 products across 10 categories such as meat, rice, and fresh produce traced. In 2020, Walmart China added Sam's Club in China to the platform.[17] Let's learn more about VeChain.

7.4. VeChain

VeChain, based in Singapore, was founded in 2017 by Sunny Lu, the former chief information officer (CIO) of Louis Vuitton China. It was initially launched on Ethereum, but its independent mainnet called VeChainThor went live in 2018.[18] VeChainThor is its public blockchain that is 'inspired' by Ethereum, but it uses centralized governance that makes updates easier. It uses a Proof-of-Authority consensus mechanism where 101 Authority Masternode Operators are known and verified by the VeChain Foundation. Node operators include academic institutions, enterprise users, and business and technical partners.[19]

VeChain's product identifier is called a VeChainID. For high-value products, customers use the identifier embedded in a Smart Tag (NFC/RFID/QR Code) to register the VeChainID. IoT devices along the supply chain upload transactions about the product's movement/custody to VeChain. Figure 7.6 shows a sample process flow. End consumers can check and verify a product's information using the VeChain Pro mobile app or by a client interface using APIs.[20]

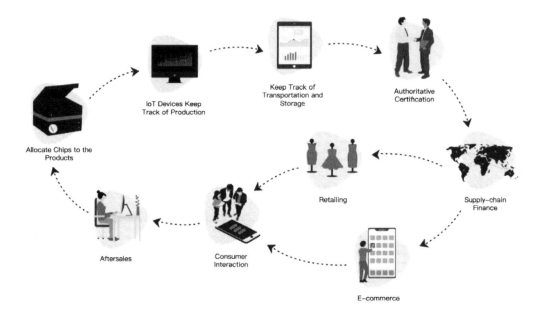

Figure 7.6: Traceability on VeChain

Source: https://www.vechain.com/product/toolchain

VeChain uses a dual-token native digital asset, VET and VTHO. VET serves as a value-transfer medium for business activities and VTHO is used to pay for transaction processing. The latter is similar to how Ethereum charges 'gas prices' to process a transaction. In VeChain, 30 percent of the transaction gas price (in VTHO) is awarded to the Authority Node Operator and 70 percent is destroyed. The design aims to prevent transaction fees (VTHO) from being directly exposed to the volatility of the price of VET. According to the VeChain white paper, *"VTHO is generated automatically via holding VETs. In other words, whoever holds VET gets VTHO and are able to use the VeChainThor blockchain for free as long as the operations performed consume less than the VTHO generated. VTHO can be transferred and traded to allow users to acquire extra VTHO for performing a larger scale of operations such as running a blockchain application.*"[21] VeChain can be explored on https://explore.vechain.org/. Figure 7.7 shows block #11,744,722, which was created on March 22, 2022.

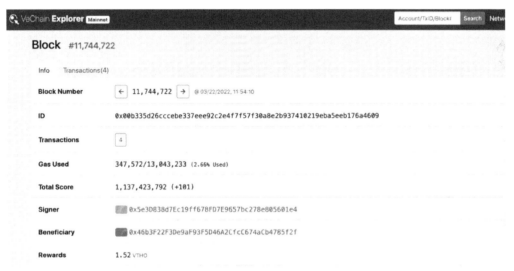

Figure 7.7: Screenshot of VeChain's Ledger

Source: https://explore.vechain.org/blocks/

Walmart China's solution traces some products on VeChain so that consumers can learn about the products, including the source, routing, and inspections from farm to retail store on the website.[22] In addition to Walmart China, VeChain's customers include luxury retailers, car manufacturers, and energy companies including H&M; LVMH (LVMH Moët Hennessy Louis Vuitton); BMW, Bayer China; ENN, BYD Auto; PICC; ENN; and Shanghai Gas.[23]

7.5. BeefChain

BeefChain, owned by American Certified Brands, LLC, is a Wyoming-based, blockchain-based solution that aims to restore equity in the US beef supply chain. The US beef supply chain includes ranchers who breed and raise cattle, sales barns where ranchers sell cattle, feedlots where cattle are fattened, and meat processors who process and package beef for sale to wholesalers and retailers. In the US, the beef supply chain is shaped like an hourglass, with many ranchers at the top, few feedlots and meat processors in the middle and many wholesalers/retailers at the bottom. In the State of Wyoming, 11,400 ranches are mostly small, family-owned ranches.[24] Only four meat processors control 85 percent of the US market.[25] On the one hand, consolidation of meat processing has lowered processing costs. On the other hand, consolidation has made supply chains vulnerable, as evidenced by the shortages caused by meat processing plant shutdowns due to COVID-19 staffing shortages and ransomware attacks.[26]

As far as equity in this supply chain, the consolidated feedlots and meat processors hold the power to set prices. The prices ranchers receive for cattle have decreased by 35 percent while retail prices have increased by eight percent since 2015.[27] Moreover, ranchers often do not share in the value of raising higher quality meat. When ranchers sell cattle, the main determinant of price is the weight of the cattle unless the rancher can prove how the cattle were raised via a US Department of Agriculture (USDA) Process Verified Program (PVP). Without PVP certification that can prove cattle were raised on grass, in open fields, and without antibiotics or hormones, the quality of the meat is not considered until after the ranchers have already sold them. The USDA quality grading happens at the processing plant based on the marbling of the meat carcass. The meat processors can charge higher prices to wholesalers/retailers for USDA prime, choice, and select cuts.

Enter BeefChain. BeefChain was co-founded by a group of Wyoming ranchers and individuals with knowledge of beef supply chains and blockchain technology in 2018. American Certified Brands, founded by Steve Lupien and others, is the holding company.

BeefChain's mission is to restore equity in the beef supply chain by verifying that cattle were grass fed, free range, and fairly treated so that ranchers can charge more money for their cattle.[28] The company uses RFID tags and blockchain technology to prove the care and provenance of cattle.

To trace cattle on a blockchain, BeefChain first had to recruit ranchers to create unique identifiers for each animal. Ranchers usually sell calves when they are one to two years old, so early tagging was a critical step in preparation for achieving traceability later. Ranchers need to tag calves' ears with machine readable tags that capture time-stamped information about the animal's birth and parentage. Each RFID tag costs about $5.00. To help make ranchers aware of the opportunity, Ogden Driskill—a well-known Wyoming rancher and politician—announced that he had tagged 323 calves from his ranch in 2018. Soon after, two other ranchers tagged their herds.[29]

Initially, BeefChain posted hashes of the tag data on Bitcoin and Ethereum. This would provide an immutable record of the first step in the supply chain.[30] The next step involved building the application and conducting a proof-of-concept (POC). BeefChain, the University of Wyoming and Avery Dennison—an RFID company—completed a POC in 2018 that traced beef raised on Murraymere Farms in Wyoming to an upscale restaurant in Taiwan. The solution used RFID tags and labels to track the movement of beef from the farm, processing plant, export, and import to the restaurant.[31] The POC showed that the solution could technically work.

The next phase involved proving that Wyoming cattle was worth more money. In 2019, BeefChain received the first USDA approval as a Process Verified Program (PVP) for a blockchain company. This allows BeefChain to audit feedlots and ranches to verify the source and age of animals; whether cattle were treated with hormones; or whether natural raising practices on grass and without antibiotics or hormones were followed.[32] BeefChain auditors now had the authorization to help more ranchers command higher prices. By 2020, Tyler Lindholm, one of BeefChain's co-founders, said that ranchers who adopted the solution see a return on investment because ranchers are commanding higher prices through the PVP certification. He said, *"Most of the ranchers know we use blockchain technology, but the main thing they care about is that they received a return on their invest of anywhere between 5 to 50 cents per pound—that's about an extra $30,000 per year per rancher."*[33] BeefChain charges ranchers a fee per head of cattle tracked in exchange for access to the technology and PVP certification. The cost is more than offset by the higher prices they now receive.

BeefChain initially posted data on Bitcoin and Ethereum, but now bases most of its development efforts on Cardano.[34] In 2020, its partnered with IOHK, the Hong-Kong based company behind the Cardano blockchain. Cardano is a public permissionless blockchain based on Proof-of-Stake. In a presentation at Cardano's 2020 conference, the President of Beefchain said *"We chose Cardano because it is secure, transparent, and scalable. They are also wonderful partners to help us grow the business."*[35] BeefChain and IOHK worked on four use cases for grass fed assurance, certification, end-to-end traceability, and consumer engagement. BeefChain deploys the auditors and IOHK and Atala Trace are the technology partners. IOHK is automating more of the process so that ranchers will have to complete less paperwork to add data, like vaccination status, to the system.

Going forward, BeefChain envisions that tokenization of cattle can broaden the rancher's financing options. Ranchers only get paid once a year when they sell the herd. Ranchers typically take out loans to finance their operations. What if ranchers sold their tokens to foster new investment models, such as fractional ownership of a cow, bull or even an entire herd? Breeding bulls, for example, can be worth $1 million, and an NFT can easily track hundreds of smaller-sized investors. Tokenization can also improve regulatory compliance. Instead of a blanket inspection to certify an entire herd for sale, NFTs tie each animal in the herd to the inspection certification and maintain that record of passing inspection even as it gets separated from the herd as it moves through the supply chain. Moreover, animal inspections across state lines could be automated by reading the RFID tag and pulling the relevant inspection data from the system.

BeefChain is next building end consumer applications so that consumers can learn who raised the meat and how the animal was treated (see Figure 7.8). Tyler Lindholm, one of BeefChain's co-founders, said that the goal is to allow end consumers to know their ranchers. *"We have the opportunity to go in many directions. Even if you are across the world, you have an opportunity to know your rancher and know how they raise their animals. You can prove it with an immutable record with blockchain technology."*[36]

Figure 7.8: Consumers will be able to scan QR codes on meat to find who raised the cattle

7.6. Everledger

Based in London, Everledger was founded in 2015 by Leanne Kemp initially with the aim to track diamonds from mines to retail stores. Kemp wanted to stop 'blood diamonds'— diamonds mined to finance conflicts in such places as Sierra Leone, Liberia, Angola, and the Ivory Coast—by better tracking the warranties associated with fair trade practices established by the United Nations. The United Nations created the World Diamond Congress to define the standards, which it subsequently passed in 2003. Known as the 'Kimberly Process Certification', the process requires sellers of rough and polished diamonds to insert a warranty declaration on invoices that reads:

> *"The diamonds herein invoiced have been purchased from legitimate sources not involved in funding conflict and in compliance with United Nations resolutions. The seller hereby guarantees that these diamonds are conflict free, based on personal knowledge and/or written guarantees provided by the supplier of these diamonds."*[37]

Everledger tracks diamonds by first creating a unique digital twin version of the physical diamond with machine vision. Machine vision specifies 40 meta data points using high resolution photographs (see Figure 7.9). Everledger worked with IBM to build the blockchain application on Hyperledger Fabric. The blockchain tracks a complete provenance history around each diamond, including the origin, allotment, rough state, planning, cutting, polishing, and certification.[38] According to the CEO, over 1 million diamonds were represented on the ledger by March 2017.[39] According to Coindesk, Everledger and its network of partners covered 40 percent of the diamonds in circulation by 2020.[40]

Everledger has since expanded its business model to authenticate and track other valuable assets such as art, batteries, critical minerals like lithium and cobalt, fashion, gemstones, insurance, luxury goods, and wines and spirits. The Everledger platform offers various products.[41] 'Capture' is the main product that traces a part's provenance. 'Amplify' is an API plug-in for eCommerce retailers, allowing them to insert the provenance of a product tracked on Everledger onto their websites.[42] As of early 2022, Everledger has raised nearly $40 million from investors, earned about $31 million a year in revenue, and had 224 employees.[43]

Although Everledger was first to market with tracking diamonds, others have since entered the market. In May of 2018, De Beers tracked 100 high-value diamonds from the mine to the retailer using a blockchain, which eventually led to a spinoff called **Tracr**. Canadian-based Lucara Diamond uses **Clara**, another blockchain-based tracker.[44]

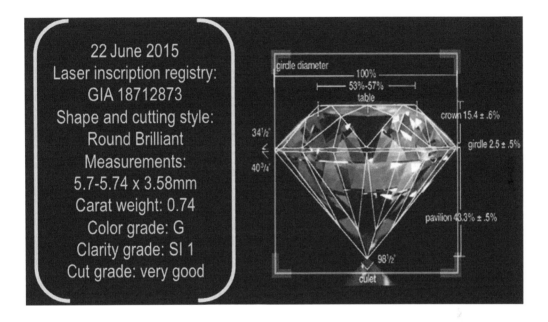

Figure 7.9: Everledger's digital identifier for a fair trade diamond

Source: https://www.youtube.com/watch?v=GAdjL-nultl

It's solution tracks diamonds from 'mine to finger'.[45] In January 2019, Russia's Ministry of Education and Science introduced its own blockchain solution for responsible diamond trade, which was developed by a Russian startup called **Bitcarat.com**.[46] At the time of this writing during the Russian invasion of Ukraine in 2022, it's difficult to assess the status of this initiative; the website roadmap had not been updated since 2020.

7.7. OpsChain Traceability

EY is a global professional services network based in London, with over 300,000 employees. EY's blockchain strategy has been unique among enterprise leaders for its early commitment to the use of public blockchains for enterprise transactions. EY believes that private-permissioned blockchains are not the end-game due to vendor lock-in, lack of scalability, and lack of interoperability. EY sees the benefits of public blockchains, such as Ethereum, as (a) an ability to participate without investing in significant technology and hosting a node; (b) all relevant information remains on the public blockchain and available to all participants, even if the project fails or various individuals leave the project; and (c) an increased ability to leverage upcoming blockchain approaches and upgrades through community development so that the participants in the use-case specific network can focus on business rules, transactions, and governance and not the underlying development of a blockchain platform. To help enterprise adoption of public blockchains, EY has contributed to open-source code bases—most notably Nightfall and the Baseline Protocol—that use zero-knowledge proofs (ZKPs) to execute confidential transactions on public blockchains. (ZKPs are explained in Chapter 10).

Here we focus on EY's OpsChain Traceability solution, used for supply chain traceability. Its history began with WineChain. EY developed WineChain in 2018 to authenticate wines and to restore trust in a marketplace plagued by fakes—counterfeit wines are a multi-billion-dollar business.[47] The solution is a hybrid with a public blockchain for verification of wine authenticity and a private blockchain for value transfer. For wine authenticity, each wine bottle is tokenized as an ERC-721 token and posted to Ethereum; the token is transformed to a QR code that is affixed to the wine bottle's label. By 2020, EY had tokenized 11 million unique wine bottles with an ERC-721 token.[48] Customers can scan the code with their smartphones and get verification that the wine is authentic (see Figure 7.10). Consumers can learn about when and where grapes were harvested, bottling date, lot number, quality of sulphites, and other data. For value transfer, vineyards, wine producers, brokers, importers, wholesalers, distributors, and retailers rely on Quorum—a private network version of Ethereum—to exchange value and to track the bottles as they move through the supply chain.[49] EY chose Quorum in anticipation of a pivot from private to public networks; building on Quorum with public blockchains in mind minimizes the recoding required to switch to Ethereum in the future.

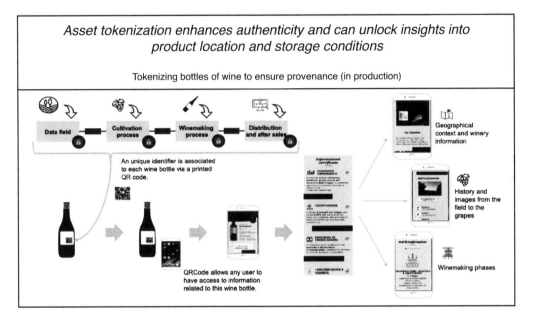

Figure 7.10: EY's WineChain Solution

Source: EY, with permission

While small scale counterfeits might occur—say by consuming a fine wine, re-using the wine bottle, and re-selling the fake—the perpetrator would be caught if they tried to scale the solution; the winery still has chain of custody visibility and would be able to pinpoint the common source of repeated quality complaints, and identify this discrete point of failure in the process.

In 2019, EY deployed the TATTOO Wine Market place with partners including Blockchain Wine Pte. Ltd for the Asia-Pacific market. 'TATTOO' stands for traceability, authenticity, transparency, trade, origin, and opinion. It has an interface to SAP; SAP is an enterprise application used by many companies in the supply chain. Thus, most customers using TATTOO are using a hybrid solution, with their private internal systems connected to EY's public OpsChain Traceability solution.[50]

When Ethereum's transaction fees escalated, EY evolved the OpsChain Traceability from Ethereum to Polygon. We introduced Polygon in the Aave case study in Chapter 5. Polygon is a layer 2 solution for Ethereum that processes transactions in the Polygon network and bundles them for posting on Ethereum. Polygon is faster than Ethereum because it uses Proof-of-Stake and is it has lower transaction costs than Ethereum.

In addition to wine, the OpsChain Traceability solution is used by Birra Peroni (Asahi Group) for beer, by Spinosa for mozzarella cheese, by Merck Animal Health for animal vaccines, and by other clients for chickens, eggs, and fresh produce.[51]

7.8. DL Freight

DL Freight is a blockchain-enabled solution for freight invoice and payment processing developed by Walmart Canada and DLT Labs. The case study begins in summer 2018 within the supply chain and logistics organization of Walmart Canada. Leaders wanted to address the problems with freight invoicing. While Walmart Canada has its own fleet of 2,000 trailers used for shipments to the stores, it also relies on 70 third-party freight carriers—some large-sized and some small-sized—to move over 500,000 loads per year.[52] A single freight invoice can have up to 200 data elements from various partners in the supply chain. Because each partner maintains its own systems of record, Walmart Canada's information often conflicted with their partners' information. Walmart Canada was frustrated with the time and resources needed to verify carriers' variable charges (called accessorial charges) on invoices. Before DL Freight, Walmart Canada and its freight carriers disputed 70 percent of invoices. It took days, weeks and even months to settle them, resulting in administrative expenses rising to about 20 percent of transportation costs.[53] Freight carriers were not getting paid in a timely manner, and both sides were spending too much money on reconciliations.

Walmart Canada engaged DLT Labs as its technology partner. DLT Labs is a Toronto-based technology platform developer that had built a *configurable* platform based on Hyperledger Fabric. Configuring an existing platform was much faster and cheaper than coding and testing a custom-built application. Once configured, the solution was audited by Walmart Canada and its parent company, Walmart Inc. The configuration, testing and compliance cycle for the production pilot took only eight months from conception to live deployment.

In addition to technology, the solution also involved significant business process redesign. Before DL Freight, freight carriers generated an invoice after the final delivery of a shipment, which is when Walmart Canada saw the invoice for the first time. Walmart had to investigate all the unexpected accessorial charges that appeared on an invoice. As shown in Figure 7.11, the freight invoice process before the adoption of DL Freight required 11 steps. The value-adding steps are the ones that process data about the shipment, including confirming shipment details (Step 1), dispatching (Step 2), accepting or rejecting delivery (Step 3), issuing a correct invoice (Step 7), and paying the invoice (step 11). All the other steps involved reviewing data and reconciling any discrepancies within the freight carrier's data.

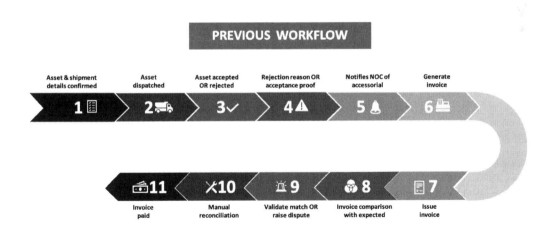

Figure 7.11: Freight invoice process before implementing the DL Freight solution

Source: Reproduced with permission from Walmart Canada and DLT Labs

307

After DL Freight was implemented, the invoice was jointly built in near real time with data from Walmart Canada and the freight carrier. The 'happy path' of the reengineered freight invoice process requires just five steps—i.e., the flow that triggers no exceptions or error conditions (see Figure 7.12).

In Step 1 of the revised process, Walmart Canada's Transportation Management System (TMS) serves as the source of truth for the tender and contracting data. The TMS uploads the shipment tender (using EDI 204 data standard) to the DL Freight platform to initially populate the invoice with shipment details, load details and delivery instructions. Known charges are added to the invoice, including fuel, planned stops and hazardous materials handling charges. Carriers interact with DL Freight—either directly through APIs or through a portal—for tender approvals. DL Freight sends a tender-acceptance notification to the TMS (using EDI 990 data standard). The connections between freight carriers' systems and DL Freight are depicted in Figure 7.13.

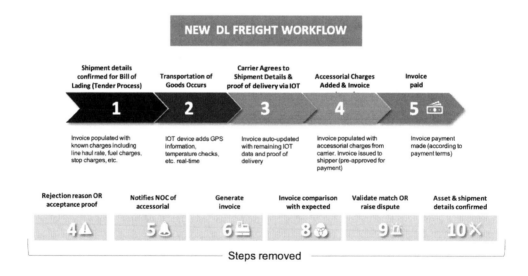

Figure 7.12: Freight invoice process after implementing the DL Freight solution

Source: With permission from Walmart Canada and DLT Labs

During Step 2, IoT devices that track temperatures, GPS locations and times are read and posted in near real time to DL Freight as the shipment moves along the transportation route. The automatic uploads are done via FourKites, a system that collects and consolidates data from the IoT devices. Some smaller carriers without sophisticated IoT device systems enter their data manually. IoT data triggers variable accessorial charges that are added to the invoice along the way, such as charges for wait times and layovers. Most transaction approvals are automated using smart contracts.

In Step 3, Walmart Canada's distribution centers connect to DL Freight to verify receipt of goods via proof of delivery. GPS reads confirm delivery to the final destination.

During Step 4, the freight carrier agrees the shipment details and proof of delivery and completes the invoice by adding any final accessorial charges. With payments pre-approved, the invoice is issued to Walmart Canada and is paid according to payment terms recorded in the smart contract. The countdown clock for payment terms, such as *"pay the invoice in net 35 days"*, does not start until the parties had agreed to the final invoice. With DL Freight, invoices are agreed soon after final delivery, ensuring that carriers get paid the right amount within the pre-agreed timeframe. In short, carriers have certainty about the amount they will be paid and receive the payments faster.[54]

After Walmart Canada and its freight operators adopted a blockchain-enabled solution in March 2020, invoice disputes fell from 70 percent to less than 2 percent, invoices were finalized within 24 hours—instead of days, weeks or longer—costs were reduced, and relationships improved. As of Summer 2021, DL Freight had processed 340,000 invoices worth $450 million. Preparing these invoices involved 57.1 million IoT messages and 2.6 million temperature updates.

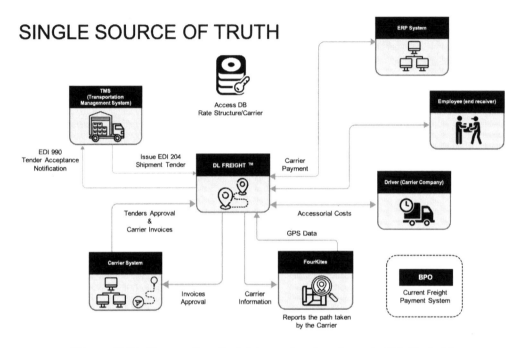

Figure 7.13: Connecting freight carriers' systems to DL Freight

Source: Reproduced with permission from DLT Labs

7.9. VeriTX

Colonel James Allen Regenor, USAF(ret) founded VeriTX in 2019. VeriTX was incorporated in Delaware, with its head office in East Aurora, New York. VeriTX's mission is to create trusted digital supply chain solutions based on three pillars: data integrity, process integrity and performance integrity. VeriTX is positioned at the convergence of Industry 4.0 and Web 3.0. The net result of this convergence is a new modality of logistics, which Regenor calls digital, following the first three modalities of land, sea, and air. The core of the VeriTX solution portfolio is a marketplace, a business-to-business platform for the buying and selling of digital and physical assets that also records trusted maintenance and lease information, powered by blockchain technology.[55]

VeriTX had nearly finished its Series A funding round for $5 million in March 2022.

The platform has been built and tested with many POCs with global strategic partners. Most recently, the US Air Force awarded VeriTX a contract valued at $2 million in September of 2021. VeriTX serves as the prime contractor for a layered approach to data security, protecting critical supply chains and increasing Air Force readiness.[56]

Although VeriTX was founded in 2019, it has a longer history dating back to when Regenor joined Moog in 2013 after retiring from 31 years of military service in the US Air Force. Regenor was hired partly for his scenario-based planning skills to help Moog envision future business directions. While working at Moog, Regenor imagined a completely decentralized manufacturing process in which military and commercial customers could print parts where they need them, when they need them. The scenario went as follows:

> *"Imagine a scenario where lives depend upon a mission being flown off the deck of an aircraft carrier far out at sea. The only available aircraft has just been grounded with a failed critical part. There is no part inventory on the carrier. But we do have a 3-D printer and a stock of powder aboard. A technical data package is available for the part, and a replacement is quickly printed. You are the responsible person who needs to get this part quickly fitted to the aircraft and to sign the plane off as safe and ready to fly. How would you know if the newly printed additive manufacturing part you are holding in your hand is good for use?"*[57]

The challenges to realize such a decentralized manufacturing process—particularly in such a highly regulated context—were enormous. What if the 3-D printing instructions had been tampered with by a cyber-terrorist? Or what if the instructions were counterfeit? Military and commercial users would need a way to guarantee that the part that came off the printer was authentic and that the part was ready for use. Furthermore, the newly printed part would need to be tracked over its entire lifetime, so it would need an embedded unique ID when it came off the printer. Military and commercial users would need a decentralized network with the highest security. Technically, Regenor and his team quickly realized that blockchain technologies might be the ideal technical solution: a decentralized blockchain application for decentralized additive manufacturing.[58] The size of the potential market is large. The US military is moving to digital supply chains, with an estimated market size for digital aircraft parts of $3.1 billion by 2025.

Trying to launch a new business within a traditional business like Moog proved to be a slow process. Professor Clayton Christensen's Theory of Disruptive Innovation—discussed in Chapter 11—found that traditional businesses had a hard time disrupting themselves, and that spin-offs or investments in startups were better routes. Ultimately, Regenor decided to depart Moog in May of 2018 to accelerate development and to make the solution independent. He said, *"To be successful, we need VeriTX to be a neutral third-party platform."* Regenor stayed on as a consultant with Moog as he launched VeriTX. While Regenor was named on the patents (along with other Moog employees), Moog owns the patents, so VeriTX licenses the patents from Moog. In late 2019, Moog became a strategic partner with VeriTX, as aligned with Christensen's Theory.

Among all the supply chain cases discussed in this Chapter, the VeriTX solution is the most disruptive to traditional supply chain ecosystems. Figure 7.14 compares the processes for centralized versus decentralized manufacturing.

It's an entirely new kind of supply chain. The potential business value is enormous, such as significantly less downtime, lower inventory costs, lower customs fees, and lower shipping and transportation costs.[59] The main military benefit is improved mission readiness rates and the commercial benefit is increased asset up time. The platform yields metadata and part data that can be used to inform predictive and prescriptive maintenance solutions. Today, most parts are fly-to-fail which is extremely inefficient and costly. Much efficiency can be gained, and costs reduced by enacting a prescriptive model.

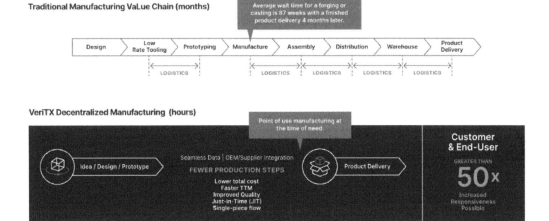

Figure 7.14: Centralized *vs.* decentralized manufacturing

Source: With permission from VeriTX

From a process perspective, VeriTX digitizes and decentralizes the parts manufacturing process by breaking it down into four steps:

1. *"Sellers design parts digitally. This includes the idea, prototype and final design of parts ranging from traditionally forged metal engine parts to polymer-molded interior parts used in aircraft cabins.*
2. *Sellers upload parts on VeriTX platform. All the necessary information such as pricing, specifications, and provenance is included.*
3. *Buyers purchase digital parts. The platform enables the exchange of digital assets, which will eventually become tangible in the last step.*
4. *Push to point-of-use, then 3D print. For those who do not have 3D printing machines, VertiTX has machine partners who can print the parts and have them ready for pick-up or delivery."* [60]

For step 2, sellers assign and upload unique identifiers on VeriTX's platform. The part identification method varies with use case and material type. For 3D printed parts, each part can be printed with an embedded unique hash 'watermark' that can be viewed with a camera on a smart phone app. The hash would be permanently stored on the blockchain at time of origin.

For metal parts, Moog did a POC with Alitheon, a company that uses simple mobile phone cameras and proprietary software to transform 54,000 unique surface characteristics of individual objects into a unique digital ID—no tags are appended, the object serves as its own identifier! (See Figure 7.15.)

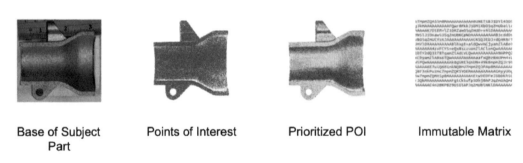

| Base of Subject Part | Points of Interest | Prioritized POI | Immutable Matrix |

Figure 7.15: Creating unique IDs from 54,000 unique surface areas for metal parts

Source: https://www.moog.com/news/blog-new/VeriPart-linking-digital-to-physical.html

Alitheon's software can scan the object at any time with a mobile phone, and if the object was previously recorded on the blockchain, the software authenticates the object and provides a match confidence score.[61] For the POC, Moog sent 20 metal parts to Alitheon for scanning, which Alitheon then sent back to Moog. Moog scanned them upon receipt, matched them with Moog's ID, and then brutalized the materials by dropping them on concrete floors, grinding them with handheld motors, and grit blasting the parts. Moog sent these worn parts back to Alitheon, which was still able to identify the unique parts, even when only 3,700 unique surface features remained on the original parts.[62]

The blockchain application leverages smart contracts to track the part's every movement and every transfer of ownership (see Figure 7.16).[63] Modules also analyze data—such as predicting part failures—and aggregate parts information to a dashboard (see Figure 7.17).

Figure 7.16: VeriTX tracks the process from part design and printing to delivery

Source: With permission from VeriTX

Next, we cover some of VeriTX's pilots.

As mentioned above, US Air Force awarded VeriTX a contract valued at $2 million in 2021. Regenor explained, *"VeriTX always talks about the fourth modality of logistics as being based on data, process, and performance integrity. For the US Air Force, VeriTX is responsible for data integrity. We built a solution called Fortis to follow the data provenance for any part. Beyond that, we can also ascertain whether anything has been altered in the documents, which is critical for environments that need to assume 'logistics under attack'."* For the Fortis application, the solution demo was built on

315

a private-permissioned version of Ethereum. VeriTx is working with a partner to potentially develop quantum key pairs for this solution in anticipation that advances in quantum computing will break the private-public keys pairs used in today's blockchains (see Chapter 10 for more on quantum).

As the beta version advances, the solution will likely become a hybrid. The part of the solution that records the hashes of transactions will likely move to Algorand. The part of the solution that does forensics and analytics to determine who or what executed transactions will operate on a private network. Regenor explained, *"It's a highly secure design in a zero trust environment with enabled quantum resistant protocols per National Security Memorandum-8."[64]*

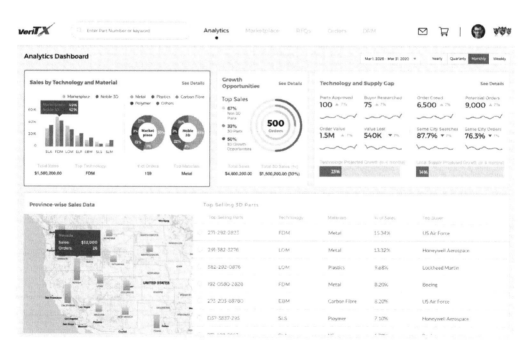

Figure 7.17: VeriTX's dashboard

Source: With permission from VeriTX

Regenor chose Algorand after examining several technology providers. Algorand is a public permissionless blockchain that relies on Proof-of-Stake, which is fast, cheap, and secure. He said, *"Algorand was the ideal solution to onboard our ecosystem partners to the network, because of its flexible architecture, low transaction fees and transactional throughput scalability."*[65] Additionally, Algorand is carbon neutral; an on-chain sustainability oracle analyses each node's energy use and compensates the usage with offsetting funds to reforestation, peat management and wind-energy projects managed by ClimateTrade.[66] Algorand also has a clawback feature that allows an authorized address to revoke assets from an account if they breach certain contractual obligations.

In another POC for a military application, VeriTX proved a massive improvement in moving to decentralized manufacturing. Before a solution like VeriTX, it takes up to 265 days for a replacement part to be ordered and delivered for the F15-Eagle fighter plane. On the VeriTX marketplace, the Department of Defense can place a buy order for a metal aircraft part to be 3D printed on-demand and delivered in just 6 hours.[67]

In the commercial airline space, Regenor and his team did a much-publicized live test of producing a 3D replacement part for a business-class seat for an inbound aircraft in 2019. The Boeing 777-300 aircraft left from Auckland New Zealand, and while it was in flight, it radioed Air New Zealand maintenance facility in Auckland to report the part broken. Although the part is not critical, it would deem the seat unsellable. The maintenance facility ordered the digital part from its supplier, Singapore-based ST Engineering (STE). STE pushed the order to Moog to print the part in Los Angeles. Using a mobile printer, Regenor printed the part and it was replaced 30 minutes after the Boeing 777-300 landed in Los Angeles by the maintenance crew.[68] Regenor explained, *"We proved that we could whittle a 43 day lead time down to an hour. Digital logistics fundamentally changes supply chains."*[69]

VeriTX's next commercial applications focus on 'rotables'. Rotables are aircraft parts that can be fixed and re-used. Commercial airlines can create sustainment opportunities to reuse, rebuild, and overhaul parts that would otherwise be discarded.

VeriTX has also forayed into the medical parts business. When Regenor realized that his platform could help with the medical devices needed to battle COVID-19, he leapt into action. He founded a new company, Rapid Medical Parts, in March 2020. He rallied his global network of partners, and in just 12 days, the Pentagon awarded his company a contract for converting the abundant supply of sleep apnea machines into ventilators. The conversion requires additional parts that Rapid Medical Parts printed, and at a tenth of the cost of a new ventilator. After the contract was completed, the need to convert sleep apneas waned because industrial ventilator manufacturers were able to meet demand. In sharing his story with us, Regenor said, *"We all answer the call. Some run towards the cannons and others dig in. I have always run towards the cannons."*

7.10. Conclusion

IBM Food Trust, VeChain, BeefChain, Everledger, OpsChain Traceability, DL Freight, and VeriTX show how ecosystem platforms can help to improve supply chains. They improve supply chain visibility, authenticate products, remove friction points in trade, reduce administrative costs, and reduce time wasted on paperwork. Our sampling of cases demonstrates multiple ways to identify products and multiple uses of blockchain, including private-permissioned, private-permissionless, and public-permissionless solutions. We also saw several hybrid solutions.

Beyond our cases, there are many other blockchain-enabled supply chains. For example:

- OpenSC, cofounded by the World Wildlife Fund and Boston Consulting Group, helps Austral Fisheries to trace fish from 'bait to plate'.[70]

- Provenance is a UK-based company that provides supply chain authenticity and traceability for many clients, including Grass Roots Farmer' Cooperative, based in Little Rock Arkansas.

- Minnesota-based Cargill traced 200,000 turkeys from 70 farms to retail stores.[71]

- France-based Carrefour traced milk and other products. Carrefour reported that the application boosted sales for products traced on a blockchain and are accessible to consumers via QR codes. [72]

- US-based Bumble Bee Foods traced fish (with SAP).[73]

- CONA built a blockchain-based solution for Coca-Cola bottlers. It was initially built on a private permissioned network but may move to a to a public-permissionless solution.[74]

It's interesting to ponder whether more supply chain applications will pivot from private to pubic blockchains based on innovations discussed in Chapter 10, such as zero-knowledge proofs and layer 2 solutions.

For those interested in a deeper examination of blockchains in supply chains, *Integrating Blockchain into Supply Chain Management* by Remko Van Hoek, Brian Fugate, Marat Davletshin, and Matthew Waller is recommended.[75] In the next chapter, we explore uses blockchain solutions for credentials.

Citations

[1] ReportBuyer Press Release (Aug 27, 2018). The global food and grocery retail market size is expected to reach USD 12.24 trillion by 2020, https://www.prnewswire.com/news-releases/the-global-food-and-grocery-retail-market-size-is-expected-to-reach-usd-12-24-trillion-by-2020--300702659.html

[2] World Health Organization (2020). Food Safety, https://www.who.int/news-room/fact-sheets/detail/food-safety

[3] Spink, J., Embark, P., Savelli, C., and Bradshaw, A. (2019). Global perspectives on food fraud: results from a WHO survey of members of the International Food Safety Authorities Network (INFOSAN). *npj Sci Food* 3, 12. https://www.nature.com/articles/s41538-019-0044-x

[4] Grossman, E. (October 25, 2016). Did slaves produce your food? https://civileats.com/2016/10/25/did-slaves-produce-your-food-forced-labor/

[5] Statista (2020). Total retail and food services sales in the United States from 1992 to 2018; https://www.statista.com/statistics/197569/annual-retail-and-food-services-sales/

[6] CDC (2020). Burden of Foodborne Illness: Findings, https://www.cdc.gov/foodborneburden/2011-foodborne-estimates.html

[7] FDA list of recalls: https://www.fda.gov/safety/recalls-market-withdrawals-safety-alerts

[8] https://www.fsis.usda.gov/recalls

[9] Food Waste: Rescuing US Cuisine. https://www.rescuingleftovercuisine.org/e?gclid=Cj0KCQiA4NTxBRDxARIsAHyp6gBqhPgXvYsvwoDJHRewOeXi5nv1sK8f1oMw5BP0AtNnseRDNRYkvqgaAgu5EALw_wcB

[10] For a case study on Mediledger, see:

Mattke, Jens; Maier, Christian; Hund, Axel; and Weitzel, Tim (2019) "How an Enterprise Blockchain Application in the U.S. Pharmaceuticals Supply Chain is Saving Lives," *MIS Quarterly Executive*: Vol.18: Iss. 4, Article 6.

For case studies on TradeLens, see:

Jensen, Thomas; Hedman, Jonas; and Henningsson, Stefan (2019) "How TradeLens Delivers Business Value With Blockchain Technology," *MIS Quarterly Executive*: Vol. 18: Iss. 4, Article 5.

Sarker, S., Henningsson, S., Jensen, T., and Hedman, J. (2021). Use Of Blockchain As A Resource For Combating Corruption In Global Shipping: An Interpretive Case Study, Journal is Management Information Systems, 38(2) pp. 338-373.

[11] https://www.ibm.com/blockchain/resources/7-benefits-ibm-food-trust/

[12] Kamath, R. (2018). Food Traceability on Blockchain: Walmart's Pork and Mango Pilots with IBM, *The Journal of The British Blockchain Association*, 1(1), 1-12.

[13] UPC 038900006198 is associated with Dole Crushed Pineapple In Its Own Juice, 8 oz https://www.upcitemdb.com/upc/38900006198

[14] What are Key Responsibilities for a Trust Anchor? https://www.ibm.com/blockchain/solutions/food-trust/food-industry-technology#1797811

[15] https://www.ibm.com/blockchain/solutions/food-trust/food-industry-technology#1797811

[16] IBM Press Release (October 23 2018), *IBM and Microsoft Announce Partnership Between Cloud Offerings*, https://www.pbsnow.com/ibm-news/ibm-and-microsoft-announce-partnership-between-cloud-offerings/

[17] Cream and Partners (June 1, 2020) Walmart China Brings Together Sam's Club and VeChain to Take One Step Further Towards Blockchainization With Safe Food Traceability Platform, retrieved March 22, 2022 from https://creamandpartners.com/walmart-china-brings-together-sams-club-and-vechain-to-take-one-step-further-towards-blockchainization-with-safe-food-traceability-platform/

[18] https://www.investopedia.com/terms/v/vechain.asp#

[19] VeChain's Proof of Authority. Retrieved March 23, 2022 from https://docs.vechain.org/thor/learn/proof-of-authority.html

[20] https://www.vechain.com/product/toolchain

[21] VeChain white paper https://www.vechain.org/whitepaper/

[22] Palmer, D. (June 25, 2019) Walmart China Teams with VeChain, PwC on Blockchain Food Safety Platform. Coindesk, https://www.coindesk.com/walmart-china-teams-with-vechain-on-blockchain-food-safety-platform

Mitra, R. (August 28, 2019). VeChain partners with Walmart, BYD, DNG VL and BMW. FXStreet. https://www.fxstreet.com/cryptocurrencies/news/vechain-partners-with-walmart-byd-dng-vl-and-bmw-201908280048

Consumer view: https://traceability.walmartmobile.cn/walmart/p/10000919067888862973

[23] https://www.cbinsights.com/company/vechain/competitors-partners

[24] Food traceability: The Beefchain solution, Cardano 2020 Conference, https://youtu.be/9zukeh-iqC4

[25] Reuters (June 17, 2021). How four big companies control the U.S. beef industry. Retrieved March 24, 2022 from https://www.reuters.com/business/how-four-big-companies-control-us-beef-industry-2021-06-17/

[26] Reuters (June 17, 2021). How four big companies control the U.S. beef industry. Retrieved March 24, 2022 from https://www.reuters.com/business/how-four-big-companies-control-us-beef-industry-2021-06-17/

[27] Pollard, A. (June 9, 2021). 'Big Four' Meatpackers Are Crushing Small Ranchers. Retrieved March 24, 2022 from https://prospect.org/power/big-four-meatpackers-crushing-small-ranchers/

[28] Ledger Insights (July 24, 2020). "Proof of Steak": using blockchain to transform food-tracing of beef. Retrieved March 24, 2022 from https://www.ledgerinsights.com/proof-of-steak-blockchain-food-beef-traceability/

[29] Del Castillo, M. (May 17, 2018). Free-Range Beef Bound By The Blockchain, retrieved March 24, 2022 from https://www.forbes.com/sites/michaeldelcastillo/2018/05/17/free-range-beef-bound-by-the-blockchain/?sh=61cb6244796a

[30] Blockchain for Food: The Case of BeefChain (May 10, 2021). https://www.youtube.com/watch?v=ZHrUhJNc1H0

[31] University of Wyoming Press Release (February 12, 2019). First-Ever Blockchain Beef Shipment Traced from Wyoming to Taiwan. Retrieved March 24, 2022 from https://northernag.net/first-ever-blockchain-beef-shipment-traced-from-wyoming-to-taiwan/

[32] Pirus, B. (April 25, 2019). BeefChain Receives First USDA Certification For A Blockchain Company. Retrieved March 24, 2022 from https://www.forbes.com/sites/benjaminpirus/2019/04/25/beefchain-receives-first-usda-certification-for-a-blockchain-company/?sh=3b9146447607

[33] Food traceability: The Beefchain solution, Cardano 2020 Conference, https://youtu.be/9zukeh-iqC4

[34] Pirus, B. (April 25, 2019). BeefChain Receives First USDA Certification For A Blockchain Company. Retrieved March 24, 2022 from https://www.forbes.com/sites/benjaminpirus/2019/04/25/beefchain-receives-first-usda-certification-for-a-blockchain-company/?sh=3b9146447607

[35] Food traceability: The Beefchain solution, Cardano 2020 Conference, https://youtu.be/9zukeh-iqC4

36 Food traceability: The Beefchain solution, Cardano 2020 Conference, https://youtu.be/9zukeh-iqC4

37 https://en.wikipedia.org/wiki/Kimberley_Process_Certification_Scheme

38 https://everledger.io/industry-solutions/diamonds/

39 Presentation by Everledger's CEO at IBM Interconnect: https://ibmgo.com/interconnect2017/?cm_mc_uid=19734726856314943335282&cm_mc_sid_50200000=1494367094&cm_mc_sid_52640000=1494367094 (About an hour and 15 minutes into the video)

40 Allison, I. (March 24, 2020). Everledger Looks Beyond Blood Diamonds With ESG Supply Chain Collaboration, Coindesk, retrieved March 21, 2022 from https://www.coindesk.com/business/2020/03/25/everledger-looks-beyond-blood-diamonds-with-esg-supply-chain-collaboration/

41 Overview of Everledger: https://youtu.be/SY2VsIL9DKY

'Capture' product: https://youtu.be/bhqYgqhnnKc

Everledger wine supply chain: https://youtu.be/GKBxZVEzMNU

42 Everledger revenues and competitors. Retrieved March 21, 2022 from https://www.everledger.io/industry-solutions/

43 https://growjo.com/company/Everledger

44 O'Neal, S. (February 6, 2019). Diamonds are blockchain's best friend, *CoinTelegraph*, https://cointelegraph.com/news/diamonds-are-blockchains-best-friend-how-dlt-helps-tracking-gems-and-prevents-fraud

45 https://www.lucaradiamond.com/clara/

46 https://bitcarat.com/

47 Micallef, J. (December 1, 2018). What's In Your Cellar? Counterfeit Wines Are A Multi-Billion Dollar Problem, Forbes, https://www.forbes.com/sites/joemicallef/2018/12/01/whats-in-your-cellar-counterfeit-wines-are-a-multi-billion-dollar-problem/#70f541ad1c83

48 Sharma, T. (July 16th, 2019). Know the Authenticity of Your Wines, https://www.blockchain-council.org/blockchain/know-the-authenticity-of-your-wines-eys-blockchain-platform-for-wine-traceability/.

49 *Restoring trust in the wine industry, from grape to glass*, EY https://www.ey.com/en_us/global-review/2018/restoring-trust-in-the-wine-industry

[50] EY Press release (November 13, 2019). EY blockchain platform supports Blockchain Wine Pte. Ltd. to launch TATTOO Wine marketplace across Asia Pacific. Retrieved March 23, 2022 from https://www.ey.com/en_gl/news/2019/11/ey-blockchain-platform-supports-blockchain-wine-pte-ltd-to-launch-tattoo-wine-marketplace-across-asia-pacific

[51] EY Press Release (April 16 2019). EY Ops Chain industrializes the blockchain at scale for enterprises. Retrieved March 23, 2022 from https://www.ey.com/en_gl/news/2019/04/ey-ops-chain-industrializes-the-blockchain-at-scale-for-enterprises

[52] *Walmart Uses Blockchain to Fix 'Broken' Freight Audit and Payment Process,* SupplyChainBrain, November 1, 2020, available at https://www.supplychainbrain.com/articles/32130-walmart-canada-fixing-a-broken-freight-audit-and-payment-process-with- blockchain.

[53] Ibid.

[54] Hamilton, S. *MOBI Community Innovation Lecture: The partnership between DLT Labs and Walmart Canada,* MOBI, September 24, 2020, available at https://dlt.mobi/mobi-community-innovation-lecture-the-partnership-between-dlt-labs-and-walmart-canada/.

[55] https://veritx.co/

[56] VeriTX news release (September 22, 2021). VeriTX Awarded US Air Force Contract to Create Secure Digital Fabric, retrieved March 21, 2022 from https://potomacofficersclub.com/news/veritx-awarded-us-air-force-contract-to-create-secure-digital-fabric/

[57] Small, G., *Additive Manufacturing Reshaping Logistics*, retrieved March 10, 2020 from http://www.moog.com/news/blog-new/IntroducingVeripart_Issue3.html

[58] Regenor, J. (April 18th 2017), *Industry Impact: Aerospace Supply Chain*, presentation at the Blockchain for Business Conference at MIT, Cambridge Massachusetts

[59] Small, G., *Additive Manufacturing Reshaping Logistics*, retrieved March 10, 2020 from http://www.moog.com/news/blog-new/IntroducingVeripart_Issue3.html

[60] VeriTX Use case, Retrieved March 20, 2022 from https://www.algorand.com/ecosystem/use-cases/veritx

[61] Alitheon website. https://www.alitheon.com

[62] Moog Press Release (2019). VeriPart™ – Linking Digital to Physical, https://www.moog.com/news/blog-new/VeriPart-linking-digital-to-physical.html.

[63] Regenor, J., op. cit., April 18, 2017.

[64] https://www.whitehouse.gov/briefing-room/presidential-actions/2022/01/19/memorandum-on-improving-the-cybersecurity-of-national-security-department-of-defense-and-intelligence-community-systems/

[65] VeriTX press release (October 22, 2020). VeriTX Teams with Algorand to Deliver Leading Digital Marketplace for Aerospace Manufacturing, retrieved March 21, 2022 from https://www.algorand.com/resources/ecosystem-announcements/veritx-algorand-deliver-digital-marketplace-for-aerospace-manufacturing

[66] Algorand press release (2021). Algorand Pledges to be the Greenest Blockchain with a Carbon-Negative Network Now and in the Future, retrieved March 24, 2022 from https://www.algorand.com/resources/algorand-announcements/carbon_negative_announcement

[67] VeriTX Use case, Retrieved March 20, 2022 from https://www.algorand.com/ecosystem/use-cases/veritx

[68] Davies, S. (July 17, 2019). Moog's connecting flight to distributed manufacturing, TCT Magazine, https://www.tctmagazine.com/3d-printing-news/moogs-connecting-flight-to-distributed-manufacturing/

[69] James Regenor, presentation to the Blockchain Center of Excellence, December 3, 2019.

[70] https://opensc.org/case-studies.html

[71] Grass Roots Farmer's Cooperative (February 10, 2019). From Pasture to Plate – Trace The Journey of Your Food. https://www.grassrootscoop.com/blog/from-pasture-to-plate-trace-the-journey-of-your-food/

Bloch, S., and Fassler, J. (Novemeber 23, 2018) Why Car "blockchain-based" turkeys obscure more than they reveal. The Counter, https://thecounter.org/cargill-blockchain-traceable-turkey-contract-farming-reality-thanksgiving/

[72] Weick, M. (December 11, 2019). 2019 Saw the End of Blockchain Tourism, *Coindesk*, https://www.coindesk.com/2019-saw-the-end-of-blockchain-tourism

[73] O'Neil, S. (July 7, 2019). Blockchain for Food, How the Industry Makes Use of the Technology. *CoinTelegraph*, https://cointelegraph.com/news/blockchain-for-the-food-how-industry-makes-use-of-the-technology

[74] Ledger Insights (August 2020). Coca Cola bottlers to trial public Ethereum for supply chain transparency. Retrieved March 24, 2022 from   https://www.ledgerinsights.com/coca-cola-bottlers-coke-blockchain-ethereum-baseline/

[75] Van Hoek, R., Fugate, B., Davletshin, M., and Waller, M. (2019). *Integrating Blockchain into Supply Chain Management*, Kogan Page, London.

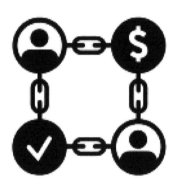

Chapter 8

Business Applications for Credentials

> *What's inside:* Self-sovereign identity (SSI) is a decentralized and automated approach for issuing, holding, and verifying credentials. SSI was introduced in Chapter 1 as one of the major movements leading us to a decentralized Web 3.0. In this chapter, we further explore the pain points with centralized approaches to credentials and how SSI solves them. We explore two case studies. The UK National Health Service (the NHS) developed a digital staff passport to verify health professionals' qualifications and credentials to expedite staff transfers during COVID-19. iDatafy developed SmartResume and a job market platform where individuals' education and skills are verified by authorized issuers so that hiring companies find qualified talent.

Learning objectives:

- Explain the principles and architectural features of SSI.
- Contrast onboarding staff before and after an SSI solution.
- Contrast the hiring process before and after an SSI solution.
- Map the NHS's Digital Staff Passport and iDatafy's SmartResume to the Blockchain Application Framework.
- Describe the governance process for the Digital Staff Passport and SmartResume applications.

8.1. Overview of self-sovereign identity and credentials

Self-sovereign identity (SSI) is a movement spearheaded by global communities to decentralize and automate the issuing, holding, and verifying of credentials made about subjects. It's part of the imperative to evolve the World Wide Web from centralized control by institutions to decentralized control by individuals. SSI empower individuals to possess and control attestations made about them by authorized issuers—like a driver's license or a university diploma—and to provide a more secure and private version of the Internet.

Let's begin by first understanding the terminology. SSI is an unfortunate label, because we—like many academics—view identity as a psychological construct defined by self or as a social construct defined by one's social group. From our perspective, governments and organizations do not provide individuals with 'identities'. Instead, governments and organizations provide individuals with 'credentials', defined as attestations made about subjects by authorized issuers. SSI is all about automating the ecosystem for credentials that comprise issuers, holders, verifiers, and governing authorities. Let's first look at holders since all readers hold credentials.

What are some of your credentials? To answer the question, look inside your physical wallet. Perhaps you have a driver's license issued to you by your State or government; a student ID card issued by your university; a credit card issued by your bank; a membership card issued by a roadside assistance company; a health insurance card issued by your health insurance provider; an awards card issued by your favorite restaurant, or a COVID-19 vaccination card issued by your local health care provider. Your physical wallet holds physical proofs of your credentials, supplied to you by authorized issuers. You present these cards to verifiers as proof of your credentials, such as when you rent a car, borrow a book from your university library, pay your tuition, request a tow truck when your car breaks down, or prove your vaccination status when you travel abroad.

SSI aims to create digital versions of credentials that you will carry around in a digital SSI wallet. You'll have them all in one convenient place. You'll control who gets to see them—that's where the term 'self-sovereign' comes in. These credentials are made about you, the credential holder, and you should have the right to decide with whom to share them. When a verifier requests to see them, you'll decide what to offer as proof.

Student readers will relate to the classic SSI example. When bar tenders need proof that you are of legal drinking age, they ask to see your driver's license. The bar tenders only need to see your date of birth, but they also see your name and address. With an SSI digital wallet, you will just share proof that you are over the legal drinking age, but you'll keep your name and address hidden. This is called the SSI **data minimization** principle, which increases your **privacy**. Moreover, the bar tenders will trust your proof because the digital credentials will be machine verified. The bar tenders' app will look up your State's or issuing body's public key on a public registry (most likely a blockchain registry) to ensure it—and only it—could have created your digital driver's license. The issuer's digital signature of your credential will be verified in seconds. Now you can understand why we think a better labeling of the SSI movement is 'self-sovereign verifiable credentials'—but alas, SSI is the entrenched term, and we shall proceed with that nomenclature.

Back to your physical wallet. Now let's think about the online relationships you have with all those issuers. While your credentials exist in digital form somewhere, you have no control or direct access to them. You have online relationships with some of the issuers, such as your university, bank, insurance company, etc., but they control the online relationship via accounts and passwords. Even if you decide to end a relationship by 'deleting' your account, all you have really accomplished is to deny yourself access to the account. The organizations control the accounts and decide their fate. So from your perspective as the holder of these credentials, you have very little agency. That is another problem SSI aims to solve for holders. Instead of accounts and passwords, you will have equal power in online relationships via peer-to-peer connections.

If SSI only benefited the holders, the other ecosystem participants would have no incentive to adopt the solution. SSI is also designed to solve their pain points. Institutions—including issuers and verifiers—also suffer high costs and high cybersecurity threats from managing accounts and passwords. Every password reset costs, on average, $70.[1] Centralized identity models are honey pots that lure cyber thieves. SSI's peer-to-peer connections offers them a better way to manage their online relationships with us.

Issuers and verifiers also face another problem that SSI solves. Many credentials are fraudulent. One of the most common frauds is claiming a university degree that was not earned. According to *The New York Times*, more than 50,000 doctorates are purchased from diploma mills every year—which exceeds the quantity legitimately awarded.[2] Can you imagine trusting a doctor who never went to medical school? Or a lawyer who never went to law school? Legitimate issuers and verifiers also suffer the consequences of fraudulent claims. Imagine you are the hospital that hired a fake doctor or the law firm that hired the fake lawyer. SSI makes sure that only authorized issuers can create the digital credentials.

Now we are ready to bring these ideas together to examine the *ecosystem* for credentials. The 'trust diamond' visually represents the roles involved in an ecosystem for credentials. Let's use university diplomas as examples. In Figure 8.1, the **governing authority** set rules in the ecosystem by specifying the types of credentials allowed/required in the ecosystem and by specifying who is allowed to issue, hold, and verify credentials. For the University of Arkansas ecosystem, the Board of Trustees of the University of Arkansas is the governing authority. For the University of Wyoming ecosystem, the Board of Trustees of the University of Wyoming is the governing authority. Boards of Trustees have the final say on decisions about degree programs, minimum credit hours, staff qualifications, and designate which campuses are authorized **issuers** of which diplomas. Governing authorities publish their governance frameworks, typically on a website.[i] Students who meet all the requirements for diplomas are the **holders** of

---

i University of Arkansas governance website: https://www.uasys.edu/leadership/

   University of Wyoming governance website: https://www.uwyo.edu/regs-policies/section-1-governance-and-structure/

credentials. **Verifiers** are the individuals and institutions who need proof of diplomas, such as companies that want to hire them. Normally, a hiring company requires transcripts to come directly from the university. This process costs time and money, delaying the onboarding of new employees. SSI solves this problem as well.

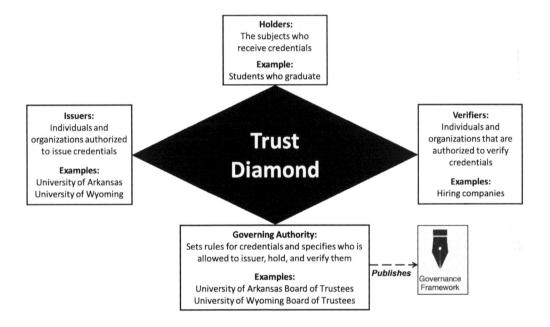

Figure 8.1: The roles involved in an ecosystem for credentials

Many standards-making bodies, open-source working groups, and organizations have been working on SSI and verifiable credentials for years. The Trust over IP (ToIP) Foundation in one prominent group. Founded in May of 2020 by 27 organizations (including the University of Arkansas' Blockchain Center of Excellence), ToIP's mission is to provide a robust, common standard and complete architecture for Internet-scale digital trust. ToIP is managed by the Linux Foundation as an open-source community. ToIP identified 11 principles of SSI, many of which we have discussed already—

decentralization, user control and agency, verifiability & authenticity, privacy and minimal disclosure (see Figure 8.2). The power of the SSI model is that anything that needs a credential is an SSI use case, including a person, a group, an organization, an animal, a physical thing, a digital thing, or a logical thing. That is SSI's first principle, the principle of representation. So the SSI model is not just about people, although our two use cases do focus on humans as holders.

1. Representation
2. Interoperability
3. Decentralization
4. Control & Agency
5. Voluntary Participation
6. Equity & Inclusion

6. Usability
7. Portability
8. Security
9. Verifiability & Authenticity
10. Privacy & Minimum Disclosure
11. Transparency

Figure 8.2: The Principles of SSI

Source: https://trustoverip.org/wp-content/uploads/2021/10/ToIP-Principles-of-SSI.pdf

So far, we've made a lot of promises about SSI. In practice, SSI is still a maturing technology, but the two cases in this chapter have managed to meet many of SSI's aspirations (see Table 8.1).

The National Health Service (the NHS) is the publicly-funded national healthcare system in the United Kingdom (UK). The NHS developed a digital staff passport to verify health professionals' qualifications and credentials so that healthcare staff could be moved quickly around hospitals during the COVID-19 crisis. This application makes use of two architectural features of SSI:

1. Online relationships are peer-to-peer—no need for accounts and passwords

2. The public key infrastructure is decentralized—no need to rely on trusted third parties

The application went live in the summer of 2020, just when the pandemic was stressing hospitals' resources to their limits. The NHS's solution reduced the average onboarding time of doctors from two days to a few minutes. If an organization the size of the NHS—with over 1.1 million employees and which operates in one of the most highly regulated industries—can gain value from SSI, it suggests that many other organizations can gain value as well.

Enterprise	Enterprise Type	Application	Status as of 2022
National Health Service (the NHS)	Public sector	Digital staff passport	Production pilot went live in Summer of 2020. 102 hospitals are registered. The NHS plans to expand the ecosystem and types of credentials.
iDatafy's Smart Resume	Private company	Digital resume and job acquisition platform	Platform is in Beta version, with 25 issuers, 70 verifiers, and 175,000 SmartResumes created (but not necessarily activated).

Table 8.1: Blockchain application examples for credentials

iDatafy's SmartResume is a digital resume where issuers create an individual's credentials, but individuals control access rights to their own resume. The SmartResume platform is more than just a certified digital resume, it is a job acquisition platform that matches qualified job seekers with hiring organizations. While this case study does not use peer-to-peer connections or a decentralized PKI, it still meets many of the aspirations of SSI including verifiable credentials secured by blockchain technology, user control over who sees their credentials, minimal data exposure, voluntary participation, and data privacy.   This case study is fascinating because of the size of the ecosystem. Whereas the NHS solution was adopted within one ecosystem, namely the NHS system of hospitals, SmartResume is bringing hundreds of issuers and verifiers to the platform. Building this vast ecosystem consumed most of iDatafy's efforts, which will be difficult for competitors to replicate.

8.2. The National Health Service[ii]

The story starts in 2019. the NHS was working with several stakeholders to solve the problem of processing staff transfers. More than 1,200 NHS hospitals employ more than 1.1 million people. Every time staff members move from one hospital to another hospital, all their credentials must be re-verified because the NHS hospital systems operate independently and manage their own human resources (HR). Staff must fill in multiple forms to prove their identity, credentials, and prior employment, and nearly half are required to travel to complete the onboarding process in person. Moreover, staff often retake training unnecessarily because they cannot prove their existing credentials. [3]

Given that the NHS frequently ranks among the five largest employers worldwide, the scale of the problem is huge. The NHS onboards or moves staff more than 1 million times per year. Junior doctors, for example, move an average of 10 times during training. More than 100,000 person-days are spent each year verifying junior doctors. The lost hours are worth about £22 million; more importantly, doctors are not caring for patients while waiting for their credentials to be verified. [4]

In 2019, the NHS developed a vision to *"enable staff to more easily move from one NHS employer to another".* [5] The solution would rely on a digital staff passport to share HR records, as well as statutory and mandatory records. Staff members would carry their credentials on their smartphones and control who might see them. The vision was that:

---

ii The NHS case was coauthored Erran Carmel (see contributors)

- All staff would have access to a digital staff passport.

- All workforce (HR) systems would be interoperable.

- All staff would experience a more efficient and focused induction, recognizing previous training and experience. [6]

The NHS envisioned that, in the long term, a staff member's digital wallet would aggregate and hold multiple credentials. It foresaw a solution that is 'future proof', based on open standards and open software for interoperability, thereby avoiding vendor lock-in. For example, the NHS sought to avoid requiring staff to buy a specific phone or to rely exclusively on one vendor's digital wallet. For these reasons, the NHS became interested in SSI and adopted WC3's verifiable credential standard for the digital representation of credentials and OpenID Connect standards for online identification.[7] Figure 8.3 depicts the trust diamond for this application.

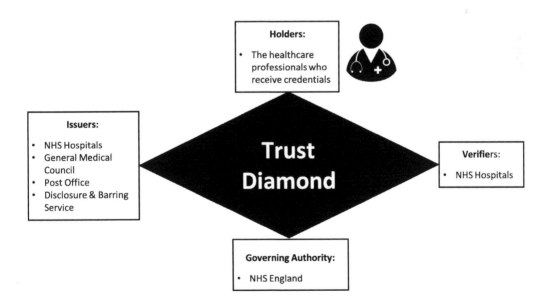

Figure 8.3: The trust diamond for the digital staff passport application

NHS England is the primary **governing authority**. NHS England requires various credentials for a doctor to work in its hospitals, such as a nationally recognized proof of identity (e.g., passport), a General Medical Council (GMC) professional registration license, specific medical certifications (e.g., advanced life support, infectious disease), a Disclosure and Barring Service (DBS) criminal-background check, and prior employment credentials. The doctors (and other healthcare professionals) are the **holders** of the credentials. Hospitals, GMC, the Post Office, and DBS serve as **issuers** of credentials, but the hospitals become **verifiers** when a healthcare professional begins work at their facility. Again, each hospital needs to verify credentials before onboarding any new employee, even for staff who have worked at other NHS hospitals.

The NHS convened a minimal viable ecosystem (MVE) to build the pilot solution. The MVE comprised NHS England, NHSX[iii], General Medical Council (GMC), NHS trusts (e.g., Blackpool Teaching Hospitals, NHS Foundation Trust) and technology providers Accenture, IBM, Oracle, Microsoft, Evernym (since acquired by Avast), and Truu. The technology providers worked on different parts of the pilot solution. For example, Evernym and Truu built the SSI digital wallet, while Microsoft provides the Azure-based cloud service. The MVE spent nine months documenting the before-and-after processes. The 2019 NHSX pilot was ready just before COVID-19 hit, but the pandemic increased the urgency to onboard staff, thereby accelerating the rollout. The NHS anticipated that staff mobility needs would escalate because of COVID-19, and that many new facilities with intensive-care beds and ventilators would be erected.[8]

The production version, referred to as the 'COVID-19 Digital Staff Passport', commenced rollout in early summer 2020. The COVID-19 Digital Staff Passport was named for why it was deployed, i.e., to quickly verify skills and credentials during the pandemic; it did not capture or track COVID-19 immunization status. The solution comprises many component parts, such as interfaces to HR systems, but in this chapter, we focus on how the edge technologies automate the trust diamond. Specifically, we

---

iii NHSX is a joint unit between the UK Department of Health and Social Care, the NHS England, and the NHS Improvement.

cover SSI digital wallets and the blockchain-enabled public key infrastructure (PKI) that is used to machine verify credentials.

For the production pilot, the NHS adopted Evernym's SSI wallet, called Connect.me. Figure 8.4 shows some user screens. The figure, of course, shows fictitious data since it would be against the SSI privacy principle to share real data. The first screen displays the peer-to-peer connections that replace accounts and passwords. The second screen shows the holder's credentials. The credentials were created by authorized issuers who invited the holder to upload them to the holder's wallet. The third screen shot shows how the holder shares credentials with verifiers. We'll explain how all this works from a process perspective in a minute.

An SSI solution relies on a digital trust registry, which is almost always a public blockchain-enabled registry. Its primary use is to serve as a decentralized public key infrastructure (PKI). Before SSI, issuers and verifiers rely on trusted-third parties called certificate authorities (CAs) to certify digital signatures. As we learned in Chapter 3, digital signatures use a public key to verify that only the sender with possession of the private key could have sent the message. PKI is also used to ensure that users are connecting to the right website. CAs store organizations' public keys on their centralized registries. Just as most holders do not like that their accounts and passwords are controlled by organizations, most issuers and verifiers do not like that certificate authorities control their public keys. SSI allows issuers and verifiers to control their own public keys, managed by a decentralized PKI.[9]

For the NHS digital staff passport, only two things need to be stored on the decentralized registry: the public keys of the governing authority and issuers and the data format (called a schema) for the credentials. The NHS chose to use the Sovrin Network for its decentralized PKI. The Sovrin Foundation, a nonprofit organization, manages the Sovrin Network and provides support for the network's open-source governance, operations, and community engagement. It uses distributed ledger technology. The PKI is distributed across a network of over 80 authorized nodes in six Continents. The Sovrin Network is a public-permissioned blockchain, meaning anyone can use it, but you need permission to operate a validator node.[10]

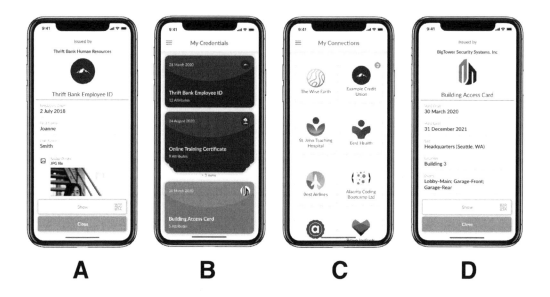

A B C D

A: The holder receives a credential issued by an authorized issuer

B. The holder's wallet stores credentials shared by multiple issuers

C. The holder's collection of peer-to-peer connections

D. The holder shares a credential with a verifier

Figure 8.4: Example of an SSI wallet

Source: https://www.evernym.com/wp-content/uploads/2020/10/connectme-ui-1024x476.jpg

To set up the application, NHS England, serving as the governing authority, made the first entry on the Sovrin Network to publicize its public key and data schema. Next, each hospital that joins creates and posts its public key to the trust registry on the Sovrin Network. When a hospital is in the role of an *issuer* of a verifiable credential, the hospital's app uses the NHS England data schema to format the credential and signs the digital credential with the hospital's private key. When a hospital is in the role of a *verifier* of a credential, its app looks up the public key on the Sovrin Network to make sure the credential was signed by an authorized issuer. The private keys and credentials are stored locally on SSI digital wallets. To be clear: credentials are NOT stored on the public registry and holders do not need to publish public keys. It's a very lightweight use of blockchain. Under the hood, there are several new enabling technologies, most notably of which is a new type of identifier called a decentralized identify (DID). See the glossary for more on DIDs.

Let's use a fictitious scenario to understand how credentials are issued, held, and verified in the application. Dr. Julia Madden is being transferred from a hospital in Oxford to a hospital in London. In Figure 8.5, Dr. Madden's first stop is Oxford's HR department. The HR person thanks her for her service and asks, *"Before you move to London, would you like to try a new digital onboarding process that takes only a few minutes, or do you prefer the old manual process which takes a couple of days?"* The HR person also explains the additional benefits, such as carrying all required credentials in one convenient place on her phone, providing backup and recovery of her credentials in case her phone is lost or damaged, and controlling who sees her credentials. Dr. Madden agrees to try the new application. The HR person instructs Dr. Madden to download the Evernym's Connect.Me SSI digital wallet app from Apple or Google. The next key step is **identity binding** to ensure that credentials are created for Dr. Madden. The HR person retrieves information from the employee database including verification with a photo of Dr. Madden from the hospital's database.

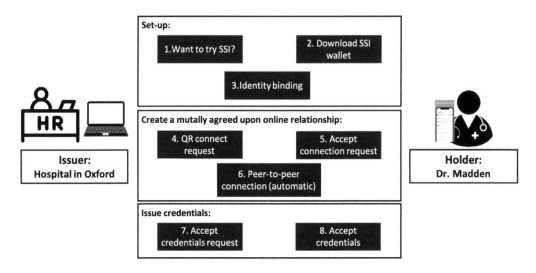

Figure 8.5: Outgoing staff HR transfer process

Once the individual's identity is confirmed, the next steps establish a relationship between the Oxford hospital and Dr. Madden. HR sends Dr. Madden a QR code to request a peer-to-peer connection. The QR code includes the hospital's public key and connection invitation. One can think of the QR code as a sort of public email address and email invite for this hospital. She accepts the invitation on her SSI wallet. When Dr. Madden scans the QR code, a unique and private peer-to-peer connection is established inside each side's SSI wallet. It's all automatic—no accounts or passwords are needed. The wallets keep track of the relationship and both sides have equal power to delete the relationship when they want.

Next, the HR person sends Dr. Madden's SSI wallet a request to upload her verifiable credentials. These credentials were extracted from the HR system and formatted for the SSI app. Dr. Madden must accept the invitation before her credentials are added to her SSI wallet. (Unlike cryptocurrency wallets where a sender can air drop cryptocurrency into someone's digital wallet without the holder's permission, holders are in complete control of who they connect with and what data goes in their SSI digital wallets.) She accepts the invitation and *voilà*, she has proof of citizenship, medical licenses, specialty licenses, and criminal background checks all in one convenient place and under her control.

Dr. Madden arrives at her new job in London and meets with HR. The HR person is glad Dr. Madden selected to onboard with the SSI app because her credentials can be verified in a few minutes (see Figure 8.6). First, HR sends her a connect request. After Dr. Madden accepts the invitation on her phone, her SSI wallet now keeps track of two peer-to-peer relationships, one with her prior hospital in Oxford and one at her new place of employment in London. Next, HR asks Dr. Madden to prove her credentials. She opens her app and sends her verified credentials to HR. The verifier's app doesn't just accept Dr. Madden's credentials, the app first pings the Sovrin Network to retrieve the public key from the hospital in Oxford to verify that it—and only it—could have created Dr. Madden's credentials. Dr. Madden is now ready to start work.

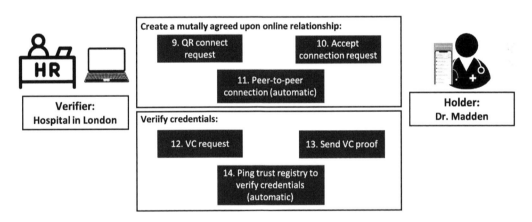

Figure 8.6: Incoming HR staff transfer process

The NHS established a support center to assist passport adopters with any questions, concerns, or issues through its business services organization. The center provides three tiers of support. The most frequent issues are minor connection problems, such as a lack of cellphone service coverage in some areas of a hospital.

As of March 2022, 102 NHS hospitals have registered to use the system.[11] The NHS did not disclose the number of staff adopters.

The NHS summarized the positive experience to date, including:

- **Staff control:** Staff control their own digital identity, employment checks, credentials, and core skills training.

- **Staff empowerment:** Staff are empowered at every step to accept, reject, and share information.

- **Transparency:** Staff know who has seen their information and for what purpose, ensuring their privacy and security.

- **Single sources of truth:** One verifiable credential is issued and is interoperable, reducing duplication.

- **Time savings:** Instead of spending days to onboard, the process takes only a few minutes.

- **Valid data:** Verifiers now have a machine-readable way to automatically verify holders' claims.

- **Better healthcare services:** Healthcare providers more quickly get to the core business of caring for patients.[12]

For the first phase of the application, NHS hospitals operate on a property of **transitive trust**. If Hospital A (like the Oxford hospital in our scenario) has verified that a doctor has a GMC professional registration license, it issues the doctor a verifiable credential of that license. Other hospitals in the network can use that verification as proof that the doctor is licensed. In future releases, the ecosystem will expand to include the GMC, Post Office, DBS, immunization providers, and other issuers. The NHS also plans to adopt multiple wallets to prevent vendor lock-in and to expand identity binding to include biometrics.

Figure 8.7 maps the digital staff passport to the Blockchain Application Framework developed in Chapter 3. This figure only captures the part of the end-to-end solution that touches the Sovrin Network to verify the digital signatures.

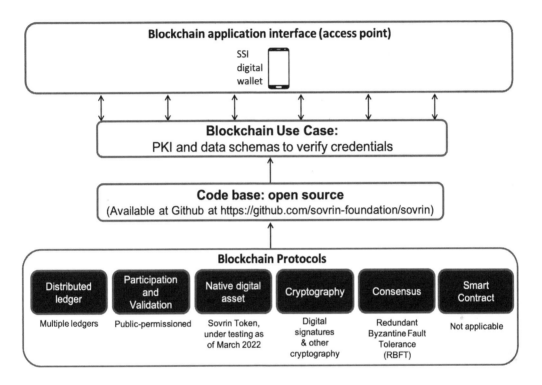

Figure 8.7: Sovrin Network mapped to the Blockchain Application Framework

Distributed ledger. According to the Sovrin Foundation's technical white paper, the Sovrin Network maintains four distributed ledgers, each structured as a set of sequenced transactions:

1. *"**The Identity ledger** is the primary ledger—the system of record for all identity records written by Sovrin identity owners.*

2. *"**The Pool ledger** is the system of record for what Sovrin nodes are permitted, at any one point it time, to serve as validator or observer nodes. The Pool ledger stores the outcome of node votes on the Voting ledger. This ledger plays a key role in verified node discovery.*

3. *The Voting ledger is where votes among trustees and stewards are held to propose, confirm, or revoke different permissions, e.g., whether a node is permitted to serve as a validator or observer node.*

4. *The Config ledger holds network-wide configuration data set by the Sovrin Foundation Technical Governance Board and approved by the Board of Trustees. Examples include: How many trustee votes are required to approve a new trustee. How many steward votes are required to approve a new steward. What time intervals should be used by nodes when posting throughput metrics.*"[13]

The Sovrin Network's identity ledger stores public keys, data schemas for formatting credentials, revocation registries for issuers to easily revoke a holder's credential, and agent authorization policies for holders to easily revoke access, say in the instance of a lost smartphone. The ledger is open to the public and may be viewed at https://indy-scan.io/txs/SOVRIN_MAINNET/domain or https://sovrin-mainnet-browser.vonx.io/. To look up the NHS's transactions, search for the NHS-X COVID-19 EO.[14]

Native digital asset. Sovrin's native digital asset is called the Sovrin Token. It was still in a testing phase as of early 2022. In the future, it could be used to provide an independent payment option for the Sovrin Network.[15]

Consensus. The Sovrin Network is a public-permissioned network, meaning that anyone may submit transactions, but only authorized stewards may run validator nodes. The Sovrin Foundation has legal agreements with the validator nodes. Its consensus mechanism is an enhanced version of the RBFT (Redundant Byzantine Fault Tolerant) protocol.[16] Observer nodes are authorized to read the ledger (see Figure 8.8).

Smart Contract. Sovrin's technical documents do not mention smart contracts.

Code base. The code case is available at https://github.com/sovrin-foundation/sovrin.

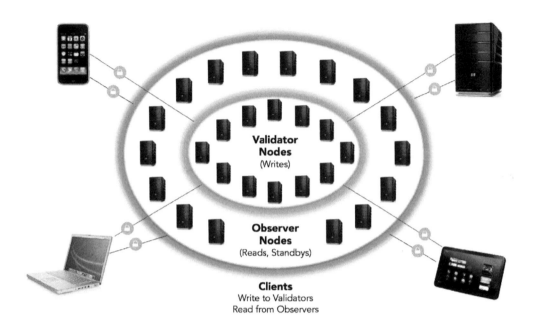

Figure 8.8: Incoming HR staff transfer process

Source: Sovrin Foundation[17]

Application interfaces. The Sovrin Network is accessed through an SSI digital wallet. By August 2020, three SSI wallets were compatible with the Sovrin Network: Trinsic, Lissi, and Connect.me.[18]

There is no need for APIs. According to the technical write paper, *"Many systems integrate with APIs in order to exchange the same kind of information that is inside verifiable claims. With verifiable claims, data is conveyed by the person or organization presenting the claim rather than through a preprogrammed API integration. Your business can use the information in a verifiable claim without any API integration, without a contract, or even without a preexisting business relationship."*[19]

Governance. The Sovrin Foundation's Board of Trustees is the approving body for decisions about the Sovrin Foundation. *"Members are selected to represent diverse expertise from across multiple industries and geographies, ensuring that special interests—whether commercial, governmental, or otherwise—do not unduly influence decision."*[20] The Sovrin Foundation published its Sovrin Governance Framework (SGF), which serves as the legal foundation of the Sovrin Network.[21] The SGF Working Group (SGFWG) developed the framework, and it was approved by the Board of Trustees. As far as changes to the code base, Hyperledger Indy manages the ledger code base and Hyperledger Aries manages the wallet standards. Changes must be approved by the Hyperledger Technical Steering Committee (TSC) (see Chapter 4).

8.3. iDatafy SmartResume

"37% of 'bad hires' are the result of credential or skill misrepresentation."

PwC Research[22]

Before presenting the SmartResume solution, we must first understand better the talent acquisition challenges it's designed to overcome. Despite all the advanced Human Resource (HR) practices, investments, and technology innovations, we have yet to solve adequately this talent acquisition problem: ***How can we create a trustworthy job market that efficiently matches qualified job seekers with hiring organizations?***

Peter Cappelli, the George W. Taylor Professor of Management at the Wharton School and director of the Center for Human Resources, summarized the challenge nicely in a *Harvard Business Review article*: *"Businesses have never done as much hiring as they do today. They've never spent as much money doing it. And they've never done a worse job of it."*[23]

Today's talent acquisition solutions include hundreds of job market and social media platforms like CareerBuilder, Indeed, LinkedIn, and Monster. According to one study, social media is now the most-used channel for recruitment efforts: 77 percent of recruiters

346

used LinkedIn, followed by Facebook (63 percent) and Instagram (35 percent).[24] While such solutions do have the advantages of convenience and scale, they equally frustrate job seekers and recruiters. Distrust happens on both sides of the market. Specifically, recruiters doubt applicants' self-reported credentials and skills, while job seekers distrust that hiring companies and platforms keep their data private and select applicants in an unbiased manner. These misgivings are warranted.

Many applicants inflate their skills or make fraudulent claims on their resumes. Job sites and social media platforms do not verify credentials. Subsequently, fraud and inflated resumes remain problematic. A recent survey found that 75 percent of employers caught applicants lying on their resumes.[25] Consequently, hiring companies spend significant resources to investigate a job candidate's claims. Verification slows down the process and increases costs. On average, it costs companies $4,129 per hire,[26] but costs can be as high as $40,000 per position for highly skilled workers.[27] Moreover, honest job applicants grow weary of the assumption of duplicity.

Hiring organizations and recruiters struggle with selection bias. Social media and many job site platforms reveal people's race, gender, age, religion, affiliations, and life-style choices, and recruiters may (in)advertently dismiss candidates based on this data rather than based on their qualifications. Some large companies have turned to artificial intelligence (AI) to modernize recruitment, but so far results have done little to reduce biases. For example, Amazon's AI recruiting tool was designed to search for keywords based on past engineering candidates' resumes. Since most engineers were male in the past, the AI tool learned to prefer male applicants. Amazon abandoned the tool after the gender bias was revealed.[28] Social media, job site platforms, and AI tools are not the only sources of selection bias; relying on referrals from current employees creates a homogeneous applicant pool because people tend to refer people who are similar to them.[29]

Data privacy protection is another concern for all parties. Hiring organizations—particularly those 60 percent of companies that outsource recruiting—need to make sure applicant data is properly handled. In the US, for example, the Family Educational Rights and Privacy Act (FERPA) protects the privacy of student education records. Generally, schools must have written permission from the parent or eligible student before releasing any information about a student's education record. Increasingly, data privacy regulations like the European Union's General Data Protection Regulation (GDPR) and California Consumer Privacy Act (CCPA) have increased data protection more broadly. Despite these regulations, many job sites and recruiters routinely collect information on applicants like email addresses, phone numbers, age, ethnicity, photos, and other personal information.[30]

The scale of the job acquisition challenges is huge. According to the United States Department of Labor, there were 75.6 million job hires in the US in 2021.[31] On average, there were 250 applications for each corporate job listing,[32] suggesting that hiring organizations processed about 19 billion applications. Furthermore, the process does not always end successfully; millions of job openings went unfilled in 2021.[33] Isn't it time to re-invent job acquisition? iDatafy thinks so, and subsequently developed the SmartResume solution to restore trust in the job search process.

iDatafy, a company founded by David Wengel in Little Rock, Arkansas in 2011, created the SmartResume platform and career network to instill trust in the talent acquisition process. The platform prevents fraudulent claims by applicants, eliminates selection bias, and ensures data privacy compliance. The SmartResume platform is similar to LinkedIn or Upwork, but with *verified* credentials secured by blockchain technology. Wengel's vision is to make the SmartResume platform, *"the world's most trusted resume and certified career network."*

To launch the career network, iDatafy needed to attract a critical mass of issuers and holders before hiring organizations would find the platform useful. The platform is free for issuers and holders. The platform also is free for verifiers during the Beta version period, but hiring companies eventually will pay a fee to connect, recruit and hire certified job talent on the platform.

The first credentialing organization was the Sam M. Walton College of Business at the University of Arkansas. In 2018, the Walton College was just about to launch the Blockchain Center of Excellence (BCoE), and the Dean of the College, Matt Waller, was looking for a blockchain project where the college could help lead in the development and implementation of an actual solution. He met Wengel shortly after the Walton College's first *Blockchain for Business Conference* in April of 2018. Waller thought the SmartResume context of credentialing students seemed a perfect fit:

> *"If you think about it, colleges and universities have been issuing diplomas and transcripts for hundreds of years, but they have never actually issued certified resumes to their students, despite the colleges being in a position as a trusted authority to do so."*

Matthew Waller, dean of the Sam M. Walton College of Business, University of Arkansas, and first adopter of SmartResume[34]

Waller convened meetings with leaders within the Walton College and across campus to determine the university's role in the initiative, including the campus CIO, the vice chancellor for economic development, the founding director of the BCoE, the chair of the information systems department (ISYS), and the associate vice provost from the registrar's office. While most of the leaders were supportive of the idea, they were initially concerned about adding another IT project given the campus was in the middle of an enterprise resource planning (ERP) replacement. They did not want to build an interface to pull student records from a system that was about to be replaced. Wengel listened. iDatafy created a simple process for issuers to extract and verify data, initially with spreadsheets, while iDatafy did the cleanup and formatting for verifiable credentials.

iDatafy realized that rather than sell to one campus at it time, the ecosystem could be built faster with an agreement with the University of Arkansas System—the centralized administration for public institutions of higher learning in the State. Michael Moore, vice president for academic affairs for the University of Arkansas System saw the value.

"A couple of things were appealing to me from the University of Arkansas System and eVersity perspective," he said. *"The platform provides an opportunity to elevate some of our students attending schools that might not get attention from big corporate partners. Also, it's free to use for our students."* iDatafy signed one Memorandum of Understanding (MoU) with the University of Arkansas System in 2019. By March 2020, six University of Arkansas System campuses were issuing SmartResumes.[35]

Besides public education issuers, other issuers joined the platform. For example, the Forge Institute—based in Arkansas—provides cybersecurity training and can now issue cybersecurity credentials to people who successfully complete their programs onto the SmartResume platform. iDatafy was also part of a $13.5 million grant from the US Department of Education along with the University of Arkansas and Shorter College to issue SmartResumes for training participants that completed the Arkansas-based programs.[36] By early 2022, 25 issuers had created 175,000 certified SmartResumes and 70 employers had signed on.

The next phase will scale the SmartResume nationally. In February 2022, iDatafy partnered with the National Student Clearinghouse to load its Comprehensive Learner Records from the Clearinghouse's Myhub digital wallet onto the SmartResume platform. Millions of students will be able to activate a SmartResume on demand through Myhub.

Figure 8.9 maps the SmartResume platform to the trust diamond. iDatafy serves as the **governing authority** over the platform. In Chapter 2, we called this the neutral facilitator or founder-led model. To ensure trust, SmartResume has earned both Comprehensive Learner Record (CLR) and Data Privacy Certification by the IMS Global Learning Consortium. IMS Global Learning Consortium is a non-profit organization that advances technology to scale and improves educational participation and attainment affordably.[37] iDatafy's solution is also FERPA-compliant.

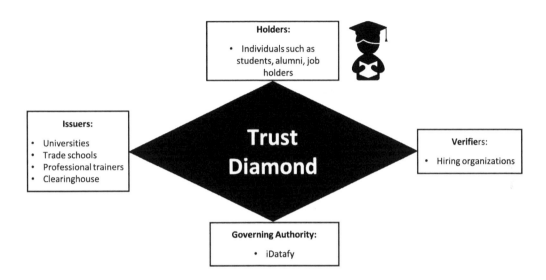

Figure 8.9: The trust diamond for the SmartResume platform

Issuers are institutions that award credentials, such as colleges, universities, trade schools, professional associations, licensing bureaus, and government organizations. In the SmartResume platform, issuers create a SmartResume on behalf of an individual by certifying educational degrees, coursework, honors, activities, awards, experiences, licenses, affiliations, research, skills, reference letters, or other certifications. The certifications appear on an individual's SmartResume as a tamper-proof badge that is secured by blockchain technology (see Figure 8.10).

As a key design decision, credentialing organizations choose the name and type of credential. This way, credentialing organizations gain value by promoting their brand. For example, the Walton College chose 'Leadership Walton' as one of its credentials. Leadership Walton is a professional development program for undergraduate business students, offering them a unique blend of academic, leadership, and career development opportunities specifically designed to guide them toward lifelong professional success.[38]

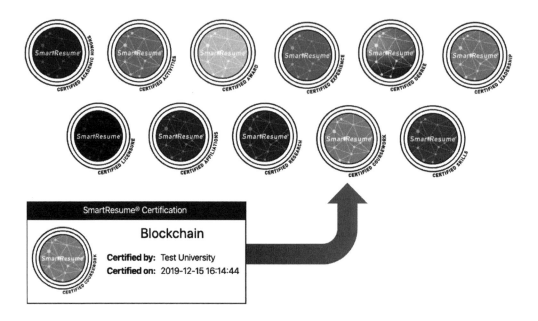

Figure 8.10: Example of SmartResume®'s certified badges
Each certification is secured on a tamper-proof ledger stored on a blockchain

By putting credentialing organizations in control, the SmartResume platform prevents users from claiming credentials they did not earn, thus protecting the organization's brand. They also gain efficiencies by credentialing a person *once*, rather than re-affirming credentials every time a person changes employment. For educational institutions, an additional benefit of joining the SmartResume platform is that it serves as a meaningful way to connect with alumni. For workforce skill certifiers—such as organizations that train and certify truck drivers; steamfitters, pipefitters, sprinkler systems installers; and heating, ventilation, and air conditioning (HVAC) technicians—the platform will provide better access for hiring companies to find qualified talent.

Holders like students, alumni, current job holders, and job seekers cannot launch their own SmartResumes. Rather, a credentialing organization must do so on the individual's behalf. However, individuals must opt in to the SmartResume platform; if an individual does not activate their SmartResume, it is not accessible by any third party. Individuals who activate their resumes can supplement their personal SmartResume with additional information, such as career objectives, hobbies, and interests. Hiring organizations can ascertain which credentials were verified by credentialing organizations by the presence of the blockchain badge and which entries were added by holders. Each individual gets one SmartResume, which may contain verified credentials from many different organizations. Individuals are in control of their job matching preferences and may grant or deny full access rights to hiring organizations.

Hiring organizations are the **verifiers,** and include any institution searching for qualified employees. Hiring organizations (or outsourced recruiters) search for qualified candidates based only on their skills, as all demographic and personal information like name and gender are masked to prevent search bias. Figure 8.11 depicts a sample resume as it would appear to a hiring organization. If an organization is interested in connecting to an individual, the platform sends the individual an email request. Hiring organizations gain efficiencies by having a qualified applicant pool, and they no longer must call each organization on a candidate's resume to verify credentials.

Let's now look under the hood. The SmartResume platform is a hybrid platform that includes a web-based interface, traditional technologies, and a permissioned blockchain ledger. iDatafy chose a hybrid solution to take advantage of the features for which blockchain technologies and traditional technologies are best suited. Blockchain technology was selected to create a tamper-proof audit trail of verified credentials in a multi-party environment. Traditional databases were selected for high performance and scalability processes, such as searching for jobs and job candidates, enhancing SmartResumes with supplemental information, mapping credentials to Standard Occupation Codes, and protecting personal information.

SmartResume®

A Resume You Can Trust.™

| Employers | Educator Institutions | Workforce Skill Certifiers | Individuals |

SmartResume   JOB APPLICANT IDATIFIER™ A46B89BZM48X

EDUCATION

Bachelor of Science in Business Administration Finance
University of Arkansas, Fayetteville, AR
Expected Graduation Date: May 2020

Honors Program GPA 3.75/4.0
Dean's List - Fall 2017 and Spring 2018

EXPERIENCE

Investment and Insurance Compliance Assistant
Arvest Asset Management, Fayetteville, AR
January 2018 - Present

- Member of the AIC Arvest Insurance team for AAM, a brokerage firm branch or Arvest Bank
- Maintained licensure files for all Arvest Insurance Agents
- Assisted with new and renewed agent appointments with insurance companies
- Performed other managerial and secretarial duties such as faxing, scanning, telephone communication with agents and companies

Orientation Leader/Mentor, Office of First Year Experience
University of Arkansas, Fayetteville, AR, May 2017 - December 2017

- Assisted with the on-going planning, implementation, and evaluation of new student orientation
- Worked as a paraprofessional in presenting and distributing information to new students and guests
- Initiated and develop open communication and interaction with students and guests
- Served as a positive role model and ambassador on behalf of the University of Arkansas

Course Reserve Assistant, Mullins Library
University of Arkansas, Fayetteville, AR, September 2016 - May 2017

- Scanned for electronic reserves, gaining proficiency with Adobe software
- Prepared usage reports of electronic reserves
- Facilitated on-going communication with professors about individual needs for reserves
- Trained new employees on software and procedure

⟶

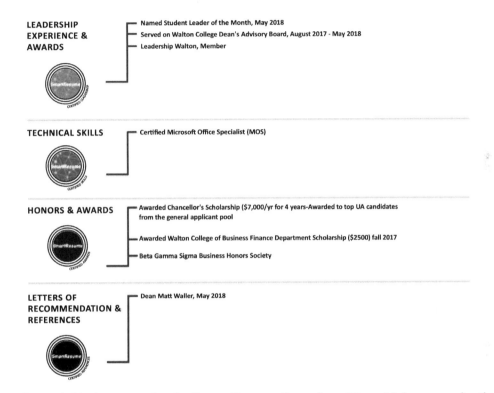

LEADERSHIP
EXPERIENCE &
AWARDS

- Named Student Leader of the Month, May 2018
- Served on Walton College Dean's Advisory Board, August 2017 - May 2018
- Leadership Walton, Member

TECHNICAL SKILLS

- Certified Microsoft Office Specialist (MOS)

HONORS & AWARDS

- Awarded Chancellor's Scholarship ($7,000/yr for 4 years-Awarded to top UA candidates from the general applicant pool
- Awarded Walton College of Business Finance Department Scholarship ($2500) fall 2017
- Beta Gamma Sigma Business Honors Society

LETTERS OF
RECOMMENDATION &
REFERENCES

- Dean Matt Waller, May 2018

Figure 8.11: An example of a SmartResume® as viewed by a hiring organization
Source: With permission from iDatafy

Andy Griebel, Chief Technology Officer (CTO), explained, *"We selected a hybrid solution. Blockchain technology provides the ability for multiple parties to verify and trust that credentials are valid. But it would be a mistake to build the entire solution on a blockchain because it would be sluggish."* From a user perspective, all the components operate seamlessly. People maneuver through the platform based on their roles, such as employers, educational institutions, workforce skill certifiers, and individuals.

Figure 8.12 maps the blockchain part of the SmartResume platform to the Blockchain Application Framework. iDatafy chose a private-permissioned blockchain where joining the network is by invitation-only and where only authorized members validate transactions. In 2018, iDatafy had examined several permissioned blockchains, but ultimately selected Hyperledger Fabric. iDatafy felt it had the most maturity and momentum at the time. However, iDatafy could switch platforms if a superior technology emerges. Andy Griebel, iDatafy's CTO said, *"Our design is flexible; we could pivot to another platform if we needed to."*

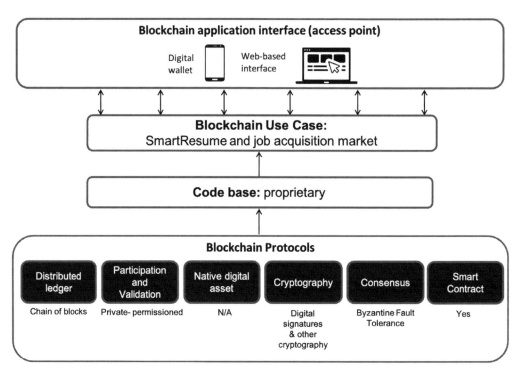

Figure 8.12: SmartResume mapped to the Blockchain Application Framework

Distributed ledger. Hyperledger Fabric structures ledgers as a chain of blocks. To comply with privacy regulations, no personal information is stored on the blockchain ledger. Instead, each SmartResume is associated with a unique Job Applicant Idatafier™. iDatafy only stores a minimum of information on the blockchain ledger associated with each credential, including the unique Job Applicant Idatafier™, credentialing organization, certification type, date, and timestamp.

Consensus: Hyperledger Fabric uses Byzantine Fault Tolerance (see Chapter 3). Consensus in Hyperledger Fabric is broken out into three phases: Endorsement, Ordering, and Validation:

1. *"Endorsement is driven by policy (requiring m out of n signatures) upon which participants endorse a transaction.*

2. *Ordering phase accepts the endorsed transactions and agrees to the order to be committed to the ledger.*

3. *Validation takes a block of ordered transactions and validates the correctness of the results, including checking endorsement policy and double-spending."[39]*

Native digital asset: Hyperledger Fabric does not use a native digital token.

Smart contracts: Hyperledger Fabric has smart contract capabilities.

Governance: iDatafy serves as the governing authority over the platform, best described as a neutral facilitator or founder-led model. iDatafy also chose a founder-led model for its SmartResume platform, with iDatafy serving as the benevolent dictator entrusted with driving results. iDatafy is a neutral party that does not compete against any partners of SmartResume because it's not a credentialing or hiring organization. Wengel said, *"iDatafy is a kind of middle person, but we're also able to stay laser focused on this, and I think it has become very clear that a dedicated persistence is needed to drive new things forward."*

User interface. The user interface is constantly evolving and improving, but Figure 8.13 provides an example of an individual resume holder's view as of March 2022. Students will also be able to access the platform through the Myhub digital wallet.

357

Business Applications for Credentials

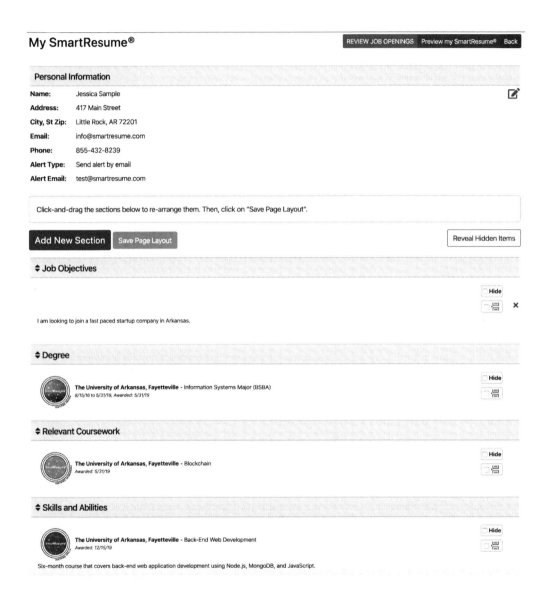

Figure 8.13: Screenshot for SmartResume® holders

8.4. Conclusion

In this chapter, we discussed SSI as a model to decentralize and automate the issuing, holding, and verifying of credentials made about subjects. We presented two cases of early adopters. Both cases ensure that credentials are created by an authorized issuer, shared with holders, and proven to verifiers (verifiable credentials). Both solutions put the holders in control of with whom to share their credentials. Both solutions integrate distributed ledgers with traditional systems of record; the NHS integrated the digital staff passport with its HR systems and iDatafy integrated the blockchain application with more traditional technologies. The NHS case is closer to the full vision of SSI—peer-to-peer connections and decentralized PKI compared to the SmartResume platform.

As of 2022, more SSI applications are in production, including an app for Syrian refugees set up by the World Food Program; digital health passes to create COVID-19 status credentials for vaccinations, tests, and approved recovery; and the Canadian government's issuance of business licenses.[40] But SSI is still a young technology. In 2021, Gartner positioned 'SSI Decentralized Identity' at the peak of inflated expectations on its famous Hype Cycle.[41] This seems like a correct judgement. After all, SSI is an ecosystem play. And ecosystems are hard and slow to build. The major lesson from the SmartResume case is that building the ecosystem consumed most of iDatafy's time and resources, but this erects a barrier to entry because competitors will not easily be able to replicate it. Dave Wengel, founder and CEO, iDatafy said:

> *"Obviously, there are people out there doing blockchain diplomas, blockchain transcripts, and blockchain credential matching. No one has, to our knowledge, anywhere in the world, built a certified resume. Even if someone were to copy what we are doing, we know how difficult it is to build a community."*

With time, more organizations will build SSI capabilities. Upgraded versions of the technology will be released and standards in provisional status today will be finalized. Gartner anticipates that SSI will pull out of the 'trough of disillusionment' between 2023 and 2026. But as we noted in Chapter 4, industries and companies within industries adopt technologies at different rates.

Citations

[1] Douglas, A. (2020). Are Password Resets Costing Your Company? Retrieved November 3, 2021 from https://www.bioconnect.com/are-password-resets-costing-your-company/

[2] National Student ClearingHouse. Your Organization's Reputation on the Line: The Real Cost of Academic Fraud. Retrieved March 15, 2022 from https://nscverifications.org/wp-content/uploads/2016/06/CostOfAcademicFraud.pdf

[3] The NHS (2020/2021). We are the NHS: People Plan for 2020/2021. Retrieved December 2, 2021, from https://www.england.nhs.uk/wp-content/uploads/2020/07/We-Are-The-NHS-Action-For-All-Of-Us-FINAL-March-21.pdf

[4] *The Independent* (August 4, 2021). NHS entrepreneurs are revolutionising staffing checks. Retrieved October 31, 2021, from https://www.independent.co.uk/news/business/business-reporter/nhs-entrepreneurs-revolutionise-staffing-checks-b1883780.html

[5] Graham, P. (2021). Enabling Staff Movement & Digital Staff Passports, NYHDIF Conference presentation, November 11/12, 2021.

[6] Graham, P. (2021). Enabling Staff Movement & Digital Staff Passports, NYHDIF Conference presentation, November 11/12, 2021.

[7] The W3C was founded in 1994 by Tim Berners-Lee, inventor of the World Wide Web. W3C oversees W3C/IETF standards for the Internet protocol suite; communities include the Decentralized Identifier Working Group and the Verifiable Credentials Working Group. The Verifiable Credentials Data Model is available at: https://www.w3.org/TR/vc-data-model/ OpenID Connect allows verification of user identity based on the authentication performed by an Authorization Server, as well as to obtain the user's basic profile information in an interoperable. See: https://openid.net/connect/

[8] Microsoft (March 15, 2021). The NHS rapidly meets clinical demands using verified credentials. Retrieved January 19, 2022, from https://customers.microsoft.com/en-us/story/1348169400682329017-nhs-foundation-trust-health-provider-m365

[9] Allen, C., Brock, A., Buterin, V., Callas, J., Dorje, D., Lundkvist, C., Kravchenko, P., Nelson, J., Reed, D., Sabadello, M., Slepak, G., Thorp, N., and Wood, H. (2015). Decentralized Public Key Infrastructure. https://github.com/WebOfTrustInfo/rwot1-sf/blob/master/final-documents/dpki.pdf

[10] https://sovrin.org/

[11] For a list of participating hospitals, see https://beta.staffpassports.nhs.uk/registered-organisations

[12] Graham, P. (2021). Enabling Staff Movement & Digital Staff Passports, NYHDIF Conference presentation, November 11/12, 2021.

[13] Sovrin Foundation (2016). The Technical Foundations of Sovrin. Retrieved March 17, 2022 from https://www.evernym.com/wp-content/uploads/2017/07/The-Technical-Foundations-of-Sovrin.pdf

[14] https://indyscan.io/txs/SOVRIN_MAINNET/domain?page=1&pageSize=50&filterTxNames=[]&sortFromRecent=true&search=C19EOJobRole

[15] Sovrin Foundation (February 25, 2020). https://sovrin.org/sovrin-foundation-launches-test-token-for-decentralized-identity-network/

[16] https://www.evernym.com/wp-content/uploads/2017/07/The-Technical-Foundations-of-Sovrin.pdf

[17] Sovrin Foundation (2016). The Technical Foundations of Sovrin. Retrieved March 17, 2022 from https://www.evernym.com/wp-content/uploads/2017/07/The-Technical-Foundations-of-Sovrin.pdf

[18] Sovrin Foundation (August 27, 2020). Interoperability Series: Sovrin Stewards Achieve Breakthrough in Wallet Portability. Retrieved March 17, 2022 from https://sovrin.org/sovrin-stewards-wallet-portability/.

[19] Sovrin Foundation (2018). Sovrin™: A Protocol and Token for Self-Sovereign Identity and Decentralized Trust. Retrieved March 17, 2022 from https://sovrin.org/wp-content/uploads/Sovrin-Protocol-and-Token-White-Paper.pdf

[20] Sovrin Foundation Board of Trustees: https://sovrin.org/team/

[21] Sovrin Foundation Governance Framework: https://sovrin.org/library/sovrin-governance-framework/

[22] Ledger Insights (2019). PwC launches blockchain credentialing solution, https://www.ledgerinsights.com/pwc-blockchain-smart-credentials/

[23] Cappelli, P. (2019). Your Approach to Hiring is All Wrong, Harvard Business Review, https://hbr.org/2019/05/recruiting

[24] Jobvite (2018). Recruiter National Survey, https://www.jobvite.com/wp-content/uploads/2018/11/2018-Recruiter-Nation-Study.pdf

[25] CareerBuilder (2017). 75% of HR Managers Have Caught a Lie on a Resume. http://press.careerbuilder.com/2017-09-14-75-of-HR-Managers-Have-Caught-a-Lie-on-a-Resume-According-to-a-New-CareerBuilder-Survey

[26] Turczynski, B. (January 9, 2020), 2020 HR Statistics: Job Search, Hiring, Recruiting & Interviews,

Zety, https://zety.com/blog/hr-statistics#job-search-statistics

[27] National Student Clearing House (2016). The real cost of academic fraud. https://nscverifications.org/wp-content/uploads/2016/06/CostOfAcademicFraud.pdf

[28] Hamilton, I. (October 10, 2018). Amazon built an AI tool to hire people but had to shut it down because it was discriminating against women, Business Insider, https://www.businessinsider.com/amazon-built-ai-to-hire-people-discriminated-against-women-2018-10

[29] Fatemi, F. (October 31, 2019). How AI is Uprooting Recruiting, *Forbes,* https://www.forbes.com/sites/falonfatemi/2019/10/31/how-ai-is-uprooting-recruiting/#43c6540f46ce

[30] Smits, J. (2018). Privacy in recruitment – Securing your candidate's data, https://cammio.com/blog/privacy-in-recruitment/

[31] US Bureau of Labor Statistics (March 9, 2022). Job Openings and Labor Turnover Summary. Report USDL-20-0243. https://www.bls.gov/news.release/jolts.nr0.htm

[32] Turczynski, B. (January 9, 2020), 2020 HR Statistics: Job Search, Hiring, Recruiting & Interviews, Zety, https://zety.com/blog/hr-statistics#job-search-statistics

[33] US Bureau of Labor Statistics (February 11, 2020). Job Openings and Labor Turnover Summary. Report USDL-20-0243. https://www.bls.gov/news.release/jolts.nr0.htm

[34] Quote from Adkison, M. (February 18, 2020). U of A Partners with Blockchain Company for Innovative Resume-Building Program https://walton.uark.edu/insights/smart-resume.php

[35] Idatafy press release (March 19, 2020). UA System Institutions Issue World's First Certified SmartResumes, retrieved March 18, 2022 from https://www.uasys.edu/news/ua-system-institutions-issue-worlds-first-certified-smartresumes/

[36] University of Arkansas press release (Feb 15, 2021), U of A Partners in State Training Project for Arkansans Hit Financially by COVID, Retrieved March 18, 2022 from https://news.uark.edu/articles/55950/u-of-a-partners-in-state-training-project-for-arkansans-hit-financially-by-covid

[37] IMS Global Learning Consortium press release (May 17, 2021). IMS Global Learning Consortium Members Implement Learner-Centered Standard for Demonstrating Evidence of Educational Achievement, retrieved March 18, 2022 from https://www.imsglobal.org/article/ims-global-learning-consortium-members-implement-learner-centered-standard-demonstrating

[38] Leadership Walton. https://walton.uark.edu/career/leadership-walton.php

[39] Hyperledger Foundation (2017). Hyperledger Architecture, retrieved March 18, 2022 from https://www.hyperledger.org/wp-content/uploads/2017/08/Hyperledger_Arch_WG_Paper_1_Consensus.pdf

[40] Russ Juskalian, Inside the Jordan refugee camp that runs on blockchain (2018), Technology Review, April 12, 2018; Lacity, M., and Carmel, E. (2022). "Verifiable credentials in the token economy," in Lacity, M. and Treiblmaier, H. (editors) Blockchains and the Token Economy: Theory and Practice, Palgrave, London.

[41] Maturity of Decentralized Identity as of August 2021. Image: https://emtemp.gcom.cloud/ngw/globalassets/en/newsroom/images/graphs/v2-hc-emerging-tech-2021.png

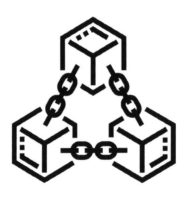

Chapter 9

Business Applications for Media

What's inside: Digital platforms like social media have amplified the creation and distribution of fake news. Fake news threatens not only our trust in the press, but has wide-ranging negative effects on politics, business, health, and society. We present an example of authenticating real news with a solution called ANSAcheck, developed by Agenzia Nazionale Stampa Associata (ANSA)—Italy's top news wire service—and Ernst & Young (EY)—one of the world's largest professional services firms. ANSAcheck's underlying blockchain technology provides verifiable authentication as to source, updates, and reposting of legitimate news stories. The solution uses Ethereum and Polygon.

Learning objectives:

- Define fake news.
- Describe how human biases make people susceptible to fake news.
- Critique the solutions to combat fake news, including the use of blockchains.
- Describe how ANSAcheck uses blockchain to prevent imposter news.
- Generate ideas for additional ways to prevent fake news.

9.1. The fake news problem

Fake news is the deliberate spread of verifiably false information under the disguise of being an authentic news story. There are many types of fake news, including news satires and parodies intended to entertain. For example, Orson Welles' 1938 radio adaptation of H.G. Wells' *The War of the Worlds* was designed as entertainment in the format of a serious radio broadcast. The broadcaster (CBS), writers, and actors were surprised to learn that more than one million listeners thought it was an actual news bulletin.[1]

Beyond entertainment, this chapter focuses on fake news fabrication, where there is no implicit understanding between the author and the audience that the story is concocted. We examine fake news designed to purposely misinform. The most common fake news fabrications are **political**, aiming to spread false information about politicians and public policies; **anti-scientific**, aiming to spread false information on such subjects as aliens, vaccines, diseases, cures, and nutrition; and **economic**, aiming to manipulate markets, stock prices, and to sell fraudulent products.[2]

The practice of creating and disseminating fake news for personal gain is not new. Consider these three stories from the past:

Back in the first century, Octavian became emperor of the Roman Empire, in part because he created fake news about his rival. Octavian portrayed Marcus Antonius (Mark Anthony) as Cleopatra's puppet and published a false document that claimed Anthony's last will requested that he be buried with the Ptolemaic pharaohs.[3] In Ancient Rome, the dissemination of fake news would require handmade copies of documents and the use of 'praecones' (town criers), as depicted in Figure 9.1. Readers might be familiar with the praeco from the HBO series *Rome*. The citizens of Rome faced the same challenge we face today: How could they know whether the news was legitimate?

Figure 9.1: A town crier disseminated news in ancient Rome

Source: Adapted from https://imperiumromanum.pl/wp-content/uploads/2019/08/792b8997970b433b06b1 0721bd89900e.jpg

As an example of scientific fake news, a reporter for the *New York Sun* in 1835 posted several stories that astronomers discovered a civilization on the moon, including humanoids with bat wings. Many people believed the stories, and sales of the newspaper increased by 50 percent, which was the presumed aim of the story. [4]

Figure 9.2: Humanoids with bat wings hoax of 1835

Source: https://upload.wikimedia.org/wikipedia/commons/f/fb/Great-Moon-Hoax-1835-New-York-Sun-lithograph-298px.jpg

Moving to an example of fake news designed to manipulate the value of a stock, in 1814, Lord Cochrane, a Radical member of UK Parliament and a naval officer, along with other conspirators, bought £1.1 million in UK government-based stocks. Cochrane then proceeded to spread false news that Napoleon was dead in an attempt to raise stock values. (Napoleon lived until 1821.) The fake news was spread to the British Admiralty via telegraph and by word of mouth at many English inns. It worked. The stock price soared until the hoax was revealed. Lord Cochrane was imprisoned, fined, and stripped of his naval rank.[5]

Fast-forward to the twenty-first century, in which digital technologies have amplified the creation and distribution of fake news. Today, humans quickly propagate false information via Internet searches, comments on posted content, and by clicking 'like' and/or 'share.'

Consider the massive dissemination of fake news stories during the 2016 United States (US) presidential election. The preponderance of these bogus stories were pro-Donald Trump and anti-Hillary Clinton.[6] In one study by economic professors at New York University and Stanford University, 115 pro-Trump fake stories were shared on Facebook 30 million times, and 41 pro-Clinton fake stories were shared 7.6 million times.[7] Among the top fake stories were claims that Pope Frances endorsed Trump, which was shared or commented on 960,000 times; and that WikiLeaks confirmed that Hillary Clinton sold weapons to ICIS, with 789,000 shares.[8] Both stories have since been removed. According to BuzzFeed news, there were more fake news story engagements (8.7 million) on Facebook than legitimate news story engagements (7.3 million) in the months leading to the US election.[9] Another academic study found that 25 percent of the 171 million tweets on Twitter in the five months prior to the 2016 election were fake or seriously erroneous news.[10] Although much of the misinformation was attributed to the British political consulting firm, Cambridge Analytica,[11] Russia successfully inserted fake news on Facebook and Twitter during the 2016 US election according to testimony presented to a US Senate Judiciary Committee.[12] Academic scholars have done post-election surveys to determine whether voters were swayed by fake news, but a direct causal link from fake news exposure to voting behavior is difficult to ascertain.

Of course, fake news is not limited to the United States; it is a worldwide phenomenon. In the United Kingdom (UK), the *Independent* reported in 2020 that Brittany Kaiser, prior business development director of Cambridge Analytica, claimed that the elections in at least 68 countries included many of the same disinformation tactics seen during the US presidential election and the UK's Brexit vote in 2016.[13]

Fake news stories have serious societal consequences. Fake news undermines the public's confidence in the free press and, moreover, when believed, results in a misinformed citizenry.[14] A 2019 global survey of more than 25,000 Internet users found that 44 percent said their trust in media has declined as a consequence of fake news.[15] It's not just the trust of the press that is at stake; fake news inflames social conflict; results in poor health outcomes (like swallowing bleach to avoid COVID-19); gives rise to radicalism and terrorism; undermines the integrity of elections; manipulates markets; and so much more.[16]   In short, fake news threatens the social trust we have in our institutions and in each other.

9.2. Why do people believe fake news?

Academic studies have rigorously sought to uncover the scope of the problem and why people believe fake news to be true. Stanford University researchers conducted field experiments and surveys with 7,804 US students from middle school, high school, and universities. The study found that, across the board, most students were not able to differentiate between fake news and real news. Most high-schoolers, for example, simply accepted the picture in Figure 9.3 as fact. More than 80 percent of middle-schoolers believed that advertising content was a real news story.[17] According to a 2019 global survey of more than 25,000 Internet users, 86 percent admitted to believing at least one fake news story. [18]

Why do so many people believe what they see and read? While our coverage of the research here is far from exhaustive, it highlights that humans are generally poor at identifying false information and that some personality traits and demographic factors affect this propensity.

Figure 9.3: Can you spot the fake news?

Source: Wineburg, McGrew et al. (2016).[19] Taken from https://imgur.com/gallery/BZWWx.
Originating from a Twitter post by @san_kaido

Human cognitive biases. More than 50 years of research on human decision-making shows that human behavior systematically deviates from what rational choice models predict.[20] Instead, humans are highly influenced by numerous cognitive biases. According to an article in *Science*, *"research demonstrates that people prefer information that confirms their pre-existing attitudes (selective exposure), view information consistent with their pre-existing beliefs as more persuasive than dissonant information (confirmation bias), and are inclined to accept information that pleases them (desirability bias)."*[21]

371

There are more than 200 identified human cognitive biases.[22] Other biases include compassion fade bias, pro-innovation bias, and framing bias. Compassion fade bias is the human tendency to have more compassion for a few known victims and less compassion for many anonymous ones. Pro-innovation bias is defined as 'the tendency to have excessive optimism towards an invention or innovation's usefulness throughout society, while often failing to identify its limitations and weaknesses.'[23] Framing bias is 'the tendency to draw different conclusions from the same information depending on how that information is presented.'[24]

One interesting twist on human biases is that many people recognise these partialities in others but underestimate their influences on themselves. This is called the 'biased blind spot'. An academic survey of 1,299 people in the US investigated individuals' perceptions about the effect of fake news on others. As predicted, individuals in this study thought that fake news had greater effects on out-group members (those from a different political party) than in-group members.[25]

With so many human biases, people tend to select news sources that support their ideologies, known as 'echo chambers'.

Repetition. Another academic study shows that individuals are more likely to accept familiar information as true, suggesting that the more a person is exposed to a fake news story, the more he or she will believe its contents.[26] This makes the proliferation of fake news even more worrisome.

Personality traits. While common vernacular would suggest that some people are more *gullible* than others, some academics call this trait 'reflexive open-mindedness'. Reflexive open-mindedness is defined as 'a tendency to unthinkingly accept incoming information as being valid and true.'[27] In three studies with 1,606 participants, professors from the University of Regina and MIT examined the associations of an individual's psychological profile with their perceptions of the accuracy of fake news. Across the studies, individuals with a general tendency of reflexive open-mindedness tended to believe fake news regardless of the familiarity of the news source or the presence/ absence of the headline's source.[28]

Demographic factors. These studies illuminate the demographic factors of people who are better or worse at identifying fake news. For example, a study by professors at New York University and Stanford presented both real and fake news stories about the 2016 US presidential election to people after the election. Respondents were asked to judge whether the stories were true or false. Respondents who spent more time consuming news, those with higher education, and older people were better at discerning real and fake news.[29]

We have thus established that fake news is a problem, and that human biases, traits, and demographic factors contribute to the belief in fake news. Next, we examine the means to combat fake news.

9.3. Means to combat fake news

The commonly used solutions to combat fake news today are deployed after the fact— they aim to detect or punish fakes after the stories have already been disseminated. These include:

- **Fact-checking websites.** According to Duke University, there are more than 100 nonpartisan groups worldwide that provide fact-checking services.[30] These include professional sites like FactCheck.org, Snopes.com, and BBC's Reality Check.

- **Legal liability.** The United Nations' 1948 Universal Declaration of Human Rights places freedom of the press as a human right: *"Everyone has the right to freedom of opinion and expression; this right includes freedom to hold opinions without interference, and to seek, receive, and impart information and ideas through any media regardless of frontiers".*[31] Many countries protect the freedom of the press in their constitutions. For example, the First Amendment to the US Constitution guarantees freedom of the press in America.[32] Because a free press is a hallmark of any democracy, government regulations to prevent fake news is not generally welcome as a solution. Today, a defamation lawsuit by someone hurt by the story is the main legal recourse against fake news. Defamation liability also extends to anyone who republishes it.[33] It is quite clear, however, that the threat of litigation is an inadequate deterrent.

- **Education.** As suggested by the demographic factors that contribute to a person's propensity to believe untruths, an educated citizenry is a powerful tool to combat fake news. Numerous examples of lesson plans for people of all ages are available online. Readers can act by fact checking stories themselves, unsubscribing to news from specific outlets, changing the way they use social media, and flagging a story they suspect is made up.

- **AI Solutions.** Social media platform providers rely on AI tools to identify and prevent the spread of fake news. AI solutions are designed to ingest and categorize large amounts of data, a task that is too expensive to do by humans on social media platforms with millions of posts per day. Many AI solutions are designed to detect and flag fake news by searching for sensational words, by checking the geolocation of the source, and by assigning reputation scores to particular sites based on the accuracy of facts.[34]

Mark Zuckerberg, Facebook's founder and CEO, for example, mentioned AI as a solution to fake news more than 30 times during his testimony to Congress after the 2016 presidential election.[35] Jump ahead to 2020, and Facebook was using AI to block fake news about COVID-19. By April 2020, Facebook had deleted fifty-million posts full of falsehoods about the coronavirus.[36]

Twitter reported in 2019 that use of AI was identifying and removing 50 percent of abusive tweets.[37] However, Twitter does not always delete fake news posts, but sometimes simply flags them. For example, Twitter flagged hundreds of Donald Trump's posts as 'disputed' after the 2020 presidential election.

Following the insurrection at the US Capitol on January 6, 2020, by Trump supporters, Twitter, Facebook, Snapchat, Instagram, YouTube, and Shopify restricted/blocked Trump's social media accounts. Such actions by social media platforms beg a deeper debate about freedom of speech versus the prevention of illegal actions spawned by fake news.[38] Where should the line be drawn?

We also note that AI contributes to the problem of fake news: Deepfakes are content manipulated by artificial intelligence, such as a video altered to make the speaker appear to say something she did not say. Microsoft launched a deepfake detector for videos and images in September 2020.[39] This Video Authenticator uses AI to analyze a still photo or video to provide a percentage chance, or confidence score, that the media is artificially manipulated. It works by detecting elements imperceptible to humans. The DeepTrust Alliance (a 501(c)) is also tackling deepfakes. Kathryn Harrison, former Director of Global Product Management for IBM Blockchain Platform, started DeepTrust because she believed a coalition of industry, civil society, and services is needed to *"create the standards that verify the origins of content to combat digital fakes."*[40] So, here we have examples of good AI fighting bad AI.

But, the battle is young. So far, the AI-driven solutions, such as Facebook's Deeptext and Google's Perspective software, are better at tagging hate speech than detecting fake news.[41] More recently, some news media outlets have turned to blockchain technologies.

Blockchain solutions. Gartner, a Global IT research and advisory company, estimates by 2023, thirty percent of world news (including videos) will rely on blockchain technologies for authentication.[42] There will likely be multiple blockchain-enabled solutions that provide services such as establishing content authenticity, tracking provenance of content over time, blacklisting imposters, spotting deepfakes, and tying digital content to the physical world—for example, by tagging the GPS location of a photo.[43]

Many of these solutions aim to prevent **imposters,** a type of fake news story that appears to be from a legitimate news agency.[44] According to an article in *Science*, imposters are *"particularly pernicious in that it is parasitic on standard news outlets, simultaneously benefiting from and undermining their credibility."*[45]

ANSAcheck is one such example of using blockchain technology to prevent imposters.

9.4. ANSAcheck

"We were attacked in the past when fakes news were tagged as ANSA news. We contributed to the problem because we cannot know who created and published fake news. With ANSAcheck, imposters cannot do that anymore because if it doesn't have an ANSAcheck tag, we didn't publish it."

Stefano De Alessandri, CEO and managing director, ANSA

ANSAcheck was developed by Agenzia Nazionale Stampa Associata (ANSA), Italy's top news wire service, along with Ernst & Young (EY), one of the world's largest professional services firms. Associata (ANSA) was founded as a not-for-profit news cooperative in 1945 after WWII. ANSA was created to serve as an independent news agency, free from the control of the Italian government and private groups. Headquartered in Rome, today it has 36 Italian-based news organizations in the cooperative, with 78 offices around the world.[46] According to the Reuters Institute Digital News Report 2020, ANSA is Italy's most trusted news source.[47]

On average, ANSA transmits 3,700 news stories, 1700 photos, and 60 videos each day to digital platforms, including the Internet, TV broadcasts, and cellular networks.[48] Ninety percent of ANSA's activities are business-to-business (B2B), providing original, professional-based information to the media industry. The remaining 10 percent of its activities are business-to-consumer (B2C) on its website (https://www.ansa.it/), which displays a subset of the news it creates.

Like most legitimate news outlets, ANSA has suffered from several imposter stories. In March 2020, for example, there were at least three imposter stories related to COVID-19. One falsely reported Italy's first death as that of a 24-year-old female. Another announced false homemade COVID-19 cures.[49] And a third falsely reported on COVID-19 policies by the Italian government. The fake stories were distributed using the ANSA brand, format, and signature.[50]

Stefano De Alessandri, ANSA's CEO and managing director, said, *"Fake news is one of the biggest challenges facing traditional media organizations and social media platforms, as it undermines the trust they have built with the public and advertisers, undermining their strategic asset that is their reputation. If we lose trust, we lose everything."*[51]

Instances like these prompted ANSA to launch the ANSAcheck project. The goal was to create an innovative solution to provide a guarantee for the origin of an ANSA-created story and for that story to be traced through is entire history of updates and reposts. EY knew that blockchain technologies could provide the tamper-resistant authenticity of the story, traceability of the story over time, and would allow readers or publishers to verify the story at any point in time.

In Phase I, completed in March 2020, ANSAcheck was deployed on ANSA's website. The system works by assigning a unique hash ID to an ANSA-created news story.[52] If even one letter in the story is changed, the system will detect that it is not identical to the original story. Story IDs are batched and posted every 15 minutes to half-hour to Ethereum, a public blockchain network, thereby creating a permanent record of the story on the public blockchain. The blockchain creates a tamper-resistant record that includes the story ID, transaction ID, timestamp, and the block number on Ethereum's ledger where the transaction is stored.

EY selected Ethereum because they believe it is the safest and most mature platform.

Each ANSA story that is secured on the blockchain is accompanied with an ANSAcheck sticker (see Figures 9.4 and 9.5) to signal its authenticity to readers. (ANSAcheck is language sensitive, so viewers who translate the website from Italian to another language will not see the specific stickers adhered to each news story; English-translation users will just see an explanation of the ANSAcheck solution as depicted in Figure 9.5.)

Figure 9.4: ANSAcheck sticker

This sticker appears on all ANSA stories posted on ANSA's website

Source: www.ansa.it

Users can click on the ANSACheck sticker to query Ethereum about the source of the story (see Figures 9.6 and 9.7). If ANSA updates the story, another entry is recorded on Ethereum and linked back to the original entry to form a chain of provenance. The solution registers about 3,000 news stories per day.

The ANSAcheck solution is comprised of three components: a JavaScript library, the notarization system, and the user interface (see Figure 9.8).

Each publisher on the platform maintains a private JavaScript library that contains its original news stories. Using EY's OpsChain Traceability solution, JavaScript libraries are connected to the notarization system. The notarization system is responsible for posting the entry on the public Ethereum blockchain and has a backend system that offers publishers the ability to join the blockchain solution.

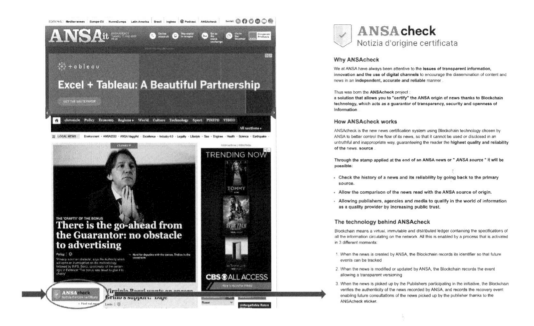

**Figure 9.5: ANSA Homepage with pointer to ANSAcheck description
(August 11, 2020)**

Source: www.ansa.it (Google translation to English)

Each registered publisher obtains a digital wallet to store their private keys for writing to the Ethereum blockchain. The user interface features a frontend dashboard for news distribution monitoring. This system allows news wire services like ANSA to track reposted news, including third-party reposts.

EY manages the transactions for posting on Ethereum using a smart contract. Interested readers may view the original smart contract: https://etherscan.io/address/0xdc6b769db 419e69c5f163048e880a02986d30376

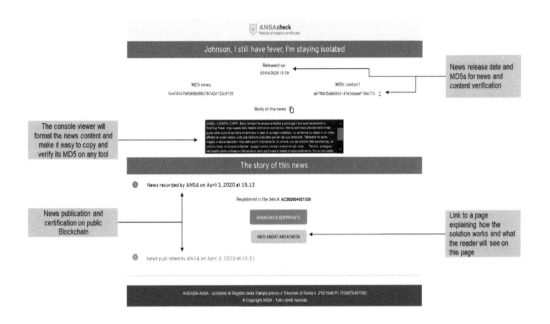

Figure 9.6: Story verification on the blockchain

When users click on the ANScheck sticker, the console viewer displays the transaction details stored on the blockchain. Each story gets a unique ID using MD5 cryptography. In this example, the story headline is 'Johnson, I still have a fever, I am staying isolated' and the unique story ID is 5b45634 7bf699bb9807b742e132c9120. This story was created on April 3, 2020 and the Block ID is AC202004031330

Source: With permission from EY

The smart contract mitigated the risk of ether's price volatility by postponing the processing of new stories if the current cost of ether is too high. EY also kept transaction costs low by batching multiple news stories within a single transaction. Initially, EY was posting a batch of stories every 15 minutes, with an average cost per story of 6 cents. Then, EY was batching roughly 500-600 new stories every six hours, so the cost per transaction dropped to around 0.006 dollars per story. To reduce transaction costs even

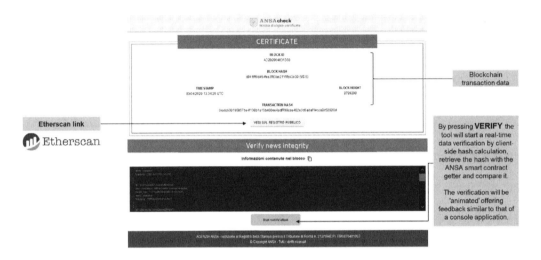

Figure 9.7: Query of the story on Ethereum via the console

In this image, users can see where the story is stored on the Ethereum blockchain. The story was added to Ethereum block number 9799299 on April 3, 2020 at 01:34:26 Coordinated Universal Time (UTC). The unique transaction hash is 0xadc600195857be4f138b1a15b400ee4adf799cae462e3d6abaf1ecca8c52928d. By pressing the verify button on the console, the application performs a real-time verification of the story.

Source: With permission from EY

further, EY moved from Ethereum to Polygon in 2021. Polygon is a second layer of Ethereum, so it maintains public blockchain standards but with less costs of tokenization. The new contract is here:

https://polygonscan.com/address/0xdc6b769db419e69c5f163048e880a02986d30376

By December 2021 more than 2.5 million ANSA news stories had been posted on the blockchain. Approximately 72 percent of readers had clicked on the ANSAcheck explanation tab to learn more about it; 38 percent of people who viewed the article actually clicked on the sticker to perform the validation.

Solution Components:
Web module, news notarization system and monitoring dashboard

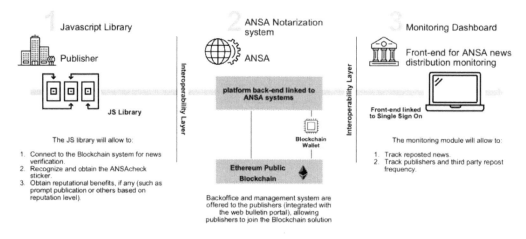

Figure 9.8: Solution components

Source: With permission from EY

Mr. De Alessandri said of Phase I, *"It's not the definitive solution on fake news, but rather the first pass. ANSA is a serious company that employs professional journalists and checks everything that we publish. This first pass does not guarantee the complete accuracy of the contents; rather, it guarantees that this piece of news comes from ANSA, not from someone else."* [53] The solution will be enhanced with new features and launched on a platform as learning is incorporated from Phase I.

EY plans to add other services to the ANSAcheck solution. Giuseppe Perrone, EY's blockchain HUB MED leader said, *"The solution will become more sophisticated in terms of functionality and components, such as fact-checking functions, semantic language analysis, and picture data protection."* In the first generation of the solution, a story must be an identical copy of the original, as a change to even a single letter will signal that the source is not the original. In the next generation, the solution will provide a measure of overlap, similar to the plagiarism software familiar to many students. This way, publishers who repost a story can add their own commentary while still verifying the original news source.

9.5. Conclusion

One of the key findings from human bias research is that many of us think other people are more susceptible to fake news than we are ourselves. In reality, most of us have believed a fake news story that we later discovered was verifiably false. While we are encouraged by the use of blockchains to authenticate news sources, no single solution will eradicate fake news. All parties in the ecosystem, including governments, journalists, publishers, social media platforms, and citizens, have roles to play. What ideas, technical and nontechnical, do you have for preventing the creation and dissemination of fake news?

Citations

[1] Hadley, C., Gaudet, H. and Herzog, H. (1940) *The Invasion from Mars: A Study in the Psychology of Panic with the Complete Script of the Famous Orson Welles Broadcast*. Princeton: Princeton University Press.

[2] Lazer, D., Baum M., Benkler Y. et al. (2018) *Science* 359 (6380): 1094–1096.

[3] MacDonald, E. (2017) The fake news that sealed the fate of Antony and Cleopatra. *The Conversation*, 13 January.

[4] The original story can be found at the Internet Archives. Available at: www.archive.org/stream/moonhoax00Lock/moonhoax00Lock_djvu.txt (accessed 6 April 2021).

[5] Johnson, P. (2002) Civilising Mammon: Fraud and Profit in Nineteenth-Century London. Article, London School of Economics and Political Science. Available at: www.web.archive.org/web/20110223134926/http://www.fathom.com/feature/121984/ (accessed 6 April 2021).

[6] Silverman, C. (2016) This Analysis Shows how Fake Election News Stories Outperformed Real News on Facebook. *BuzzFeed News*, 16 November.

[7] Allcott, H. and Gentzkow, M. (2017) Social Media and Fake News in the 2016 Election. *Journal of Economic Perspectives* 31(2): 211–236.

[8] Silverman, C. (2016) This Analysis Shows how Fake Election News Stories Outperformed Real News on Facebook. *BuzzFeed News*, 16 November.

[9] Silverman, C. (2016) This Analysis Shows how Fake Election News Stories Outperformed Real News on Facebook. *BuzzFeed News*, 16 November.

[10] Bovet, A. and Makse, H. (2019) Influence of fake news in Twitter during the 2016 US presidential election. *Nature Communications* 10: Article 7. Available at: www.nature.com/articles/s41467-018-07761-2 (accessed 6 April 2021).

[11] Zuboff, S. (2019) *The Age of Surveillance Capitalism*. New York: Public Affairs.

[12] Senate Judiciary Committee (2017) Extremist content and Russian disinformation online: Working with tech to find solutions. Available at: www.judiciary.senate.gov/meetings/extremist-content-and-russian-disinformation-online-working-with-tech-to-find-solutions (accessed 6 April 2021).

[13] Wood, V. (2020) Fake news worse during election campaign than Brexit referendum, whistleblower says. *The Independent*, 27 January. Available at: www.independent.co.uk/news/uk/politics/brexit-fake-news-2019-election-facebook-cambridge-analytica-brittany-kaisar-eu-referendum-a9304821.html (accessed 6 April 2021).

[14] Jang, S. and Kim, J. (2018) Third-person effects of fake news: Fake news regulation and media literacy interventions. *Computers in Human Behavior* 80(1): 295–302.

[15] Ipsos Public Affairs and the Centre for International Governance Innovation (2019) CIGI-Ipsos Global Survey: Internet Security & Trust. Available at: www.cigionline.org/internet-survey-2019 (accessed 6 April 2021).

[16] (2020) Fake social media accounts root cause of riots; plea in SC seeks to weed them out. *Asian News International,* 4 March. Available at: https://search.proquest.com/docview/2370335878?accountid=8361 (accessed 6 April 2021).
Margetts, H. (2019) Rethinking Democracy with Social Media. *The Political Quarterly*, 90(1): 107–123.
Muqsith, M. (2019) Effect Fake News for Democracy. *Jurnal cita hukum*, 7(3): 307–318.

[17] Wineburg, S., McGrew, S. et al. (2016) Evaluating Information: The Cornerstone of Civic Online Reasoning. Stanford Digital Repository. Available at: http://purl.stanford.edu/fv751yt5934 (accessed 6 April 2021).

[18] Ipsos Public Affairs and the Centre for International Governance Innovation (2019) CIGI-Ipsos Global Survey: Internet Security & Trust. Available at: www.cigionline.org/internet-survey-2019 (accessed 6 April 2021).

[19] Wineburg, S., McGrew, S., (2016) Evaluating Information: The Cornerstone of Civic Online Reasoning. Stanford Digital Repository. Available at: http://purl.stanford.edu/fv751yt5934 (accessed 6 April 2021).

[20] Santos, L. and Rosati, A. (2015) The Evolutionary Rots of Human Decision Making. *Annual Review of Psychology*, 66: 321–347.

[21] Lazer, D., Baum, M., Benkler, Y. et al. (2018) *Science* 359(6380): 1094–1096.

[22] List of human cognitive biases: https://en.wikipedia.org/wiki/List_of_cognitive_biases

[23] https://en.wikipedia.org/wiki/List_of_cognitive_biases.

24 https://en.wikipedia.org/wiki/List_of_cognitive_biases.

25 Jang, S., and Kim, J. (2018) Third-person effects of fake news: Fake news regulation and media literacy interventions. *Computers in Human Behavior* 80(1): 295–302.

26 Swire, B., Ecker, U.K.H., and Lewandowsky, S. (2017) The role of familiarity in correcting inaccurate information. *Journal of Experimental Psychology: Learning, Memory and Cognition, 43*(12), 1948–1961.

27 Pennycook, G., and Rand, D. (2020) Who falls for fake news? The roles of bullshit receptivity, overclaiming, familiarity and analytic thinking. *Journal of Personality*, 88: 185–200.

28 Pennycook, G., and Rand, D. (2020) Who falls for fake news? The roles of bullshit receptivity, overclaiming, familiarity and analytic thinking. *Journal of Personality*, 88: 185–200.

29 Allcott, H., and Gentzkow, M. (2017) Social Media and Fake News in the 2016 Election. *Journal of Economic Perspectives*, 31(2): 211–236.

30 Duke Reporters' Lab. Available at: www.reporterslab.org/fact-checking/ (accessed 6 April 2021).

31 United Nations (1948) Universal Declaration of Human Rights. Available at: www.un.org/en/about-us/universal-declaration-of-human-rights (accessed 6 April 2021).

32 In the US, the First Amendment to the Constitution guarantees freedom of the press. "Congress shall make no law respecting an establishment of religion, or prohibiting the free exercise thereof; or abridging the freedom of speech, or of the press; or the right of the people peaceably to assemble, and to petition the Government for a redress of grievances."

33 Haskins, J. (2019) Fake News: What Laws Are Designed to Protect. Available at: www.legalzoom.com/articles/fake-news-what-laws-are-designed-to-protect (accessed 6 April 2021).

34 Maruti Techlabs (2020) Is artificial intelligence the key to combat fake news? Available at: www.marutitech.com/artificial-intelligence-fake-news/ (accessed 6 April 2021).

35 Woolley, S. (2020) We're fighting fake news AI bots by using more AI. That's a mistake. *MIT Technology Review*. Available at: www.technologyreview.com/2020/01/08/130983/were-fighting-fake-news-ai-bots-by-using-more-ai-thats-a-mistake/ (accessed 6 April 2021).

36 Some, K. (2020) Facebook uses AI to fight coronavirus misinformation and fake news. Available at: www.analyticsinsight.net/facebook-uses-ai-fight-coronavirus-misinformation-fake-news/ (accessed 6 April 2021).

37 Newcomb, A. (2019) Twitter Says A.I. Is Now Removing Over Half of Its Abusive Tweets Before

They're Flagged. Fortune Magazine, 24 October. Available at: www.fortune.com/2019/10/24/twitter-abuse-tweets/ (accessed 6 April 2021).

[38] Hutchinson A (2021) President Trump Banned from Various Social Networks After US Capitol Riots. 7 January. Available at: www.socialmediatoday.com/news/president-trump-banned-from-various-social-networks-after-us-capitol-riots/593007/ (accessed 6 April 2021).

[39] Burt T and Horvitz E (2020) New Steps to Combat Disinformation. Microsoft press release, 1 September. https://blogs.microsoft.com/on-the-issues/2020/09/01/disinformation-deepfakes-newsguard-video-authenticator/ (accessed 6 April 2021).

[40] DeepTrust Alliance. Available at: www.deeptrustalliance.org/about (accessed 6 April 2021).

[41] Woolley S (2020) We're fighting fake news AI bots by using more AI. That's a mistake. *MIT Technology Review*. Available at: www.technologyreview.com/2020/01/08/130983/were-fighting-fake-news-ai-bots-by-using-more-ai-thats-a-mistake/ (accessed 6 April 2021).

[42] Gartner (2019) Gartner Top Strategic Predictions for 2020 and Beyond. Available at: www.gartner.com/smarterwithgartner/gartner-top-strategic-predictions-for-2020-and-beyond/ (accessed 6 April 2021).

[43] Mearian L (2020) How blockchain could help block fake news. *ComputerWorld*, 17 February. Available at: www.computerworld.com/article/3526427/how-blockchain-could-help-block-fake-news.html (accessed 6 April 2021).

[44] Wardle Claire (2017) Fake news. It's complicated. *First Draft*, 16 February. Available at: www.firstdraftnews.org/latest/fake-news-complicated/ (accessed 6 April 2021).

[45] Lazer D, Baum M, Benkler Y et al. (2018) *Science* 359(6380): 1094–1096.

[46] https://en.wikipedia.org/wiki/Agenzia_Nazionale_Stampa_Associata

[47] Newman, N., Fletcher, R., Schulz, A., Andi, S., and Nielsen, R. (2020). Reuters Institute Digital News Report. https://reutersinstitute.politics.ox.ac.uk/sites/default/files/2020-06/DNR_2020_FINAL.pdf

[48] De Alessandri, S. and Perrone, G. (2020). Going public: EY Global Blockchain Summit 2020.

[49] Sephton C (2020) ANSA will put the sources and history of 1,000 news stories a day on a publicly available blockchain, but bigger challenges lie ahead. *Modern Consensus*, 8 April. Available at: www.modernconsensus.com/people/media/its-brand-used-to-spread-fake-news-italian-media-outlet-turns-to-blockchain/ (accessed 6 April 2021).

[50] De Alessandri S and Perrone G (2020) Going public: EY Global Blockchain Summit 2020.

[51] De Alessandri S and Perrone G (2020) Going public: EY Global Blockchain Summit 2020.

[52] A hash is an algorithm for transforming one input into a different output. Given a specific input, the identical output will always be reproduced. A good hash algorithm makes it practically impossible to determine the input value based on the output value, which is why hashes are called one-way functions. ANSAcheck uses the MD5 hashing algorithm, which always produces a 128-bit output.

[53] De Alessandri S and Perrone G (2020) Going Public: EY Global Blockchain Summit 2020.

PART III

Road to Maturity

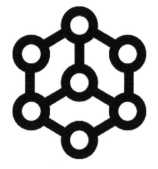

Chapter 10

Technical Challenges and Emerging Solutions

What's inside: Blockchain is growing up! What started with Bitcoin in 2009 has resulted in a $2 trillion global economy within 13 years. The technical innovations continue. In this chapter, we look at emerging technical innovations for efficient resource consumption, security, performance, scalability, anonymity, confidentiality, and interoperability. We explain how the technical innovations work at a high-level, often using images and analogies so that non-technical readers may understand their purpose.

Learning objectives:

- Evaluate solutions for efficient resource consumption.
- Evaluate solutions for security threats.
- Evaluate solutions for performance and scalability.
- Evaluate solutions for anonymity & confidentiality.
- Describe three methods for cross-chain transaction processing.

10.1. Introduction

So far in our learning journey, we'd covered the foundations of blockchains for Web 3.0 and highlighted many live applications across a variety of industries. This is our first chapter in the 'Road to Maturity' section of the book. This chapter focuses on developments aiming to improve blockchain technologies. We specifically address solutions for the massive resource consumption for certain protocols; security; performance and scalability; anonymity for public blockchains; confidentiality for private blockchains; and interoperability. We've also included some behavioral practices that readers can take to reduce their risks when using these technologies. There are three things every reader must do: first, protect your private keys; second, protect your private keys; and third, protect your private keys! By the end of this chapter, readers will be well equipped to understand the debates and conversations around these technologies. Readers will be able to explain some quite sophisticated technical concepts, such as the threat of quantum computing, zero-knowledge proofs (interactive and non-interactive), and interoperability methods for cross-chain transaction processing (notaries, sidechains, and hash-time locked contracts (HTLCs)). It sounds intimidating at first, but our coverage will ease the learning journey.

10.2. Resource consumption

"It's worth the price; a single security breech costs an average of $3.8 million"

Don and Alex Tapscott, authors of Blockchain Revolution[1]

Computers that run blockchain nodes consume resources in the form of electricity. The computational intensity of a given blockchain's consensus protocol is the main driver of resource consumption. Recalling from Chapter 3, Bitcoin and Ethereum use the safest, yet computationally most resource-demanding protocol called Proof-of-Work. Bitcoin's first miners back in 2009 could successfully compete for a block reward using their desktop computers. As Bitcoin's price skyrocketed, miners shifted to specialized hardware and shared computational power through mining pools. Specifically, Bitcoin requires an Application-Specific Integrated Circuit (ASIC). Ethereum mining requires a Graphics Processing Unit (GPU). Proof-of-Work is admittedly a resource hog for both of these public networks. In order to compete, large mining centers have been established (see Figure 10.1 for an example).

Figure 10.1: Bitcoin mining site in Bowden Sweden

Source: https://coinscage.com/wp-content/uploads/2017/05/bitcoin-mining-farm-1.jpg

Digiconomist, a site that tracks blockchain energy consumption, calculated that by 2022, each bitcoin transaction required 2,140 kilowatts of electricity; Ethereum used 264 kilowatts of electricity per transaction. A single transaction's electricity consumption is enough to power an average US household for 73 days for Bitcoin and 9 days for Ethereum.[2] As the quote from Don and Alex Tapscott suggests, many people believe that this expense is worthwhile in order to secure the blockchains.

Mining pools are incentivized to erect data centers near a low cost source of electricity. For this reason, large mining pools had sprung up in China due to cheap electricity. China controlled over 80 percent of the mining power over Bitcoin until it became illegal in 2021.[3] As of April 2022, the US took up the slack and now it is the largest miner of Bitcoin, with 35 percent of the mining power.[4] Within the US, the price of electricity varies greatly across the 50 States (see Figure 10.2). Louisiana has the lowest average cost of electricity for mining one Bitcoin, at $3,224 per bitcoin. Hawaii and Alaska were the most expensive at $9,483 and $7,059 per bitcoin respectively.[5]

Figure 10.2: Electricity cost per kilowatt hour in US

*Source:https://image.cnbcfm.com/api/v1/image/106950410-1633024899325-023955_GEI_*
ElectricityPriceMap_Handout_2020_1_Page_1.jpg?v=1633025034&w=1910&ffmt=webp

People are finding ways to reduce electricity costs. For example, ***EZ Blockchain*** developed a solution that converts the natural gas flaring waste from drilling and refining into electricity to power cryptocurrency mining. EZ Blockchain uses portable gas electric generators to power mobile data centers (see Figure 10.3). The business model helps drilling and refining companies reduce CO_2 emissions while generating money from cryptocurrency mining. As of 2022, EZ Blockchain has delivered 13 mobile mining units, primarily in North Dakota.[6]

Liquid immersion cooling is another innovation that reduces the electricity costs consumed by mining equipment. The liquid—called a dielectric coolant—is designed to have zero electrical conductivity but good heat conductivity, which reduces the heat, power consumption and noise of mining equipment. Engineered Fluids, a US-based company, claims its immersion solution saves 35 percent off electricity costs.[7]

Figure 10.3: EZ Blockchain mining

Generators convert natural gas flaring to electricity to power portable data centers for mining cryptocurrencies.

Source: https://www.ezblockchain.net/

Some public blockchains rely on less computationally intensive consensus algorithms compared to Proof-of-Work. For example, Cardano uses Proof-of-Stake and EOS uses Delegated Proof-of-Stake consensus protocols for public blockchains that consume much less energy. Permissioned blockchains rely on some form of Byzantine Fault Tolerance, which requires very little energy consumption—about as much energy as it takes to run an email server.

10.3. Security

One of blockchain's greatest selling points is heightened security over centralized systems that have single points of failure. In Chapter 3, we learned that blockchain applications still function properly even if a high percentage of nodes are faulty—or even malicious—promising unbeatable resiliency and 100 percent availability. If blockchains are so secure, why do we hear about so many heists and breaches? There are vulnerability points in today's blockchain technologies, particularly from digital wallets, young code bases, poorly-written smart contracts and the possibility of 51 percent attacks. Additionally, quantum computing poses a future security threat.

10.3.1. Digital wallet security

Most heists on blockchains happen at the vulnerable access points of digital wallets where private keys are stored. As noted in Chapter 3, once a hacker steals a private key, they control the asset and can easily transfer funds to another address. While users may store their digital wallets on their own devices, most users rely on centralized exchanges. Exchanges are a lucrative target for hackers because some exchanges control millions of private keys. We already covered one of the largest heists at *Mt. Gox*. But that was back in 2014. Jumping ahead, single attacks have stolen hundreds of millions of dollars' worth of crypto.[8] Among them was $650 million stolen from the ***Ronin Network*** in 2022, a layer 2 solution for Ethereum. The attacker stole private keys to eventually control five of the nine validator nodes, so this was also a 51 percent attack. In 2021, Poly Network had $610 million stolen, but eventually worked with the hacker to return most of the money.[9] We naturally worry about the risk implications of these incidents, but risks can be mitigated. In addition, readers can enact practices for selecting exchanges and managing their wallets:

- Select exchanges with investment insurance. The largest crypto exchanges—Binance, Coinbase and Gemini—now have insurance to compensate users.

- When using an exchange, select services that require more than just one factor authentication; in addition to a private key, the service might require a biometric identifier, pass phrases, photo, or other identifiers.

- Use separate wallets for each exchange or blockchain.

- Keep very little money in 'hot' wallets that are connected to exchanges or to the Internet.

- Keep most crypto offline in a 'cold' wallet; keep the cold wallet backed up on multiple devices.

- Print private keys on paper and store them in a vault. Or better yet, divide private keys across multiple pieces of paper and store parts in different secure locations.

- Monitor the wallet's approvals and delete ones that are no longer needed, such as if you withdraw from a staking pool.[10]

- Keep wallet software updated.

10.3.2. Code base security

Although much less frequent than the heists of private keys from digital wallets, many blockchains have had heists resulting from software weaknesses in the code base. These typically happen within the first year of launch when the code base is still very new. The Bitcoin blockchain was hacked in August 2010 when someone exploited a software vulnerability to create 184 *billion* bitcoins, a highly suspicious act given the maximum money supply is only 21 *million* bitcoins.[11] A hacker of Ripple was able to transfer 1000 bitcoins from an address that had only .0001 bitcoins in 2014.[12] As software updates are implemented, new vulnerabilities could be introduced. For example, a serious bug in a

Bitcoin Core update was discovered in 2018 that could have brought down the network with a denial-of-service attack, a type of malicious attack that floods a network with so many transactions that it disrupts service for legitimate users. Fortunately, the Bitcoin Core developers spotted it and fixed it before hackers could exploit it.[13] Although the source code was fixed quickly, these episodes offer an important warning.

As discussed in Chapter 3, **n-versioning** is a practice that helps to secure code bases. With n-versioning, independent software teams code the detailed functionality in different programming languages to improve fault tolerance and redundancy.

10.3.3. Smart contract security

As defined in Chapter 3, a decentralized autonomous organization (DAO) is an organization or company that is run entirely by rules encoded as computer programs in smart contracts that execute on a blockchain. To illustrate the security concerns of a smart contract, we shared the story of a particular DAO, confusingly named *The DAO* (as opposed to 'a' DAO), in Chapter 2. As a reminder: the thieves exploited a weakness in the smart contract launched on the Ethereum blockchain. The Ethereum community debated whether to roll back the ledger and return the money or to let the theft occur to maintain the immutability of the ledger. The decision was made to let miners vote, weighing their votes by their hashing power. The miners voted for a hard fork—a permanent divergence in the Ethereum blockchain. The blocks were rolled back and the stolen ether was returned. Those miners who refused to follow the fork proceeded mining with the original code, leaving us with Ethereum (fork followers) and *Ethereum Classic* (non-fork followers), where the thief can still cash out.

Other smart contract heists and vulnerabilities have come to light, such as with the smart contracts running Parity, POWH Coin, LastWinner and Fomo3D:

- *Parity* was launched by Gavin Wood, co-founder of Ethereum in 2017. Someone was able to exploit a weakness in the smart contract to steal $30 million worth of ether.[14]

- *POWH Coin* was deemed by many as a Ponzi scheme where new investors pay earlier investors.[i] But worse than the business model, *white hat hackers*—ethical hackers who help to identify security defects—found a flaw in the smart contract that operated the *POWH Coin.* In 2018, *black hat hacker(s)*—criminals that exploit security defects for their own advantage—exploited an unsigned integer underflow opportunity, thereby enabling them to withdraw an infinite number of POWH's tokens. [15]

- *Last Winner* and *Fomo3D* are gambling smart contracts launched on Ethereum that share over 90 percent of code. In August 2018, AnChain identified five Ethereum addresses on Last Winner that exploited a flaw in the smart contract code to steal $4 million.[16]

Auditing a smart contract before deployment is a practice to improve smart contract security. In Chapter 5, we learned that Aave hires five independent auditors before deploying any smart contract. Many professional services firms now offer these services. For example, EY has a smart contract and token review service for blockchain clients. According to EY, *"the Smart Contract & Token Review solution allows users to customize tests and reports, identify vulnerabilities, and mitigate risks in the token deployment process and the code underlying of smart contracts."*[17]

10.3.4. Fifty-one percent attack

How likely can someone commandeer more than 50 percent of the hashing power? And where are the biggest threats? For large public blockchains, the threat comes from the concentration of power by mining pools. We'll specifically look at the threats of concentration of power for Bitcoin and Ethereum. For smaller-sized public blockchains, a single hacker may find it worthwhile to overtake the network if the hacker's electricity costs are lower than the amount of cryptocurrency he or she could steal through a double spend. We'll examine the 51 percent hacks that happened at Verge; ZenCash; Bitcoin

---

i   A Ponzi Scheme is form of fraud in which the first investors get paid from later investors; there is no revenue generated from legitimate returns on investments.

Gold and Ethereum Classic. Private blockchains are not concerned with a 51 percent takeover; indeed, many private blockchains are operated under a 'benevolent dictator' governance model discussed in Chapter 2.

Focusing on Bitcoin, the main threat of a 51 percent takeover comes from the concentration of power from mining pools (see Figure 10.3). **Poolin, F2Pool, SlushPool**, and **Antpool** are among the largest mining pools. In theory, the miners could possibly collude. Also note that more than 50 percent of the winning miners cannot be identified. According to Blockchain.com, *"mining pools could suddenly decide to change their tag or input addresses, leading to a decrease of their labelled contribution and an increase in the UNKNOWN labels."*[18]

The China-based company, **Bitmain,** poses another interesting threat. Bitmain is both the world's largest bitcoin mining hardware manufacturer with 70 percent market share and owner of Antpool, one of the largest mining pools. Antpool mined around 10 percent of all blocks as of this writing (see Figure 10.4). Being the largest provider and consumer of bitcoin mining hardware poses a serious conflict of interest. In April 2017, it was discovered that Bitmain built-in a 'backdoor' program within its Antminer hardware so that the company could easily seize control and shut down other miners competing with its mining pool. Here's how this could occur:

'The firmware checks-in with a central service randomly every one to 11 minutes. Each check-in transmits the Antminer serial number, a hardware identification number and IP address. Bitmain can use this check-in data to cross check against customer sales and delivery records making it personally identifiable. The remote service can then return 'false' which will stop the miner from mining.'[19]

Dubbed 'Antscape', Bitmain apologized and posted updates to the firmware.[20]

Hashrate Distribution

An estimation of hashrate distribution amongst the largest mining pools

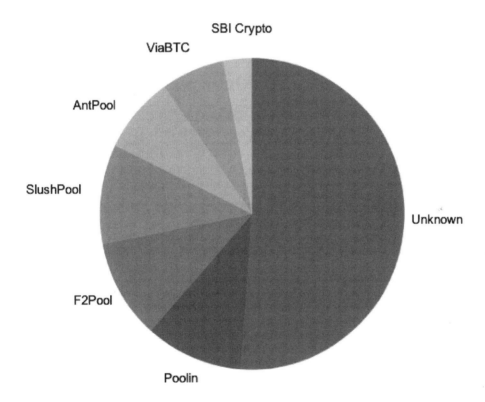

Figure 10.4: Bitcoin's largest winning mining pools on April 4, 2022

Source: https://blockchain.info/pools

Ethereum also tracks its top miners on https://etherchain.org/miner. On April 4, 2022, ***Ethermine, f2pool2***, and ***Hiveon Pool*** were the top mining pools (see Figure 10.5). Ethermine alone controlled more than 25 percent of the Ethereum network on this day, but Ethereum is more decentralized than Bitcoin.

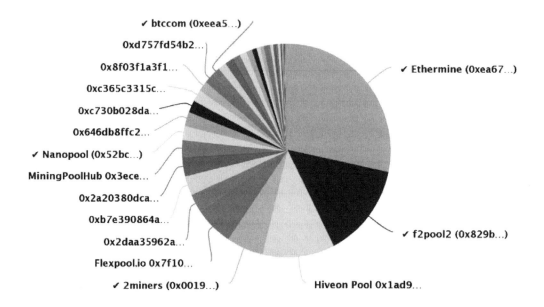

Figure 10.5: Ethereum's largest winning mining pools on April 4, 2022

Source: https://www.etherchain.org/charts/miner

Given that blockchains are supposed to be completely distributed applications, the dominance of a few key mining pools does pose a risk. A 2018 study by Professor Sirer and his colleagues found that 'both Bitcoin and Ethereum mining are very centralized, with the top four miners in Bitcoin and the top three miners in Ethereum controlling more than 50 percent of the hash rate... The entire blockchain for both systems is determined by fewer than 20 mining entities.'[21]

Although Bitcoin and Ethereum have not suffered a 51 percent takeover, other blockchain networks have, including the Ronin Network, discussed above. Verge; ZenCash; Bitcoin Gold and Ethereum Classic have also suffered 51 percent attacks:

- At *Verge* (XVG), a privacy coin, a 51 percent takeover happened three times in 2018. In the first takeover, hackers stole $1 million worth of cryptocurrency. In the second takeover, they stole $1.8 million and prevented others from processing transactions. During the third takeover, over 142 million XVG were stolen.[22] Each time, developers sought to implement patches, but hackers were still able to spoof timestamps to double spend XVG.[23]

- *ZenCash* (ZEN) suffered a 51 percent attack in June of 2018 by a private miner with a large mining operation. By double-spending, the hacker swiped over $550,000 worth of its cryptocurrency. In this hack, the developers responded quickly with a patch.[24]

- *Bitcoin Gold* (BTG) experienced a 51 percent hack in January 2020; the hacker reorganized nearly 30 blocks to double spend $70,000 worth of the cryptocurrency.[25]

- Of all the 51 percent attacks, the one at *Ethereum Classic* is considered the most troubling. As noted above, Ethereum Classic was the 'non-fork' followers after the DAO attack on Ethereum in 2016. As early as 2018, white hats warned that a 51 percent takeover of Ethereum Classic could happen by spending as little as $2,216 in electricity.[26] In January of 2019, a hacker gained control of 51 percent of the network and stole over $1 million worth of the cryptocurrency. A few days later, the hacker voluntarily returned $100,000 to one of the exchanges it robbed, Gate.io. It's unclear why the hacker returned the money to this exchange, and not to others it stole from, like Coinbase.[27]

One way to prevent a 51 percent attack is to initiate a delay. This was proposed by the ZenCash team (now called Horizen). Horizen is a fork of Zcash, which is a fork of Bitcoin. The team proposed to update their proof-of-work consensus algorithm with a delay function that would penalize miners who are preparing for such an attack. *"Because a 51 percent attack requires a miner to produce blocks in secret before posting them to the blockchain, a delay function allows for penalties that make such attacks prohibitively expensive."*[28] A delay would increase the cost of a 51 percent attack by a factor of ten.

10.3.5. Quantum computing

Blockchain's cryptography is deemed secure because today's digital computers don't have enough computational power to make brute force guessing of a private key based on knowing only the public key feasible. According to one source, today's digital computer would take billions of years to randomly guess a private key that matches a public key.[29] Looking far ahead, some people are concerned that the cryptography we deem to be secure today may become vulnerable in the future. Keeping in mind that permissionless blockchain records are immutable and *forever* public, there is indeed a risk that future technologies could break the cryptography that protects the blockchains of today. Quantum computing is one such risk.

Quantum computing will speed computers in such a way that brute force searches that are impractical today could be practical in the future.[30] How? Today's digital computers are based on binary digits, called 'bits', which represent the state of a computation with a '0' or a '1'. Today, we make digital computers faster by processing more bits per second, but each bit can still only represent one computation. Quantum computers change this; they are based on quantum bits, called 'qubits', which can simultaneously represent multiple states and therefore do multiple calculations at the same time. A 30-qubit computer could do one billion calculations simultaneously.[31] Some have estimated that it would take a 317 million qubit computer to hack Bitcoin in an hour.[32] Currently, IBM's 127-qubit Eagle is the fastest quantum computer, so we have time to find a solution.[33]

According to Dr. Atefeh (Atty) Mashatan, Director of the Cybersecurity Research Lab at Ryerson University, there are two options: *"either replace the vulnerable components of existing platforms with quantum-resistant alternatives or go back to the drawing board and design new blockchains that are not quantum-vulnerable. The latter is much easier than the former."* To quantum-patch an existing blockchain, cryptographic keys would need to be replaced with much larger key sizes, which will further hinder scalability. All of the balances from the old addresses would need to be transferred to new addresses stored in new quantum-resistant wallets. However, the patch would only work if the public key had not been previously broadcast. Dr. Mashatan explained, *"If a public key is broadcast and the associated wallet still contains some funds, an adversary who has access to an attack-capable quantum computer can find the corresponding private key and, consequently, impersonate the wallet owner and use the remaining funds."*[34]

In 2022, JPMorgan Chase announced that it had developed and tested a quantum resistant blockchain network in partnership with Toshiba and Ciena. The network is called 'QKD', which stands for quantum key distribution. According to CoinTelegraph, *"QKD utilizes quantum mechanics and cryptography to enable two parties to exchange secure data and detect and defend against third parties attempting to eavesdrop on the exchange. The technology is seen as a viable defense against potential blockchain hacks that could be conducted by quantum computers in the future."*[35]

10.4. Performance and scalability

Although performance and scalability affect each other, they are conceptually distinctive. Performance is about the length of time it takes for a transaction to be processed in a system; scalability refers to the *throughput,* i.e., how many transactions can be processed per second. Performance and scalability issues are significantly greater for public, permissionless blockchains than for private, permissioned blockchains. We'll examine them separately.

10.4.1. Performance and scalability challenges of public blockchains

Because the *a priori* trust among trading partners is nil in a public blockchain, the computer networks need a lot of computational power to validate transactions and to constantly monitor the integrity of records. All this computation slows down performance and throughput. As we saw in the huge adoption surges in 2017 and 2021, Bitcoin and Ethereum struggled to process transactions within the targeted windows. Moreover, settlement times are not fast enough for transactions requiring nearly instantaneous reaction times, such as IoT devices that monitor the status of critical systems, or for retail applications where a customer will certainly not wait around for a transaction to settle. Additionally, public blockchains like Bitcoin and Ethereum are considered too small in scale to handle the volumes that will be required for many enterprise applications. For example, PayPal handles about 193 transactions per second, SWIFT—the global provider of secure financial messaging services—processes about 329 messages per second,[36] and Visa handles 1,667 transactions per second (and claimed it could accommodate up to 56,000 transactions per second).[37]

Ethereum's scalability problem was really highlighted when one smart contract for the game *CryptoKitties* started using 10 percent of Ethereum's network capacity in November of 2017. Cryptokitties created a backlog of tens of thousands of transactions.[38] Ethereum's PoW consensus algorithm requires that every node processes the code in a smart contract, which is not only slow, but expensive.[39]

One consequence of public blockchains' lack of scalability is higher transaction costs. For the early years of Bitcoin, transaction fees were indeed very small, averaging about 11 cents (in $US) per transaction in June 2014 and 28 cents in December of 2016.[40] When the network is not congested, very small fees are enough to incentivize miners. For a specific example, we found a successful transaction on March 12th 2017, where a person offered just 45 cents worth of bitcoins to transfer over $8200 worth of bitcoins.[41] However, when the network is congested, miners cannot include all of the newly validated transactions in the next block, so the miners' algorithms select the transactions offering the highest fees. As Bitcoin traffic exploded in December of 2017, fees skyrocketed to as high as $55 per transaction.[42] During peak times in 2017, senders offering smaller fees sometimes waited days to be added to the blockchain, or worse, their orphaned transaction eventually dropped out and needed to be resent.[43] Moving ahead to 2021/2022, Figures 10.6 and 10.7 show the average transaction fee per transaction in US dollars for Bitcoin and Ethereum. Keep in mind, these are *averages*—senders who want to guarantee that their transaction is included in the next block offered fees as high as hundreds of dollars' worth of bitcoin or ether.

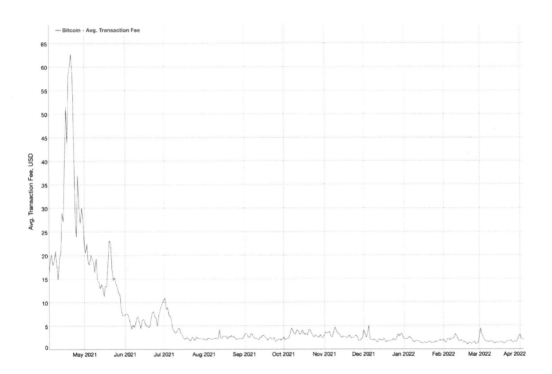

**Figure 10.6: Average transaction fee on the Bitcoin network
2021-2022 in US Dollars**

Source: https://bitinfocharts.com/comparison/bitcoin-transactionfees.html#1y

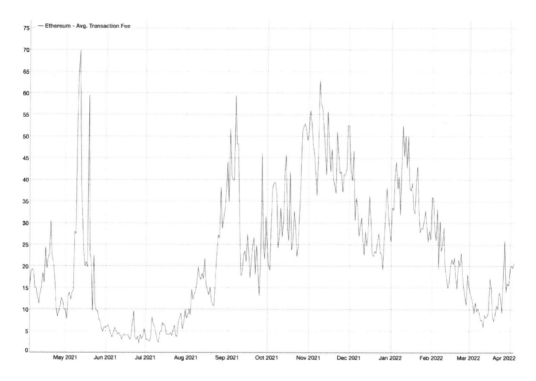

**Figure 10.7: Average transaction fee on the Ethereum Network
2021-2022 in US Dollars**

Source: https://bitinfocharts.com/comparison/ethereum-transactionfees.html#1y

Performance and scaling solutions for public blockchains. Open source communities and private enterprises have already implemented some innovations and continue to develop new solutions to improve public blockchains. Getting a globally diverse set of decentralized developers and miners to agree to upgrades is a considerable effort that can take years of negotiations and emergency meetings.[44] When the community cannot agree, splinter groups launch 'hard forks', which are permanent, divergent paths off of the original blockchain. This is why we now have not only the original Bitcoin, but Bitcoin XT; Bitcoin Classic; Bitcoin Gold; and Bitcoin Cash. Moreover, forks of forks happened when infighting continued. For example, Bitcoin Cash is a 2017 hard fork of Bitcoin, aiming to increase the size of blocks and to keep transaction fees low. The following year, the Bitcoin Cash community fought over two proposed upgrades, which prompted one faction to create a hard fork of Bitcoin Cash called Bitcoin SV (SV for 'Satoshi Vision'). Thus, the communities do not always agree on technical upgrades. Here, we highlight two of the major performance and scaling solutions for Bitcoin, called Segregated Witness and the Lightning Network. We also cover innovations for Ethereum, including Proof-of-Stake, sharding, and layer 2 solutions (see Table 10.1).

Bitcoin	Ethereum
Segregated Witness: Separates digital signature from transactions to increase block size, fix transaction malleability and enable layer 2 solutions; Implemented August 2017.	**Proof-of-Stake:** Block validators are selected based on their stake in the network, such as how many coins or how long coins have been owned. Uses less electricity than Proof-of-Work and creates blocks faster. Beacon Chain is in test mode as of April 2022.
Layer 2 – Lightning Network: Off-chain payment channels to process intermediate transactions; Explorer: https://explorer.acinq.co/ Available to SegWit adopters in 2017.	Although there are many layer 2 solutions, we focus on Polygon. Polygon was founded in 2017; Polygon PoS explorer: https://polygonscan.com/
	Sharding: Divides Ethereum into multiple chains called shards; planned for 2023.

Table 10.1: Examples of performance and scalability solutions

For Bitcoin, **Segregated Witness**, called 'SegWit'[45], has been the biggest protocol change in Bitcoin since its inception. It improved Bitcoin in a number of ways. First, SegWit squeezed more transactions into a block by moving digital signatures (called 'witnesses') from the sender's address to a new part of a Bitcoin block. By segregating the signatures, block sizes increased from 1 megabyte to possibly 4 megabytes, thus improving throughput. This innovation also solved **transaction malleability**, the possibility for a hacker to alter a digital signature before it is added to a block, which would change the transaction ID. The recipient would still receive the bitcoins, but the sender would not be able to find it by searching for the transaction ID (see Glossary for more).

Not all of the Bitcoin miners welcomed SegWit. Some miners did not like the design, which moved the anchor for the signatures from being embedded in the Merkle Root to the first transaction in the block (called the coinbase transaction) used to reward the winning miner.[46] Another issue was the deployment strategy: SegWit was released as a 'soft fork', which means than non-SegWit adopters could still mine Bitcoins. Some miners thought it would be cleaner (yet more difficult) to release as a hard fork. Many emergency meetings occurred among the Bitcoin community as SegWit was being debated. SegWit had a rocky adoption[47], but was activated as a soft fork to the Bitcoin Core in August 2017.[48] Two years later, a little less than half of Bitcoin transactions used SegWit, probably because people were slow to upgrade wallets. A faction of the mining community—representing about 2,000 nodes—decided to completely walk away from Bitcoin by creating a hard fork called **Bitcoin Classic** in May of 2016.[49]

SegWit enabled the use of the **Lightning Network**. The Lighting Network is a layer 2 solution that tracks intermediate transfers of funds off-chain and only posts the value of the initial credit and the final account balance transfers to the blockchain. The solution helps unclutter the blockchain with intermediate transactions. Functionally, it's like opening up a bar tab. A person secures a bar tab with a credit card, orders several drinks (or sends a few drinks back), and then settles the final bill with one payment. To be clear: transactions are not publicly broadcast, but they are encrypted and routed from the payer to the payee via intermediate nodes.[50] On this day in April 2022, 18,410 Lightning Network nodes were operational, and they were processing 82,128 payment channels.[51]

Turning our attention to Ethereum, a number of performance and scalability solutions have planned for 'Ethereum 2.0'.[52] The vision is to make Ethereum more scalable to support thousands of transactions per second, more secure, and more sustainable. Ethereum's roadmap calls for a phased solution that includes:

1. Beacon Chain to introduce Proof-of-Stake in parallel to Ethereum mainnet's Proof-of-Work

2. The Merge to pivot Ethereum's mainnet from Proof-of-Work to Beacon Chain's Proof-of-Stake

3. Shard Chains for sharding.

Sharding will involve segmenting the validation process so that not every Ethereum node validates every transaction. If adopted, each shard in Ethereum would act like its own blockchain, but shards would be merged on the main chain by a sharding manger smart contract.[53] As for the status, the Beacon Chain test net went live in 2020. A new token, called ETH2, was used for Beacon Chain as a validator reward, but all references to ETH2 tokens or calling the upgrades 'Ethereum 2.0' are being phased out. [54] The Merge is estimated to happen in late 2022 and Shard Chains in 2023. Vitalik Buterin, Ethereum's co-founder, said, *"Ethereum 1.0 is a couple of people's scrappy attempt to build a world computer; Ethereum 2.0 will actually be the world computer."*[55]

Several layer 2 solutions run atop of Ethereum's mainnet. Here we cover the Raiden Network, Plasma, and Polygon.

The *Raiden Network* runs on top of Ethereum. Heiko Hees, CEO and founder of Brainbot in Germany, launched the Raiden Network as a high-speed network for micropayments on Ethereum.[56] Described as similar to the Lightning Network, the basic idea is to switch from a model where all transactions hit the shared ledger on the blockchain (which is the bottleneck) to a model where users can privately exchange messages which sign the transfer of value. Raiden nodes connect to Ethereum nodes using an API. The processing of a million, confidential transactions per second is possible, because they are not added to the blockchain. Furthermore, transaction fees are reported to be 'tiny'.[57]

By 2022, Layer 2 solutions based on ***Plasma*** have become popular. Plasma was designed by Vitalik Buterin and Joseph Poon. Polygon, OMG Network, Gazelle, LeapDAO, and Gluon are customized versions of the Plasma framework.[58] As we learned in previous chapters, Aave, EY OpsChain Traceability, and ANSAcheck use Polygon to lower transaction costs and to speed transactions while using the Ethereum blockchain for settlements.

Polygon (formerly Matic Network) was founded in 2017 by Jaynti Kanani, Sandeep Nailwal, and Anurag Arjun. Polygon's mission is to bring the world to Ethereum. *"Polygon believes in Web3 for all. Polygon is a decentralized Ethereum scaling platform that enables developers to build scalable user-friendly dApps with low transaction fees without ever sacrificing on security."* Polygon is a suite of solutions already in production, including Ethereum sides chain based on Proof-of-Stake ('Polygon PoS'); zero-knowledge proof rollups to allow low-cost and scalable token transfers ('Polygon Hermez'); a modular framework for building public or private blockchains that are compatible with Ethereum ('Polygon Edge'). Polygon Nightfall is operating in a testnet as of April, 2022.[59] Polygon PoS had 140 million unique addresses by April 2022 and was processing over 3 million transactions per day.[60] Over 10,000 dApps had been deployed on Polygon PoS for NFTs, decentralized exchanges, decentralized finance, games, metaverses, and DAOs.

10.4.2. Performance and scalability of private blockchains

Private-permissioned blockchains solve the performance and scaling challenges by limiting the number of nodes needed to validate transactions and by allowing private messaging and channels among trading partners. Many permissioned blockchain protocols create divisions of labor, so some nodes might be validating transactions while other nodes might be sequencing their outputs, and still others may be adding sequenced blocks to the ledger. Subsequently, permissioned blockchain protocols like Corda, Quorum and Hyperledger Fabric can settle transactions within seconds.

As of 2022, the exact scalability of private blockchains is an unknown, as few have been adopted to scale. However, most private blockchains claim they are highly scalable. For example, IBM tested Hyperledger Fabric within its cloud data center and reported throughput of 3,000 transactions per second with latency of under a second.[61] *FastFabric* aims to increase Hyperledger Fabric transactions from 3,000 to 20,000 per second. Developed by professors at the University of Waterloo and University of Massachusetts, FastFabric improved throughput by separating the hardware for committer and endorser nodes; separating metadata from transaction data; introducing parallelism and caching; and moving world-state key-value stores to light-weight-in-memory stores.[62]

10.5. Anonymity

Within many public blockchain, every transaction's sending address, receiving address and amount is transparent to anyone with access to the Internet. For example, Figure 10.8 illustrates an example of an actual Bitcoin transaction that took place on February 25, 2016 at 10:24:44 am. The public has no easy way to identify the trading partners, yet the world can observe the transaction took place.[63]

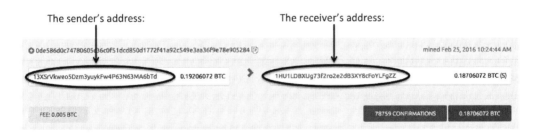

Figure 10.8: A Bitcoin transaction that occurred in Block 400000 on Feb 25, 2016

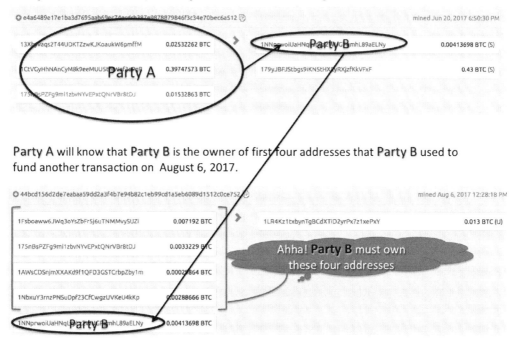

Figure 10.9: Meta patterns that can arise from a blockchain's transparency

Although public blockchains are anonymous in that no personal identities are revealed on the ledger, meta patterns can emerge where identities could be revealed. For example, many transactions are funded with multiple addresses, so patterns can emerge where one party can track another party's transactions. Figure 10.9 illustrates how this can occur. If Party A sends value to an address owned by Party B on one date, Party A can later determine additional addresses owned by Party B when Party B spends the coins. Consequently, it is more apt to describe Bitcoin (and Ethereum) as 'pseudo-anonymous'. This was something Satoshi Nakamoto acknowledged in his white paper. Nakamoto recommended that new addresses should be generated for new transactions: *"As an additional firewall, a new key pair should be used for each transaction to keep them from being linked to a common owner. Some linking is still unavoidable with multi-input transactions, which necessarily reveal that the same owner owned their inputs. The risk is that if the owner of a key is revealed, linking could reveal other transactions that belonged to the same owner."*[64]

Open-source communities are working to address these issues. We examine two such solutions: zero knowledge proofs and CryptoNotes.

10.5.1. Zero-knowledge proofs

Zero-knowledge proofs (ZKPs) were developed by Shafi Goldwasser, Charles Rackoff, and Silvio Micali in 1985.[65] Zero-knowledge proofs are a method for one party to verify possession of a piece of information to other parties without revealing the information. In general, there are two types of zero-knowledge proofs: challenge-response and non-interactive.

As a simple example of a ***challenge-response ZKP***, suppose Alice wants to prove to Bob that she knows the exact number of jellybeans that fills a large jar without telling Bob the exact number (see Figure 10.10). What might Alice do to convince Bob she knows the amount? Alice could instruct Bob to take any number of jellybeans out of the jar after she leaves the room. Bob makes his choice. Alice re-enters the room and Bob exits the room. Alice recounts the beans and compares the current count with the previous count to calculate exactly how many jellybeans (if any) Bob removed. When Bob returns, Alice tells Bob exactly how many jellybeans he took. If Bob thinks Alice made a lucky guess, rounds of the same choice could be made over and over again. Eventually, Bob will be convinced that Alice possesses the knowledge of the exact number of jellybeans without her ever revealing the number. A challenge-response ZKP has some limitations: the challenge-response is coordinated for known parties; iterations can slow performance; and the results are probabilistic rather than deterministic because Alice could get lucky by guessing the correct number.

Figure 10.10: Jellybean example for a challenge-response zero-knowledge proof

Most blockchain applications use another type of ZNP, called *a non-interactive zero-knowledge proof.* These ZKPs do not require iterations; someone can prove to the *public* that they know something.

Proving someone solved a Sudoku puzzle is a common example to illustrate a non-interactive ZNP.[66] A Sudoku puzzle has nine rows and nine columns. Within the puzzle, there are nine squares. Puzzles start with some cells filled in (see left side of Figure 10.11). To solve the puzzle, one must find a unique solution so that the numbers one through nine appear exactly once across each row, down each column, and within each square (see right side of Figure 10.11 for the solution). Suppose there is a contest to see who solved the puzzle first. Suppose Alice won. How might Alice convince everyone she solved the puzzle first without revealing the solution? Alice could construct an algorithm that takes the numbers from each *row* and randomly shuffles them; Takes the numbers from each *column* and randomly shuffles them; and takes the numbers within each *square* and randomly shuffles them. If the result shows 27 collections of nine numbers with each collection containing the numbers one through nine, Alice can prove she solved the puzzle without revealing the solution.

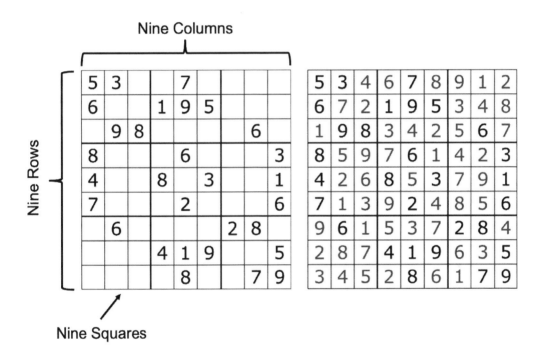

Figure 10.11: A Sudoku puzzle and its solution

On the left side of the figure, a Sudoku puzzle has some cells filled in. The challenge is to find the solution so that the numbers one through nine appear exactly once across each row, down each column, and within each square. The right side of the figure shows the solution.

Source: https://en.wikipedia.org/wiki/Sudoku [67]

In blockchain applications, non-interactive ZKPs are used to guarantee that transactions are valid without revealing information about the sender, receiver, and/or transaction. Zcash, Quorum, EY's Nightfall, MediLedger, and many other blockchains use ZKPs. Zcash, for example, uses a cryptographic zero-knowledge proof called 'zk-SNARK',[68] which stands for 'Zero-Knowledge Succinct Non-Interactive Argument of Knowledge.'[69]

EY's Nightfall is a smart contract protocol that uses non-interactive ZKPs. Nightfall allows parties to exchange tokens on a public blockchain (Ethereum) in a way that protects their privacy by masking the sender, receiver, and amounts of the exchange while still preventing a double spend. Essentially, Nightfall is a confidential escrow service for ERC-20 (fungible) and ERC 721 (non-fungible) tokens.

Here we provide a high level overview; it is meant to convey the principles. Let's assume Alice wants to send Token T to Bob. At the start of the transaction, Alice's wallet currently has possession of the private key that controls the ownership of Token T recorded on the blockchain. To safely send the token to Bob in a way that prevents Alice from double spending it and ensures that only Bob can retrieve it (or that she can retrieve it before Bob does if the agreement goes sour), the following steps are executed. First, Alice's wallet creates a token commitment by using her private key to put Token T in escrow controlled by a smart contract (called a shield contract) on the blockchain. The shield contract takes control over the token. Alice's software creates a token commitment for Bob using Bob's public key and a secret key only Alice knows. Alice sends Bob's token commitment to the shield contract. Alice's software also creates Alice's nullification of Alice's token commitment so she will no longer have control over the token *if* Bob retrieves it. Alice's nullification is sent to the shield contract. Offline, Alice sends the secret key, Bob's token commitment, and the token ID to Bob. This message happens *offchain*, so it's important this message is secured to prevent someone other than Bob from using it. Bob can now take possession of Token T by proving to the shield contract he knows the secret key. When Bob is ready, his software uses the secret key to nullify his token commitment and issues a PayToAddress command to move control of the token to Bob's wallet. When the transaction is finished, the balance in the shield contract is zero and Bob has the private key that controls Token T in his wallet. Alice will no longer be able to retrieve it.

There seems to be a lot of steps here, but each step is necessary. Why doesn't Alice just send the money to Bob's wallet directly like Bitcoin does? The way Bitcoin works, recipients cannot prevent people from sending value to their addresses. In Bitcoin (and in many public blockchains), anyone can 'air drop' money into someone's wallet without their permission. Many individuals want—and certainly enterprises need—to control their receivables. Nightfall enables that; the recipient has to pro-actively retrieve the tokens from the shield contract.

According to Chen Zur, EY Partner/Principle and US Blockchain Practice Leader, *"With Nightfall, there is no way for anyone to know that Alice and Bob did a transaction between them. All you know is that one of the wallets sent some tokens to another wallet, but there's no way to know what happened between them. And that's the first step. We are developing this further to also include contract rules for purchase agreements, such as terms and conditions, but what we have right now and what is in the public domain is the ability to move tokens between two wallets without anyone knowing what happened."*

By 2020, EY had shown that running Nightfall on the public Ethereum was less expensive than using traditional private networks for high-value, low-volume transactions. A Canadian customer was using it to trace the provenance of high-value medical equipment.[70] In 2021, EY released Nightfall 3 as open source, which combined ZKP with a new model for validating transactions more efficiently, called 'optimistic rollup'. Paul Brody, EY Global Blockchain Leader, said, *"Based on EY experience, ZK-Optimistic roll-ups are currently among the most effective in balancing security incentives and mathematical efficiency for running private transactions on the public Ethereum network. As we have in the past, we are again contributing this code into the public domain to speed up enterprise adoption of this technology."[71]*

10.5.2. CryptoNote and Monero

CryptoNote is another protocol used in blockchains that offers more privacy than those used in Bitcoin and Ethereum. CryptoNote's transactions cannot be followed through the blockchain in a way that reveals who sent or received coins.[72] Monero is an example of a blockchain that uses the CryptoNote protocol. To understand how little information is revealed on Monero's public blockchain, see Figure 10.12.

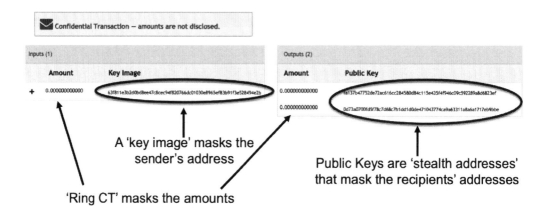

Figure 10.12: An example of a Monero transaction [73]

Monero uses 'ring signatures' and a 'key image' to hide the sender's address; a 'stealth address' (also called a public key) to hide the recipient's address(es); and 'ring confidential transactions' to mask amounts. These innovations create complete anonymity, but do so in a way that prevents a double spend.

To understand how Monero works, we'll begin with the wallet. Every Monero wallet has two sets of private-public key pairs—one for viewing, one for spending:

The ***view key pair*** is comprised of a private view key and public view key. An account owner needs the private view key to find transactions associated with his or her wallet address on the blockchain.

The *spend key pair* is comprised of a private spend key and public spend key. The private spend key can only be used once, meaning that if someone wants to spend money from an address, one must spend all of it. As we will see, this architecture helps to prevent double spending.

A Monaro address is a concatenation of the *public spend key* and the *public view key*.

Let's walk through a transaction to see how the algorithms work. Suppose Alice wants to send four Monero to Bob. Her digital wallet will select an address or addresses that contains more than four Monero because Alice needs to offer the Monero miners a small transaction fee. The wallet selects an address with ten Monero in it. Again, the protocol requires that all ten Monero are consumed in the transaction. So, for this transaction, the wallet will send money to two addresses: Bob's address and a new address for Alice's change of 3.99 Monero (so the miner gets .01 Monero).

To create the input side of the transaction, Alice's wallet uses the unique private spend key stored only in her wallet that is associated with the public spend key. To create the output side of the transaction for Bob, Alice needs Bob's address (comprised of Bob's public spend key and a public view key). These will be used to create a new 'spend-one-time-only' public key for Bob. This public key serves as a 'stealth address' to mask Bob's real address. Alice will also get a new address for her change (see right side of Figure 10.12).

To process the transaction, Monero masks Alice's identity (or more specifically, masks her public spend key) by creating a 'ring signature' comprised of Alice's signature and a number of decoys selected from past Monero transactions stored in the blockchain. A 'key image' is derived from the output Alice sent, but it's impossible to know which address produced the key image to an outsider (see left side of Figure 10.12). To an outsider, any of the decoys could have used their private key to sign the transaction and create the key image, but really only Alice did. (Note: the more decoys requested, the more resources consumed, so higher fees will be needed to incentivize miners to include the transaction.)

To prevent a double spend, miners only need to make sure that the key image appears nowhere else in the blockchain. Thus, the key image is the main way Monero makes sure the private key was not used before to spend the amount.

So how does Bob's wallet find the money Alice sent if it's not visible on the blockchain? Bob's wallet scans the blockchain with his private view key to find the output. Since part of the new public spend address contains the public view key he sent to Alice, the private view key pair can find the transaction and lay claim to it. Once the output is detected, it is retrieved and put into Bob's wallet. Then, his wallet calculates a one-time private spend key that corresponds with the public spend key. Only he can spend it with his wallet's private spend key.

Finally, to mask the amounts, Monero uses 'ring confidential transactions' or 'RingCT'. This protocol uses a 'range proof' to prove to miners that the inputs of a transaction are equal to the outputs, but miners do not know the value of either.

While zero knowledge proofs and CryptoNotes are effective at masking senders, receivers, and amounts, the blockchain protocol is not the only threat to anonymity. If wallets are transacting over the Internet, messages will contain other revealing information like an IP address. To achieve true anonymity, senders and receivers would need to use a network that masks IP addresses, like Tor or the Invisible Internet (IP2) protocol. For example, the illegal marketplace website, Silk Road, chose Bitcoin as its payment application and Tor as its network (see Glossary for the story of Silk Road).

10.6. Confidentiality

"The issue is that some companies are afraid that information that's being collected for the blockchain will be used for other purposes. So let's say I'm a pharmacy. If I verified all the products I have on hand, I'm announcing my inventory. Companies are concerned that this added intelligence could be used for other purposes such as contract negotiations, etc."

Bob Celeste, CEO and Founder of the Center for Supply Chain Studies[74]

MULTI-LEDGERING

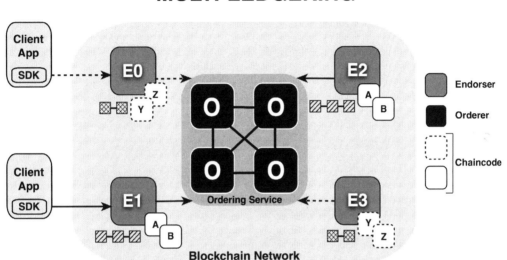

- PEERS **E0** AND **E3** CONNECT TO THE ▨ CHANNEL FOR CHAINCODES **Y** AND **Z**
- PEERS **E1** AND **E2** CONNECT TO THE ▧ CHANNEL FOR CHAINCODES **A** AND **B**

Figure 10.13: Channels in Hyperledger Fabric

Fabric allows parties to use a software development toolkit (SDK) to code smart contracts (called chaincodes) to create separate ledgers for different agreements

Source: https://www.altoros.com/blog/wp-content/uploads/2017/04/hyperledger-fabric-v1-general-availability-multi-ledgering-

Moving from public, permissionless blockchains to private, permissioned blockchains, we obviously cannot allow anonymity among trading partners. Regulations require that enterprises know the identity of their customers, employees, and suppliers. However, enterprises are concerned about confidentiality. With one shared ledger, how do we allow some folks to view transactions while preventing other folks from viewing transactions

423

when we are all sharing a blockchain application? Chapter 3 already presented *Quorum* as an example of a solution. With Quorum, participants can execute private and public smart contracts so that the ledger is segmented into a private state database and a public state database.[75] Within a single ledger, all nodes can view Quorum's public states, but only those nodes party to private contracts can view private states.

Hyperledger Fabric uses the concept of channels. Channels provide a data-partitioning capability, so that only those parties with permission to use the channel are able to see it.[76] Confidential transactions are encrypted with secret keys known only to their originators, validators, and authorized auditors. Smart contracts (called Chaincode in Fabric) specify a channel's parties and the rules by which assets can be created and modified on the channel's ledger (see Figure 10.13).[77]

10.7. Interoperability

Interoperability is the ability for one system to use another system. Among all of the technical challenges, interoperability is the most important one to solve to truly realize an 'Internet of Value'.[78] Traditional companies like Accenture and IBM; startups like Aion, Cosmos, and Polkadot; and blockchain consortia like the Hyperledger Foundation, all have interoperability projects underway. There is clearly a need for blockchain interoperability to seamlessly interconnect:

- multiple public blockchains (e.g. Bitcoin and Ethereum)
- multiple private blockchains (e.g. Hyperledger Fabric and R3)
- public and private blockchains (e.g. Ethereum and Hyperledger Fabric)
- blockchains with legacy systems (e.g. MediLeder and SAP; Ripple and SWIFT)

Interoperability requirements include:[79]

'All or none' atomicity: An interoperability solution should ensure that *all* the actions associated with a cross-chain transaction execute, or *all* the actions should fail; no partial executions should be allowed. For example, if Alice records her assets on Chain A and she wants to send some value to Bob who records his assets on Chain B, an interoperability solution should ensure that (a) Alice's account is debited AND Bob's account is credited or (b) that NEITHER action occurs.

Universality: An interoperability solution should be universal by not requiring a custom program to be built for each new chain.

No need for trusted third parties (TTPs): An interoperability solution should not rely on centralized trusted third parties. If this criterion is required, it will eliminate the interoperability solutions that rely on notaries (explained below).

Source code availability: An interoperability solution's source code should be available for audit so that other criteria can be assessed.

Developer and user friendly: An interoperability solution should be easy to use by developers and seamless to end-users.

All interoperability approaches 'get into' applications though Application Programming Interfaces (APIs) (see Glossary).

10.7.1. Three ways to connect blockchains

There are three common ways for connecting two or more blockchains:

1. **One-time asset pass** where an asset is 'destroyed' on chain A before being 'created' on chain B.

2. A **cross-chain oracle** where one chain needs to read data from another chain. One-way reads are also called 'one-way pegs'.

3. **Cross-chain transaction processing** where two or more blockchains want to coordinate operations so that a single asset can be used by more than one chain. These are also called 'two-way pegs'.

Among these three, cross-chain transaction processing is the holy grail of interoperability; the first two are relatively easy to accomplish.

1. One-time asset pass. Enterprises and individuals want the ability to switch blockchain solutions. Since digital ledgers are immutable, how is this done technically? One way is to 'burn' the asset on one blockchain and then recreate it on a different blockchain (see Figure 10.14). A *proof-of-burn* is an algorithm that sends value to a verifiably un-spendable address that permanently locks that value on chain. For Bitcoin, this could be achieved by using the scripting language for the transaction in a way that would ensure the value could never be redeemed. For example, setting the 'txout' to only execute if $2 = 3$.[80] For Ethereum, there are known burn addresses, such as address 0x0000000000000 0000000000000000000000000dEaD, where tokens can be credited but never withdrawn.[81]

2. Cross-chain oracle. A cross-chain oracle is a one-way read of data from one chain by another chain. The term **oracle** refers to the external data needed from a source chain to perform some operation in a destination chain. *BTC Relay* was one of the first cross-chain oracles. BTC Relay allowed users of applications developed on the Ethereum platform to pay with bitcoins. Developed by Joseph Chow, BTC Relay is an open-source smart contract that was deployed on the Ethereum blockchain in May of 2016.[82] The open-source community conveyed much enthusiasm for it and was seen as an important application of Satoshi Nakamoto's *Simple Payment Verification (SPV).*[83] (SPV proofs are explained below and in the Glossary.)

BTC Relay stored Bitcoin's blockchain headers inside of Ethereum, thus maintaining a mini-version of the entire Bitcoin blockchain. An application developer inside Ethereum could query BTC Relay to verify a transaction on the bitcoin network.[84] BTC Relay automatically executed with no trusted third parties. BTC Relay was quite fascinating in how it incentivized people to keep adding new Bitcoin blocks to the smart contract, on average, every ten minutes. 'Relayers' who submit new Bitcoin block headers to BTC Relay contract got paid a small transaction fee when other developers queried BTC Relay to verify a transaction.[85] BTC Relay was in essence a 'program' that read from one chain to 'prove' existence and then is used as a 'true/false' or as a value in the Ethereum platform. Despite the excitement of BTC Relay in 2016, the last transaction was in October 2018.[86] Increased competition and alternative oracles provide more than just Bitcoin pegs—they also provide other external resources that are 'authenticated' with proofs.

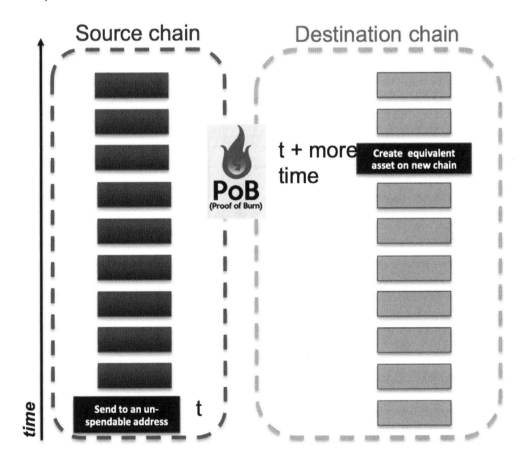

Figure 10.14: Proof-of-Burn is one way to 'destroy' assets on one blockchain and 'recreate' them on another

3. Cross-chain transaction processing. For cross-chain transaction processing, a two-way peg is needed. With a two-way peg, an asset must be 'locked' in the source chain before actions on the destination chain are taken. When the destination chain is finished processing, it locks the asset in the destination chain so that the source chain can once again take control (see Figure 10.15).

We've covered three ways to connect blockchains. Next, we look at three examples of technical strategies for blockchain interoperability.

10.7.2. Technical strategies for interoperability

In 2016, the R3 blockchain consortium commissioned Vitalik Buterin, the inventor of Ethereum, to investigate strategies for blockchain interoperability.[87] He described three blockchain interoperability strategies:

1. **Notaries:** A single third party or multiple parties coordinate cross-chain operations.[88]

2. **Sidechains/relays**: A smart contract inside one blockchain automatically validates and reads events in another blockchain.

3. **Hash-locking**: Two or more blockchains coordinate operations using the same hash trigger. Operations can also be coordinated by adding a time-out feature to the shared hash feature, creating what are called hash-time locked contracts (**HTLCs**).

Notaries. Notaries are the simplest way to connect two or more blockchains. A notary has control of locks on both chains. A notary must operate full nodes (running the software and storing the entire ledger) for all of the chains to which it connects. This ensures that notaries are grabbing transactions as quickly as possible and have visibility to the entire set of transactions. Notaries may rely on just a single custodian or on multiple custodians. *A single notary* connects two or more blockchains using one trusted third party (see Figure 10.16)

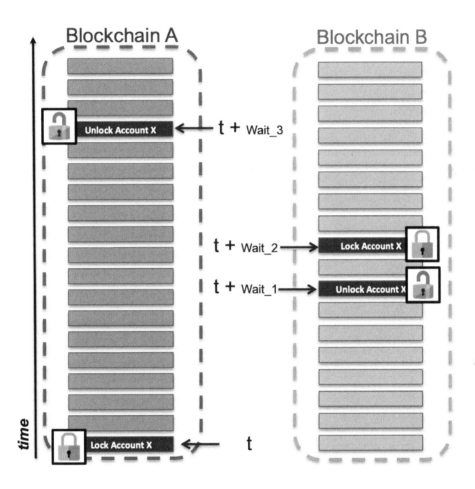

Figure 10.15: Blockchain time delays in cross-chain transactions

At time t, Chain A locks the address on Chain A and indicates an address on Chain B. That transaction requires some time for the Chain A nodes to reach consensus. After the wait, Chain B creates the equivalent number of assets on Chain B. (Assets are not moved across chains but are replaced with equivalent assets on Chain B). Chain B executes its transactions, locks the address, and indicates an address on Chain A. Some time must pass for the Chain B nodes to reach consensus. After a wait, Chain A unlocks the address and it is back in control of the asset.

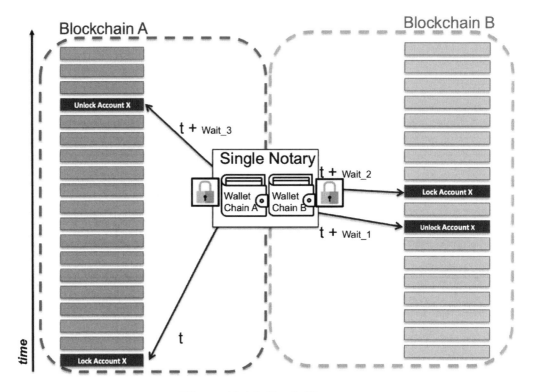

Figure 10.16: Single Notary

In this figure, a centralized exchange runs full nodes for both chains. It controls the wallets and locks for addresses stored on both chains. It is the simplest interoperability solution but relies on trusting one centralized party.

Source: Figure adapted from Lerner (2016)[89]

Exchanges are common examples of single notaries. Exchanges allow users to easily buy and sell cryptocurrencies and to exchange cryptocurrencies for fiat currencies; but that convenience comes at the acceptance and trust of centralized control, and with the risks of a single point of failure. Cyber-thieves target exchanges because of the large honeypot of value stored all in one place.

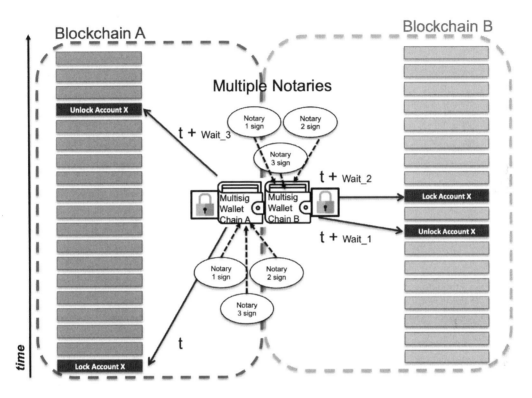

Figure 10.17: Multiple notaries

In this figure, an exchange runs full nodes for both blockchains. It holds the wallets and locks for addresses stored on both chains, but funds are only released when n of m signatures from federation members are signed. It is a simple interoperability solution, but relies on trusting the federation.

Source: Figure adapted from Lerner (2016)[90]

A multi-signature notary, or federation, relies on multiple, independent custodians (see Figure 10.17). Multi-signature addresses require multiple users to sign a transaction before it can be broadcast onto the blockchain network.[91] This method is more secure than a single notary, but trust remains centralized within the hands of a few entities. Typically, algorithms require that a majority of the notaries validate a transaction or event.

More specifically, the federation requires that '*n* of *m*' members sign the transaction.

BitGo was the first multi-signature wallet, launched in August of 2013. The BitGo wallet required two out of three signatures, of which BitGo was one signatory. In 2015, the exchange Bitfinex adopted BitGo, providing all its customers with BitGo's multi-signature wallets. In 2016, Bitfinex was hacked and the perpetrator used the keys to steal $60 million from the exchange.[92] Since that fateful event, BitGo recovered and has reached many milestones, including providing multisignature wallets for 100 coins.[93]

By 2022, BitGo served as custodian to more than $64 billion in digital assets, which are insured by a policy with Lloyds.[94] In addition to BitGo, other popular multi-signature wallets include Armory, Coinbase, CoPay, and Electrum.[95]

Sidechains/Relays. Sidechains and relays provide the functions of a notary, but rely on automatically executing algorithms instead of on custodians. Back et al. (2014) first conceived of 'pegged sidechains' as a way for bitcoins and other ledger assets to be transferred between multiple, independent blockchains.[96] For these authors, a sidechain is a two-way peg to a parent chain (or main chain) that allows assets to be interchanged at a predetermined rate. But the term is relative to the asset, not to the network. For this reason, Vitalik Buterin laments the term 'sidechain' in his white paper on interoperability. He argued that it is better to use the phrase, *"a relay of chain A exists on chain B"* or *"D is a cross-chain portable digital asset with home ledger A that can also be used on chain B."* [97] According to Back et al. (2014), sidechains should:

- run in parallel to main chains

- allow free movement to/from the main chain

- be firewalled so theft in one chain cannot be replicated in the other chain

- allow for different consensus algorithms

- be fully independent from the main chain

- be fast and efficient[98]

Liquid is an example of a federated sidechain to the Bitcoin blockchain. Developed by Blockstream, it allows members to settle Bitcoin transactions in seconds. According to its website, the federation of members include exchanges, traders, and financial institutions from nine countries across four continents.[99] Readers can view Liquid transactions on https://blockstream.info/liquid/.

Many sidechains/relays use Satoshi Nakamoto's *Simple Payment Verification* (SPV). The idea is that someone can prove that their transaction is included in a valid block and that many other valid blocks were built on top of it. Nakamoto (2008) described SPV as a way to verify bitcoin transactions without running a full network node. Rather, one only needs to maintain a copy of the block headers and then find the security links (called a *Merkle tree* branch, see Chapter 3 or Glossary) to the transaction to prove it was verified and accepted by the network. SPV shows that *"tokens have been locked up on one chain so validators can safely unlock an equivalent value on the other chain."[100]* Figure 10.18 illustrates that SPV Proofs can be used to coordinate cross-chain transactions without relying on a notary but instead relying only on the algorithmic proofs.

Hash-time locked contracts (HTLC). HTLCs are a clever way to coordinate transactions across two blockchains by relying on the same data trigger, called a 'secret key', 'private key' or 'preimage'. Figure 10.19 shows how it works. Alice initiates a smart contract on one blockchain that locks value into an address with the hash of the secret key so that one of two things happen: The receiver, Bob, either retrieves the value in the address using the secret key (this is the 'hash lock') and his digital signature, or the contract expires and returns the value to Alice (this is the 'time lock'). So how will Bob get the secret key in a safe manner? Bob creates a smart contract on his chain and locks value using the same hash of the secret key. Alice must reveal the secret key (and her digital signature) to unlock the value in the Bob's contract. The instance that happens, Bob's smart contract learns the secret key and uses it to unlock the value on Alice's smart contract. It's a simple, yet brilliant, solution that eliminates counter-party risks.

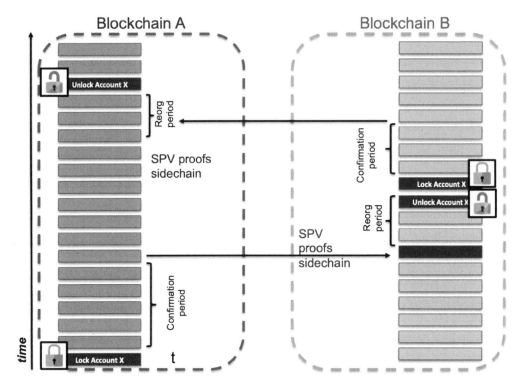

Figure 10.18: Cross-chain transactions using
Simple Payment Verification (SPV) Proofs

SPV proofs run automatically and thus do not rely on TTPs. Chain A locks the
asset and then must wait until the transaction has settled and more valid blocks have
been created on top of it so that parties are confident that they are dealing with the
longest, and thus most valid, chain. After the confirmation period, an SPV proof can
be submitted to Chain B. Chain B now has to wait, a time called the 'reorg period'.
It's possible, another party may submit an SPV proof that contradicts the previous
SPV proof. Chain B will select the SPV with the longest chain. Once confident
the SPV proof is valid, it unlocks the asset on Chain B, executes transactions, locks
the asset, and waits for the transaction to settle before sending an SPV proof back
to Chain A.

Source: Figure adapted from Lerner (2016) [101]

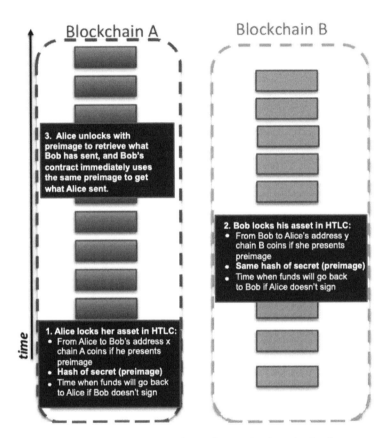

Figure 10.19: Conceptual rendering of a hash-time locked contract (HTLC)

Interledger, Hyperledger Cactus, Cosmos, Polkadot, Harmony, WanChain, Chainlink, Hybrix and Loom are important cross-chain solutions.[102] To get a sense of how they work, we cover Interledger and Cactus.

Interledger Protocol. The Interledger Protocol (ILP) accommodates HTLCs. Two Ripple engineers published the ILP's white paper back in 2015. In 2021, the Interledger Foundation was formed. Its mission is *"a non-profit advocate for the web, promoting innovation, creativity, and inclusion by advancing open payment standards and technologies that seamlessly connect our global society."[103]*

435

For a given payment, the ILP protocol sends many micropayments with confirmations between micropayments to minimize the risk that a node could steal or fail to send a payment through a network (see Figure 10.20). ILP uses 'cryptographic escrow' that *"conditionally locks funds to allow secure payments through untrusted connectors."*[104] For a given transaction, the ILP recognizes three types of participants: sender, routers, and receiver. Routers (also called 'connectors') are nodes that find a trust path between the sender and receiver. Nodes use the same hashlock for HTLCs across the paths.[105] (For a detailed example of how HTCLs flow through an end-to-end transaction, see https://interledger.org/rfcs/0022-hashed-timelock-agreements/.) While HTLCs are used, they still require that the Interledger Module be updated and installed for each of the ledgers (blockchains) that are being interacted with. This means that as new platforms come online, if they do not follow a standard the protocol recognizes, one needs to be added.

Hyperledger Cactus. Founded in 2020, Cactus is one of the projects managed by the Hyperledger Foundation. Accenture and Fujitsu donated the source code. Cactus is a pluggable, enterprise-grade framework for transacting across multiple blockchains. The first version was released in March 2022 and awaiting community review. It has ledger connectors to Hyperledger Besu; Hyperledger Fabric; Hyperledger Indy; Hyperledger Iroha; Hyperledger Sawtooth; Corda; Go-Ethereum; Quorum; and Xdai.[106]

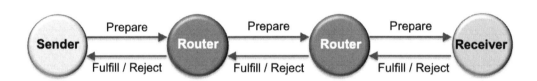

Figure 10.20: The Interledger Protocol

An aggregate payment is split into multiple micropayments. Each micropayment is routed over a network and a fulfillment confirmation must be received before sending the next micropayment.

Source: https://interledger.org/overview.html

10.8. Conclusion

We have thus outlined the major technical challenges and emerging solutions as of 2022. To test your understanding of this chapter and previous chapters, pretend you are at a dinner party. Do you feel confident enough to participate in conversations with your family and friends when they say things like:

- *"I care about the environment, so I don't want anything to do with crypto."*

- *"I worry about losing my bitcoins to quantum computers, but I don't know what quantum computers are or how they might steal my bitcoins, but I'm worried."*

- *"Zero knowledge proof make no sense—how can someone claim they know something without saying it? Are we just supposed to trust them?"*

- *"Bitcoin is 100 percent anonymous. That's why it's used mostly by criminals."*

- *"Cryptocurrencies are a Ponzi Scheme."* or *"Digital assets are nothing but air."*

- *"Crypto is completely outside the bounds of regulations, attractive mostly to rogue governments."*

- *"What do you mean blockchains are secure? You hear about multi-million-dollar thefts every week!"*

Citations

[1] Tapscott, D. and Tapscott, A (2016), *Blockchain Revolution*, Penguin, New York City

[2] https://digiconomist.net/bitcoin-energy-consumption

https://digiconomist.net/ethereum-energy-consumption

[3] Tuwiner, J. (December 20, 2019), *Bitcoin Mining Pools*, https://www.buybitcoinworldwide.com/mining/pools/

[4] NBC Meet the Press (March 31, 2022). Cryptocurrency: The Wild West, Viewed April 4, 2022 on https://www.nbcnews.com/meet-the-press/video/cryptocurrency-the-wild-west-136697925853

[5] Sedgwick, K. (December 21, 2017), *These Are The Five Cheapest US States for Bitcoin Mining*, https://news.bitcoin.com/these-are-the-five-cheapest-us-states-for-bitcoin-mining/

Sharma, R. (February 21, 2018). 5 Best States for Bitcoin Mining (And the Worst). https://www.investopedia.com/news/five-best-states-bitcoin-mining-and-worst/

[6] https://www.ezblockchain.net/blog.html

[7] https://www.engineeredfluids.com/for-crypto-currency

[8] Thompson, P. (January 5, 2020). https://cointelegraph.com/news/most-significant-hacks-of-2019-new-record-of-twelve-in-one-year, *CoinTelegraph*, https://cointelegraph.com/news/most-significant-hacks-of-2019-new-record-of-twelve-in-one-year

[9] Tsihitas, T. (April 4, 2022). Worldwide cryptocurrency heists tracker (updated daily). Retrieved April 4, 2022 from https://www.comparitech.com/crypto/biggest-cryptocurrency-heists/

[10] Nahar, P. (August 31, 2021). What are 51% attacks in cryptocurrencies? Retrieved April 4, 2022 https://economictimes.indiatimes.com/markets/cryptocurrency/what-are-51-attacks-in-cryptocurrencies/articleshow/85802504.cms?utm_source=contentofinterest&utm_medium=text&utm_campaign=cppst

[11] Shrem, C. (2019), "Bitcoin's Biggest Hack in History: 184.4 Billion Bitcoin from Thin Air," *Hackernoon*, https://hackernoon.com/bitcoins-biggest-hack-in-history-184-4-ded46310d4ef

[12] *Stellar and Ripple Hacked: Justcoin to the Rescue*, Oct 14th, 2014, https://cointelegraph.com/news/stellar-and-ripple-hacked-justcoin-to-the-rescue

[13] Kaul, K. (September 23, 2018). 'High Severity' Bug in Bitcoin Code Capable of Crashing the Cryptocurrency – Detected and Fixed, LiveBitcoinNews, https://www.livebitcoinnews.com/high-severity-bug-in-bitcoin-code-capable-of-crashing-the-cryptocurrency-detected-and-fixed/

[14] Morisander (March 23, 2018). The biggest smart contract hacks in history or how to endanger up to US $2.2 billion, *Medium*, https://medium.com/solidified/the-biggest-smart-contract-hacks-in-history-or-how-to-endanger-up-to-us-2-2-billion-d5a72961d15d

[15] Morisander (March 23, 2018). The biggest smart contract hacks in history or how to endanger up to US $2.2 billion, *Medium*, https://medium.com/solidified/the-biggest-smart-contract-hacks-in-history-or-how-to-endanger-up-to-us-2-2-billion-d5a72961d15d

[16] AnChain.AI (Aug 22, 2018). Exposing An $18 Million USD Smart Contract Vulnerability, Medium, https://medium.com/@AnChain.AI/largest-smart-contract-attacks-in-blockchain-history-exposed-part-1-93b975a374d0

[17] https://www.ey.com/en_gl/blockchain-platforms/smart-contract-token-review

[18] https://blockchain.info/pools

[19] Crypto Mining Blog (April 27th, 2017), *BitMain Up for Another Scandal with Antbleed Backdoor*, http://cryptomining-blog.com/8634-bitmain-up-for-another-scandal-with-antbleed-backdoor/

[20] Rowley, J. (April 27th, 2017), *Tensions Persist as Traders Largely Shake Off The 'Antbleed' Bitcoin Backdoor Scandal*, https://news.crunchbase.com/news/tensions-persist-traders-largely-shake-off-antbleed-bitcoin-backdoor-scandal/

[21] Gencer, A.E., Basu, S., Eyal, I., cen Renesse, R., and Sirer, E.G, (January 15th, 2018), *Decentralization in Bitcoin and Ethereum*, https://arxiv.org/pdf/1801.03998.pdf

[22] Avan-Nomayo, O. (May 29, 2018). Strike Three? Verge suffers third suspected 51 percent attack, Bitcoinist, https://bitcoinist.com/strike-three-verge-suffers-third-suspected-51-percent-attack/

[23] Hertig, A. (June 5, 2018). Verge's Blockchain Attacks are Worth a Second Look. *Coindesk*, https://www.coindesk.com/verges-blockchain-attacks-are-worth-a-sober-second-look

[24] Horizen (June 8, 2018). ZenCash's Statement on Double Spend transaction. https://blog.horizen.global/zencash-statement-on-double-spend-attack/

[25] Martin, J. (January 27, 2020). Bitcoin Gold Blockchain Hit by 51 percent attack leading to $70K double spend, *CoinTelegraph*, https://cointelegraph.com/news/bitcoin-gold-blockchain-hit-by-51-attack-leading-to-70k-double-spend

[26] Varsheney, N. (May 30, 2018). Here's how much it costs to launch a 51% attack on PoW cryptocurrencies, https://thenextweb.com/hardfork/2018/05/30/heres-how-much-it-costs-to-launch-a-51-attack-on-pow-cryptocurrencies/

[27] Zmudzinski, A. (January 13, 2019). Ethereum Classic 51% hackers allegedly returned $100,000 to crypto exchange, *CoinTelegraph*, https://cointelegraph.com/news/ethereum-classic-51-attackers-allegedly-returned-100-000-to-crypto-exchange

[28] O'Leary, R. (September 13, 2021). A Solution to Crypto's 51% Attack? Fine Miners Before It Happens. Retrieved April 5, 2022 from https://www.coindesk.com/tech/2018/10/10/a-solution-to-cryptos-51-attack-fine-miners-before-it-happens/

[29] Sharma, N. (November 5th, 2017), *Is Quantum Computing an Existential Threat to Blockchain Technology?* https://singularityhub.com/2017/11/05/is-quantum-computing-an-existential-threat-to-blockchain-technology/ - sm.00009y4jmx95sdww11rov5gdjdlzo

[30] Schneier, B. (2015), *NSA Plans for a Post-Quantum World*, https://www.schneier.com/blog/archives/2015/08/nsa_plans_for_a.html

[31] Sharma, N. (November 5, 2017), *Is Quantum Computing an Existential Threat to Blockchain Technology?* https://singularityhub.com/2017/11/05/is-quantum-computing-an-existential-threat-to-blockchain-technology/ - sm.00009y4jmx95sdww11rov5gdjdlzo

[32] Ravisetti, M. (February 8, 2022). Quantum hackers could break bitcoin in minutes, but don't panic just yet. Retrieved April 5, 2022 from https://www.cnet.com/science/quantum-hackers-could-break-bitcoin-in-minutes-but-dont-panic-just-yet/#:~:text=Bingo%2C%20it'd%20take%20about,larger%20number%2C%22%20he%20said.

[33] Gent, E. (November 22, 2021). IBM's 127-Qubit Eagle Is the Biggest Quantum Computer Yet. Retrieved April 5, 2022 from https://singularityhub.com/2021/11/22/ibms-127-qubit-eagle-is-the-biggest-quantum-computer-yet/

[34] Email interview with Mary Lacity, February 20, 2020.

[35] Quarmby, B. (February 18, 2022). JPMorgan unveils research on quantum resistant blockchain network, retrieved April 5, 2022 from https://cointelegraph.com/news/jpmorgan-unveils-research-on-quantum-resistant-blockchain-network

[36] SWIFT Fin Traffic & Figures, https://www.swift.com/about-us/swift-fin-traffic-figures

[37] *Bitcoin and Ethereum vs Visa and PayPal – Transactions per second*, Altcoin Today, April 22nd 2017, http://www.altcointoday.com/bitcoin-ethereum-vs-visa-paypal-transactions-per-second/

[38] BBC News (December 5, 2017), *CryptoKitties craze slows down transactions on Ethereum*, http://www.bbc.com/news/technology-42237162

Wong (December 4th, 2017), *The Ethereum network is getting jammed up because people are rushing to buy cartoon cats on its blockchain*, https://qz.com/1145833/cryptokitties-is-causing-ethereum-network-congestion/?utm_source=MIT+Technology+Review&utm_campaign=d6185c2892-EMAIL_CAMPAIGN_2017_11_02&utm_medium=email&utm_term=0_997ed6f472-d6185c2892-156469793

[39] Sfox (May 24, 2019). Ethereum 2.0: What the Next Three Years of Ethereum Will Look Like, https://blog.sfox.com/ethereum-2-0-what-the-next-three-years-of-ethereum-will-look-like-b366a46f9704

[40] This website tracks average bitcoin transaction fee: https://bitinfocharts.com/comparison/bitcoin-transactionfees.html

[41] The second transaction on block 456958 shows a miner was paid by the sender .00036955 bitcoins to add this to the transaction to the block. On March 12, one bitcoin was worth $1232.99, so miner received 45 cents that day to include this transaction https://blockexplorer.com/block/0000000000000000015c7bd17dc9a82f457a8aed35bc6606cca57cb5932deb7e

[42] To track average bitcoin transaction fee, see: https://bitinfocharts.com/comparison/bitcoin-transactionfees.html

[43] *Bitcoin's Transaction Backlog Hits All-Time High, Fees Skyrocket*, May 11th, 2017, http://www.trustnodes.com/2017/05/11/bitcoins-transaction-backlog-hits-all-time-high-fees-skyrocket

[44] Van Wirdum, A. (August 23, 2017). The Long Road To SegWit: How Bitcoin's Biggest Protocol Upgrade Became Reality, Bitcoin Magazine, https://bitcoinmagazine.com/articles/long-road-segwit-how-bitcoins-biggest-protocol-upgrade-became-reality

[45] For a technical explanation of segregated witness, see http://learnmeabitcoin.com/faq/segregated-witness

[46] If you look at a Bitcoin block, the first transaction is the miner's reward, called a Coinbase. Rewards earned by a 'coinbase' transaction cannot be spent until they receive 100 confirmations in the blockchain.

[47] Van Wirdum, A. (August 23, 2017). The Long Road To SegWit: How Bitcoin's Biggest Protocol Upgrade Became Reality, Bitcoin Magazine, https://bitcoinmagazine.com/articles/long-road-segwit-how-bitcoins-biggest-protocol-upgrade-became-reality

[48] Bitcoin Magazine. What is SegWit? https://bitcoinmagazine.com/guides/what-is-segwit

[49] Reiff, N. (June 25, 2019). A History of Bitcoin Hard Forks, Investopedia, https://www.investopedia.com/tech/history-bitcoin-hard-forks/

[50] https://explorer.acinq.co/faq

[51] https://explorer.acinq.co/

[52] Ethereum 2.0 Phases https://docs.ethhub.io/ethereum-roadmap/ethereum-2.0/eth-2.0-phases/

[53] DistrictOx, Ethereum Sharding Explained, https://education.district0x.io/general-topics/understanding-ethereum/ethereum-sharding-explained/

[54] https://ethereum.org/en/upgrades/

"One major problem with the Eth2 branding is that it creates a broken mental model for new users of Ethereum. They intuitively think that Eth1 comes first and Eth2 comes after. Or that Eth1 ceases to exist once Eth2 exists. Neither of these is true. By removing Eth2 terminology, we save all future users from navigating this confusing mental model."

[55] Edgington, B. (August 28, 2018). State of Ethereum Protocol #1, Consensys, https://media.consensys.net/state-of-ethereum-protocol-1-d3211dd0f6

[56] Hertig, A. (May 31st, 2016), *Will Ethereum Beat Bitcoin to Mainstream Microtransactions?*, https://www.coindesk.com/ethereum-bitcoin-mainstream-microtransactions/

[57] *The Raiden Network: High Speed Asset Transfers for Ethereum*, http://raiden.network/

[58] https://www.blockchain-council.org/ethereum/best-ethereum-layer-2/

[59] https://polygon.technology/

[60] As we learned in previous chapters, Aave, EY OpsChain Traceability, and ANSAcheck use Polygon to lower transaction costs and speed transactions while using the Ethereum blockchain for settlements.

[61] IBM Research (February 2, 2018). Hyperledger Fabric: A Distributed Operating System for Permissioned Blockchains. https://www.ibm.com/blogs/research/2018/02/architecture-hyperledger-fabric/

[62] *What Is Hyperledger? How the Linux Foundation builds an open platform around the blockchain projects of Intel and IBM*, https://blockgeeks.com/guides/what-is-hyperledger/

Gorenflo, C., Lee, S. and Keshav, L. FastFabric: Scaling Hyperledger Fabric to 20,000 Transactions per Second. https://arxiv.org/pdf/1901.00910.pdf

[63] To further protect privacy, users are advised to generate new addresses every time they receive bitcoins to prevent previous trading partners from detecting usage patterns.

[64] Nakamoto, S. (2008), *Bitcoin: A Peer-to-Peer Electronic Cash System*, p.6, https://bitcoin.org/bitcoin.pdf

[65] https://blockonomi.com/zero-knowledge-proofs/

[66] Lexie (December 7, 2017). Zero-knowledge proofs explained Part 2: Non-interactive zero-knowledge proofs. https://www.expressvpn.com/blog/zero-knowledge-proofs-explained-non-interactive-zero-knowledge-proofs/

Zhu, N. (April 8, 2019). Understanding Zero-knowledge proofs through illustrated examples, Medium, https://blog.goodaudience.com/understanding-zero-knowledge-proofs-through-simple-examples-df673f796d99

[67] https://upload.wikimedia.org/wikipedia/commons/thumb/e/e0/Sudoku_Puzzle_by_L2G-20050714_standardized_layout.svg/500px-Sudoku_Puzzle_by_L2G-20050714_standardized_layout.svg.png

[68] *What are zk-SNARKs?*, https://z.cash/technology/zksnarks.html

[69] *What are zk-SNARKs?*, https://z.cash/technology/zksnarks.html

[70] EY (October 23, 2019). Transforming the business lifecycle with Nightfall, https://www.youtube.com/watch?v=SUtTy9RoXb0

[71] EY Press release (July 1, 2021). EY contributes a zero-knowledge proof layer 2 protocol into the public domain to help address increasing transaction costs on Ethereum blockchain. https://www.ey.com/en_gl/news/2021/07/ey-contributes-a-zero-knowledge-proof-layer-2-protocol-into-the-public-domain-to-help-address-increasing-transaction-costs-on-ethereum-blockchain

[72] van Saberhagen, N. (October 17, 2013). CryptoNote v 2.0 https://bytecoin.org/old/whitepaper.pdf

[73] https://moneroblocks.info/tx/898764c111ed490300fa58623c905ae335737a98ab28c49af34c8d9045915f82

[74] Personal interview with Mary Lacity

[75] Quorum White Paper, available at https://github.com/jpmorganchase/quorum-docs/blob/master/Quorum Whitepaper v0.1.pdf

[76] Cocco, S. and Singh, G. (March 20th, 2017), *Top 6 technical advantages of Hyperledger Fabric for blockchain networks*, https://www.ibm.com/developerworks/cloud/library/cl-top-technical-advantages-of-hyperledger-fabric-for-blockchain-networks/index.html

[77] https://medium.com/chain-cloud-company-blog/hyperledger-vs-corda-pt-1-3723c4fa5028

[78] Ross, C. (December 5th, 2016), *Blockchain Brings Us into The Future, But Only After It Drags Up the Past: Interoperability Becomes an Actual Issue Again*, http://www.horsesforsources.com/blog/christine-ferrusi-ross/the-interoperability-problems-blockchain-brings_120616

Ross, C. (April 18th 2017), *Simplify Blockchain by Refusing to Let Interoperability Issues Bog You Down*, posted on http://www.horsesforsources.com/Simplify-Blockchain-Refusing-Interoperability-Issues_041817

[79] The technical requirements come from several sources, particularly from Jin, H., Dai, X., Xiao, J. (2018), Towards a Novel Architecture for Enabling Interoperability Amongst Multiple Blockchains, *IEEE 38th International Conference on Distributed Computer Systems*, pp. 1203-1211. We also relied on:

Treat, D., Giordano, G., Schiatti, L., Borne-Pons, H. (Oct 22, 2018), *Connecting ecosystems: Blockchain integration*, Accenture White Paper, https://www.accenture.com/us-en/insights/blockchain/integration-ecosystems

Hardjono, T., Lipton, A., and Pentland, A. (2018), *Towards a Design Philosophy for Interoperable Blockchain Systems*, MIT Connection Science, https://arxiv.org/pdf/1805.05934.pdf

[80] https://en.bitcoin.it/wiki/Proof_of_burn

[81] View a burn address on Ethereum at: https://etherscan.io/address/0x000000000000000000000000000000000000dead

[82] Hallam, G. (May 2, 2016). *The BTC Relay is live! Bitcoin can now exist on the Ethereum blockchain.* Post to Reddit: https://www.reddit.com/r/Bitcoin/comments/4hhtwh/george_hallam_the_btc_relay_is_live_bitcoin_can/

[83] Nakamoto, S. (2008), Bitcoin: A Peer-to-Peer Electronic Cash System, https://bitcoin.org/bitcoin.pdf

[84] http://btcrelay.org/

[85] Ethereum, *Welcome to BTC Relay's Documentation!*, https://btc-relay.readthedocs.io/en/latest/index.htm

[86] BTC Relay's transactions can be viewed at https://etherscan.io/address/0x41f274c0023f83391de4e0733c609df5a124c3d4

[87] Buterin, V. (September 9, 2016). *Chain Interoperability*, https://static1.squarespace.com/static/55f73743e4b051cfcc0b02cf/t/5886800ecd0f68de303349b1/1485209617040/C hain+Interoperability.pdf

[88] For our interoperability discussion, notaries are trusted third parties. There are also projects in which smart contracts can serve as a notary, such as POEX.io that is used to 'time stamp' a document.

[89] Lerner, S. D. (April 2016). *Drivechains, sidechains, and hybrid 2-way peg designs*, https://uploads.strikinglycdn.com/files/27311e59-0832-49b5-ab0e- 2b0a73899561/Drivechains_Sidechains_and_Hybrid_2-way_peg_Designs_R9.pdf

[90] Lerner, S. D. (April 2016), *Drivechains, sidechains, and hybrid 2-way peg designs*, https://uploads.strikinglycdn.com/files/27311e59-0832-49b5-ab0e- 2b0a73899561/Drivechains_Sidechains_and_Hybrid_2-way_peg_Designs_R9.pdf

[91] https://en.wikipedia.org/wiki/Multisignature

[92] Higgins, S. (August 3, 2016), *The Bitfinex Bitcoin Hack: What We Know (And Don't Know).* News Article, CoinDesk

[93] Press release (November 15, 2018). *BitGo First to Deliver Multi-Signature Security for Over 100 Coins and Tokens*, https://www.businesswire.com/news/home/20181115005640/en/BitGo-Deliver-Multi-Signature-Security-100- Coins-Tokens

[94] See: https://www.bitgo.com/newsroom/press-releases/bitgo-announces-over-64-billion-in-auc-and-appoints-cassandra-lentchner-president-for-the-bitgo-trust-companies;

On insurance, see:

Kharif, O. (February 19, 2019). *Crypto Startup Offers Insurance Against Quadriga Wallet Dilemma*, Bloomberg, https://www.bloomberg.com/news/articles/2019-02-19/crypto-startup-offers-insurance-against-quadriga-wallet-dilemma

[95] Gaurav (December 2, 2021). What is Multi-Signature Wallet? 5 Best Multisig Wallets. https://coincodecap.com/multi-signature-wallet

[96] Back, A., Corallo, M., Dashjr, L., Friedenbach, M., Maxwell, G., Miller, A., Poelstra, A., Timón, J., and Wuille, P. (Oct 22 2014), Enabling Blockchain Innovations with Pegged Sidechains, https://blockstream.com/sidechains.pdf

[97] Buterin, V. (September 9, 2016), *Chain Interoperability*, https://static1.squarespace.com/static/55f73743e4b051cfcc0b02cf/t/5886800ecd0f68de303349b1/1485209617040/C hain+Interoperability.pdf

[98] Back, A., Friedenbach, M., Miller, A., Poelstra, A., Timon, J., and Wuille, P. (Oct 22, 2014). *Enabling Blockchain Innovations with Pegged Sidechains*, https://blockstream.com/sidechains.pdf

[99] https://blockstream.com/liquid-faq/

[100] *SPV, Simplified Payment Verification*, Bitcoin.Org glossary.

[101] Lerner, S. D. (April 2016), *Drivechains, sidechains, and hybrid 2-way peg designs*, https://uploads. strikinglycdn.com/files/27311e59-0832-49b5-ab0e- 2b0a73899561/Drivechains_Sidechains_and_ Hybrid_2-way_peg_Designs_R9.pdf

[102] Soni, P. (October 10, 2021). All about Blockchain Interoperability in 2022. https://www.analyticssteps. com/blogs/all-about-blockchain-interoperability-2022

[103] https://interledger.org/about-us/

[104] Thomas, S., and Schwatz, E, (2015), *A Protocol for Interledger Payments*, https://interledger.org/ interledger.pdf

[105] Hashed-Timelock Agreements (HTLAs) https://interledger.org/rfcs/0022-hashed-timelock-agreements/

[106] Somogyvari, P. and Takeuchi, T. (March 17, 2022)

Chapter 11

Innovations: If You Build It, Will They Come?

What's inside: By now, readers have substantial evidence that Web 3.0 is upon us. So far, we covered over three dozen blockchain-based applications that are live today. We know that many readers are likely enthused by blockchain innovations and may have their own ideas for new blockchain-based applications. In this chapter, we analyze the first generation of applications with the goal of helping readers vet their ideas for future innovations. If you build it, will individuals or organizations adopt it?

Learning objectives:

- Apply the insights from the theories of Diffusion of Innovations, Institutional Isomorphism, and Disruptive Innovation to analyze the creation, adoption, and dissemination of existing blockchain applications.

- Apply the insights from the theories to analyze your own ideas for an innovation.

- Defend the suitability of using blockchain technologies for a given innovation.

- Apply ethical design principles to analyze innovations.

11.1. Introduction

In this chapter, we reflect on what we have learned from the first 13 years of blockchain solutions and what it suggests for assessing the potential of new innovations.

Let's begin by listing the applications we've examined in this book. Figure 11.1 categorizes the applications by two governance decisions, namely, rights of participation and rights of validation. We can think of these as a list of winners as of this writing—they survived the arduous journey from idea, proof-of-concept, production pilot, to launch. Most innovations do not. At any moment in time, there are millions of innovations at different stages of development and most innovations fail before or shortly after launch. According to one study, less than 10 percent of innovation ideas make it to implementation.[1] Once implemented, another study found that only 40 percent of innovations generated positive returns.[2] In the crypto/blockchain space, The China Academy of Information and Communications Technology (CAICT) found that 92 percent of over 80,000 blockchain projects have failed already; the average lifetime was 1.22 years.[3]

After deployment, only a few live deployments scale, meaning they become widely adopted by the target ecosystem. If they continue to adapt, they can survive for a long time, else they will be replaced with the next generation of innovations. The cycle of innovation for blockchains follows known patterns described by time-tested theories on innovations.

In this chapter, we cover three innovation theories, namely, the theories of Diffusion of Innovations, Institutional Isomorphism, and Disruptive Innovation (see Figure 11.2). These theories will help us to not only assess the blockchain applications we've learned about in Figure 11.1, but they will help readers analyze their own ideas for innovations.

Why did we write this chapter? As Directors of blockchain centers, we are approached by people with hundreds of ideas each year for blockchain-based applications. In our experience, too many people jump to the selection of blockchain technologies before fully assessing whether the innovation is worth pursuing in the first place. Before asking whether a proposed innovation should be built with blockchain technologies, innovators should ask a different question, such as: does the innovation generate enough value so that it will likely to be adopted?

		Who can operate a validator node?	
		Permissionless *(Anyone)*	**Permissioned** *(Requires permission, selection, or election)*

Who can submit transactions?	**Public**
	(Anyone)
		QUADRANT 1: Public permissionless
		
		• Aave • Litecoin
		• ANSAcheck • Lightning
		• BeefChain Network
		• Brave BAT • Monero
		• Binance • Namecoin
		• Bitcoin • Polygon
		• Cardano • Santander's bond
		• Dogecoin issuance
		• EOS (node validators) • Tether
		• Ethereum • USD Coin
		• Ethereum Classic • VeriTX
		• IOTA • WineChain
		  (authenticity)
		  • Zcash
			QUADRANT 2: Public-permissioned
			
			• EOS (block producers)
			• Ripple
			• NHS Staff Passport's PKI on Sovrin
			• Stellar
			• VeChain

	Private *(requires keys to access)*	**QUADRANT 4: Private-permissionless** • Nightfall protocol • Baseline protocol	**QUADRANT 3: Private-permissioned** • DL Freight • Everledger • IBM Food Trust • KoreConX • MediLedger • SmartResume • TradeLens • VeriTX • WineChain (value exchange)

Figure 11.1: Blockchain-based applications covered in this book

Just because an innovation is 'new' does not mean that is has value. The proposed innovation must generate more value to the target market than the costs expended, and the risks incurred. Innovators face a daunting 'innovation-embeddedness' challenge; innovations must be assimilated within complex institutional, political, regulatory, social, economic, and existing technology systems.[4]

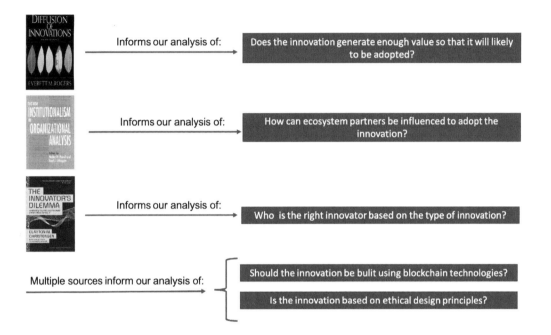

Informs our analysis of: Does the innovation generate enough value so that it will likely to be adopted?

Informs our analysis of: How can ecosystem partners be influenced to adopt the innovation?

Informs our analysis of: Who is the right innovator based on the type of innovation?

Multiple sources inform our analysis of: Should the innovation be bulit using blockchain technologies? Is the innovation based on ethical design principles?

**Figure 11.2: Is an innovation worth pursuing?
Does it need blockchain technologies?**

The potential value of an innovation to the target market must be great enough to overcome all the hurdles. To help answer the question about the value of the innovation, our first analysis draws on Everett Rogers' Diffusion of Innovation Theory. This theory distinguishes between innovations targeted at individuals and organizations. Rogers' theory describes different factors that affect adoption rates in these two markets.

If the target market is organizations, our second analysis draws on Paul DiMaggio and Walter Powell's theory of Institutional Isomorphism. This theory is particularly useful for innovators trying to build minimal viable ecosystems for organizational adopters. It answers the question: How can the first organizational adopters influence other ecosystem partners to adopt the solution to achieve network effects? The theory is particularly useful for better understanding the adoption of private-permissioned applications in Quadrant 3 of Figure 11.1.

Our third analysis draws from Clayton Christensen's Theory of Disruptive Innovation. It helps to answer the question: who is the right innovator for this type of innovation? This theory distinguishes between two types of innovators, namely entrants and incumbents, and between two types of innovations—disruptive and sustaining. Usually, entrants are nimble startups whereas incumbents are usually large organizations that dominant current markets. This theory provides insights as to why new entrants dominate the public-permissionless quadrant and why incumbents dominate the private-permissioned quadrant of Figure 11.1.

After vetting the worthiness of an innovation idea, innovators are ready to focus on the design of the innovation. Here we cover two analyses: should the innovation be built using blockchains? Is the innovation based on ethical design principles? Again, our major point is that the technology selected to implement an innovation idea should come *after* establishing that the innovation idea has merit. Let's jump in.

11.2. Is the innovation likely to be adopted?

An innovation needs to generate net value that exceeds the costs to develop, test, launch, educate the market, maintain, and support the innovation. Costs include investments of time, money, and resources. Innovations need to be worth the risks, such as the risks of low adoption rates, risks of unanticipated harmful consequences, and risks of unintentional breach of laws or regulations. Fortunately, decades of research has unveiled the characteristics of innovations and the characteristics of adopters to help us answer the question: is the innovation likely to be adopted?

According to Everett Rogers' Diffusion of Innovation Theory, an innovation is an idea, practice, or object that is perceived as new by an individual or by an organization. Rogers studied the speed by which innovations are adopted by members of a social system.

The target social system may comprise individuals, organizations, or both. Bitcoin, for example, can be adopted by individuals because a single person can decide to own or to mine bitcoins. Bitcoin can also be adopted by organizations. For example, Overstock.com was among the first retailers to accept bitcoins as payment; the University of Nicosia was the first university to accept bitcoins as tuition payments. Rogers teaches us that the decision-making process for individuals is different from the decision-making process for organizations. We'll get to that insight in a moment, but first we need to understand the role of time in the diffusion of innovations.

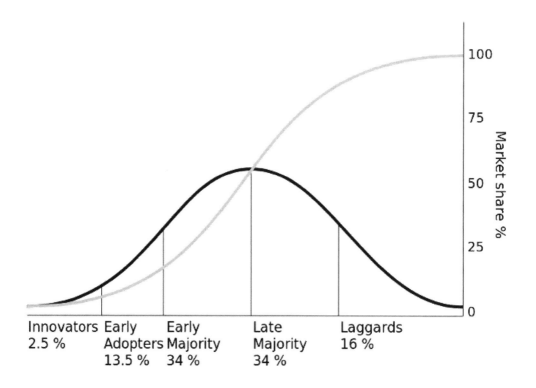

Figure 11.3: Rogers' diffusion of innovation adoption curve

Source: https://upload.wikimedia.org/wikipedia/commons/thumb/1/11/Diffusion_of_ideas.svg/800px-Diffusion_of_ideas.svg.png

Many innovations, Rogers argued, have an s-shaped curve, which plots the number of adopters as a cumulative frequency over time (see Figure 11.3). He called the first set of adopters 'innovators' and the last set of adopters 'laggards'. Of course, some individuals and organizations may never become aware of an innovation or may choose to never adopt an innovation; these are called 'non-adopters'.

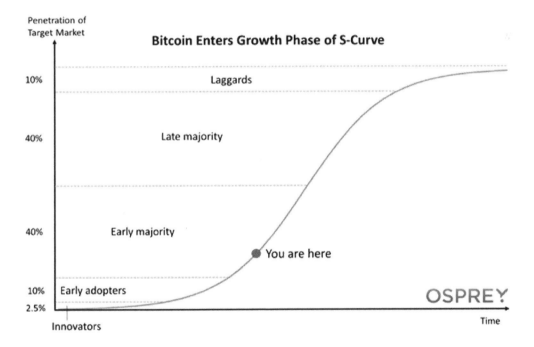

Figure 11.4: Bitcoin mapped to Rogers' adoption curve in 2021

Source: https://ospreyfunds.io/wp-content/uploads/scurve.png

Let's apply Rogers' s-shaped curve to analyze Bitcoin. As of 2022, about 22 percent of Americans own bitcoins, which places Bitcoin in the 'early majority' phase of dissemination.[5] This analysis is consistent with other people's attempts to map Bitcoin to Rogers' adoption curve (see Figure 11.4). Even though Bitcoin is our most mature blockchain application, it is still in the early stages of diffusion—at least according to this theory. Bitcoin may become more broadly diffused if it ever becomes widely accepted by most merchants or if many countries accept it as legal tender for the payment of debts (such as announced by El Salvador in 2021). Let's get to know more about the target markets.

11.2.1. Factors that determine individual adoption

For individuals, Rogers' theory posits that attributes of the individual, attributes of the innovation, communication channels, and the social system determine adoption or non-adoption rates (see Figure 11.5).

Individual's attributes. For individuals, early adopters are more likely than late adopters to possess these characteristics:

- More formal education
- More likely to be literate
- Higher social status
- Greater upward social mobility
- Belong to larger social networks
- Greater empathy
- Less dogmatic
- Greater ability to deal with abstractions
- Greater rationality
- Greater intelligence
- Higher ability to cope with uncertainty
- Higher aspirations
- Less fatalistic, better attitudes
- Have more change agent contact
- Greater exposure to mass media

- Seek information about innovations
- Higher degree of opinion leadership

Readers might be surprised that age is not on the list. According to Rogers, age is a puzzle—some research finds it to be important, other research does not.

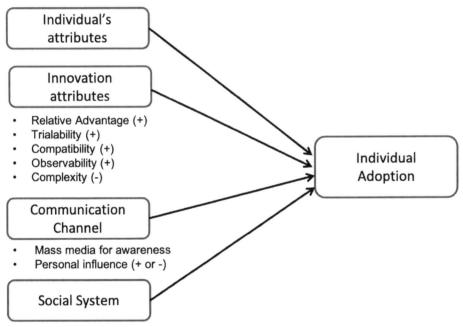

Figure 11.5: Determinants of individual adoption

Source: Adapted from Rogers (2006); Callahan (2004)

Innovation attributes. Among the factors depicted in Figure 11.5, the attributes of an innovation are the most influential; they account for between 49 to 87 percent of the variance in adoption rates. The five attributes that make people want to adopt innovations are relative advantage, trialability, compatibility, observability, and complexity (see Figure 11.6).[6]

Innovation Attribute	Description	Effect on Adoption Rate
Relative Advantage	*"The degree to which an innovation is perceived as better than an idea it supersedes."* The innovation may be better economically, functionally, environmentally, or socially.	⬆
Trialability	*"The degree to which an innovation may be experimented with on a limited basis."* Trialability reduces uncertainty.	⬆
Compatibility	*"The degree to which an innovation is perceived as being consistent with the existing values, past experiences, and needs of potential adopters."*	⬆
Observability	*"The degree to which the results of an innovation are visible to others."*	⬆
Complexity	*"The degree to which an innovation is perceived as difficult to understand and use."* The more complex the solution, the slower it will be adopted.	⬇

Figure 11.6: Five attributes of innovations
Source: Adapted from Rogers (2006)

Among the five, ***relative advantage***—the degree to which an innovation is perceived as better than an idea it supersedes—is the most important.   Relative advantage is closely related to 'perceived usefulness', the degree to which an individual believes the innovation will increase their performance/utility/productivity.[7] Who has the capability, credibility, and domain expertise to design an innovation that is better than what people currently use? The answer is: innovators with deep subject matter expertise.   Let's use VeriTX, a case study from Chapter 7, as an example. Colonel James Allen Regenor had years of expertise in the Air Force to understand deeply the problem of parts inventory on aircraft carriers and at forward operating bases. He knew first-hand the missions that were delayed because of missing or damaged parts. His innovation was to place 3-D printers at critical locations to print parts when and where they are needed. He came up with the idea for VeriTX. The potential advantage is clear: increased mission-critical rates. When pitching to investors, he established the relative advantage of VeriTX over competing solutions, including other solutions based on 3D printing (see Figure 11.7). Other innovators are encouraged to follow his model for demonstrating relative advantage.

VERITX IS UNIQUE

Company	3D Print Based	Data Encryption	Blockchain Fortification	Data Rights Managed IP	Counterfeit Part Mitigation	Data Lakes	CMMC Ready
VeriTX	✓	✓	✓	✓	✓	✓	✓
Honeywell GoDirect		✓	✓		✓	✓	
skywise		✓				✓	
Authenticiti	✓	✓					
Identify3D	✓	✓		✓			
(icon)	✓	✓					
(icon)	✓	✓					
LINK3D	✓	✓					
ZIPPY	✓	✓	✓				
Block.Aero		✓	✓				
GE Aviation		✓	✓			✓	

2 Patents Awarded

VeriTX

Figure 11.7: VeriTX's relative advantage

Source: With permission from VeriTX

Let's assess Bitcoin using Rogers' theory. What is Bitcoin's relative advantage? From Nakamoto's white paper, Bitcoin has a relative advantage over other payment systems because counter-party risks are mitigated with cryptography and with an incentivized

457

community of miners instead of relying on trusted third parties; it enhances privacy over traditional payment systems; it lowers transaction costs compared to traditional payment systems; and it bypasses government fiat currencies.

Trialability is the degree to which an innovation may be experimented with on a limited basis. How would you rate Bitcoin's trialability? Bitcoin can be tried for the first time by becoming a miner, by downloading a digital wallet and finding someone to send bitcoins to the wallet, or by purchasing bitcoin on an exchange. The easiest way to try Bitcoin is to use an exchange, which is what most people choose. By using an exchange, the adopter has just wiped-out Bitcoin's relative advantage of no trusted third parties, enhanced privacy, and no government oversight. How can we reconcile the conflict between relative advantage and trialability? For many individuals, Bitcoin is an investment, so to them, Bitcoin's relative advantage is that it offers higher potential returns than other investments options or it increases the diversity of their investment portfolios. From our analysis of Bitcoin, we can immediately understand the subjective nature of assessing the attributes of an innovation.

Let's move on to *compatibility*. To what degree is Bitcoin perceived as being consistent with existing values, past experiences, and needs? In the early days of Bitcoin, the first adopters were largely cypherpunks, Libertarians, and individuals with deep technical expertise. Bitcoin is highly compatible with those values. How has the compatibility of Bitcoin evolved over time?

How *observable* is Bitcoin? Initially Bitcoin was only observed by the cypherpunks, Libertarians, and individuals on the mailing lists. Blockchain.com was the first company to build a web-based Bitcoin explorer in 2011 so that anyone with access to the Internet could view Bitcoin's distributed ledger. Of course, individuals had to proactively choose to observe Bitcoin; they had to search for and find an explorer. Bitcoin is even more observable today because news of Bitcoin is pushed to passive observers by mainstream media.

Complexity is the degree to which an innovation is perceived as difficult to understand and use. The more complex the solution, the slower it will be adopted. Complexity is the inverse of 'ease of use', defined as the degree to which a person believes that using a particular system would be free of effort.[8] Compared to many innovations, Bitcoin is complex to understand. Not every person will understand what we learned in Chapter 3 regarding distributed ledgers, consensus mechanisms, smart contracts, cryptography, and digital assets! While not every Bitcoin user needs to understand how the technology works, they do need to understand how to acquire and use it.

Communication channels are another important factor; people are much more likely to adopt an innovation if they learned about it from people they know and trust rather than from mass media. Can you remember when you first learned about Bitcoin? Was it from a personal communication or a mass media communication channel?

Social systems also influence adoption rates. Social systems include change agents who champion adoption, and opinion leaders who are known for their competence and expertise. Opinion leaders may either encourage or discourage adoption. As far as incentives, mandating adoption increases adoption rates, but the quality of mandatory adoptions—as measured by satisfaction and frequency of use—is often lower compared to voluntary adoption. Innovators can encourage voluntary adoption by offering behavioral incentives. David Callahan, co-founder of the think tank Demos and Inside Philanthropy, identified three classes of incentives: remunerative, moral, and coercive. *Remunerative incentives* provide material rewards like money for adopting the target behavior. *Moral incentives* present behavioral decisions as 'the right thing to do' and provides intrinsic rewards such as positive self-esteem or extrinsic rewards such as praise and admiration from others. *Coercive incentives* provide unease, displeasure, or even punishments for not adopting the target behavior.[9]

Let's apply these concepts about incentives to Bitcoin. Figure 11.8 is an excerpt from Satoshi Nakamoto's white paper. Which of the three types of incentives did Satoshi Nakamoto use?

6. Incentive

By convention, the first transaction in a block is a special transaction that starts a new coin owned by the creator of the block. This adds an incentive for nodes to support the network, and provides a way to initially distribute coins into circulation, since there is no central authority to issue them. The steady addition of a constant of amount of new coins is analogous to gold miners expending resources to add gold to circulation. In our case, it is CPU time and electricity that is expended.

The incentive can also be funded with transaction fees. If the output value of a transaction is less than its input value, the difference is a transaction fee that is added to the incentive value of the block containing the transaction. Once a predetermined number of coins have entered circulation, the incentive can transition entirely to transaction fees and be completely inflation free.

The incentive may help encourage nodes to stay honest. If a greedy attacker is able to assemble more CPU power than all the honest nodes, he would have to choose between using it to defraud people by stealing back his payments, or using it to generate new coins. He ought to find it more profitable to play by the rules, such rules that favour him with more new coins than everyone else combined, than to undermine the system and the validity of his own wealth.

Figure 11.8: Role of incentives in the Bitcoin white paper

Source: Nakamoto (2008)[10]. Bitcoin: A Peer-to-Peer Electronic Cash System https://bitcoin.org/bitcoin.pdf

Nakamoto offered remunerative incentives to miners in terms of a financial block reward and transaction fees to support the network. Nakamoto designed coercive influences to punish miners if they attacked the network; miners would suffer a net financial loss. Now think about the incentives for Proof-of-Stake and Practical Byzantine Fault Tolerance blockchain networks. Which types of incentives do they use?

Let's change the target market from individual adoption to organizational adoption.

11.2.2. Factors that determine organizational adoption

Rogers's Theory considers three factors that lead organizations to adopt innovations: top management wants it; innate characteristics of the organization; and top management is linked to other external innovation champions/adopters such as consultants and leaders from peer or aspirational organizations (see Figure 11.9).

Leadership support. For organizations, much power rests with senior management. Organizations cannot pursue every new idea. Instead, innovation projects are prioritized based on alignment with the organizational strategy and its potential value, often measured as a projected return on investment. In most organizations, new innovations must be integrated with existing innovations. Senior management has the power to assign top talent and financial resources to important innovation projects; engage influential stakeholders such as business sponsors, IT, legal, and human resources; hire consultants to assist in building capabilities; prepare the organization for changes caused by the innovation, such as training existing employees or authorizing new positions.

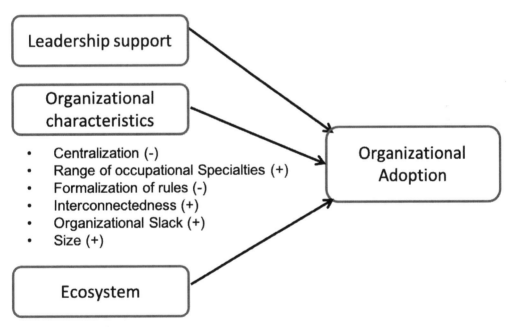

Degree to which organizational members are linked to other individuals who are external to the system (like consultants, other CEOS, CIOS, Boards, professional peers, etc.)

Figure 11.9: Determinants of organizational adoption

Source: Adapted from Rogers (2006)

461

Applying Roger's theory, we can see the role senior leaders played in adoptions at the NHS, DL Freight, IBM Food Trust, and TradeLens. Senior leaders from NHS England wanted to find a better way to onboard staff, leading to the allocation of resources for the adoption of the digital staff passport. Walmart Canada's leaders wanted to reduce the number of invoice disputes, leading to the adoption of DL Freight. Walmart's leaders wanted to reduce food waste and increase food safety, leading to the adoption of the IBM Food Trust. Senior leaders from Maersk wanted to better track shipping containers and to reduce administrative costs, leading to the development of TradeLens. Conversely, senior leaders can also kill an adoption. Below we introduce the story of a failed healthcare consortium. As you will learn, the C-suite executives did not want any innovation that would disrupt their current business models and terminated the consortium.

Innovators need to understand the organizational power structure when trying to get an organization to adopt an innovation. The innovator must make sure they are influencing/selling to the leader with enough power to authorize and support the adoption. These leaders must be convinced of the value of the innovation. If the leader is inaccessible, innovators can also approach opinion leaders that in turn influence the leaders.

Organizational characteristics. For organizations, early adopters are more likely than late adopters to possess these organizational characteristics:

- More decentralized in structure
- Employs a broader range of occupational specialties
- Has fewer formal rules (less bureaucratic)
- Is highly interconnected to other organizations
- Has more slack resources; that is, uncommitted resources
- Has more employees

You might be surprised that Rogers claimed that larger organizations are more innovative than smaller organizations. A meta analysis of adoption studies supports the claim: large organizations were more likely than smaller organizations to adopt information technology innovations.[11] An additional insight: organizational size is confounded with other variables like slack resources and a broader range of occupational specialties. The theory of Disruptive Innovation, discussed below, will further illuminate the finding by distinguishing between the types of innovations pursued by incumbent organizations—which are often large organizations—than those pursued by entrants.

Ecosystem. In the case of blockchain-based innovations, which are ecosystem solutions, we need to stretch Rogers' theory from focusing on a single organizational adoption to focus on adoption by multiple organizations within an ecosystem. Blockchains are multi-party systems—they only function if a critical mass of the targeted ecosystem partners adopts the solution. Reflecting again on our cases, NHS England had to convince the independent NHS hospitals to adopt the digital health passport. Walmart had to convince freight carriers to adopt DL Freight. Walmart had to convince food supply chain partners to use IBM Food Trust. Maersk had to convince ports, terminals, and even competitors to adopt TradeLens. How might ecosystem partners sway the holdouts? We can answer that with another theory: the theory of Institutional Isomorphism.

11.3. How can ecosystem partners be influenced to adopt the innovation?

Developed by Paul DiMaggio and Walter Powell, this theory models the process of homogenization among organizations facing similar environmental conditions.[12] Essentially, the theory seeks to answer the question: Why do organizations within an industry eventually change (from the Latin root 'morph') to become more alike (from the Latin root 'iso')? Another version of this question is: How can we get organizations to conform? DiMaggio and Powell posited that organizations adopt similar structures, processes, philosophies, practices, and technologies through three mechanisms of influence, namely, coercive, normative, and mimetic (see Figure 11.10):[13]

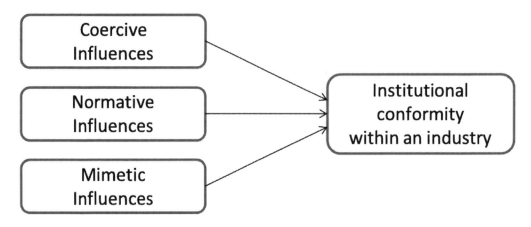

Figure 11.10: Three influences that pressure institutions to conform

Source: Adapted from DiMaggio and Powell (1991) [14]

Coercive influences come from political pressures exerted on an organization by other organizations upon which they are dependent. Government regulations and powerful trading partners' mandates are examples of coercive influences. Although 'coercive' has a negative connotation, coercive influences can be effective for promoting a greater good. Government regulations, for example, aim to protect consumers, investors, citizens, children and the environment.

Within the context of blockchains, several interviewees thought government regulations would be the fastest route to mass adoption. For example, one interviewee thought new US government regulations would be the way to force the adoption of better healthcare processes that could be enabled with blockchains. He said: *"The government may need to step in at some point. All we have to do is have a couple of use cases, and then we go public about it and say, 'This is the kind of thing we could do. Why can't we do this with healthcare?' We let the government ask, 'Why aren't you doing this?' Then, there's going to be a bunch of payers who say, 'Oh, this is going to be bad for the consumer.' What are they talking about? Consumers are getting screwed to the nth degree right now. There have never been higher insurance rates."*

In addition to governments, powerful trading partners can also influence adoption. For example, in September of 2018, Walmart and Sam's Club required its major suppliers of fresh, leafy greens to join the IBM Food Trust. Direct suppliers were required to conform to one-step back traceability by January 31, 2019 and end-to-end traceability through vertical partners by September 30, 2019. Its letter to suppliers explained that food safety (a greater good) is a shared responsibility that is only achieved through collaboration with supply chain partners. Recognizing that adoption would place burdens on its suppliers, the letter reads in part, *"To assist you in meeting this new Walmart business requirement, we have worked closely with IBM and other food companies to create a user-friendly, low-cost, blockchain-enabled traceability solution that meets our requirements and creates shared value for the entire leafy green farm to table continuum."*[15]

Normative influences arise from norms of professionalism.[16] In the context of blockchains, standards-making bodies and working groups/consortia discussed in Chapter 4—like GS1; IEEE; ISO; Hyperledger Foundation; Enterprise Ethereum Alliance; Global Blockchain Business Council; and BiTA—provide normative influences. Powerful blockchain advisors like Accenture; ConsenSys; Deloitte; EY; KPMG; HfS; IBM; PwC; and Wipro influence their client's blockchain directions. Tapscotts' Blockchain Research Institute is also a major influencer in the space, featuring early enterprise adopters in its programs and offering thought leadership on creating an 'Internet of Value'. Returning to our cases, NHS, Walmart, and Maersk engaged technology partners to not only build capabilities, but also to normalize the acceptance of the solutions.

Mimetic influences arise from the perception that peer organizations are more successful; by mimicking peer behavior, the organization aims to achieve similar results. Mimetic influences are particularly strong when environmental uncertainty is high, goals are ambiguous, and when technologies are poorly understood.[17] iDatafy has built three successful consortia since 2011, with the SmartResume being the most recent. CEO Dave Wengel said that whenever he approaches a new consortium member, the first question asked is usually, *"Who else is using this?"* It's important to pick early adopters who are influential and well-regarded in the ecosystem. For the SmartResume project, Wengel knew he had to start the consortium with a large, influential academic credentialing organization. (Wengel would not recruit any hiring organizations until the career network was large enough to warrant their attention.) Wengel invited Matt Waller, the dean of the Sam M. Walton College of Business at the University of Arkansas, to become the first member in summer of 2018. As the flagship business school in the state, the Walton College had the prominence to influence other adopters. Also recall IBM's strategy to attract 'anchor tenants' like Maersk and Walmart for its major blockchain applications, which can be considered mimetic influences.[18] One interviewee thought this was an effective strategy: *"There's also a little bit of a herd mentality. People are afraid to be left out."*

As a caveat, DiMaggio and Powell stress that the three influences are analytically distinctive but may not be empirically indistinguishable; the influences may work in tandem.

11.4. Who is the best innovator for this type of innovation?

To answer this question, we turn to the great business theoretician Professor Clayton Christensen to provide us with a richer vocabulary and a theoretical framework. Professor Christensen was a chaired professor of management at Harvard Business School until his death in 2020. He spent decades studying and theorizing on technology and business model innovations. Beginning with his first book on the subject, the *Innovator's Dilemma*, published in 1997,[19] Christensen studied how market leaders rise and fall based on their capacity to exploit innovations. This theory describes two types of innovations—disruptive and sustaining. He defined **disruptive innovation** as a *process* by which an innovation creates a new market that eventually disrupts an existing market, thereby displacing the incumbent enterprises that currently dominate a market.[20]

The classic example of a disruptive innovation is Henry Ford's assembly line that produced the Model T automobiles in 1908. Although the automobile was invented in 1886, early models cost so much money that they did not disrupt the traditional mode of transportation—the horse and buggy. Ford's invention of the assembly line dramatically reduced the costs of producing a car. It was the invention of the assembly line that produced the inexpensive Model T that disrupted the horse and buggy market.

What's most relevant to our blockchain discussion is Christensen's theory on WHO creates disruptive innovations. Christensen considered two types of enterprises—entrants and incumbents. New entrants are more likely to create truly disruptive innovations. New entrants, such as inventors and startups, have little to lose, are less risk averse, and are unconstrained by legacy investments and bureaucracy. Incumbents are the existing market leaders—the traditional enterprises that dominant a market. Christensen observed that incumbents find it very difficult to break their successful business models; they view it as irrational to cannibalize revenues from existing products to replace it with a risky disruptive innovation. Instead, incumbents focus on **sustaining innovations**, i.e., those innovations that improve products and services within existing markets. You can think of sustaining innovations as incremental innovations, such as new models of an iPhone or software upgrades. Figure 11.11 captures the essence of Christensen's Theory.

Readers might wonder: why don't incumbents see the disruption coming? Keep in mind thousands of innovations fail; incumbents cannot monitor every possible source of disruption. Many times, it's too late to pivot when a real threat emerges. Consider Blockbuster, founded in 1985 in Dallas Texas. Its business model was based on retail brick-and-mortar stores that rented videos to customers. The videos in those days were stored on physical devices (e.g., DVD, VHS, Blu-Ray). It had 9,000 stores at its peak of success (in 2004). Netflix was founded in 1997, a year when Blockbuster earned $3.54 billion in revenues. The next year, Netflix lost $11 million while Blockbuster continued to grow—tiny Netflix hardly seemed a threat to Blockbuster. One can imagine Blockbuster's Board of Directors laughing at the thought that this little entrant foretold its ultimate demise. Initially, Netflix mailed videos stored on physical devices to customers. When the Internet advanced enough to transmit large digital files, Netflix easily pivoted from mail delivery to digital streaming services whereas Blockbuster could not. Blockbuster was too incumbered by its retail model and it went bankrupt in 2010.[21]

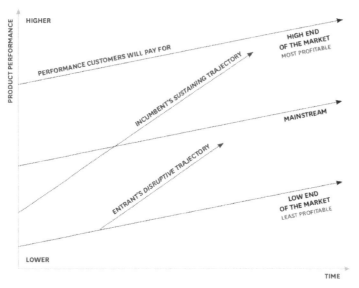

THE DISRUPTIVE INNOVATION MODEL

This diagram contrasts *product performance trajectories* (the red lines showing how products or services improve over time) with *customer demand trajectories* (the blue lines showing customers' willingness to pay for performance). As incumbent companies introduce higher-quality products or services (upper red line) to satisfy the high end of the market (where profitability is highest), they overshoot the needs of low-end customers and many mainstream customers. This leaves an opening for entrants to find footholds in the less-profitable segments that incumbents are neglecting. Entrants on a disruptive trajectory (lower red line) improve the performance of their offerings and move upmarket (where profitability is highest for them, too) and challenge the dominance of the incumbents.

Figure 11.11: Theory of Disruptive Innovation

Source: Christensen, C., Raynor, M., and McDonald, R. (2015), 'Disruptive Innovations', Harvard Business Review, 93(12): 45-53. https://hbr.org/resources/images/article_assets/2015/11/R1512B_BIG_MODEL_360.png

However, incumbents are not necessarily doomed to fail. Keep in mind the human capacity to learn. Nearly every Master of Business (MBA) student has read Christensen's work. Boards of Directors are more aware of the possible threat from entrants than they were two decades ago. But being aware of the threat does not diminish the real barriers incumbents must overcome in terms of legacy investments, pressure to produce positive quarterly earnings reports, and bureaucratic structures that can stall the pursuits of disruption. According to Christensen's theory, incumbents' best chances for pursuing disruptive innovations are to spin off an independent business unit once an innovation looks promising or to simply acquire a promising entrant.

Equipped with Christensen's theory, let's return to our blockchain analysis. Let's begin with some general observations of the applications in the public-permissionless quadrant of Figure 11.1. Think about the degree to which do you agree or disagree with the following conjectures.

Conjecture 1: New entrants largely develop disruptive innovations and launch them primarily on public-permissionless blockchains.

As a general finding, it seems that entrants in the public-permissionless quadrant for Figure 11.1 are creating disruptive innovations based on entirely new models. Satoshi Nakamoto invented Bitcoin, a peer-to-peer payment application that eliminates the need for trusted third parties—or to use Christensen's term, to by-pass the 'incumbents'. Vitalik Buterin invented Ethereum and launched it with cofounders Mihai Alisie; Amir Chetrit; Charles Hoskinson; Anthony Di Iorio; Joseph Lubin; Gavin Wood; and Jeffrey Wilke. Ethereum is a platform for deploying decentralized applications (dApps)—anyone can build on it; it's a completely new way to deploy software applications. In Chapter 5, we studied one Ethereum dApp called Aave; it manages a completely decentralized market for lending and borrowing—no need to use traditional banks. While the applications in the public-permissionless quadrant have not destroyed the markets for government fiat currencies or for traditional banks, we likely are witnessing a disruptive innovation process underway. A $2 trillion crypto/blockchain market is not to be ignored.

Let's turn our attention to the private-permissioned blockchains in Quadrant 3 of Figure 11.1. Our second conjecture is:

Conjecture 2: Incumbents primarily develop sustaining innovations and primarily launch them on private-permissioned blockchains.

So far, private-permissioned blockchain applications are primarily created by incumbents, the large enterprises that dominate their markets; their innovations are best characterized as sustaining innovations. These first-generation applications are delivering business value, but most of the solutions do not disrupt, transform, or obliterate existing market structures. Incumbents came together to uplift all parties in an ecosystem rather than to eliminate any one of them. As a general observation, no parties were threatened with disintermediation. They can be characterized not as a tidal wave of disruption but as a rising tide that lifts all ships. DL Freight is an example. Walmart Canada and its freight carriers both benefit from the shared invoice; it's a sustaining innovation that improves and supports the existing freight carrier relationships.

In general, these first-generation private-permissioned applications do not eliminate trusted third parties but often introduce new ones. The TTPs take on different roles; rather than sit in the middle of transactions, these TTPs manage network-level services, such as operating network nodes, protecting digital wallets on behalf of clients, enforcing access rules set up by members, and managing software updates. For example, IBM is the solution provider for Everledger, we.trade, TradeLens, and the Food Trust. IBM has no role in mediating the peer-to-peer transactions among trading partners—IBM cannot even interpret the data on the private channels. However, IBM is the cloud provider for the validator nodes, secures the networks, manages the software (including upgrades) and enforces access rules set up by participants. Beyond our sample of applications, a 2020 HfS Research survey of 318 respondents from Global 2000 companies that found only six percent of enterprise blockchain applications intend to remove intermediaries.[22] Again, our point is that private-permissioned blockchains are primarily developed by incumbents seeking sustaining innovations, as described by Clayton Christensen.

Let's pose another conjecture based on another of Christensen's insights pertaining to the difficulty for incumbents to pursue disruptive innovations:

Conjecture 3: Incumbents cannot easily pursue disruptive blockchain innovations from within.

Here we introduce a failed US-based healthcare provider consortium. The consortium comprised ecosystem partners with representatives keen on redesigning healthcare claims processing. The consortium members knew the solution had to be disruptive rather than sustaining, but they had difficulty convincing the senior leaders from their respective organizations. One of consortium's representatives was the head of innovation for a large healthcare payer. He said, *"You see some things, particularly in radiology, where a patient pays $800 for an MRI in a physician's office, and ours cost $2,400. Which do you*

470

think somebody's going to go to for an MRI? There's a point where you have to disrupt yourself."[23] He tried for a few years to evangelize the message to senior management. He continued: *"We need to design a consumer-centric, transparent healthcare system. I want to use blockchains to disrupt the current system, because it will be insolvent in ten years if we don't."* Two years later, he left the company and the consortium after concluding that healthcare payers don't want to be disrupted—they make money by sitting on huge stores of cash. He said: *"Payers don't want claims to be streamlined with a blockchain. One of them told me he took it to their executives for review and was told, 'don't bring this back up...it is career limiting for you.' That's what we are fighting against. They can see losing money if claims are immediately adjudicated."* The consortium eventually disbanded.

Many other blockchain innovation leaders we met in 2018 to 2020 from large traditional enterprises, left their organizations to start blockchain ventures or advisory firms. In addition to the head of innovation of the healthcare provider mentioned above, blockchain leaders from CME Group, JP Morgan, Moog, and the State of Illinois also left to start their own companies. Blockchain leaders could not drive disruptive innovations from within because business sponsors within traditional enterprises blocked or failed to support disruption. One departed leader said, *"It is very difficult to disrupt an organization from the inside. We were excited to build a digital ledger on top of systems of record, but the business sponsors just wanted to recreate the old models on the new world, so we lost support."* So if disruptive innovation from within is too difficult for incumbents, they can pursue alternative routes:

Conjecture 4: Incumbents can pursue disruptive blockchain innovations with outside investments/spinoffs.

Christensen theorized that incumbents could pursue disruptive innovations by investing or acquiring entrants, or by spinning off independent business units. Recall the VeriTX case from Chapter 7. While working at Moog Aircraft, Colonel James Allen Regenor began working on a business-to-business blockchain-enabled solution for printed parts.

This was a completely disruptive innovation, as it would pivot Moog from traditional, centralized manufacturing of parts to decentralized, 3-D printing of parts. Ultimately, Regenor decided to depart Moog in 2018 to accelerate moving from POCs to live production. Regenor stayed on as a consultant with Moog as he launched VeriTX and Moog is one of its partners.

Conjecture 5: Incumbents can buy innovations as a service.

Incumbent enterprises do not necessarily have to build innovations with ecosystem partners. They can allow others to build them and then buy them as a service. We've seen some examples in public-permissioned blockchains in Quadrant 2 of Figure 11.1. For example, we learned that Ripple's customers are primarily institutional enterprises like banks, corporates, payment providers and exchanges. They gain benefits from engaging Ripple, but they did not all participate or invest in its development. For banking customers, Ripple promises that banks will capture new revenue by booking new corporate and consumer clients, reduce their transaction costs, and provide one integration point and a consistent experience for rules, standards and governance.[24]

State Street, a US-based global financial services firm, reached the buy/partner-versus-build conclusion after years of internal development. In September of 2016, State Street hired a new Chief Technology Architect (CTA), in part because of his long history with open-source projects. Over the next few years, the internal blockchain team grew to over 100 people. It was using Hyperledger Fabric to build an open-source permissioned blockchain solution to create a single book of record. The idea was to eliminate the need for reconciliations across hundreds of databases.[25] In May 2019, the CTA left State Street to co-found a startup. In December of 2019, State Street cut at least 100 blockchain developers. Doug Brown, head of alternative financing solutions at State Street, told Coindesk, *"there is a real question about whether it's worth their time to build that infrastructure, the cost to do it, the staffing to do it."* [26] Rather than build an in-house DLT solution, State Street thought it was time to rely more on outside providers. According to Ralph Achkar, managing director of digital products at State Street in London, *"I think the choice in approaching that space was, do we need to have all of these resources internally, or can we actually build partnerships and work with other providers in the market?"*[27]

In summary, Christensen's Theory of Disruptive Innovation informs the process by which entrants can overtake incumbents with disruptive innovations.

Assuming the first three analyses indicate that the innovation is likely to be adopted and that the right innovator is leading the effort, we are finally ready to ask whether the innovation should be built using blockchain technology.

11.5. Should the innovation be built using blockchain technologies?

We've already learned a bit about the suitability of blockchains in Chapter 3 when we talked about the trust boundary. We compared traditional distributed databases with blockchain's distributed ledgers. We noted that traditional distributed databases are centrally controlled so that a single organization can decide to alter records or access rules; blockchains are distributed—no one entity has the power to roll back or alter history. All the nodes in a traditional distributed database environment trust each other, and therefore fewer verifications are required.[28] Trust is not presumed among nodes in a blockchain distributed ledger, so every event must be checked and rechecked, which is one reason why traditional distributed databases are magnitudes faster than blockchains.[29]

Based on several sources, the following four prompts help innovators decide whether the innovation would benefit from blockchain technologies:[30]

1. If the proposed innovation affects **multiple parties**, it's a potential blockchain use case. If it just solves a problem for one party, blockchain is not likely useful. The only exception we've seen is that sometimes a single organization has independent business units that act as multiple independent parties. The 1200 independent hospitals at NHS England is an example.

473

2. If the transactions require **multiple parties to write**, it's a potential blockchain use case. If one party writes the transactions and other parties just need to read the data, it's not a strong blockchain use case—use a traditional database and grant read access.

3. If there is a compelling reason for trading partners to prefer **mitigating counter-party risks with automation and incentivized communities** instead of relying on trusted third parties, it strengthens the use of blockchains. But as we saw in the private-permissioned blockchains quadrant of Figure 11.1, TTPs were not eliminated, but they took on different roles.

4. If the trading partners **need an immutable record of events**, it's a potential blockchain use case. Immutability guarantees that data has not been tampered with once it's been added to the ledger. Immutability is a key difference between blockchains and traditional distributed ledgers. On the other hand, some transactions don't need permanent records; perhaps, for example, we don't need to have a full record of every social media post.

Let's consider immutability a bit more. It's appropriate to think of a blockchain as a state machine based on all prior transactions. The power of blockchain is that one can recreate the current state (like current account balances) from all prior transactions because the transactions never change. Immutability does not mean that parties are forever beholden to errors. Errors can be remedied by issuing counter transactions. Counter transactions are easier to accomplish in private networks where parties know each other than in public networks where parties are pseudo-anonymous. In a public network, we've seen the example of a hacker of Ethereum Classic voluntarily giving back $100,000 to Gate.ui. Most hackers do not voluntarily submit reverse transactions. Under that circumstance, the community who controls 51 percent of the network's computer power have the power to roll back the ledger, as we saw in the 2016 DAO attack on Ethereum. It's an extremely contentious event to roll back a public blockchain ledger because it destroys the property of immutability.

In addition to the four common prompts, we propose a fifth prompt:

5. If the application involves **digital assets that are hard to monetize**, it's a potential blockchain use case.

With the proliferation of cryptocurrency exchanges, blockchain platforms, and DeFi, blockchains are becoming the easiest way to digitize, monetize, and exchange assets. Whereas a few years ago traditional databases had the default advantage and innovators had to defend the use of blockchains, it's becoming reversed for some use cases. For example, the National Collegiate Athletic Association (NCAA) ruled in 2021 that student athletes could monetize their name, image, and likeness (NIL), allowing them for the first time to seek money from endorsements, merchandise, and use of their social media accounts. Many student athletes are creating NFTs of video clips and selling them on blockchain platforms because it's now the easiest, fastest, and cheapest way to access global markets.[31]

Sometimes we fall prey to 20st century thinking about 21st century technologies. Much of the 20th century was about using digital technologies to represent things and events in the physical world. For example, replacing a physical check book with digital transfers of value using an app or replacing a physical token of a credential with a verifiable digital credential. The 21st century is shaping up to be natively digital where we work, learn, travel, socialize and play in completely virtual worlds called 'metaverses'. Virtual digital worlds need digital assets and digital money. It's hard to imagine metaverses without blockchain, a conjecture we defend in the final chapter.

Once readers are convinced that an innovation is a blockchain use case, then they must decide which type of network is most suitable.

Public networks should be the default because they prevent vendor lock-in, do not require investments in infrastructure, and easily onboard new users. Private networks are still warranted—as of 2022—when special circumstances prevail, such as when countries require that data must be stored within their own jurisdictions or for military applications that warrant the exponential investment in private network cybersecurity.

The degree to which public and private blockchains will continue to develop in parallel, converge, intersect, or otherwise have one supplant the other, remains uncertain. But we've established where the disruptive innovations are primarily happening—on public networks. For organizations, early indications suggest that confidential (rather than anonymous) transactions over public blockchains may become the dominant model (i.e., private-permissionless networks from Quadrant 4 in Figure 11.1). Transactions in this quadrant use zero-knowledge proofs to simply verify that trading partners have systems of record that match—no data is stored on the ledger, just the mathematical proof that parties agreed to an event.

At this point, if an innovation idea has survived the analyzes performed in this chapter, we are ready for the final assessment: Is the innovation based on ethical design principles?

11.6. Ethical by design

Innovators should design innovations based on ethical principles rather than just on legal compliance, profit maximization, or for the benefit of one group at the exclusion of others. It helps to have an overarching ethical framework, so here we extract common ethical principles from several sources. We reviewed ethical principles from the Berkman Klein Center for Internet and Society at Harvard University; the Trust Over IP (ToIP) Foundation (discussed in Chapter 8); the Ada Lovelace Institute; the World Economic Forum; Christopher Allen's *The Path to Self-Sovereign Identity*; Kim Cameron's *The Laws of Identity*; and Kaliya Young's *The Domains of Identity*.[32] The most common ethical design principles are in Table 11.1. Our advice: innovators should explicate their ethical design principles and provide evidence that the innovation meets or exceeds the principles.

Ethical design principle	Description
Promotion of human values and environmental sustainability	Innovations should promote values by helping humans flourish, by bettering society, and by protecting and preserving our natural world. Increasingly investors are using ESG (Environmental, Social and Governance) criteria to assess innovations. For example, many investors are choosing blockchain projects with alternative consensus mechanisms to Proof-of-Work because of environmental concerns.
Privacy and minimum disclosure	Innovations should protect privacy. The right to privacy is viewed as an inalienable human right. Humans have the right to have data rectified in cases of errors. Humans have the right to erasure, which means that personally identifiable data should not be stored on an immutable ledger. Humans have the right to reveal only the minimum amount of data needed to accomplish a task. For example, SmartResume was designed so that hiring organizations search for qualified candidates based only on their skills, as all demographic and personal information are masked.
User control and agency	Innovations should protect individuals' rights to make purposive actions regarding things that affect them. Individuals have the right to control the access to and processing of data collected about them. Individuals should be able to monetize their own data. For example, NHS staff possess and control access to their verifiable credentials.
Voluntary participation	Innovations should be voluntary to use; alternative solutions to accomplish the same tasks should be available. For example, NHS staff volunteer to use the digital staff passport; adoption is not mandated.

Ethical design principle	Description
Equity, fairness, inclusion, and non-discrimination	Diverse viewpoints should be included in the conception, design, testing and implementation of an innovation. Innovations should be widely available.
Safety and security	Innovations should be safe to use; potential negative consequences should be explained, and risks mitigated. Innovations should have end-to-end security, perform as intended, and be resistant to being compromised by unauthorized parties.
Transparency and explainability	Innovations should be transparent about how data is created, processed, updated, and deleted; Innovations should provide explanations on how the innovation reaches decisions. Open-source software helps to meet this ethical principle since the code can be seen and audited.
Portability and interoperability	Innovations should not lock-in users. Innovations should protect the individual's rights to change platforms and to take their data with them without excessive costs, inconveniences, or other roadblocks. Interoperability helps prevent lock-in and promotes portability.
Professional responsibility	Humans design innovations. Innovators should call on their professionalism and integrity to ensure that the appropriate stakeholders are consulted, and long-term effects are considered. As innovators, we have a responsibility to make sure that solutions are accurate, multiple parties are invited to collaborate, and scientific methods are used to assess results.

Table 11.1: Ethical design principles

11.7. Conclusion

The aim of this chapter was to give readers tools to analyze innovations targeted at individuals, organizations, or both. Readers should have a deeper admiration for the three-dozen blockchain innovations in Figure 11.1 that survived the perilous journey from conception to implementation. Readers should also have obtained new vocabulary and theoretical frameworks to assess their own ideas for innovations. Hopefully we've conveyed that not every application will benefit from blockchain technologies but that every application should be built on ethical design principles! The more ideas readers generate and critically evaluate, the more likely they will invent something of value. We conclude this chapter with some inspirational quotations:[33]

"The best way to have a good idea is to have a lot of ideas."

Linus Pauling, Nobel Prize winning chemist

"The difficulty lies not so much in developing new ideas as in escaping from old ones."

John Maynard Keynes, economist

"Don't worry about people stealing your ideas. If your ideas are any good, you'll have to ram them down people's throats."

Howard Aiken, computer pioneer

Citations

[1] Day, J. (2022). Innovation Metrics: Ideation Rate vs. Implementation Rate. https://ideascale.com/inno-vation-metrics-ideation-rate-vs-implementation-rate/

[2] Jovana (2020). 20 innovation-related statistics that we can learn from in 2020. https://innovationcloud.com/blog/20-innovationrelated-statistics-that-we-can-learn-from-in-2020.html

[3] James, A. (2018). 92% of Blockchain Projects Have Already Failed. https://bitcoinist.com/92-blockchain-projects-already-failed-average-lifespan-1-22-years/#:~:text=BET%26WIN-,92%25%20of%20Blockchain%20Projects%20Have%20Already%20Failed,Average%20Lifespan%20of%201.22%20Years&text=More%20than%2080%2C000%20projects%20claiming,the%20hottest%20buzzword%20in%20business.

[4] Lacity, M. and Willcocks, L. (2018), *Robotic Process and Cognitive Automation: The Next Phase*, SB Publishing, Stratford-upon-Avon, UK.

[5] https://explodingtopics.com/blog/blockchain-stats

[6] Rogers, E.M., *Diffusion of Innovations*, New York, Free Press, 2006, fifth edition.

[7] Davis, F.D. (1989). Perceived Usefulness, Perceived Ease of Use, and User Acceptance of Information Technology, MIS Quarterly 13(3): 319–340.

[8] Jeyaraj, A., Rottman, J., and Lacity, M. (2006). "A Review of the Predictors, Linkages, and Biases in IT Innovation Adoption Research, *Journal of Information Technology*, 21(1), pp. 1-23.

[9] Callahan, David (2004). *The cheating culture: Why more Americans are doing wrong to get ahead.* Harcourt.

[10] Nakamoto (2008). Bitcoin: A Peer-to-Peer Electronic Cash System https://bitcoin.org/bitcoin.pdf

[11] Op. cit. Jeyaraj et al. 2006.

[12] Mizruchi, M., and Fein, L. (1999) The Social Construction of Organizational Knowledge: A Study of the Uses of Coercive, Mimetic, and Normative Isomorphism, *Administrative Science Quarterly*, Vol. 44, 4, 653-683

[13] Op. cit. DiMaggio, P. and Powell, W. (1991).

[14] Op. cit. DiMaggio, P. and Powell, W. (1991).

[15] Walmart Food Traceability Initiative Fresh Leafy Greens (September 24, 2018). https://corporate.walmart.com/media-library/document/blockchain-supplier-letter-september-2018/_proxyDocument?id=00000166-088d-dc77-a7ff-4dff689f0001

[16] Op. cit. DiMaggio, P. and Powell, W. (1991).

[17] Ibid, p. 71.

Mizruchi, M., and Fein, L. (1999) The Social Construction of Organizational Knowledge: A Study of the Uses of Coercive, Mimetic, and Normative Isomorphism, *Administrative Science Quarterly,* Vol. 44, 4, 653-683.

[18] Marie Wieck, GM of IBM Blockchain, speaking at Consensus 2017: https://ibmgo.com/interconnect2017/search/?q=blockchain&tags=all&categoryType=video

[19] The theory of disruptive innovation was developed by Clayton Christensen over two decades, beginning with his first book published in 1997, *The innovator's dilemma: when new technologies cause great firms to fail,* Harvard Business School Press. For a thoughtful and current synopsis of the theory, see Christensen, C., Raynor, M. and McDonald, R. "What Is Disruptive Innovation?," *Harvard Business Review* (93:12), December 2015, pp. 45-53.

[20] https://www.christenseninstitute.org/disruptive-innovations/

[21] https://www.drift.com/blog/netflix-vs-blockbuster/

[22] Gupta, S., Duncan, S., Mondal, T., and Madhur, M. (2020). *HfS Top Enterprise Blockchain Services*, HFS Research.

[23] Personal interview with Mary Lacity

[24] https://ripple.com/use-cases/

[25] Lacity, M. (2018), *A Manager's Guide to Blockchains for Business*, SB Publishing, Stratford-Upon-Avon, UK.

[26] Quoted in Allison, I. (August 8, 2018). *Inside State Street Bank's Blockchain Deliberations, Coindesk*, https://www.coindesk.com/state-street-opens-up-about-its-internal-blockchain-debate

[27] Allison, I. (December 3, 2019). State Street Slashes DLT Developer Team as Bank Rethinks Blockchain Strategy, *Coindesk* https://www.coindesk.com/state-street-slashes-dlt-developer-team-as-bank-rethinks-blockchain-strategy

[28] Brown, R. (November 8, 2016) "On distributed databases and distributed ledgers", posted on https://gendal.me/2016/11/08/on-distributed-databases-and-distributed-ledgers/

[29] Diedrich, H. (2016). *Ethereum: blockchains, digital assets, smart contracts, decentralized autonomous organizations*, Wildfire publishing.

[30] Pedersen, Asger B.; Risius, Marten; and Beck, Roman (2019) "A Ten-Step Decision Path to DetermineWhen to Use Blockchain Technologies," *MIS Quarterly Executive*: Vol. 18: Iss. 2, Article 3. Available at: https://aisel.aisnet.org/misqe/vol18/iss2/3

Büyüközkan, G., and Tüfekçi, G. (2021). A decision-making framework for evaluating appropriate business blockchain platforms using multiple preference formats and VIKOR. Information Sciences, Vol. 571, pp. 337-357.

Farshidi, Siamak & Jansen, Slinger & España, Sergio & Verkleij, Jacco. (2020). Decision Support for Blockchain Platform Selection: Three Industry Case Studies. IEEE Transactions on Engineering Management. 10.1109/TEM.2019.2956897.

[31] Dolan, J. (2021). NCAA Ruling: What Does it Mean for College Athletes Getting Paid? Retrieved April 20, 2022 from https://wavve.co/ncaa-ruling-meaning-for-college-athletes-getting-paid/#:~:text=What%20is%20the%20NCAA%20Ruling,receive%20for%20playing%20college%20sports.

[32] Examples of Ethical Principles:

Allen, C. (2016). The Path to Self-Sovereign Identity. Retrieved July 12, 2021from http://www.lifewithalacrity.com/2016/04/the-path-to-self-soverereign-identity.html

Trust over IP Foundation (2020). Governance Stack Design Principles. Retrieved July 13, 2021 from https://wiki.trustoverip.org/pages/viewpage.action?pageId=71755&preview=%2F71755%2F71758%2FGS+Design+Principles.docx

Fjeld, J., Achten, N., Hilligoss, H., Nagy, A., and Srikumar, M. (2020). Principled Artificial Intelligence: Mapping Consensus in Ethical and Rights-based Approaches to Principles for AI, Research Publication No. 2020-1, The Berkman Klein Center for Internet & Society, https://cyber.harvard.edu/publication/2020/principled-ai

World Economic Forum (2020) Presidio Principles Foundational Values for a Decentralized Future. Retrieved July 13, 2021 from http://www3.weforum.org/docs/WEF_Presidio_Principles_2020.pdf

Young, K. (2020). The domains of identity: A framework for understanding identity systems in contemporary society. Anthem Press, London.

[33] https://www.brainyquote.com/topics/ideas-quotes

Chapter 12

The Future of Blockchains and Web 3.0

What's inside: Readers are invited to think about the future of blockchains and Web 3.0. To inform the discussion, we first look back to illustrate that many Web 3.0 innovations are combinations and extensions of prior innovations. We illustrate the concept of combinatorial innovation with Bitcoin, Ethereum, and metaverses. The battle for a decentralized Internet is far from won because powerful economic forces often favor centralized ownership and control. We are accustomed to free services online in exchange for allowing third parties to monetize our data. Web 3.0 can succeed if we continue to develop economic funding models and behavioral incentives, and widely educate people on using Web 3.0 technologies that are designed to enhance privacy, autonomy, and inclusion.

Learning objectives:

- Apply the concept of combinatorial innovations to analyze Bitcoin, Ethereum, metaverses, and beyond.
- Debate Web 3.0's aspirations for decentralization and inclusivity: are they pipedreams or inevitabilities?
- Identify the main challenges to realizing Web 3.0.
- Debate whether or not enterprises are prepared for Web 3.0's disruption.

12.1. Introduction

We've nearly completed our learning journey together. We've covered much ground, including the aims and aspirations of Web 3.0. We've argued that the decentralization of economic and social activities is a way to restore global trust, and that blockchains serve as the decentralized digital infrastructure. By now, all readers know that blockchain technology is decentralized because each computer node in the network is a peer, with no single computer in charge. We've made a crucial distinction between technology decentralization and governance decentralization; blockchain decisions may be made by decentralized or centralized governance structures. Recall from Chapter 2 that governance decisions comprise a portfolio of decision-making rights over the mission/vision, the funding model, rights of participation, rights of validation, rights of overrides, and governance residence.

As of 2022, we are still missing universal components to realize the full vision for Web 3.0. We have not yet realized the full power of individual self-sovereignty, asset/token transfers across chains, and a truly seamless and friendly user experience. But today we can more easily see the possibilities.

If we want to exchange value without relying on institutions, we need a large percentage of the population to understand and use blockchain-based applications. Cryptocurrencies promise to be the money 'of the people, by the people, for the people', but as of 2022, the lack of user diversity falls short of our Web 3.0 aspirations for inclusion. According to CNBC, 62 percent of cryptocurrency investors are white; 67 percent are men; and 66 percent are under age 45.[1]

As college professors, we hope that education can bridge the gap, but we struggle to attract diverse students to our blockchain classes. How can we do better? The University of Wyoming is implementing State-wide high school, community college, and university education. The University of Arkansas launched a Women in Blockchain Initiative to support and promote female participation.[2] We welcome your ideas for increasing diversity in the blockchain space.

So, what does the future of blockchains and Web 3.0 hold? As argued in this book, we believe that the future is not deterministic; individuals and organizations do not just sit around and wait for the future to happen, they actively create it. What will the next innovations bring? The seeds for the next 'big thing' are already here if we are wise enough to see them because many innovations are 'combinatorial', meaning that new innovations come from combining and extending existing innovations.[3] For this final chapter on the future of blockchains, we speculate on metaverses as the next combinatorial 'big thing', but readers may have other ideas.

Also for this final chapter, we sought the advice of people on the front lines of Web 3.0 innovation. They addressed some big questions:

- Are Web 3.0 aspirations for decentralization and inclusivity a pipedream or an inevitability?
- What are Web 3.0's greatest challenges?
- Are enterprises prepared for Web 3.0's disruption to their business models?

Their insights are presented throughout this chapter in their own words.

12.2. Combinatorial innovations, metaverses, and beyond

A futurist from Deloitte once stated that all futuristics are really historians. To think about the future of Web 3.0, we first look back to illustrate that many new innovations are combinations and extensions of prior innovations. Bitcoin is an example of a combinatorial innovation (see Figure 12.1).

Bitcoin would not have been possible without a number of prior innovations, including the development of the Internet itself, as covered in Chapter 1. Before Bitcoin, Nick Szabo conceived of decentralized **digital cash** in 1998 as Bit Gold, but it was not implemented.[4] David Chaum launched DigiCash in 1990—the first live cryptocurrency of significance.[5] While an important breakthrough, DigiCash was centrally controlled in that the company's system performed the validations. Nakamoto combined many ideas in the Bitcoin white paper, such as Wei Dai's concept for b-money—a distributed cryptocurrency with a **public ledger** in 1998; **timestamping** from a 1999 multi-authored paper; cryptographic **Merkle trees** for security from Merkle's 1980 paper; Hashcash for denial of service counter-measures, published in 2002; and **proof-of-work** from Dwork and Naor's 1993 paper.[6] Nakamoto brought these prior inventions together to create a peer-to-peer payment application, launched in 2009.

Now let's look at some key innovations that led to Ethereum. The 2014 Ethereum white paper by Vitalik Buterin is based on Bitcoin—it's mentioned 77 times. While clearly a fan of Bitcoin, Buterin noted that Bitcoin's scripting language lacks Turing-completeness (among other limitations). By including a Turing complete programming language, Ethereum could serve as a platform to code and deploy new dApps. Buterin also sites Nick Szabo's ideas; in addition to inventing Bit Gold, Szabo also developed the **smart contract** idea in 1998 and secure property ownership in 2005. Combining these prior innovations to create something new, Buterin foresaw that three types of decentralized applications would run on Ethereum: financial applications; semi-financial applications; and governance applications like online voting. His white paper specifically mentions **decentralized autonomous organization (DAOs)** seven times, stable-value currencies one time and non-fungible assets once.[7] From the launch of Ethereum in 2015, we saw many seeds of Buterin's ideas some to life.

Chapter 4 covered the importance of the Ethereum token standards, including the **ERC-20** token standard for fungible tokens, initially proposed by Fabian Vogelsteller and Vitalik Buterin in 2015.[8] The **ERC-721** token standard for non-fungible tokens was proposed in 2018 by William Entriken, Dieter Shirley, Jacob Evans, and Nastassia Sachs.[9] The combination of Ethereum, token standards, and DAOs led us to the explosion of **digital assets, DeFi,** and **NFT markets**, as we discussed several times already.

Jumping to the top of Figure 12.1, follow the trail of innovations that brings us to **metaverses**, which are virtual realities in which users interact with other users in

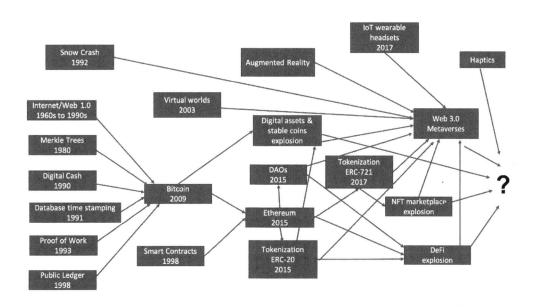

Figure 12.1: Combinatorial innovations in Web 3.0 landscape leading us to metaverses and beyond

computer-generated environments. The term 'metaverse' was first mentioned in a 1992 science fiction novel called ***Snow Crash*** by Neal Stephenson. Some people refer to 'the' metaverse (singular) while some people refer to metaverses (plural). When metaverse is used in singular form, it refers to the idea of ONE futuristic, universal, and interoperable virtual world, just as we have ONE physical world. Metaverses (plural) are where we are today, with multiple virtual worlds that cannot yet interact with one another, let alone exchange value, or transport your avatars, virtual goods, and virtual money across metaverses. But we are getting ahead of ourselves. Let's return to the foundational innovations that led to Web 3.0 versions of metaverses.

Linden Lab launched Second Life in 2003 as one of the first **virtual worlds** of note. Second Life has centralized governance (owned and operated by Linden Lab) and has a centralized architecture. It is different from multi-player games because there are no organized games. Second Life may best be thought of as an '**Internet of Place**'. Users create digital representations of themselves called 'avatars', login, and then visit virtual places and interact with other avatars in those same virtual places (see first image in Figure 12.2). Individuals are not charged to create avatars on the platform, but Linden Labs charges for its land. Second Life has the notion of digital assets. Second Life has its own digital money, called 'Linden dollars', for users to buy, sell, or rent land and goods. Linden Labs—as the benevolent dictator—has the power to ban users and to delete places. For example, Linden Labs deleted Woodbury University's land from Second Life after users in the land behaved in a racist and harassing manner.[10] Users interact with Second Life with a keyboard and mouse. In all, Second Life is a Web 2.0 version of a metaverse.

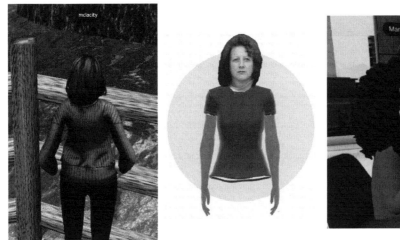

Figure 12.2: Mary Lacity's avatar in Second Life, Spatial, and Horizon Workroom

**Figure 12.3: Augmented reality: Pokémon Go (left)
and maintenance instructions (right)**

Sources: https://9to5mac.com/2017/12/20/ar-pokemon-go-arkit/pokemon-go-arkit-5/
https://www.i-scoop.eu/wp-content/uploads/2017/08/Augmented-reality-Industry-4.0-concept.jpg

In addition to virtual reality innovation, **augmented reality** lays digital content over physical surroundings, allowing users to be in virtual and physical worlds simultaneously. Pokémon Go, released in 2016, is an example (see left side of Figure 12.3). In this game, users download the mobile app, create avatars, and use their mobile phone's camera to overlay the virtual world to the user's physical surroundings. When the app overlays a Pokémon character into the landscape, users try to capture Pokémon creatures by throwing virtual balls at them. The app is controlled and governed by Niantic, which earns revenues by selling advertisements.[11] Thus, Pokémon Go is another example of a Web 2.0 application.

In addition to games, augmented realities are used in businesses, such as overlaying instructions onto a physical machine to assist workers (see right side of Figure 12.3). Augmented reality is anticipated to affect manufacturing, design, construction, retail, transportation, government, and professional services.[12]

IoT wearable innovations make virtual words more immersive. Instead of interacting with two-dimension virtual worlds on a flat screen, users wear gear over their eyes to experience a three-dimensional virtual reality. One of the first IoT virtual reality headsets was the Oculus Rift, which Palmer Luckey raised $12.5 million through Kickstarter in 2012 to build. Facebook bought Oculus in 2014 for $2 billion. In 2021, Facebook broke its promise to Palmer Lucky by introducing ads on Oculus headsets.[13] Facebook, now called Meta, owns and controls metaverses such as Horizon Workrooms. Meta's metaverse has centralized governance and architecture. To use Oculus headsets, a user must have a Facebook logon ID and password. As users interact in metaverses, the headset gathers all sorts of data that is sent to Meta. So far, Meta's metaverse is a Web 2.0 application.

There are Web 3.0 versions of metaverses built on blockchains, including Decentraland, Somnium, and Cryptovoxels (see Table 12.1). There are also Web 3.0 metaverse platforms specifically for gaming, including The Sandbox, Axie Infinitym, Enjin, and Gala.[14] These metaverses make use of fungible tokens to serve as 'money' in the metaverse; non-fungible tokens to represent digital assets like virtual land, virtual products, and virtual services (like an event access pass); DAOs to govern the metaverse; blockchain platforms to verify and permanently store metaverse transactions on a distributed ledger; and NFT marketplaces to conveniently buy and sell digital assets without needing to be inside the metaverse. They are decentralized in architecture and some metaverses—like Decentraland—have completely decentralized governance managed by a DAO.

Metaverse	Platform	VR headset enabled	Description	Fungible token market cap on May 10, 2022
Decentraland Launched in 2017	Ethereum	No	Decentraland set a maximum limit of 90,000 plots of virtual land, represented by ERC-721 NFTs, and bought with ERC-20 fungible tokens called MANA with a total money supply of 2.2 million, managed by a DAO.[15] NFTs can be bought on OpenSea.	$2.1 billion
Somnium Launched in 2018	Ethereum; Polygon; OpenSea	Yes	Somnium does not have a maximum number of plots of virtual land; Land is represented by ERC-721 NFTs and bought with ERC-20 fungible tokens called CUBE with a total money supply of 100 million or with other crypo on the OpenSea marketplace. Somnium uses Polygon to keep transaction costs low.[16]	$33 million
Voxels Launched in 2018	Ethereum; OpenSea	Yes	Voxels had 7694 parcels of virtual land on this day in 2022; represented by ERC-721 NFTs and bought with ERC-20 fungible tokens called VOXEL with a total money supply of 300 million.[17]	$52 million

Table 12.1: Web 3.0 metaverses

We anticipate that metaverses will irrevocably alter the business, social, educational, political, and economic landscape of our world. CB Insights estimates that metaverses will be a $1 trillion market within eight years.[18] One can easily envision that within a decade (or sooner), many young people will earn most of their income and spend much of their money in metaverses. There will be new jobs created, such as virtual real estate agents, virtual fashion designers, virtual bodyguards, and virtual babysitters. Universities will develop new curricula and offer remote learning in a metaverse. For example, VictoryRX hosted a Metaversity tour for University of Arkansas faculty where we toured the campus, performed a chemistry experiment, attended an art class, and dissected a huge pig from outer space in our space suits (see Figure 12.4).

Figure 12.4: VictoryRX hosted a Metaversity tour for
University of Arkansas faculty

Events in the metaverse will offer new experiences; instead of watching a sporting event as a spectator, fans will be able to pick their views, such as watching the game from a player's point of view, the referee's point of view, or even from the view of objects like the football, hockey puck, or baseball! Metaverse scalability allows millions instead of thousands of people to attend live events. With the advancement of **haptics**—technologies that provide a sense of touch—we can imagine even more use cases, such as *feeling* what the players feel. Ever wonder what a tackle really feels like in a professional football game? Or what an Olympic ski jumper experiences? Or a brain surgeon?

It's easy to imagine both utopian and dystopian consequences. On the utopian side, millions of people might inexpensively gain access to work, education, places, events, and ideas, leading to more inclusion. In a metaverse, people with physical disabilities may gain mobility.[19] Perhaps the combination of haptics and metaverses will allow us to really feel—thus to really empathize—with whom we interact. On the dystopian side, the negative consequences of addiction, bullying, and threats to our humanness from two-dimensional social media/digital games could be escalated in three-dimensional metaverses.[20] Surveillance Capitalism could get MUCH worse—instead of just tracking our interactions with websites and ad clicks, tech giants can hear everything we say and watch everything we do. In addition to monetizing this personal data, the ability to manipulate our behaviors in a metaverse is terrifying.

Returning to the ideas of Chapters 1 and 2, whom do we trust with operating a metaverse? Do we trust centralized architectures where one or a few organizations control the nodes in the network, and thus the data and transactions or do we trust decentralized crowds of independent node operators? As far as governance, will we prefer the speed, efficiency, and clear accountability of centralized governance or the low abuse of power, inclusion, freedom, and privacy from decentralized governance? Before you answer, consider the economics. Most users are accustomed to free services from technology providers in exchange for the tech provider owning and monetizing our data. A major impediment to Web 3.0 decentralized governance is the lack of economic models—it's hard to compete with free. Forbes contributor Alison McCauly wrote, *"Web3 communities are still looking for business models that reduce the cost of decentralization, which inherently shifts the expense of the network to the people who use it."[21]* Another economic challenge is the funding of software development. Meta invested $10 billion in metaverse development in 2021, and the user experience is much richer compared to Web 3.0 metaverses like Decentraland.

Next, we bring in our first two experts to further discuss metaverses. Kathryn Carlisle, Senior Managing Director, BCoE at University of Arkansas, encourages individuals and companies to see *"the bigger picture."* Melanie Cutlan, Managing Director of Accenture's Technology Incubation Group and Blockchain practice, calls for businesses to develop metaverses responsibly.

Kathryn Carlisle, Senior Managing Director, BCoE at University of Arkansas

Be wary of not seeing the forest through the trees—metaverses are NOT just virtual reality or gaming. Companies that quickly jump to talking about how they are going to have a presence in virtual realities for their metaverse strategy are getting it wrong. The concept of the metaverse is so much more. The metaverse is the meta layer of data that translates between our physical and digital worlds. The essence of it is in our self-sovereign identity and the data that we own, and that we can take across the metaverse with us. It's where you can log in and experience one digital world and then easily move to another through both virtual reality or augmented reality. The metaverse will seamlessly move through your entire life, whether it's in the real world or in virtual spaces, and you own that identity that characterizes the connectedness in-between. In reality, we can use our VR headsets or smartphones as augmented reality displays to then contextualize the world that we are living in with that described meta-layer on top of it. The context in which you can see Web 3.0 through that data layer then becomes much richer vs. an immersive city center or shopping mall.

Melanie Cutlan, Managing Director of Accenture's Technology Incubation Group and Blockchain practice

We've seen incredible developments in the blockchain, distributed ledger and tokenization space over the last decade. So have you, given your decision to explore them more in depth. But, as with any revolutionary innovation, it's easy to miss the broader implications of the underlying technology shift, even if you're watching closely.

Greater than the sum of its parts: *To understand the true impact of these technologies on business and society, you must think about their combinatorial effects. Blockchain will intersect with other emerging technologies to create a radically new set of experiences that connect the physical and virtual worlds.*

Nowhere is this more apparent than in the metaverse.

*At Accenture, we see the metaverse as a **continuum that spans the spectrum of digitally enhanced worlds, realities and business models**. It applies across all aspects of our lives, from consumers to workers and across the entire enterprise; from 2D to 3D; and enabled by cloud, blockchain, digital twins, edge technologies and beyond. As the next evolution of the Internet, the metaverse will be a continuum of rapidly emerging capabilities, use cases, technologies and experiences.*

*In parallel, Web3 will enable the metaverse through an important innovation—the Internet of Ownership. While many metaverse solutions seek to unify our experiences on a new set of platforms, Web3 is changing the way data moves through our systems. This new approach to data establishes a **foundation of trust that grounds the new spaces in real-world value**. It is this innovation that ultimately underpins the Internet of Ownership and enables the linkage between our traditional economies and institutions and those forming in the metaverse.*

The ownership of identity, audiences, assets and more represent a shift towards individuals gaining more say and value from their experiences on the web today. This is due to the promise of blockchain and other technologies creating unique verifiable

495

digital identities for people and things, and enabling everything from digital currencies to new products, Smart Contracts and more. These technologies will rewire interactions, applications, commerce, and the business models behind them.

Building reality responsibly: As we evolve the Metaverse Continuum, we must seize the opportunity to ensure that it is developed with responsibility at the core. From ownership of data, to inclusion and diversity, to sustainability and through to security and personal safety, this work must begin now.

We are on the threshold of a new decade of digital transformation, and at a defining moment for those looking to shape the future. The Metaverse Continuum will transform not only how consumers interact with each other, but also how businesses interact with customers, how work is done, what products and services companies offer, how they make and distribute them, and fundamentally how they operate their organizations.

As you look to apply your new blockchain knowledge, your ability to reimagine opportunities in this context will set you apart. How does the ownership of data and the design of virtual experiences relate to sustainability? Product development? Customer engagement?

These are the questions we're asking now, ones that future leaders like you may one day answer as we design the new world together.

12.3. Web 3.0 aspirations for decentralization and inclusivity: pipedream or inevitability?

This book is enthusiastic about blockchains and Web 3.0, but it's important to understand that there are critics with compelling arguments that Web 3.0 is a pipedream. Critics with deep technical knowledge on how the Internet operates have written articles such as *Web 3.0 is Bullshit*[22] and *Blockchain Gaslighting*.[23] (Gaslighting is manipulating others with false narratives which makes them doubt their perceptions and beliefs.) They point to (1) technical limitations of blockchain's compute, bandwidth, and storage capabilities; (2) statistics about the centralization of Bitcoin and Ethereum such as *"just 0.01% of bitcoin holders controls 27% of the currency in circulation"* and (3) dismantling big Tech will leave us worse off. On this last point, David Rosenthal, author of *Blockchain Gaslighting*, wrote: *"If a system is to be decentralized, it has to have a low barrier to entry. If it has a low barrier to entry, competition will ensure it has low margins. Low margin businesses don't attract venture capital. VCs are pouring money into cryptocurrency and 'Web 3.0' companies. This money is not going to build systems with low barriers to entry and thus low margins. Thus the systems that will result from this flood of money will not be decentralized, no matter what the sales pitch says."* [24]

To add to the discussion, we invited additional experts to contribute their thoughts. Sandra Ro, the CEO of Global Blockchain Business Council (GBBC), speaks to the great responsibility of Web 3.0 and the vital importance of collaboration and human centered design. Dan Conway, Teaching Professor at the University of Arkansas, titled his contribution as *Guns, Germs, Steel, and Tokens* to make the point that Web 3.0, so far, erects more fences in its architecture than drivers of community. Yorke Rhodes, Director of Transformation, Blockchain at Microsoft, offers a more nuanced analysis of decentralization.

Sandra Ro, CEO of Global Blockchain Business Council (GBBC)

The promises of Web 3.0, decentralization, digital assets, and blockchain technology connote the democratization of access, power, and inclusion, yielding a better, trust-enabled, and more functional world. Yet, if we are not mindful, not deliberate in our ethics alongside our technical ingenuity, we could enable a much worse outcome: a fully digitized surveillance society with clear disregard for an individual's privacy, security, and rights, coupled with a further widening of the digital divide between the 'digital haves and have nots', controlled by a handful of digital masters.

I am reminded of a gathering of technologists, academia, members of clergy and non-

profit organizations at The Vatican for 'The Common Good in the Digital Age' sponsored by Dicastery for Promoting Integral Human Development[25] and the Pontifical Council for Culture[26], 26-28 September 2019, where His Holiness Pope Francis encouraged each of us to think about technological solutions in the context of its impact to all of society, especially the most vulnerable, the most excluded.[27]

During the three days, we, as leaders from many different backgrounds and walks of life, worked together. How would we impact society positively with digital tools and technology? Alone, we can enable limited change. Together, across unlikely collaborations, with academia, private sector, governments and yes, even religious and / or other institutions, we can make sure we keep each other in check: to remind ourselves to keep breaking down the silos and echo chambers, to prioritize how we educate, to enable the digital access of opportunities and wealth generation to many, not just a few.

As the changemakers, entrepreneurs, and leaders of Web 3.0, we have a great responsibility to build the world we want, and make sure the next generation of companies, organizations, and networks do not leave behind those who often lose out the most as the 'digitization of everything' continues. I, for one, am dedicated to furthering 'human-centric', responsible technology to solve real world problems by working with others, who share this common view, this common good.

Dan Conway, Teaching Professor at the University of Arkansas

"Who will provide the grand design: what is yours and what is mine?"

Don Henley, The Last Resort, Hotel California

In his 1999 book, 'Guns, Germs, and Steel, the Fate of Human Societies', Jared Diamond presents a compelling narrative summarizing human history where state power and control generally result from use of superior weapons, devastation by disease, and relative advantages in technology. It is the perspective of an evolutionary biologist, and it chronicles how the inequities of today came to be.

498

But there is one more new frontier—a new virtual world built on digital tokens. While regulatory uncertainty somewhat clouds this new world (and the illusion of ownership clouds common sense), the question of the impact on human society and resulting inequities remain. Who will provide the grand design in this new world? It appears we need a fourth element to the three proposed by Dr. Diamond. I put forth digital access tokens for consideration: Guns, Germs, Steel, and Tokens.

It is said that good fences make good neighbors. But what is a good fence? Is it one that denies access yet permits enough tease to induce covet of the neighbor's greener grass? Is it an impenetrable fence where the gatekeeper alone strictly controls access? Is it a fence that can be overcome only by bad neighbors with superior guns, germs, and steel?

The metaverse is a land dense with fences. The haves, those with the right access tokens, may pass freely through the gates into the highlands of inequity. Those without access tokens are unceremoniously denied and left behind in the valley of the unworthy.

What is the future of blockchain? Web 2.0, or social media, is anti-social and anti-human when used to divide and fuel suspicion of others. Web 3.0 appears to have more fence in its architecture than drivers of community. Where are the DAOs that have inclusion and shared growth as strategic components of their models? I would be encouraged if inclusion was as prevalent as fences, and if the brilliance employed in the blockchain industry sought to use the opportunity for increasing human unity.

Yorke Rhodes, Director of Transformation, Blockchain at Microsoft

We are in an exciting time in digital transformation brought on by ever present technical improvements and innovations. Web 3.0 is the latest step change wave of transformation on a global scale. It brings with it a new design paradigm, opportunities and threats, and many nuanced definitions. Like every transformation before it, there is a bell curve of adoption from innovators through laggards. In many ways, Web 3.0 has crossed the chasm, while we are still very early in understanding and adoption. The future certainly looks bright from a systems design perspective on this open, inclusive substrate. But we must design with intentionality.

For example, what is decentralization and is it a binary on/off quality or does it exist on a spectrum? On a spectrum, I like to use the term 'sufficient decentralization', which can be realized with diligence and practical adherence to the principles of this term. The goal of decentralization is to minimize dependence on systemic central actors that could overtake the system. Thus, paying attention to the potentially centralizing tendencies of scale is quite important. This means monitoring key metrics that show centralization happening and putting in place incentives to prevent them from being solidified.

Take for example client diversity in Ethereum, one of the key points of decentralization that fights against single party control. This is not a static one-time problem. It can be molded over time with multiple levers used to incentivize actors to sufficiently decentralize client usage. If client code bases need attention, that is another lever of action.

With sufficient decentralization, a root of trust in a publicly maintained distributed system utility can be achieved. This means the public utility becomes the source of trust without a single entity, party, or sovereign nation being able to take control of that root. Sufficient decentralization means dominant actors cannot arbitrate who can use and benefit from the utility of the distributed system.

Along these axes, inclusivity, which also can be defined on a spectrum of multiple attributes, is achievable.

Some argue that costs create a barrier to entry in these systems and often point to Ethereum Layer 1 gas fees as an example of the problem. The reality is that gas is an arbitration mechanism to scarce resources and is part of the distributed system incentive design. Gas has the effect of monetizing supply & demand on a set of resources, which is more or less a democratic approach. That being said, cost optimized approaches are always better, and hence the argument for using Layer 2 solutions at lower gas fees. Scaled up consumer experiences such as we see in Ecommerce are built on layered approaches, so a Layer 2 approach makes sense to solve for scale.

One challenge to watch out for in Layer 2 systems is the choices and compromises made in security and decentralization as the systems are brought on line. These are often done to speed time to market with a plan to address the compromises later, but the result is they become attack vectors. The Ronin Layer 2 hack is an example of a set of bootstrap comprises that became an attack surface. It is also worthwhile to think longer term and model for conditions that could cause Layer 2 fees to increase with high adoption on the Layer 2.

An example of inclusivity on a global domain is the global artist community. Only the well connected, discovered artists have had their work sold at high value. Often these artists only see a benefit on the first sale and the high values come on secondary sales. This puts local communities of artists in an information and market asymmetry model that has often impaired emerging markets. Introducing geographically diverse artists and others to an economy that isn't dependent on local buyer/seller supply and demand opens up entirely new markets for these creators on a global stage. This drives inclusion in emerging markets for creators worldwide. A similar approach is being taken for agricultural commodities by providing small hold farmers with verifiable economic history and better access to overcome the information asymmetry driven by middlemen. This provides transparency to opaque market dynamics and a path to economic growth.

Web 3.0 distributed systems technical approaches default to open systems, transparent token transfers, and systems of coordination that cross enterprise boundaries. Web 2.0 businesses have accrued value through closed walled garden systems approaches and information asymmetry. Operating on a global domain with verifiability codified into the system, inclusive of business logic, code, and transaction relationship execution at the speed of sub second transactions is complex and a wholly new paradigm. Most businesses are far from realizing the competitive risk to their existing business models, nor are they ready to embrace this approach to create new revenue and engagement opportunities.

A case in point is the amount of people hours spent on reconciliation of siloed enterprise systems that happens in supply chains and finance. This is because the systems design assumed no common reference for source data and source of truth. The last few decades of systems design have been internally focused trying to bring old legacy paper-based processes to digital.

Web 3.0 offers an opportunity to redesign systems with a more open collaborative multi-party benefit. Value chains require cross enterprise boundary coordination. Our systems design approach should embrace that to solve the digital transformation opportunities available using Web 3.0 distributed systems.

When we assume a distributed systems design paradigm on a global scale, it changes fundamental assumptions of the approach. This brings with it new challenges, better value chain design, and opportunities to fix many long-standing problems of federated systems, honey pots, reconciliation, delays, and consumer identity, consent, and data privacy.

Like the Internet, there remains a place for private transactions and information, a place for transparency, and a place for fully public transparent transactions. At no point will 100% of private business transactions, practices, and commercial agreements be fully public transactions. It's important to not fall into the design trap that assumes everything must be fully transparent. Knowing that Web 3.0 provides a hybrid systems design approach that accounts for private data, defined multi-party matrixed privacy, and fully transparent data and logic is an important nuance. Solutions do exist to protect privacy, private transactions, and in Web 3.0 to provide fully private transactions over a public blockchain substrate. A few different models leveraging some common approaches are maturing in this area. Layer 2 systems can have permissioned access as one very coarse approach. The tooling and Layer 2 approaches using zero knowledge proofs are maturing. These approaches can prove a set of conditions exist without access to the underlying private business data or relationships.

The opportunity for Web 3.0 systems design is upon us and the innovators that take advantage of this paradigm will see the fruits of their labor long before those that have slept on this transformation wave.

12.4. Web 3.0's greatest challenges

So far, we've discussed lack of economic incentives and education are Web 3.0's greatest challenges. Two experts add the lack of regulations and lack of interoperability to that list. Carol Goforth, University Professor at University of Arkansas School of Law, sees regulations as the bigger barrier to realizing the full potential of Web 3.0. Dino Farinacci, inventor, and founder of Lispers, sees lack of interoperability as the greatest challenge.

Carol GoForth, University Professor at University of Arkansas

There are innumerable opinions as to the biggest challenges facing blockchain and crypto. Some observers contend that volatility in pricing of cryptoassets is the biggest hurdle to widespread acceptance and adoption; some complain that governmental oversight and the increasing involvement of legacy financial institutions as intermediaries threatens the original goals of protecting privacy and providing peer-to-peer, democratic control; others point to the undeniable and highly publicized presence of criminals in the space; still others complain that the potential advent of quantum computing threatens the security of encryption protocols that currently protect the security of data on blockchains. While there is some truth to each of these positions, I think a bigger barrier to realizing the full potential of blockchain technology is the tendency of regulators to see things in black and white, advocating for extremes based on the false narrative that "crypto is for criminals," or the equally questionable idea that the best approach is a multi-year moratorium on regulation.

Most reputable crypto entrepreneurs appear to agree that reasonable regulation with a clearly articulated path to compliance would be ideal, while most regulators seem to be more concerned with laying claim to authority over crypto and asserting control through existing legal structures that do not mesh easily with this new and continually evolving technology. A 2022 executive order from President Biden missed the opportunity to call for Congressional intervention to balance the need for effective regulation with the legitimate need of entrepreneurs to be able to develop and implement this tremendously exciting technology.

There is both a need and role for responsible regulation in the crypto/blockchain ecosystem. That role should not, however, stifle innovation or drive it elsewhere.

Dino Farinacci, inventor, and founder of Lispers

The Internet was built with a common set of lower layers so many types of applications could run over one network infrastructure. One type of 'network of networks' that could support various types of data packets, from email to file transfer, from web to streaming video to high bandwidth conferencing.

A new set of applications that run over the Internet infrastructure use blockchain data structures. Designed to create a 'single source of truth' similar to how a typical physical ledger is used. This Internet blockchain data structure is needed so we can introduce a new concept called the 'Internet of value'. Value can be transmitted via authenticated transactions with the latest state-of-the-art cryptography. This is all goodness, but we have an evolution problem occurring. There are 100s of blockchains, each with different protocol designs, different goals, and different scaling and security requirements. The problem has occurred because this space has evolved over the past 10 years adding improvements upon the initial Bitcoin and Ethereum designs coupled with new blockchain applications that have sprung up.

The really big problem that is occurring is that there is a blockchain deployed for each application. And even if the blockchains use cryptocurrency to transmit value, the transactions, the tokens, and the security are not compatible. So there is no concept or working model where you can transmit value from a Bitcoin wallet to an Ethereum wallet. This is an enormous problem where there is no incentive to fix. Since each blockchain project wants to focus on their own value-add and applications, they don't focus on the global 'common-good'. We have a tragedy of the commons. Standards communities are getting involved to these architectural issues but the problem is too complex to come up with satisfactory solutions.

One Internet can run dozens of applications but dozens of blockchain applications cannot run over one blockchain network. We request a call to awareness.

12.5. Are enterprises prepared for Web 3.0's disruption?

Three leaders from some of the world's largest companies tackled this question. All agree that disruption is inevitable and offer insights on what disruption will look like for incumbents. Their insights resonate with Clayton Christensen's Theory of Disruption innovation, which we discussed in the previous chapter.

Dale Chrystie, Blockchain Strategist at FedEx and Chairman of BiTA Standards Council, cautions executives from incumbent organizations to disrupt or be disrupted. Chen Zur leads EY's US Blockchain practice, notes that disruption to financial services is already upon us with DeFi, but that Web 3.0 will transform many industries over the next eight years. Anouk Brumfield leads IBM's Global Blockchain Services; she urges incumbent enterprises to consider public and hybrid blockchains.

Dale Chrystie, Blockchain Strategist at FedEx

We live in a Web 2.0 world. Embracing a Web 3.0 world isn't just going to be process improvement (evolution). It will be breakthrough (revolution). And most people and enterprises don't yet realize the massive difference between the two. Web 3.0 brings a foundational shift to blockchain, peer-to-peer technology, smart contracts, self-sovereign identify, digital currency, etc. And there is no direct path from 2.0 to 3.0 on any kind of linear scale.

Even if we accept the inevitability of these things intellectually, it is still difficult to grasp

505

the gravitational pull of Web 2.0, fighting at literally every step along the way to keep people and organizations from jumping to Web 3.0. Most enterprise systems were built on 2.0. Enterprises have spent years improving those 2.0 processes, and they likely have reports, goals, and incentives, tied tightly to all of that. Many employees may have wanted to work for large companies because of what and how they influenced Web 2.0. It is not even a stretch to think of Web 3.0 in terms of a 'conflict of interest' in many ways over current Web 2.0 processes.

This is a 'disrupt or be disrupted' moment for many companies and even industries, specifically those who play a 'middleman' role. The automotive industry could serve as an analogy for these competing philosophies. Let's look at two data points on a supply and demand curve: 1) the trajectory of demand for electric vehicles (EV) and when they reach critical mass (in a very few years), and, 2) the demand for internal combustion engine (ICE) vehicles. The point where those two data points intersect is when the demand for electric vehicles quickly passes the other line, and that is the moment when the demand for ICE vehicles is dropping quickly. Long before that happens, the automotive manufacturers must have ramped up EV production because once the ICE demand starts to fall, they could find themselves out of business if they are not prepared. That is similar to what could happen with Web 2.0 vs Web 3.0.

So, while blockchain/Web 3.0 is not yet very fast, or mature or scalable, at what point do enterprises increase resource allocations to explore how to take advantage of this? Organizations will need to make investments in these technologies—which still don't make sense to many people—to prevent being left behind or disrupted by early adopters seeking to disrupt their business models. This is a unique moment in time when technology will determine that what has made enterprises successful to date will no longer make them successful in the future. They must continue to adapt and invest in these emerging technologies to ensure future success.

Chen Zur, Partner/Principal US Blockchain Practice Leader at EY

As a short introduction, I lead EY US's Blockchain practice, working on the development and adoption of public blockchain and digital assets technology. The question I would like to discuss in the next few lines is: Are enterprises prepared for Web 3.0's disruption to their business models? Or: What do we (as EY) see enterprises doing, to prepare for Web 3.0's disruption?

I would like to start by quoting Charles Darwin, "It is not the strongest of the species that survives, nor the most intelligent; it is the one most adaptable to change." (and change is indeed coming!).

I focus on financial services organizations because they are currently feeling the sense of urgency, more than any other industry in this space. Previous versions of the Internet focused on the way we consume digital content (Web 1.0) and on the distributed way we create digital content (Web 2.0). In its essence, Web 3.0 adds an 'Internet of value' layer focused on the way we own and exchange value between us, digitally. Web 3.0 also added 'digital identity, ownership and value exchange' to the core capabilities of the Internet. Naturally, financial services was the first industry we see this capability disrupt our current world, with the emergence of DeFi as an example. However, financial services is where this disruption starts, not where it ends. I truly believe that by the year 2030, Web 3.0 technology will transform many more aspects of our lives. Digital identity, metaverse, supply chain provenance, and gaming are but a few additional examples.

Anouk Brumfield, VP, Senior Partner, and Global Blockchain Services Leader for IBM

It is abundantly clear that technology drives business, but it is difficult to foresee which technologies will lead the way. We have reached a point where emerging technologies are making dramatic changes in the way we do business today, with the potential to reshape the entire century. Web 3.0 is the future of the Web.

The Web is at the core of business. Web 1.0 changed communication by allowing individuals and businesses to send and receive messages through email and research information online. Web 2.0 made the web interactive and drove business success through engagement with social media.

Now, Web 3.0 is driven by the ownership and monetization of user data. Everywhere we look, businesses are collecting, analyzing, and/or selling data. For better or worse, new technologies are making these efforts easier, safer, and more efficient.

For an example of how the ownership and monetization of data work in Web 3.0, look to the Metaverse, a digital reality where users can create environments to interact with each other and have experiences beyond their normal day to day lives. These myriad virtual experiences present yet another opportunity for companies to monetize user activity.

Blockchain will continue to undergird emerging technologies. While the jury is still out on the Metaverse, blockchain remains critical to the evolution of business because it is both extremely efficient and nearly invisible to average technology users. It lets companies manage highly secure transactions, which is both useful for internal business practices and customer-facing applications.

Blockchain has seen widespread adoption because it is the technology that underpins Bitcoin and other cryptocurrencies. Most recently, we've seen companies and individuals, in particular, putting blockchain technology to use in new ways. Take NFTs, for example. An NFT, or Non-Fungible Token, is an item that derives its value from being the only copy of itself. Because it is a highly secure ticket of authenticity, you see NFTs being used largely for digital art. By using blockchain to create the token for their creations, artists are able to sell their NFTs for tens of thousands of dollars.

Time will tell. Businesses are likely to continue the trend of using blockchain for secure transactions and communications, even as the technology creates new opportunities like NFTs in the art world. However, there is much more that businesses can do with blockchain. At a minimum, it is likely to continue to operate in the background of many business operations. Only time—and the evolution of new technologies—will show the limits and possibilities of blockchain and how it will impact how business itself develops and adapts.

In summary, there is a huge focus in the market around web 3.0, so it is important for enterprises to prepare for this market shift. Blockchain will see real-world applications this year onward. It will be on public blockchains and hybrid (private and public) blockchains. Traditional banks will consider Decentralized Finance (DeFi) space seriously and CeDeFI (Centralized and Decentralized Finance) scenarios will emerge. Web 2.0 companies will transform themselves into Web 3.0 and/or Metaverse focused companies. Web 3.0 is combination of various technologies coming together: blockchain, AI, AR (Augment Reality)/VR (Virtual Reality)/XR (Extended Reality), Data, IOT, Digital Twins, etc. Blockchain will be common layer sticking the 'Web3.0' fabric. Web 3.0 is about not only reading, writing but ownership of data—decentralization. So wallets, tokens, etc. will be key—it will be the new way of life. Web 3.0 will disrupt enterprises and enterprises that don't pivot to hybrid blockchains will be left behind.[28]

12.6. Conclusion

A technology maximum states that we overestimate technology's impact in the short term and underestimate its impact in the long term. That maxim likely rings true for the innovations we've studied in the Web 3.0 space.

Hopefully, readers by now have been given enough evidence to agree that something big is indeed afoot. Blockchains have the potential to change the way we connect online (SSI), exchange value, and monetize our own data—just as the Internet changed the way we exchange information. Blockchains show us new ways to mitigate counter-party risks, to provide reliable bookkeeping records, and to secure networks by using cryptography, digital tokens, consensus algorithms, distributed ledgers, and smart contracts. In our opinion, it's not just a pipedream; it's already a $1 to $2 trillion dollar industry. Public blockchains like Bitcoin have over a decade of operations without its ledger being hacked—that's quite remarkable considering it stores up to nearly a trillion dollars' worth of value (depending on the price of Bitcoin) and is OPEN to the public. When blunders like the 2016 Ethereum DAO attack occurs, we learn from them. Communities improve the technologies with each iteration of software development and upgrades.

Citations

[1] Cohen, J., and Wronski, L. (August 30, 2021). Cryptocurrency investing has a big gender problem. Retrieved February 3, 2022 from https://www.cnbc.com/2021/08/30/cryptocurrency-has-a-big-gender-problem.html

[2] https://blockchain.uark.edu/women-in-blockchain/

[3] Yoo, Y., Boland, R. J., Lyytinen, K., & Majchrzak, A. (2012). Organizing for Innovation in the Digitized World. *Organization Science*, *23*(5), 1398–1408. http://www.jstor.org/stable/23252314

[4] Szabo, N. (1998). Secure Property Titles with Owner Authority, Retrieved August 14, 2021 from https://nakamotoinstitute.org/secure-property-titles/

[5] Chaum, D. (1982). Computer Systems Established, Maintained and Trusted by Mutually Suspicious Groups, University of California, Berkeley.

[6] Nakamoto cited 8 papers in the Bitcoin white paper:

W. Dai, *b-money*, http://www.weidai.com/bmoney.txt, 1998.

H. Massias, X.S. Avila, and J.-J. Quisquater, *Design of a secure timestamping service with minimal trust requirements*, in 20th Symposium on Information Theory in the Benelux, May 1999.

S. Haber, W.S. Stornetta, *How to time-stamp a digital document*, in Journal of Cryptology, vol 3, no 2, pages 99-111, 1991.

D. Bayer, S. Haber, W.S. Stornetta, *Improving the efficiency and reliability of digital time-stamping*, in Sequences II: Methods in Communication, Security and Computer Science, pages 329-334, 1993.

S. Haber, W.S. Stornetta, *Secure names for bit-strings*, in Proceedings of the 4th ACM Conference on Computer and Communications Security, pages 28-35, April 1997.

A. Back, *Hashcash - a denial of service counter-measure*, http://www.hashcash.org/papers/hashcash.pdf, 2002.

R.C. Merkle, *Protocols for public key cryptosystems*, in Proc. 1980 Symposium on Security and Privacy, IEEE Computer Society, pages 122-133, April 1980.

W. Feller, "An introduction to probability theory and its applications," 1957.

[7] Buterin, V. (2014). Ethereum white paper. https://ethereum.org/en/whitepaper/

[8] https://eips.ethereum.org/EIPS/eip-20

[9] https://eips.ethereum.org/EIPS/eip-721

[10] Foster, Andrea L. (July 13, 2007). "The Death of a Virtual Campus" (PDF). The Chronicle of Higher Education. Archived from the original on May 4, 2016. Retrieved May 4, 2016.

[11] https://en.wikipedia.org/wiki/Pok%C3%A9mon_Go

[12] I-scoop (2021). Augmented reality and virtual reality trends and use cases in IIoT. Retrieved May 11, 2022 from https://www.i-scoop.eu/industry-40-virtual-reality-vr-augmented-reality-ar-trends/

[13] O'Flaherty, K. (2021). Facebook Just Gave 1 Million Oculus Users A Reason To Quit, Forbes, https://www.forbes.com/sites/kateoflahertyuk/2021/07/04/facebook-just-gave-1-million-oculus-users-a-reason-to-leave/?sh=417e22bf76f5

[14] Sensorium (March 16, 2022). Top 10 Metaverse Crypto Projects To Watch In 2022, https://sensoriumxr.com/articles/top-metaverse-crypto-projects

Christodoulou, K., Katelaris, L., Themistocleous, M., Christodoulou, P. and Iosif, E. (2022). NFTs and the Metaverse Revolution: Research perspectives and open challenges, in in Blockchain and the Token Economy, (editors, Horst Treiblmaier and Mary Lacity), Palgrave MacMillan, Houndmills, forthcoming.

[15] You may track Decentraland transactions on Ethereum:

https://etherscan.io/token/0x0f5d2fb29fb7d3cfee444a200298f468908cc942

[16] You may track Somnium Space Cubes on:

https://etherscan.io/token/0xdf801468a808a32656d2ed2d2d80b72a129739f4

[17] You may track Cryptovoxels on Ethereum:

https://etherscan.io/token/0x79986af15539de2db9a5086382daeda917a9cf0c

[18] CB Insights Research (2022). The metaverse could be tech's next trillion-dollar opportunity: These are the companies making it a reality, retrieved May 11, 2022 from https://www.cbinsights.com/research/metaverse-market-map/

[19] Olenick, M., Kim, W.C., and Mauborgne, R. (2022). Meta: Facebook's Pivot to the Metaverse. A Dystopia or Blue Ocean Utopia? Retrieved May 11, 2022 from https://www.blueoceanstrategy.com/teaching-materials/meta-facebook-pivot-to-metaverse/

[20] Porra, J., Lacity, M., Parks, M. (2019). Can Computer-Based Human-Likeness Endanger Humanness? - A Philosophical and Ethical Perspective on Digital Assistants Expressing Feelings They Can't Have. *Information Systems Frontiers*, (22), pp. 533-547.

[21] McCauley, A. (March 22, 2022). The Battle For Control Of The Metaverse: Can Open Innovation Outrun Corporate Domination? Forbes, retrieved May 11, 2022.

[22] Diehl, S. (2021). Web3 is Bullshit. Retrieved May 11, 2022 from https://www.stephendiehl.com/blog/web3-bullshit.html

[23] Rosenthal, D. (2022). Blockchain Gaslighting. Retrieved May 11, 2022 from https://blog.dshr.org/2022/01/blockchain-gaslighting.html

[24] Rosenthal, D. (2022). Blockchain Gaslighting. Retrieved May 11, 2022 from https://blog.dshr.org/2022/01/blockchain-gaslighting.html

[25] Vatican COVID-19 Commission https://www.humandevelopment.va/en.html

[26] The Pontifical Council for Culture, http://www.cultura.va/content/cultura/en.html

[27] *"In my Encyclical Letter on care for our common home, I pointed to a fundamental parallelism. The indisputable benefit that humanity will be able to draw from technological progress (cf. Laudato Si', 102) depends on the degree to which the new possibilities at our disposal are employed in an ethical manner (cf. ibid., 105). This correlation requires an adequate development of responsibility and of values alongside the vast technological progress underway."* His Holiness, Pope Francis. https://www.vatican.va/content/francesco/en/speeches/2019/september/documents/papa-francesco_20190927_eradigitale.html

https://www.digitalage19.org/Home

[28] Selig, J. (2022). The 8 Defining Features of Web 3.0. *Expert.ai*. https://www.expert.ai/blog/web-3-0/

Hayes, A. (2022). What is Blockchain?. *Investopedia*. https://www.investopedia.com/terms/b/blockchain.asp

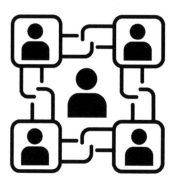

Glossary

This glossary covers terms, major events and supplemental information

Altcoins: Alternative coins are cryptocurrencies that are alternatives to Bitcoin. Initially, altcoins were created by downloading the Bitcoin Core, altering the programming code, and launching a new network. Namecoin and Litecoin are examples. As time went on, the term has become outdated.

Airdrop: the practice of sending crypto to many wallet addresses, often to promote a new cryptocurrency. Most digital wallets do not require the owner's permission to receive cryptocurrencies, so senders can search distributed ledgers to distribute tokens to millions of wallet addresses. It is considered impolite and certainly against the value of user choice to send someone crypto without their authorization. For one thing, it may have tax implications.

Anonymity: In the context of blockchains, the identity of the senders and receivers of transactions is unknown. Anonymity is different from confidentiality (see entry below).

Anti-money laundering (AML): Regulations that require financial institutions to report suspicious activity of money laundering, which is defined as an illegal practice that converts profits from crimes into what appears to be a legitimate source of cash. Sample AML regulations include the US Bank Secrecy Act of 1970; the UK Sanctions and Anti-Money Laundering Act 2018; and the European Union's AML directives in 2015 and 2020.[1]

Application Programming Interface (API): An API is a piece of software that connects two software applications so that one application can send a message to and receive a response from another application. Bitcoin, for example, has over 100 APIs. Sample Bitcoin APIs include programming code to indicate the number of blocks in the longest chain ('GetBlockCount'); to create a new bitcoin wallet ('CreateWallet'); and to list the IP addresses of all banned nodes ('ListBanned'). See https://bitcoin.org/en/developer-reference.

Asymmetric key algorithm: A type of cryptography that uses a pair of mathematically related numbers called 'keys'—one public key and one private key. Users can digitally sign messages by encrypting them with their private keys. *'This is effective since any message recipient can verify that the user's public key can decrypt the message, and thus prove that the user's secret key was used to encrypt it. If the user's secret key is, in fact, secret, then it follows that the user, and not some impostor, really sent the message.'*[2] **RSA**, **DSA**, and **ECC** are three specific examples of asymmetric key algorithms (see entries below for each).

Atomic swap: Ensures that *all* of the actions associated with a transaction execute, or *all* the actions fail; no partial executions should be allowed. For example, if Alice wants to send some value to Bob, an atomic swap ensures that either (a) Alice's account is debited AND Bob's account is credited, or (b) that NEITHER action occurs.

Benevolent dictator: A governance model in which a single person or single organization holds decision making rights, and bases decisions on the best interests of the community.

Bitcoin: This term bitcoin refers to both the Bitcoin application as a whole and to its native digital asset, the bitcoin cryptocurrency.

Bitcoin (application): The Bitcoin application is a peer-to-peer payment application. Conceived of by Satoshi Nakamoto in 2008 by combining many existing innovations, the Bitcoin network was launched live in 2009.[3] Nakamoto adopted public-private key encryption to authenticate asset ownership, a proof-of-work consensus protocol for validating transactions and adding them to the ledger, and the use of hashes and Merkle trees to secure transactions within a completely distributed, peer-to-peer, public network. Among its advances were a digital ledger structured as a chain of blocks and the creation of a native digital asset called bitcoins.

Bitcoin (cryptocurrency): Bitcoins are the native digital asset within the Bitcoin blockchain. Bitcoin was designed to be a scarce resource with a maximum money supply of 21 million bitcoins. The first 50 bitcoins were released in 2009, and the last will be released in the year 2140. Bitcoins are added to the money supply, on average, every ten minutes to reward miners for creating a new block of transactions. Every 210,000 blocks, the miner's reward cuts in half, so that more bitcoins are released in its earlier years than in later years. By early 2020, about 85 percent of the money supply has been released.

Block header: Each block within a blockchain contains a header with important information such as the block's unique ID; the number of transactions in the block; when the block was created; the size of the block (in terms of computer storage); and the pointer to the previous block. Figure G.1 provides an example of Bitcoin's block header.

Block #507980

BlockHash 0000000000000000002ac0fd Bitcoin Block 507980 | Bitcoin Block Explorer ↑154a398

Summary

Number Of Transactions	1838	Difficulty	2603077300218.5933
Height	507980 (Mainchain)	Bits	176c2146
Block Reward	12.5 BTC	Size (bytes)	973919
Timestamp	Feb 6, 2018 10:23:10 AM	Version	536870912
Mined by		Nonce	3997532233
Merkle Root	6334a61743821be369a74b116a50b...	Next Block	507981
Previous Block	507979		

Figure G.1: Example of a block header for Bitcoin

In this example, we are looking at the 507,980th block in the Bitcoin blockchain. The summary data in the header indicates that there are 1,838 transactions in the block's payload; its *'height'* is equal to its sequence in the blockchain (block 507980); *'block reward'* indicates that the winning miner earned 12.5 bitcoins for using its computer's resources to validate the transactions and to create the block; the *'timestamp'* indicates the exact second the block was created on February 6th 2018; the *'Merkle root'* shows the result of the Merkle hashing sequences (see **Merkle root** entry below) used to secure the block; the *'previous block'* is the pointer to this block's predecessor. The *'bits'* and *'size'* indicate how much computer storage is required to store this block. The *'version'* indicates which set of Bitcoin's blockchains rules to follow. The *'difficulty'* and *'nonce'* are associated with Bitcoin's Proof-of-Work consensus algorithm. Functionally, the difficulty indicates the number of lead zeros the miner's computer(s) had to find (after trillions of random tries) in order to find a unique *'blockhash'*. In this block, notice the blockhash has 18 lead zeros. The difficulty is part of the proof that the miner's computer did some serious calculations to earn the block reward (see entry for **Proof-of-Work**).

Blockchain: This term is used several ways. Sometimes the term refers broadly to what we are calling a 'blockchain application'. For example, people call Bitcoin and Ethereum 'blockchains'. The term can also be used to describe the structure of the digital ledger. With a blockchain structure, newly submitted transactions are sequenced and collected into a block (see Figure G.2). The block comprises a header and payload of transactions. The block header includes a pointer to the previous block of transactions, forming a chain of sequenced blocks over time all the way back to the first block, called the 'genesis block'.

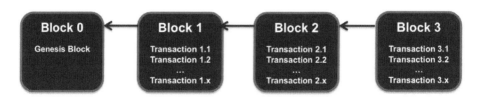

Figure G.2: Distributed ledger structured as a chain of blocks

518

Blockchain application: A blockchain application is a peer-to-peer (decentralized) network for validating, timestamping, and permanently storing transactions on a shared *distributed ledger*. *Digital assets*, native to each blockchain application, are programmable, exist only in digital form, and come with rights of use. *Consensus* algorithms validate transactions, update the ledger, and keep copies of the ledger in sync. *Cryptography* helps to secure the network. Most blockchains use *smart contracts* that apply rules to automatically execute transactions based upon pre-agreed conditions.

Byzantine fault tolerance of a system: The ability of a distributed network to function properly given that a certain number of nodes are faulty or even malicious. A general rule is that peer-to-peer distributed systems like blockchains can function properly even when up to a third of the participating nodes are faulty.

Byzantine Generals' Problem: A conceptual situation described by Leslie Lamport, Robert Shostak, and Marshall Pease (1982) to investigate how decentralized communication networks can reach agreement if some unknown number of nodes is faulty. In their metaphor, a Byzantine General represents a computer node; some generals are loyal (i.e. not faulty) and some generals are disloyal (i.e. faulty). Lamport et al. (1982) proved that decentralized networks could reach a consensus provided that two thirds of the nodes function properly.[4]

Central Bank Digital Currency (CBDC): A CBDC is digital version of fiat currency, completely controlled by the country's government.

Centralized network: See entry for **Network structures**

Code base: The set of programming instructions based on the agreed upon rules, i.e. protocols.

Coercive influences: See entry for **Institutional Isomorphism**

Confidentiality: In the context of blockchains, only authorized parties are allowed to know the identities of the parties involved or the details of the transaction.

Glossary

Consensus protocol: Consensus protocols are rules for making sure copies of the distributed ledger agree. Consensus protocols are used to counteract the **tragedy of the commons** and the **Byzantine Generals Problem** (see separate entries). Although consensus protocols vary in their validation procedures, in general, all consensus protocols seek to authenticate ownership and ensure that transactions are funded (i.e. no double spending) before adding them to the official distributed ledger. The process of validation begins when a new transaction is broadcast to the network. Computer algorithms verify legitimate ownership of the asset (based on the owner's digital signature with his or her private key) and check that the asset has not been given away before by scanning the ledger, thus preventing double spending. Which node gets to collect verified transactions and add them to the official ledger depends on the network's consensus protocol. Many consensus protocols have been used and proposed, including proof-of-work; proof-of-stake; proof-of-authority; proof-of-activity (which combines proof-of-stake with proof-of-work); proof-of-authority; proof-of-burn; proof-of-capacity; proof-of-elapsed time; proof-of-listening; and proof-of-luck.

Consortium-led innovation: In the context of a blockchain, a consortium provides a structure for competitors and ecosystem partners to cooperate to define, build, govern, and/or operate a shared blockchain application.

Coopetition: A portmanteau of two words—'cooperation' and 'competition'. Coopetition recognizes that firms have complex interdependencies. In some realms, firms that compete for market share also cooperate to achieve mutual benefits such as to define standards, to build component parts, or to reduce shared administrative and infrastructure costs.[5]

Corda: An open-source, distributed ledger platform developed by the R3 Consortium. Corda was designed to increase privacy, reduce data redundancy and increase scalability. Corda uses public-private key encryptions and hashes, and creates permanent, immutable records between trading partners. As a private protocol, participants are assigned a cryptographic identity, which is tied to a 'real world' identity, such as a legal entity identifier.[6] Once on-boarded, a party can transform a legal contract into smart contract code to transact with another Corda party or parties. Rather than distribute the entire ledger to everyone on the network, Corda creates node-to-node transactions directly between/among the parties involved in the transaction as defined in the smart contract.[7] Each Corda participant only sees the subset of data for which they are privy. This feature is implemented using **multiple composite keys** (see entry below).[8]

Corda has configurable consensus, meaning parties to a contract can pick their preferred consensus protocol, which is likely to be Byzantine Fault Tolerance (BFT) or Raft.[9] The Corda ledger is built on relational database technology, and thus does not use a block structure. It chose this structure so that participants could easily query the ledger using SQL. Data is considered 'on-ledger' if at least two parties in the system agree about the transaction's validity, whereas data held by only one party is 'off-ledger'. Corda's design is scalable since there is less network traffic and data storage, more private than most DTL protocols, and settles transactions as soon as nodes agree.[10]

As time went on, Corda's architecture evolved to the point where some people no longer consider it a blockchain; Corda lacks some of the defining characteristics of public blockchains: It does not have a native digital asset, it does not broadcast transactions, and it does not distribute a shared ledger. Indeed, Corda's main architects call Corda 'blockchain-inspired'.[11] The initial version was released in November of 2016.[12]

Counterparty risk: The risk each trading party bears that the other party will not fulfill its contractual obligations.

Credentials: Attestations made about subjects by authorized issuers.

Cross-chain oracle: One blockchain application reads data from another blockchain application. One-way reads are also called 'one-way pegs'.

Cross-chain transaction processing: Two or more blockchains coordinate operations so that a single asset can be used by more than one chain. These are also called 'two-way pegs'.

Cryptography: The science of securing data in the presence of third party adversaries using mathematical and computer algorithms.

CryptoNotes: A protocol that aims to increase the anonymity of blockchains.

Cryptocurrency exchange: A trusted third party that acts as a money transmitter or market maker for cryptocurrencies. Coinbase, Binance, and Huobi are examples.

Decentralized autonomous organization (DAO): A kind of smart contract that runs an entire organization automatically based on codified rules in a smart contract. The idea of a DAO is to create a completely independent entity that is exclusively governed by the rules that you program into it and 'lives' on the chain. This is more than using the blockchain to manage a company: instead, the code is the entire company. And it cannot be stopped.[13]

Decentralized Identifiers (DIDs): According to the W3C (2020): *"DIDs are designed to enable individuals and organizations to generate their own identifiers using systems they trust. These new identifiers enable entities to prove control over them by authenticating cryptographic proofs such as digital signatures. Since the generation and assertion of Decentralized Identifiers is entity-controlled, each entity can have as many DIDs as necessary to maintain their desired separation of identities, personas, and interactions."[14]* The W3C DID standard has three data fields (see Figure G.3). The first field is always the three letters, 'did', similar to how all web addresses start out with 'www'. The second field describes the DID method—how this particular DID creates, reads, updates, and deletes the DID. The last data field is a unique string.

Figure G.3: W3C DID data fields

Source: https://www.w3.org/TR/did-core/diagrams/parts-of-a-did.svg

A DID has four properties[15]:

1. **Persistence.** Unlike logon IDs, email addresses, or URLs, no one else has the power to revoke someone's DID.

2. **Resolvable.** Just as a URL resolves to one and only one IP Address, a DID resolves to one and only one DID document, meaning one can find meta data associated with the DID.

3. **Cryptographically verifiable.** A DID is cryptographically verifiable; whoever controls the private key is considered to be the legitimate owner of the DID. Verifiers can look up the issuer's public key to verify that only the issuer could have created the DID document.

4. **Decentralized.** A DID is decentralized; no trusted third-party registration authority is required. With SSI, a centralized public key infrastructure (PKI) is replaced with a decentralized PKI as indicated by the DID method.

Decentralized Finance (DeFi): The complete decentralization of financial transactions where parties can swap assets, lend crypto, borrow crypto without relying on any trusted third parties.

Decentralized network: See entry for **Network structures**

Delegated Proof-of-Stake (DPoS): A consensus protocol created by Daniel Larimer, founder of BitShares, Steemit and EOS.[16] With this method, anyone who possesses the cryptocurrency can vote to elect validator nodes. The validator nodes with the most votes become a 'delegate' (see Figure G.4). The algorithm takes turns selecting a leader from among the panel of delegates for a current time period. After the time period elapses, another round of voting occurs to select the next panel of delegates. Delegates are rewarded with transaction fees. DPoS settles transactions faster and with fewer resources than proof-of-work, and is more democratic than permissioned protocols.[17] EOS uses DPoS.

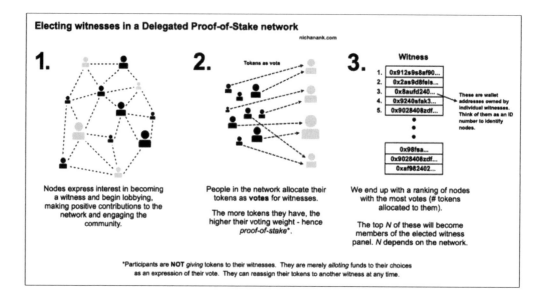

Figure G4: Delegated Proof-of-Stake (DPoS) voting process

Source: https://en.bitcoinwiki.org/upload/en/images/8/8b/Consensus-algorithms-pos-dpos.png

Democracy: A governance model where any participant has an equal vote.

Denial of Service (DoS) attack: A type of malicious attack that floods a network with so many transactions that it disrupts service for legitimate users.

Digital signature: A way to sign a transaction using a computer rather than a hand signature, thus proving one is authorized to do so (see Chapter 3 for more details).

Digital wallet: Software that stores private keys associated with addresses that hold digital assets. A digital wallet is an entry point, or interface, to many blockchains. Stored off a blockchain, the private keys are the only way to prove that one owns an asset on the distributed ledger. If the digital wallet is destroyed or hacked, there is no way to retrieve it. Thus, digital wallets are the main source of vulnerability for blockchain applications.

Directed acyclic graph (DAG): A type of graph that flows in just one direction with no feedback loops. In the context of blockchains, one-way graphs can be used to represent the time sequence of transactions. Iota's 'tangle' structures its ledger based on a DAG (see Figure G.5).

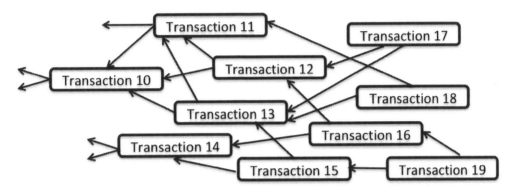

Figure G.5: Distributed ledger structured as a tangle of transactions

Disruptive Innovation: An innovation based on a new business model that targets underserved customers or creates new markets that may eventually threaten the traditional competitors' market shares. The term comes from Clayton Christensen's Theory of Disruptive Innovation.[18]

Distributed ledger: As a component of a blockchain application, a distributed ledger is a time-stamped, permanent record of all valid transactions that have occurred within a given blockchain application. Each node of the blockchain network has an identical copy; no node is in charge.

Distributed network: See entry for **Network structures**

DSA (Digital Signature Algorithm): An asymmetric key algorithm that generates private-public key pairs. Designed by David Kravitz, an NSA (National Security Agency) employee, the National Institute of Standards and Technology adopted it in the 1990s.[19]

Elliptic curve cryptography (ECC): ECC is a common method for generating private-public key pairs in blockchain applications. Basically, an ECC algorithm transforms a private key into a public key by bouncing around a large elliptic curve n number of times, where n is equal to the private key. It's theoretically impossible to figure out the private key if one only has the public key. The specific EC curve used in Bitcoin is $y^2 = x^3 + 7$ (see Chapter 3 for details).

EOS: EOS was developed by Daniel Larimer and Brendan Blumer, CTO and CEO, respectively, of Block.one. They wanted the advantages—open, secure, decentralized—of a public blockchain platform, like Ethereum, to build and operate decentralized applications, but without the latency, limited scalability, and resource intensity. The EOS mainnet was launched live in June of 2018. Anyone can view the blockchain (https://bloks.io/) and use EOS. Anyone can operate a validator node if they meet minimal criteria: an individual or organization must have a public website URL; at least one social media account; an ID on Steemit; sufficient hardware; plans to scale hardware; plans to benefit the community; telegram and testnet nodes; a roadmap; and a dividend position.[20] However, only 21 'block producers' can add blocks. The block producers are selected by a Delegated Proof-of-Stake mechanism (see glossary) in which owners of EOS cast votes in proportion to their stake.[21] Block producers are rewarded with the issuance of new EOS tokens. Blocks are produced about every 500 milliseconds, with each of the 21 producers getting a turn. On the day of this writing, EOS was trading at $2.35 and block producers were located in China (eight nodes), Singapore (three nodes), the Cayman Islands (two nodes), United States (two nodes) and BVI, Canada, Hong Kong, Japan, South Korea, and Ukraine (operating one node each).

ERC-20 tokens: Standard for creating a token for *fungible digital assets* that can be exchanged with other fungible tokens on Ethereum. Each token is interchangeable and has the same value. The token must meet mandatory requirements for defining the total money supply, specifying the number of tokens than can be transferred to a user account, providing a way to extract the balance of an account, allowing the transfer of tokens to other accounts, and checking a transaction against the money supply to prevent counterfeits. Optionally, ERC-20 tokens can be assigned a token name, symbol, and decimal value (up to 18 decimal places).[22] Aion (AION); Augur (REP); EOS (EOS); Golem (GNT); Maker (MKR); TRON (TRX); and VeChain(VET) are examples of ERC-20 tokens.

ERC-721 tokens: Standard for creating a token for *nonfungible digital assets* on Ethereum, whereby each token is unique and can have a different value than others of its kind. ERC-721 tokens can only be exchanged with other tokens of its same kind. ERC-721 tokens must meet required functions, including balance of an address; owner of a token; approval and transfer of a token. [23] CryptoKitties was the first ERC-721 token, which gained popularity in 2017; each CryptoKitty is one of a kind. Whereas CryptoKitties are native digital assets that only exist inside Ethereum, ERC-721 tokens can be used to represent unique assets outside of Ethereum with a unique digital twin inside Ethereum. EY's WineChain token is an example; EY tokenized 11 million unique wine bottles with an ERC-721 token.[24]

ERC-1155 tokens: Standard interface for a smart contract that can process fungible and non-fungible tokens. The authors of the standard describe the need as follows: *"Tokens standards like ERC-20 and ERC-721 require a separate contract to be deployed for each token type or collection. This places a lot of redundant bytecode on the Ethereum blockchain and limits certain functionality by the nature of separating each token contract into its own permissioned address. With the rise of blockchain games and platforms like Enjin Coin, game developers may be creating thousands of token types, and a new type of token standard is needed to support them. However, ERC-1155 is not specific to games and many other applications can benefit from this flexibility. New functionality is possible with this design such as transferring multiple token types at once, saving on transaction costs. Trading (escrow / atomic swaps) of multiple tokens can be built on top of this standard and it removes the need to 'approve' individual token contracts separately. It is also easy to describe and mix multiple fungible or non-fungible token types in a single contract."[25]*

Ether: Ethereum's native digital asset. Ether is not intended so much as a cryptocurrency, as much as it is a 'crypto-fuel', meaning it's a token whose main function is to pay for the Ethereum platform.[26] Like Bitcoin, ether is released through the process of mining blocks, and miners also receive the ether that senders append to their transactions to pay for them to be validated and added to the ledger. Ethereum's block reward was initially 5 ether, but it was reduced to 3 ether in 2017 and to 2 ether in 2019.[27] As of August 26, 2019, ether was trading at $188.49; the network had 8,977 active nodes[28], and 8,426,754 blocks had been added to the ledger. The total ether money supply amount is unclear;[29] a maximum of 18 million ether can be mined per year.[30]

Ethereum: Vitalik Buterin wrote the 2013 Ethereum white paper that would become the Ethereum platform when he was only 19 years old. Vitalik Buterin, Gavin Wood and Jeffrey Wilcke began work on Ethereum by launching The Ethereum Foundation, a non-profit organization based in Switzerland. According to the Ethereum Foundation: *"Ethereum is a community-driven project aiming to decentralize the Internet and return it to its democratic roots. It is a platform for building and deploying applications which do not need to rely on trust and cannot be controlled by any central authority."*[31] Ethereum's smart contracts are the primary innovation that extends a blockchain from a transaction verification and settlement protocol to a platform to launch decentralized applications (DApps). DApps can create and transact new native digitals assets besides ether, provided that they conform to **ERC-20** or **ERC-711** guidelines (see separate entries above).

Ethereum Foundation: Vitalik Buterin, Gavin Wood and Jeffrey Wilcke began work on Ethereum by launching The Ethereum Foundation, a non-profit organization based in Switzerland. The foundation was first funded in August 2014 using an Initial Coin Offering for its native digital asset called 'ether'. Ethereum went live in July of 2015, with a presale release of 60 million ether and 20 million ether retained by The Ethereum Foundation.[32] It raised over $16 million.[33]

Exchange: see **Cryptocurrency Exchange** entry.

Fabric: See **Hyperledger Fabric** entry.

Fake news: the deliberate spread of verifiably false information under the disguise of being an authentic news story.

Federation: A governance model in which decentralized groups specialize on parts of a project while coordinating with a central group.

Fork: A divergence of a blockchain into two or more separate paths. Soft forks are temporary, whereas hard forks are permanent (see Figure G.6).

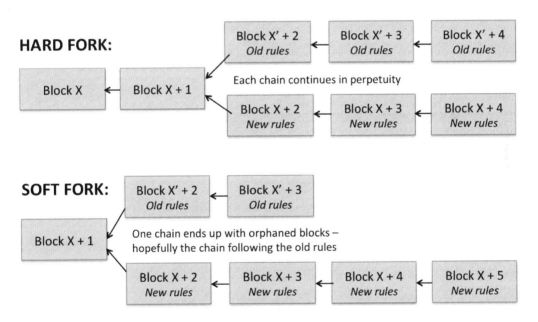

Figure G.6: Hard fork *vs.* soft forks

A hard fork is a permanent divergence in a blockchain. A soft fork is a temporary divergence in a blockchain while nodes upgrade to the new rules; mining under old rules will not win blocks, so nodes will eventually join the new chain if everything goes as planned.

Fork (Hard): Hard forks are permanent, divergent paths of a blockchain. Hard forks typically occur under two circumstances. First, someone may create their own blockchain or digital asset by copying and modifying source code. Second, hard forks can occur when the open source community disagrees on the rules of the next version of the protocol. For example, Bitcoin forked into 'Bitcoin' and 'Bitcoin Cash' when miners disagreed over a proposed upgrade in 2017. In another example, Ethereum split into 'Ethereum' and 'Ethereum Classic' when the community disagreed about remediating The DAO hack (see story in Chapter 8).

Fork (Soft): Sometimes two nodes create the next block at the same time, resulting in two versions called a soft fork. For a short while, different nodes in the network will be working off of different branches of the ledger until one is established as the longest and therefore the valid branch. Soft forks also occur during planned upgrades to the open source software. A temporary divergence in the blockchain happens when non-upgraded nodes do not follow the new consensus rules.[34] The non-upgraded nodes can still mine for a set time period, so it is up to the upgraded nodes to mine faster and become the longest, and thus, most valid chain.[35] In practice, the open source community tries to get most people to agree to the soft fork in advance.

Fungible token: a token that represents an interchangeable asset.

Governance: Defines the decision-making rights, including who and how the decisions are made.

Hash: An algorithm for transforming one input into a different output. Given a specific input, the identical output will always be reproduced. A good hash algorithm makes it practically impossible to determine the input value based on the output value, which is why hashes are called 'one way' functions. SHA-256 is commonly used in blockchains. Blockchains use hashes in many places to add layers of security. Public keys are hashed into addresses; addresses and amounts within a transaction are hashed to create a unique and secure transaction ID; transaction IDs within a block are hashed together multiple times to produce a **Merkle root** (see entry below) that resides in a block header; and all the data in the block header is hashed to create a unique and secure block ID.

Hash-Time Locked Contracts (HTLC): A type of smart contract that locks the sender's value into the contract until either the receiver retrieves the value in the address using the secret key and their digital signature (this is the 'hash lock'), or the contract expires and returns the value to the sender (this is the 'time lock').

Hexadecimal: A numbering system with 16 base numbers, often used in blockchain cryptography. The 16 numbers are usually represented as 0, 1, 2, 3, 4, 5, 6, 7, 8, 9, A, B, C, D, E, and F.

Hyperledger Fabric: Hyperledger Fabric is one of the projects sponsored by the Hyperledger Project, a non-profit organization launched by the Linux Foundation in December of 2015 to advance the application of enterprise-grade blockchains across industries.[37] Although the Hyperledger Project has other major blockchain frameworks, Fabric has received considerable media attention, thanks to its adoption by enterprises such as IBM, Wal-Mart, and Maersk.[38] Digital Asset Holdings and IBM initially contributed to Hyperledger Fabric's code base. Twenty-six other companies—including Fujitsu, GE, Hitachi, State Street, and SAP—contributed to the open source code that was released in 2017.[39] Fabric's ledger is structured as a chain of blocks and has two subsystems: 'the world state' and the 'transaction log' of all the transactions that led up to the current world state. Participants can create their own channels, which is a separate transaction ledger. Within a channel, every node gets copies of the same ledger.[40] Fabric also has a smart contracting feature, called Chaincode, which is used to connect outside applications to the world state ledger.

Hyperledger Foundation: The Linux Foundation launched this non-profit organization in December of 2015 to advance the application of enterprise-grade blockchains across industries.[41] Brian Behlendorf, the developer of the Apache Web server, serves as its first Executive Director. By January 2020, 275 corporate members were listed on its website. As of 2022, the Hyperledger Foundation had six graduated projects (Aries, Besu, Frabric, Indy, Iroha, and Sawtooth) and nine projects in incubation: Bevel, Cactus, Caliper, Cello, Explorer, Firefly, Grid, Transact, and Ursa.

Immutability: As it relates to blockchains, immutability means that a transaction or smart contract that has been added to the digital ledger can never be changed. For public blockchains like Bitcoin and Ethereum, immutability means that hacks cannot be fixed unless 51 percent of the nodes agree to the fix by rolling back the ledger and creating a hard fork. For private blockchains, authorized parties may submit transactions that reverse a prior error, but the entire transaction history that led to the current account balance will be maintained. The benefit of immutability is that trading partners can rely on one historical record for data provenance and auditability. Immutability may conflict with regulations or corporate policies that require data destruction after an elapsed period of time, but there are a number of practices to address this, such as keeping private data off chain.[44]

Initial Coin Offering (ICO): With an ICO, startups announce that they want to raise cash using an ICO by launching a new coin, i.e. a new cryptocurrency. Investors buy the coins instead of shares in a company. While there are many legitimate ICOs, investors are warned to fully vet ICO projects to avoid being scammed.

Initial DEX Offering (IDO). A funding model that allows startups to raise money on a decentralized exchange by launching a new cryptocurrency, managed by a smart contract, with no third parties involved.

Initial Exchange Offering (IEO): A funding round conducted on a cryptocurrency exchange. Investors fund their exchange wallets with coins and use those funds to buy the fundraising company's tokens. Binance, Huobi, OKEX, KuCoin, and BitMax are examples of exchanges with IEO services.[45]

Institutional Isomorphism: A theory that describes the process by which competitors within an industry become more alike in structure and adopt similar practices over time. Paul DiMaggio and Walter Powell first articulated the theory.[46] The theory identifies three pressures that lead institutions to conform: mimetic, coercive, and normative. *Mimetic influences* arise from the perception that peer organizations are more successful; by mimicking peer behavior, the organization aims to achieve similar results. *Coercive influences* come from both formal and informal political pressures exerted on an organization by other organizations upon which they are dependent. Government regulations, legal requirements, and ceremonial practices to boost legitimacy, are examples of coercive influences. *Normative influences* arise from duties, obligations, and norms of professionalism, including formal education and professional and trade associations that seek to legitimize their existence. DiMaggio and Powell wrote, *"Many professional career tracks are so closely guarded, both at the entry level and throughout career progression, that individuals who make it to the top are virtually indistinguishable"*.[47]

Interface (blockchain): An access point to a blockchain application through an application programming interface (API). For end users, interfaces include digital wallets; gateways; anchors; exchanges; web portals; and IoT devices.

Interledger Protocol (ILP): Two Ripple engineers published the ILP's white paper back in 2015. For a given payment, the ILP protocol sends many micropayments with confirmations between micropayments to minimize the risk that a node could steal or fail to send a payment through a network.

Internet-of-Things (IoT): A term that refers to connecting devices with unique identifiers to the Internet so that data can be collected from and sent to those devices.

Internet Protocol (IP) Address: This is a unique number assigned to every device connected to the Internet. It's like a street, city, state, and zip code for each device. A sample IP address (in version 4) is '172.16.254.1'.

Interoperability: The ability for one system to use another system.[48] In relation to blockchains, interoperability means one blockchain could be connected to different blockchains or to different systems of record.

Know Your Customer (KYC): Regulations that require financial institutions to verify the identity, suitability, and risks involved with maintaining a business relationship with a customer. Examples of KYC regulations include the USA Patriot Act of 2001 and the UK Money Laundering Regulation of 2017.[49]

Lightning Network: A protocol that tracks intermediate transfers of funds off a blockchain and only posts the value of the initial credit and the final account balance transfers to the blockchain. The solution helps unclutter the blockchain network by getting rid of intermediate transactions.

Liquid immersion cooling: The use of liquids—called a dielectric coolants—designed to have zero electrical conductivity but good heat conductivity, which reduces the heat, power consumption and noise of cryptocurrency mining equipment.

Meritocracy: A governance model in which power is held by individuals or organizations based on their proven ability.

Merkle root: Named after the US computer scientist, Ralph Merkle, the Merkle root is the result of a sequence of hashes between pairs of numbers. In blockchain applications, the numbers are pairs of transactions. The process to calculate the Merkle root produces a very secure block because if a single digit is altered in any individual transaction, a subsequent calculation check of the Merkle root would reveal an alteration. For a given block, the Merkle root is added to the block's header. See Chapter 3 for details.

Metaverse: A virtual reality in which users interact with other users in computer-generated environments. Metaverse is a portmanteau of 'meta' and 'universe'.

Mimetic influences: See entry for **Institutional Isomorphism**

Minimal viable ecosystem: The minimum number of ecosystem partners that are needed to successfully launch a minimal viable product. Too many participants will slow development; too few and the solution will not be useful or attractive. In the context of blockchains, IBM recommends that competitors should be included in an MVE to establish trust.[51]

Minimal viable product: An initial version of a product that has enough functionality to attract early adopters. The early adopters provide feedback to improve the product, such as proposing new features and functionality. The purposes of an MVP are to test a product with minimal resources; accelerate learning through feedback from early adopters; lay claim to the solution before competitors; and to start building a brand.[52]

Mining: See entry for **Proof-of-Work**

Mining pool: Groups of miners who pool their resources and agree to share block rewards in proportion to their contributed mining hash power. Mining pools are desirable to the average miner because they smooth out rewards and make them more predictable.[53]

Mission: A formal statement that expresses the aspirations and values of an organization or community.

Money laundering with cryptocurrencies: Criminals around the world have used cryptocurrencies for money laundering, which converts profits from crimes into what appears to be a legitimate source of cash. For example, ten men were arrested in the Netherlands in January 2016 for laundering large sums of money using bitcoins.[54] In another example, a Russian man was arrested in Greece for laundering $4 billion into virtual currency.[55] The US Drug Enforcement Agency (DEA) is concerned about the increased use of cryptocurrencies as a way to launder the revenue generated from crime, which is worth approximately $300 billion annually in the US.[56] In a 2017 report, the DEA stated, *"Emerging as a money laundering vulnerability, Bitcoin and other virtual currencies enable TCOs (Transnational Criminal Organizations) to easily transfer illicit proceeds internationally."*[57] Most exchanges now comply with anti-money laundering (AML) requirements.

MultiChain: MultiChain is the code base developed by Coin Sciences Ltd. According to its whitepaper, *"MultiChain is an off-the-shelf platform for the creation and deployment of private blockchains, either within or between organizations. It aims to overcome a* *key obstacle to the deployment of blockchain technology in the institutional financial sector, by providing the privacy and control required in an easy-to-use package. Rather than supporting a single blockchain like Bitcoin Core, MultiChain is easy to configure and can work with different blockchains at the same time.*"[58] Its consensus protocol relies on 'mining diversity'; a round robin schedule of pre-authorized nodes assigned the tasks of validating new transactions and adding them to the ledger.

Multiple composite keys: In contrast to a single private-key pair, multiple private keys are needed to authorize a transaction. It's a way for multiple parties to share an asset.

N-versioning: Independent software teams code the detailed functionality in different programming languages to improve fault tolerance and redundancy. For example, Ethereum protocols have been coded in various computer languages like Go, Rust, C++, Python, Java, and Ruby.

Network structures: A network structure describes the relationships among nodes in a network (see Figure G.7). With a centralized structure, one node is in control; the centralized node (server) receives all incoming data from other nodes and, in turn, routes data to other nodes. In a decentralized network, all nodes are peers; no one node is in charge. Data travels to its closest neighbors until all targeted recipient nodes receive the data. In computer science, a distributed network is a hybrid, resulting in a distributed network of centralized networks.[59] However, many people use the terms 'decentralized' and 'distributed' as synonyms in common vernacular.

Node: According to the Hyperledger Blockchain Performance Metrics white paper (2019), *"In the context of a blockchain network, a node is an independent computing entity that communicates with other nodes in a network to work together collectively to complete transactions. A node is a virtual entity, in the sense that it could be running on physical hardware, or as a Virtual Machine (VM) or containerized environment. In the latter case, a node could share physical hardware with other nodes in the same network. A set of nodes may be managed by the same organization.*

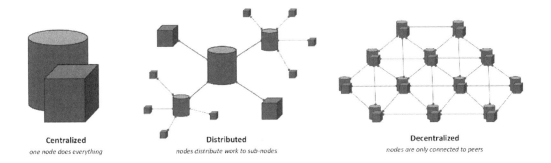

Figure G.7: Three network structures

Source: http://www.truthcoin.info/images/cent-dec-dist.jpg

For example, think of a mining pool operated by one company where a group of machines run as individual nodes doing proof of work (PoW) on a network. In most blockchain networks (Bitcoin, Ethereum, Hyperledger Burrow, Hyperledger Indy, Hyperledger Iroha, Hyperledger Sawtooth) each node plays a uniform class of roles in the network, such as generating blocks, propagating blocks, and so on. In these networks, nodes are usually referred to as peers. Such networks might require one or more nodes to take on a temporary role as a leader. This leadership role may be passed to other nodes in certain well-determined conditions. However, in some blockchain networks (such as Hyperledger Fabric), nodes are assigned one or more possible roles, such as endorsing peers, ordering services, or validating peers."[60]

Non-fungible token (NFT): a token that represents a unique, one-of-a-kind asset.

Normative influences: See entry for **Institutional Isomorphism**.

Notary: Pertaining to blockchains, a notary is a trusted third party that coordinates cross-chain operations. Cryptocurrency exchanges are common examples. Exchanges allow users to easily buy and sell cryptocurrencies and to exchange cryptocurrencies for fiat currencies; but that convenience comes at the acceptance and trust of centralized control, and with the risks of a single point of failure.

Oligarchy: A governance model in which a few people or a few institutions hold decision making rights.

Oracle: In a blockchain application, an   is an agent that finds and verifies real-world occurrences and submits this information to a blockchain to be used by smart contracts.[61]

Performance: See entry for **Systems Performance**.

Permissioned Protocol: Within a blockchain application, a permissioned protocol restricts access and confines which nodes are allowed to observe, transact, validate and add transactions to the permanent record (i.e. the distributed ledger).

Permissionless Protocol: Within a blockchain application, a permissionless protocol does not restrict access. Anyone can operate a full node and compete (or be semi-randomly assigned or voted upon) to validate and add transactions to the permanent record (i.e. the distributed ledger).

Plasma: Designed for Ethereum by Vitalik Buterin and Joseph Poon, Plasma is a 'layer 2' blockchain option designed to increase Ethereum's throughput, allowing more transactions per second.[62] *As of 2020, it is still being debated by the Ethereum community.*[63]

Polygon: Founded in 2017 by Jaynti Kanani, Sandeep Nailwal, and Anurag Arjun, Polygon is a layer 2 solution for Ethereum than reduces transaction costs and speeds transactions.

Practical Byzantine Fault Tolerance (PBFT): A consensus protocol created by Miguel Castro and Barbara Liskov in 1999.[64] With PBFT, nodes need permission to serve as validator nodes, forming a member list. Each round, a node from the member list is selected as leader. A client node sends a request to the leader node to validate a transaction. The leader node multicasts the request to all the other authorized nodes. The authorized nodes execute the request independently and then send the confirmation to each other and to the client. The client waits for a certain percentage of replies to confirm validation, typically waiting for 2/3 of the nodes to agree. The leader node changes for the next round.

As a *class* of consensus algorithms, there are many versions of PBFT, including Redundant Byzantine Fault Tolerance (RBFT) used by Hyperledger Indy[65]; Delegated Byzantine Fault Tolerance used by Antshares;[66] Quorum used by JP Morgan;[67] and Federated Byzantine Agreement used by Stellar[68]—to name but a few. PBFT versions differ by how authorized nodes are chosen and by how nodes are assigned roles. Ripple and Stellar, for example, allow participants to pick which nodes they want as validators;[69] Antshares separates bookkeeping nodes from user nodes, with the former being operated by professionals; Quorum delegates nodes to observer, voter, and maker roles;[70] R3 Corda authorizes notary and observer nodes; Hyperledger Fabric defines endorser, orderer, and committer nodes.

Privacy coin: A cryptocurrency that aims to maximize anonymity by using protocols and cryptography to mask the senders, receivers, and/or amounts while still preventing a double spend. Monero and Zcash are examples.

Private-public key pair: Two numbers that are mathematically related such that it is nearly impossible to figure out the private key if one only has access to the public key. Both keys are needed to prove ownership of a digital asset. Together, the pair serves as a digital signature. In practice, the owner of the digital asset holds the private key off the blockchain, either in a wallet the owner stores on his/her own device or in a wallet stored on an exchange or third-party provider. The public key is stored on the blockchain. (In Bitcoin, the public key is transformed into an address using a hash function.) Both keys need to 'turn' to send value. Figure G.8 is an example of a legitimate private-public key pair. (Don't bother searching for this address on a blockchain, a program created the private-public key pair for illustrative purposes.)[71]

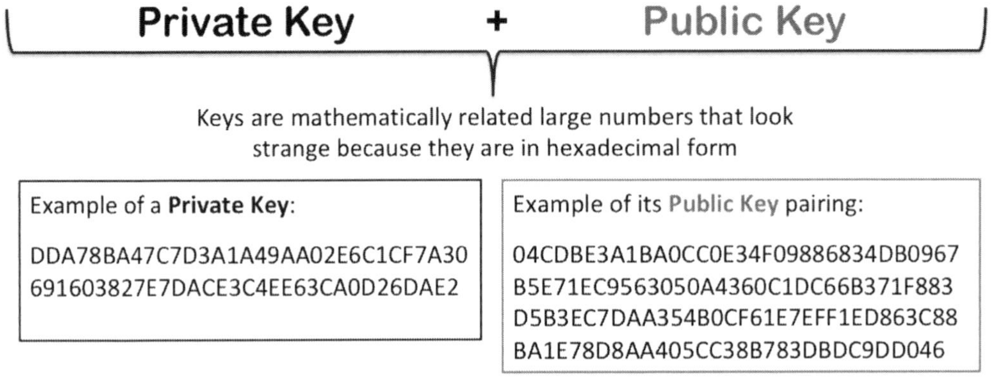

Private Key	+	Public Key

Keys are mathematically related large numbers that look
strange because they are in hexadecimal form

Example of a **Private Key**:	Example of its Public Key pairing:
DDA78BA47C7D3A1A49AA02E6C1CF7A30 691603827E7DACE3C4EE63CA0D26DAE2	04CDBE3A1BA0CC0E34F09886834DB0967 B5E71EC9563050A4360C1DC66B371F883 D5B3EC7DAA354B0CF61E7EFF1ED863C88 BA1E78D8AA405CC38B783DBDC9DD046

Figure G.8: Example of a private-public key pair

Source: http://minetopics.blogspot.com/2013/01/hiding-bitcoins-in-your-brain.html

Notice how long the hexadecimal public key is:

04CDBE3A1BA0CC0E34F09886834DB0967B5E71EC9563050A4360C1DC66B371F883D
5B3EC7DAA354B0CF61E7EFF1ED863C88BA1E78D8AA405CC38B783DBDC9DD046

To store on a blockchain, the public key gets shortened through a series of hashing processes, so it would look like this on a blockchain:

17A16QmavnUfCW11DAApiJxp7ARnxN5pGX

Proof-of-Authority (PoA): A consensus mechanism that preauthorizes nodes with the authority to validate and add transactions to a distributed ledger. The algorithm takes turns selecting a leader from among the list of authorized nodes (see Figure G.9). The leader node checks each transaction in the transaction queue; organizes valid transactions into a block; signs the block with the node's private key; and distributes the block to other nodes. The other nodes validate that the block was signed by the current leader and recheck each transaction within the block, resulting in an acceptance or a rejection of the entire block. As a permissioned consensus algorithm, it settles transactions faster and with fewer resources than permissionless algorithms, but it is more centralized.[72]

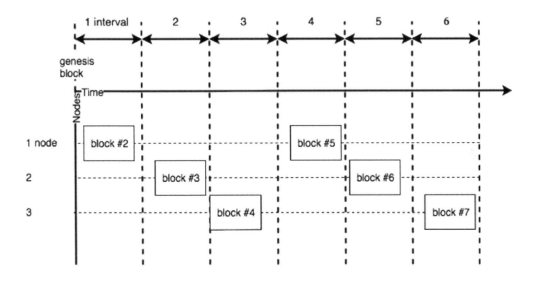

Figure G.9: Proof of Authority: Authorized nodes take turns creating blocks

Source: https://apla.readthedocs.io/en/latest/_images/block-generation.png

Proof-of-Stake: Sunny King and Scott Nadal created the 'proof-of-stake' consensus protocol for blockchains in a 2012 white paper.[73] Instead of 'mining' for coins, the protocol selects a member to 'forge' new currency as a reward for validating the transactions and creating the next block. Essentially, the selected member node is awarded a transaction fee. The member node is selected in a semi-random way; it's called a 'proof-of-stake' because the members with the highest 'stake' (i.e. have the largest account balances) are giving priority in the selection algorithm. Participants in the blockchain can estimate with some certainty which member will likely be the next 'forger'. A 'proof-of-stake' process uses much less energy than a 'proof-of-work' process. However, critics claim it is less secure than proof-of-work because people with small stakes have little to lose by voting for multiple blockchain histories, which leads to consensus never resolving.[74] Peercoin and Nxt use proof-of-stake. Ethereum may migrate to PoS.

Proof-of-Work: Cynthia Dwork and Moni Naor created the 'proof-of-work' protocol in 1993 to prevent junk email.[75] Satoshi Nakamoto adopted the 'proof-of-work' consensus protocol for Bitcoin in the 2008 white paper.[76] Ethereum also uses proof-of-work (for now). Nakamoto needed a way to find independent verifiers to validate transactions and add blocks to the blockchain without relying on trusted third parties. Nakamoto proposed to reward other nodes in the network with newly issued bitcoins when they validate all recently submitted transactions and create the next block. So that validator nodes take the task seriously, Nakamoto proposed a competition among computer nodes in the blockchain network to be the first to collect recently verified transactions into a block and then to find an acceptable block identification number (known as the blockhash) for the next block in the blockchain. It's not easy to find an acceptable number... it takes a lot of computing power to perform the brute force guesses to find a hash number that is less than the current mining 'difficulty'. The difficulty is part of the proof that the miner's computer did a significant amount of work to earn the block reward.

For the Bitcoin blockchain, a block's winning miner—or more likely, the winning mining pool—receives a set amount of bitcoins, which was 12.5 bitcoins as of March 2020, plus all the small fees that people offered miners to include their transactions in the block. A new block is mined every ten minutes on average. The miner's block reward halves every 210,000 blocks, so miners earn fewer coins with time, but the value of those coins might be substantially higher over time.

For the Ethereum blockchain, winning miners are awarded two ether per block, which are created about every 15 seconds. Sometimes ether is sent to a miner who found a solution but whose block was not included, called an uncle (or aunt) reward.[77]

The proof-of-work protocol creates a highly secure ledger, as an attacker would need to gain control of more than 50 percent of the hashing power of the network, rewrite history and find all new hashes that adhere to the protocol before other nodes notice. The cons of the protocol include slower transaction settlement times, fewer transactions processed per second, and higher electricity consumption compared to other protocols.

Protocol: A common set of rules that allow different nodes in a computer network to communicate. For example, the Internet uses the Transmission Control Protocol/Internet Protocol (TCP/IP), which is a set of protocols that specify how data should be structured, addressed, transmitted, routed, and received by nodes on the Internet. Blockchain protocols specify rules for how transactions are structured; addressed; transmitted; routed; validated; sequenced; secured; and added to the permanent record (i.e. the distributed ledger) by nodes in a blockchain network.

Pseudo-Anonymity: A blockchain application that aims to mask the identity of parties to a transaction, but whose identity may be revealed through meta data. For example, IP addresses may reveal the sender of a transaction. More commonly, when Party A sends value to an address owned by Party B on one date, Party A can later determine additional addresses owned by Party B when Party B spends the coins.

Quantum Computing: A computing architecture based on quantum bits, called 'qubits', which can simultaneously represent multiple states and therefore do multiple calculations at the same time. Quantum computing will speed computers in such a way that brute force guesses of private cryptographic keys that are impractical today could be practical in the future.

Quick Response (QR) code: A QR code is a two-dimensional code that is machine readable. QR codes are often used to track goods, and may contain information such as the manufacturer, lot number, and item number. Any number or text can be converted to a QR code. For example, Figure G.10 is QR code for 'The University of Arkansas'. If you take your camera phone and scan the QR code, you will see that the QR code is interpreted correctly.

Figure G.10. Machine-readable QR code for 'The University of Arkansas'

Quorum: Quorum is an enterprise-ready distributed ledger and smart contract platform based on Ethereum.[78] The Enterprise Ethereum Alliance officially supports Quorum.[79] Quorum was developed by J.P. Morgan, the world's third largest financial services firm, by assets of over $2.5 trillion, as an open-source, enterprise grade version of Ethereum.[80] Quorum is a private/permissioned blockchain that requires institutions to apply for permission to operate a node.[81] A key benefit is that it is designed to process and settle hundreds of transactions per second. J.P. Morgan licensed Quorum with a General Purpose License (GPL) so that the platform will be free to use. It plans to co-evolve in cooperation with Ethereum.[82] Quorum's architecture sits on top of the public Ethereum blockchain. QuorumChain is the original consensus protocol, with other Raft and Istanbul BFT protocols[83] added later.[84] As an open source project, any person or enterprise can download Quorum for experimentation. Notable adopters include Reuters;[13] Markit;[85] Microsoft;[86] Synechron;[87] BlockApps;[88] AMIS Technologies;[89] and Chronicled. Microsoft added Quorum to the Azure cloud marketplace for a trusted execution environment that is an additional layer of security.[90]

QuorumChain: The main consensus protocol used in Quorum. QuorumChain is a time-based, majority-voting algorithm that uses a smart contract to identify which nodes participate in consensus. QuorumChain has three types of nodes: voter nodes, maker nodes, and observer nodes. Voter nodes vote on which block should be added to the blockchain. Maker nodes are authorized to add the blocks after enough votes have been cast. Observer nodes receive and validate blocks, but do not vote or make blocks.[91] The ledger is segmented into a private state database and a public state database. Participants can execute private and public smart contracts. While all nodes validate public transactions, nodes can only validate private transactions if they are party to the private smart contract.[92]

R3: A blockchain consortium founded in 2014 by David Rutter, with the aim to develop a blockchain platform that could be used by global financial institutions. See Chapter 2 for more information.

Raft: A consensus protocol used in several blockchains, including Quorum. According to the Quorum white paper, *"Raft separates the key elements of consensus, such as leader election, log replication, and safety, and it enforces a stronger degree of coherency to reduce the number of states that must be considered."*[93] The elected leader node accepts requests from client nodes, replicates them to the network, and responds to the client when a quorum (>50 percent) has been reached. Raft can ensure settlement finality and has throughput of over a thousand transactions per second.

Raiden Network: A protocol that builds another layer on top of a blockchain. It was initially launched to allow for micropayments on Ethereum.[94] Described as similar to the Lightning Network, the basic idea is to switch from a model where all transactions hit the shared ledger on the blockchain (which is the bottleneck) to a model where users can privately exchange messages, which sign the transfer of value. Raiden nodes connect to Ethereum nodes using an API and claims that a million transactions per second of confidential transactions are possible (because they are not added to the blockchain).[95]

Redactable blockchain: A technical innovation that allows blockchains to be edited reliably without creating a hard fork by using secret trap door keys. The keys can only be used by authorized parties. The keys are used to find a hash collision, where two different inputs can create the same hash output. According to the seminal paper by Ateniese et al. (2017), *"The best way to grasp the concept of a redactable blockchain is to think of adding a lock to each link of the hash chain: Without the lock key it is hard to find collisions and the chain remains immutable, but given the lock key it is possible to efficiently find collisions and thus replace the content of any block in the chain. With the knowledge of the key, any redaction is then possible: deletion, modification, and insertion of any number of blocks. Note that if the lock key is lost or destroyed, then a redactable blockchain reverts to an immutable one."*[96] The secret keys are meant to be invoked infrequently—e.g., remedying egregious errors or attacks (like the DAO).

Representative Meritocracy: A governance model where people or institutions that have proven their merit are eligible to be elected to a council based on votes from other meritorious members.

RSA: RSA is an asymmetric key algorithm designed by three MIT professors—Rivest, Shamir, and Adleman—in 1977, based on multiplying two really large prime numbers.

Sandbox: A test environment that isolates software code from the live production environment, allowing people to test and experiment with the software.

Scalability: See entry for **System Scalability**.

Security Token Offering (STO): An STO is a legally compliant, licensed initial coin offering, which is only available to accredited investors.

Segregated Witness (SegWit): A protocol that increases the number of transactions that can be included in a Bitcoin block. Instead of appending a digital signature to each address within a transaction, the protocol calls for a single digital signature at block header level, thus reducing the size of transactions, enabling more transactions per block.[98]

Self-Sovereign Identity: Self-sovereign identity (SSI) is a decentralized and automated approach for issuing, holding, and verifying credentials. Holders possess and control their personal data. Online relationships are peer-to-peer—no need for accounts and passwords. The public key infrastructure is decentralized—no need to rely on trusted third parties.

SHA-256: A secure, one-way hash function commonly used in blockchains. It was designed by the US National Security Agency. It takes any-sized input value and produces a 32-byte output value using hexadecimal notation. The same input will always produce the exact same output.

Sharding: A protocol that segments the validation process for new transactions in a blockchain so that not every node validates every transaction. Its purpose is to improve system performance.

Sidechains/relays: Sidechains and relays provide the functions of a notary, but rely on automatically executing algorithms instead of on custodians. Back et al. (2014) first conceived of 'pegged sidechains' as a way for bitcoins and other ledger assets to be transferred between multiple, independent blockchains.[99] For these authors, a sidechain is a two-way peg to a parent chain (or main chain) that allows assets to be interchanged at a predetermined rate. But the term is relative to the asset, not to the network. For this reason, Vitalik Buterin laments the term 'sidechain' in his white paper on interoperability. He argued it is better to use the phrase, *"a relay of chain A exists on chain B"* or *"D is a cross-chain portable digital asset with home ledger A that can also be used on chain B."* [100]

Silk Road: Silk Road was an anonymous marketplace, and Bitcoin's most visible example of a nefarious use case. Ross William Ulbricht founded Silk Road in 2011, when he was just 27 years old.[101] The marketplace combined the anonymity of Bitcoin with the obscurity of Tor, the network protocol that masks the identity of servers. (One can spot a Tor website by the website address's suffix '.onion'). One can hardly believe

547

the audacity of Silk Road's openness (see Figure G.11 for a screen shot showing illegal drugs available for sale). After an intense search that comprised cyber and behavioral investigative methods—such as posing as drug buyers—the US Federal Bureau of Investigation (FBI) arrested Ulbricht in 2013. He was sentenced to life in prison without the possibility of parole.[102] This story is nuanced in a way that will not be covered here, but the documentary film, *Deep Web*, by Director Alex Winter, provides thorough coverage of the rise and fall of Silk Road.

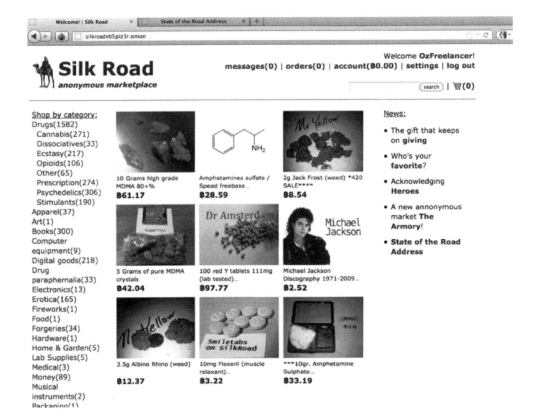

Figure G.11: Silk Road website screenshot

Source: Techrepublic[103]

Simple Payment Verification (SPV): Nakamoto (2008) described SPV as a way to verify bitcoin transactions without running a full network node. Rather, one only needs to maintain a copy of the block headers and then find the security links (called a ***Merkle tree*** branch) to the transaction to prove it was verified and accepted by the network. SPV shows that *"tokens have been locked up on one chain so validators can safely unlock an equivalent value on the other chain."*[104]

Smart Contract–Deterministic: Once deployed on the blockchain, a deterministic smart contract can execute autonomously without the need for any outside information. See Chapter 3 for more information.

Smart Contract–Non-Deterministic: Once deployed on the blockchain, a non-deterministic smart contract requires outside information to execute the terms of the agreement. The outside information is called an 'oracle'. See Chapter 3 for more information.

Smart contract: A smart contract—a concept developed by Nick Szabo in 1994—is a piece of software that stores rules for negotiating the terms of a contract, automatically verifies the contract and then executes the terms.[105] See Chapter 3 for more information.

Stable coin: A cryptocurrency that aims to create a stable store of value by pegging the digital coin to a stable asset outside of the network, such as pegging a digital coin to a fiat currency or to a commodity like gold or a barrel of oil. Tether; USD Coin; Gemini; JPM Coin; and Libra are examples.

Stakeocracy: A 'Pay to Play' governance model where individuals' or institutions' votes are weighted by the size of their investment.

Sustaining innovation: An innovation that improves the performance of an enterprise's current product or services to meet the needs of its most demanding customers. The term comes from Clayton Christensen's Theory of Disruptive Innovation.[106]

Sybil attack: A single malicious node in a network that replicates itself so many times, it takes over the network. Blockchains like Bitcoin, Ethereum and Stellar use cryptocurrencies to prevent Sybil attacks, as a Sybil attacker would run out of money.

System performance: A term used to measure how long it takes a network to process a transaction. Blockchain applications generally vary in their performance from minutes to seconds.

System scalability: A system's ability to handle an increase in workload, such as when new users are added to a system.[107] Scalability refers to the throughput, i.e. how many transactions can be processed per second.

Tragedy of the commons: This concept is defined as a situation within a shared-resource system where individual users acting independently according to their own self-interest behave contrary to the common good of all users by depleting or spoiling that resource through their collective action.[108]

Transaction costs: The effort, time, and costs incurred in searching, creating, negotiating, monitoring, and administrating a transaction between trading partners.

Transmission Control Protocol/Internet Protocol (TCP/IP): As the Internet's primary protocol, it breaks messages into packets and routes them to their destination as defined by a unique address called an 'IP address'. Every device connected to the Internet has a unique IP address including computers; mobile phones; laptops; printers; IoT devices; servers; routers, etc.

Transaction malleability: When a user creates a transaction, the digital wallet signs and sends off the transaction to the network in order to get validated and added to the digital ledger. Transactions are automatically assigned a unique transaction-ID based on its content. While the transaction is still making its way through the network, there is a way to slightly change the transaction so that it is still a valid transaction that correctly moves money as the original author intended. The small change, however, will generate a different unique transaction-ID based on the slightly revised content. The result is that a sender sending a transaction cannot be certain that the transaction will have the same ID from the moment is was created to when it finally gets mined in a block.[109]

Trust: Trust can be defined formally as *"the degree to which subject A has confident positive expectations that object B will fulfil its obligations in context C to limit L".*[110]

Trust protocol: In the context of a blockchain application, the term 'trust protocol' is defined to mean the reliance on computer algorithms rather than trusted third party institutions to verify transactions and to ensure all copies of the digital ledgers agree across nodes.

Trusted third parties: Trusted third parties—like banks, certificate authorities, and credit card companies—exist to mitigate counterparty risks, i.e. the risk each party bears that the other party will not fulfill its contractual obligations. Trusted third parties perform many vital functions, such as authenticating asset ownership and making sure accounts are funded to prevent double spending.

Turing complete: A term that refers to a computer programming language that has a full set of commands to execute every algorithm that another Turing complete programming language can execute. For example, a simple calculator with basic arithmetic functions is not Turing complete because it cannot execute if-then-else or loop logic. As it relates to blockchain codebases, a Turing complete, smart contracting feature provides the ability to code many types of agreements; but with more coding capabilities comes more risks of software vulnerabilities. Ethereum and Hyperledger Fabric, for example, do have Turing complete programming languages to code smart contracts; Ethereum's smart contracting language is called Solidity; Hyperledger Fabric's is called Chaincode. Bitcoin and Stellar do not have Turing complete smart contracts.

Verifiable credentials: The term 'verifiable credential' is a special type of credential that is machine-verifiable. More formally, W3C defines a verifiable credential as *"a tamper-evident credential that has authorship that can be cryptographically verified."*

Web 3.0: Web 3.0 is the idea that we will use the Internet for reading, writing, and execution, but that users will control and monetize their activities by decentralizing the WWW with blockchain technologies. The term is credited to Gavin Wood, co-founder of Ethereum.[111]

Zero-knowledge proof: Shafi Goldwasser, Charles Rackoff, and Silvio Micali developed the concept in 1985.[112] Zero knowledge proofs are a method for one party (or node) to verify possession of a piece of information to other parties (or nodes) without revealing the information. In general, there are two types of zero-knowledge proofs: *challenge-response* which coordinates an interaction for known parties and *non-interactive*, which do not require iterations. In blockchain applications, zero-knowledge proofs are used to guarantee that transactions are valid without revealing information about the sender, receiver, and/or transaction. Zcash, EY's Nightfall, MediLedger, and many other blockchains use zero knowledge proofs.

zk-SNARK (Zero-Knowledge Succinct Non-Interactive Argument of Knowledge): A zero-knowledge proof used in some blockchain protocols.

Here is an explanation of zk-SNARKs:

*Suppose Bob is given a hash **H** of some value, and he wishes to have a proof that Alice knows the value **s** that hashes to **H**. Normally Alice would prove this by giving s to Bob, after which Bob would compute the hash and check that it equals **H**. However, suppose Alice doesn't want to reveal the value **s** to Bob but instead she just wants to prove that she knows the value. She can use a zk-SNARK for this. We can describe Alice's scenario using the following program, here written as a Javascript function:*

```
function C(x, w) {
return ( sha256(w) == x );
}
```

*In other words: the program takes in a public hash **x** and a secret value **w** and returns true if the **SHA-256 hash** of w equals x. Translating Alice's problem using* *the function C(x,w) we see that Alice needs to create a proof that she possesses **s** such that **C(H, s) == true**, without having to reveal **s**. This is the general problem that zk-SNARKs solve.*[113]

Citations

[1] https://en.wikipedia.org/wiki/Money_laundering#Anti-money_laundering

[2] *Definition of Asymmetric Encryption*, http://hitachi-id.com/resource/itsec-concepts/asymmetric_encryption.html

Mapt course, *Asymmetric Cryptography*, https://www.packtpub.com/mapt/book/big_data_and_business_intelligence/9781787125445/3/ch03lvl1sec28/asymmetric-cryptography

[3] Nakamoto, S. (2008), *Bitcoin: A Peer-to-Peer Electronic Cash System*, https://bitcoin.org/bitcoin.pdf

[4] Lamport, L.; Shostak, R.; Pease, M. (1982), T'he Byzantine Generals Problem', *ACM Transactions on Programming Languages and Systems*. 4 (3): 387–389.

[5] Dagnino, G., ; Padula, G. (2002), *Coopetition Strategy: Towards a New Kind of Interfirm Dynamics for Value Creation*, EURAM 2nd Annual Conference, Stockholm School of Entrepreneurship, Sweden.

[6] *How is Consensus achieved in Corda?* https://discourse.corda.net/t/how-is-consensus-achieved-on-corda/1148

[7] *Welcome to Corda*, https://docs.corda.net/

[8] Corda survey responses as reported in Seibold, S., and Samman, G. (2016), *Consensus: Immutable Agreement for the Internet of Value*, KPMG White Paper

[9] Brown, R., Carlyle, J., Grigg, I., and Hearn, M. (2016), *Corda: An Introduction*, Corda White Paper, https://docs.corda.net/_static/corda-introductory-whitepaper.pdf

[10] Corda survey responses as reported in Seibold, S., and Samman, G. (2016), *Consensus: Immutable Agreement for the Internet of Value*, KPMG White Paper

Glossary

[11] *Welcome to Corda*, https://docs.corda.net/

[12] Lee, P. (November 30th 2017), *R3 releases Corda as Blockchain strains start to show*, https://www.euromoney.com/article/b12kqb9hqwgp2d/r3-releases-corda-as-blockchain-strains-start-to-show

[13] Diedrich, H. (2016), *Ethereum: blockchains, digital assets, smart contracts, decentralized autonomous organizations*, Wildfire Publishing.

[14] W3C (2020). Decentralized Identifiers (DIDs) v1.0. Retrieved July 12, 2021, from https://www.w3.org/TR/did-core/

[15] Preukschat, A. and Reed, D. (2021). *Self-Sovereign Identity: Decentralized digital identity and verifiable credentials*. Manning Publications, Shelter Island.

[16] https://en.bitcoinwiki.org/wiki/DPoS

[17] Delegated Proof of Stake, https://lisk.io/academy/blockchain-basics/how-does-blockchain-work/delegated-proof-of-stake

[18] Clayton Christensen has developed the theory of disruptive innovation over two decades, beginning with this first book, published in 1997, *The innovator's dilemma: when new technologies cause great firms to fail,* (Boston, Massachusetts, Harvard Business School Press). For a thoughtful and current synopsis of the theory, see Christensen, C., Raynor, M., and McDonald, R. (2015), *Disruptive Innovations, Harvard Business Review*, 93(12): 45-53

[19] https://en.wikipedia.org/wiki/Digital_Signature_Algorithm

[20] Ben Sigman (May 8, 2018), *EOS Block Producer FAQ* https://medium.com/@bensig/eos-block-producer-faq-8ba0299c2896

[21] To view the 21 EOS validator nodes and block producers, see https://bloks.io/vote

[22] William, M. (May 12, 2018), *ERC-20 Tokens, Explained*, Cointelegraph, https://cointelegraph.com/explained/erc-20-tokens-explained

[23] http://erc721.org/

[24] Sharma, T. (July 16th, 2019), *Know the Authenticity of Your Wines*, https://www.blockchain-council.org/blockchain/know-the-authenticity-of-your-wines-eys-blockchain-platform-for-wine-traceability/.

[25] https://eips.ethereum.org/EIPS/eip-1155#simple-summary

[26] Beigel, O. (March 3rd 2017), *What is Ethereum?* https://99bitcoins.com/guide-buy-ether-ethereum/

[27] ConsenSys (January 10, 2019), *The Thirdening: What You Need To Know*, https://media.consensys.net/the-thirdening-what-you-need-to-know-df96599ad857

[28] https://www.ethernodes.org/network/1

[29] According to discussions within the open source community, the total money supply for ether has not been established, https://ethereum.stackexchange.com/questions/443/what-is-the-total-supply-of-ether

[30] *Is the ether supply infinite?* https://www.ethereum.org/ether

[31] http://wiki.p2pfoundation.net/Ethereum, *A Next-Generation Smart Contract and Decentralized Application Platform*, posted on https://github.com/ethereum/wiki/wiki/White-Paper

[32] *Is the ether supply infinite?* https://www.ethereum.org/ether

[33] Levi, A. (May 21, 2017), *Corporate Trends in Blockchain*, CB Insights webinar presentation.

[34] *The Differences Between Hard and Soft Forks*, We Use Coins, August 23rd 2016, https://www.weusecoins.com/hard-fork-soft-fork-differences/

[35] *Hard & Soft Forking Explained*, by Loshil and @MLPFrank, https://www.youtube.com/watch?v=pdaXY1OOiWQ

[37] The Linux Foundation (January 22nd 2016), *The Hyperledger Project Charter*, https://www.hyperledger.org/about/charter

[38] Connell, J. (June 2017), *On Byzantine Fault Tolerance in Blockchain Systems*, https://cryptoinsider.com/byzantine-fault-tolerance-blockchain-systems/

[39] Groenfeldt, T. (July 13th 2017), 'Linux Foundation's Hyperledger Fabric 1.0 Ready For Production', *Forbes Magazine,* https://www.forbes.com/sites/tomgroenfeldt/2017/07/13/linux-foundats-hyperledger-fabric-1-0-ready-for-production/-624d7632902e

[40] Hyperledger Foundation, *Hyperledger Architecture, Volume 1*, https://www.hyperledger.org/wp-content/uploads/2017/08/HyperLedger_Arch_WG_Paper_1_Consensus.pdf

[41] The Linux Foundation (January 22nd 2016), *The Hyperledger Project Charter*, https://www.hyperledger.org/about/charter

[44] Reiger, A.; Guggenmos, F., Locki, J., Fridgen, G., and Urbach, N. (2019), 'Building a Blockchain Application that Complies with the EU General Data Protection Regulation', *MIS Quarterly Executive*,

18(4), pp. 263-279.

[45] Winslet, T (2019), 'Top 3 Initial Exchange Offerings (IEOs) to Watch in the Crypto Market' *The Daily Hodl*, https://dailyhodl.com/2019/04/11/top-3-initial-exchange-offerings-ieos-to-watch-in-the-crypto-market/

[46] DiMaggio, P., and Powell, W. (1991), 'The Iron Cage Revisited: Institutional Isomorphism and Collective Rationality in Organizational Fields', *The New Institutionalism in Organizational Analysis*, (Powell & DiMaggio eds), The University of Chicago Press, 63-82

[47] DiMaggio, P., and Powell, W. (1991), 'The Iron Cage Revisited: Institutional Isomorphism and Collective Rationality in Organizational Fields', *The New Institutionalism in Organizational Analysis*, (Powell & DiMaggio eds), The University of Chicago Press, 63-82

[48] Ross, C. (December 5th 2016), *Blockchain Brings Us Into The Future, But Only After It Drags Up The Past: Interoperability Becomes An Actual Issue Again*, http://www.horsesforsources.com/blog/christine-ferrusi-ross/the-interoperability-problems-blockchain-brings_120616

Ross, C. (April 18th 2017), *Simplify Blockchain by Refusing to Let Interoperability Issues Bog You Down*, http://www.horsesforsources.com/Simplify-Blockchain-Refusing-Interoperability-Issues_041817

[49] https://en.wikipedia.org/wiki/Know_your_customer

[51] Arun, J., Cuomo, J., and Gaur, N. (2019). *Blockchain for Business*, Addison-Wesley, Boston.

[52] Lenarduzzi, V., Taibi, D. (August 2016), *MVP Explained: A Systematic Mapping Study on the Definitions of Minimal Viable Product*, 2016 42th Euromicro Conference on Software Engineering and Advanced Applications (SEAA). Cyprus. pp. 112–119.

[53] Tuwiner, J. (July 13th, 2017), *Bitcoin Mining Pools*, https://www.buybitcoinworldwide.com/mining/pools/

[54] The Guardian (January 20th 2016), *Ten arrested in Netherlands over bitcoin money-laundering allegations*, https://www.theguardian.com/technology/2016/jan/20/bitcoin-netherlands-arrests-cars-cash-ecstasy

[55] Lee, T. (July 26th 2017), *Officials arrest suspect in $4 billion Bitcoin money laundering scheme*, https://arstechnica.com/tech-policy/2017/07/officials-arrest-suspect-in-4-billion-bitcoin-money-laundering-scheme/

[56] De, N. (Oct 25th 2017), *DEA Report: Bitcoin Used for Trade-Based Money Laundering*, https://www.coindesk.com/dea-report-bitcoin-used-trade-based-money-laundering/

[57] The US Department of Justice Drug Enforcement Administration (October 2017), *2017 National Drug Threat Assessment*, https://www.dea.gov/docs/DIR-040-17_2017-NDTA.pdf

[58] MultiChain White Paper (2015), https://www.multichain.com/download/MultiChain-White-Paper.pdf

[59] Institute of Network Cultures, *Beyond distributed and decentralized: what is a federated network?*, http://networkcultures.org/unlikeus/resources/articles/what-is-a-federated-network/

[60] Hyperledger Blockchain Performance Metrics White Paper (2019). https://www.hyperledger.org/resources/publications/blockchain-performance-metrics

[61] https://blockchainhub.net/blockchain-oracles/

[62] Robinson, Dan (2019). https://events.technologyreview.com/video/watch/dan-robinson-scaling-interoperability/

[63] Cuen, L. (February 11, 2020), *Plasma Became Optimism and It Might Just Save Ethereum*, Coindesk, https://www.coindesk.com/plasma-became-optimism-and-it-might-just-save-ethereum

[64] *Practical Byzantine Fault Tolerance*, Proceedings of the Third Symposium on Operating Systems Design and Implementation, New Orleans, USA, February 1999, http://pmg.csail.mit.edu/papers/osdi99.pdf

[65] Hyperledger Foundation, *Hyperledger Architecture, Volume 1*, https://www.hyperledger.org/wp-content/uploads/2017/08/HyperLedger_Arch_WG_Paper_1_Consensus.pdf

[66] Connell, J. (June 2017), *On Byzantine Fault Tolerance in Blockchain Systems*, https://cryptoinsider.com/byzantine-fault-tolerance-blockchain-systems/

[67] Quorum White Paper, https://github.com/jpmorganchase/quorum-docs/blob/master/Quorum Whitepaper v0.1.pdf

[68] Maziières, D. (2016), *The Stellar Consensus Protocol: A Federated Model for Internet-level Consensus*, White Paper, https://www.stellar.org/papers/stellar-consensus-protocol.pdf

[69] Maziières, D. (2016), *The Stellar Consensus Protocol: A Federated Model for Internet-level Consensus*, White Paper, https://www.stellar.org/papers/stellar-consensus-protocol.pdf

[70] Maziières, D. (2016), *The Stellar Consensus Protocol: A Federated Model for Internet-level Consensus*, White Paper, https://www.stellar.org/papers/stellar-consensus-protocol.pdf

[71] http://minetopics.blogspot.com/2013/01/hiding-bitcoins-in-your-brain.html

[72] Proof-of-Authority Consensus https://apla.readthedocs.io/en/latest/concepts/consensus.html#advantages-of-poa-consensus

[73] King, S., and Nadal, S. (2012), *PPCoin: Peer-to-Peer Crypto-Currency with Proof-of-Stake*, https://peercoin.net/assets/paper/peercoin-paper.pdf

[74] *Distributed Consensus from Proof of Stake is Impossible,* Andrew Poelstra, https://www.smithandcrown.com/open-research/distributed-consensus-from-proof-of-stake-is-impossible/

[75] Dwork, C., and Naor, M. (1993), *Pricing via processing: Combatting Junk Mail*, http://www.hashcash.org/papers/pvp.pdf

[76] Nakamoto, S. (2008), *Bitcoin: A Peer-to-Peer Electronic Cash System*, https://bitcoin.org/bitcoin.pdf

[77] Beigel, O. (March 3rd 2017), *What is Ethereum?*, https://99bitcoins.com/guide-buy-ether-ethereum/

[78] J.P. Morgan, Quorum, https://www.jpmorgan.com/country/US/EN/Quorum

[79] Enterprise Ethereum Alliance (July 7th 2017), *Enterprise Etherum Alliance Announces Support for Blockchain Consensus Algorithm Integration*, https://entethalliance.org/enterprise-ethereum-alliance-announces-support-blockchain-consensus-algorithm-integration/

[80] The Quorum White Paper, https://github.com/jpmorganchase/quorum-docs/blob/master/Quorum Whitepaper v0.1.pdf

[81] Hackett, R. (October 4th 2016), 'Why J.P. Morgan Chase Is Building a Blockchain on Ethereum', *Fortune Magazine*, http://fortune.com/2016/10/04/jp-morgan-chase-blockchain-ethereum-quorum/

[82] J.P. Morgan, Quorum, https://www.jpmorgan.com/country/US/EN/Quorum

[83] https://www.ethnews.com/amis-technologies-new-algorithm-handles-more-transactions-per-second

https://github.com/ethereum/EIPs/issues/650

https://ethereumfoundation.org/devcon3/sessions/bft-for-geth/

[84] Quorum White Paper, https://github.com/jpmorganchase/quorum-docs/blob/master/Quorum Whitepaper v0.1.pdf

[85] http://www.ibtimes.co.uk/how-ihs-markits-syndicated-loans-blockchain-arrived-cash-1622304

[86] Castillo, M (February 28th 2017), *Microsoft Adds JPMorgan's 'Quorum' Blockchain to Azure Platform*, https://www.coindesk.com/microsoft-azure-jpmorgans-quorum-blockchain/

[87] http://www.financemagnates.com/cryptocurrency/innovation/synechron-releases-quorum-maker-enterprise-ethereum-alliance/

[88] http://blockapps.net/

[89] Nation, J. (July 5th 2017), *AMIS Technologies' New Algorithm Handles More Transactions-Per-Second*, https://www.ethnews.com/amis-technologies-new-algorithm-handles-more-transactions-per-second

[90] Castillo, M (February 28th 2017), *Microsoft Adds JPMorgan's 'Quorum' Blockchain to Azure Platform*, https://www.coindesk.com/microsoft-azure-jpmorgans-quorum-blockchain/

[91] *QuorumChain Consensus*, https://github.com/jpmorganchase/quorum/wiki/QuorumChain-Consensus

[92] Quorum White Paper, https://github.com/jpmorganchase/quorum-docs/blob/master/Quorum Whitepaper v0.1.pdf

[93] Raft White Paper, Ongaro, D., and Ousterhout, J. (2014), *In Search of an Understandable Consensus Algorithm*, https://raft.github.io/raft.pdf

[94] Hertig, A. (May 31st 2016), *Will Ethereum Beat Bitcoin to Mainstream Microtransactions?* https://www.coindesk.com/ethereum-bitcoin-mainstream-microtransactions/

[95] *The Raiden Network: High Speed Asset Transfers for Ethereum*, http://raiden.network/

[96] Ateniese, G., B. Magri, D. Venturi and E. Andrade (2017), *Redactable Blockchain – or – Rewriting History in Bitcoin and Friends*, 2017 IEEE European Symposium on Security and Privacy (EuroS&P), Paris, pp. 111-126.

[98] For a technical explanation of segregated witness, see http://learnmeabitcoin.com/faq/segregated-witness

[99] Back, A., Corallo, M., Dashjr, L., Friedenbach, M., Maxwell, G., Miller, A., Poelstra, A., Timón, J., and Wuille, P. (Oct 22 2014), Enabling Blockchain Innovations with Pegged Sidechains, https://blockstream.com/sidechains.pdf

[100] Buterin, V. (September 9, 2016), *Chain Interoperability*, https://static1.squarespace.com/static/55f73743e4b051cfcc0b02cf/t/5886800ecd0f68de303349b1/1485209617040/C hain+Interoperability.pdf

[101] Popper, N. (2015), *Digital Gold: Bitcoin and the Inside History of the Misfits and Millionaires Trying to Reinvent Money*, Harper, New York.

Glossary

[102] Weiser, B. (May 29th 2015), Ross Ulbricht, Creator of Silk Road Website, Is Sentenced to Life in Prison, *The New York Times*, posted https://www.nytimes.com/2015/05/30/nyregion/ross-ulbricht-creator-of-silk-road-website-is-sentenced-to-life-in-prison.html

[103] Reese, H. (May 10th 2017), *How the founder of the Silk Road made millions on his illegal startup on the Dark Web*, https://www.techrepublic.com/article/how-online-marketplace-silk-road-became-the-craigslist-for-illegal-drugs/

https://tr2.cbsistatic.com/hub/i/r/2017/05/10/709e488c-6c51-407f-ae13-5115b14d86c4/resize/770x/ac1af6 17d15f84b986b574770d9a67de/screen-shot-2012-04-24-at-2-02-25-am.png

[104] *SPV, Simplified Payment Verification*, Bitcoin.Org glossary.

[105] *The Future of Blockchains: Smart Contracts*, Technode, http://technode.com/2016/11/14/the-future-of-blockchain-technology-smart-contracts/

[106] Clayton Christensen has developed the theory of disruptive innovation over two decades, beginning with this first book, published in 1997, *The innovator's dilemma: when new technologies cause great firms to fail*, (Boston, Massachusetts, Harvard Business School Press). For a thoughtful and current synopsis of the theory, see Christensen, C., Raynor, M., and McDonald, R. (2015), *Disruptive Innovations*, *Harvard Business Review*, 93(12): 45-53

[107] Castor, A. (June 14th 2017), *Hyperledger Takes on Blockchain Scaling with New Working Group*, https://www.coindesk.com/hyperledger-takes-on-blockchain-scaling-with-new-working-group/

[108] 'The tragedy of the commons' is defined as 'an economic theory of a situation within a shared-resource system where individual users acting independently according to their own self-interest behave contrary to the common good of all users by depleting or spoiling that resource through their collective action.' https://en.wikipedia.org/wiki/Tragedy_of_the_commons

[109] *Transaction Malleability*, https://en.bitcoinwiki.org/wiki/Transaction_Malleability

[110] Scheutz, S., Steelman, Z., Kuai, L., and Lacity, M. (2022). Trust in the IT artifact: a systematic review. University of Arkansas working paper.

[111] https://en.wikipedia.org/wiki/Web3

[112] https://blockonomi.com/zero-knowledge-proofs/

[113] Lundkvist, C. (2017), Introduction to zk-SNARKs with examples, https://media.consensys.net/introduction-to-zksnarks-with-examples-3283b554fc3b

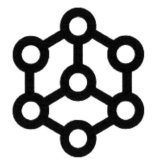

Index

A

Aave 133, 134, 215–217, 226, 244–250, 306, 399, 412, 442, 469
Accenture 18, 23, 134, 182, 185, 227, 336, 424, 436, 465, 494, 495
advisory council 68. *See also* governance
Agenzia Nazionale Stampa Associata. *See* ANSA
altcoins 108, 159, 160, 165, 515. *See also* cryptocurrencies/tokens
AML (anti-money laundering) 74, 138, 162, 234, 264, 278, 515, 535
angel investment 112, 173, 174. *See also* investment models
anonymity 64, 130, 138, 141, 163, 391, 392, 413, 420–423, 515, 522, 539, 543
 CryptoNotes 415, 422, 522
 Monero 76, 77, 108, 126, 166, 167, 204, 205, 420, 421, 422, 539
 pseudo-anonymity 165, 414, 474, 543
 Zcash 84, 126, 166, 167, 404, 418, 539, 552
 zero-knowledge proofs 167, 262, 279, 304, 319, 392, 415, 443, 476, 552
ANSA (Agenzia Nazionale Stampa Associata) 21, 53, 365, 376–382, 387
ANSAcheck 21, 53, 365, 376–382, 387, 412, 442
anti-money laundering. *See* AML
API (application programming interface) 67, 78, 515, 533.
application programming interface. *See* API
asymmetric key algorithm 516, 525, 546. *See also* cryptography
atomic swap 265, 516. *See also* interoperability

B

B3i (Blockchain Insurance Industry Initiative) 182, 184, 185. *See also* consortia/working
 groups;
Baseline Protocol 76, 82, 92, 179, 185, 304
BeefChain 285, 289, 290, 298–301, 318
benevolent dictator 63–65, 181, 357, 400, 488, 516. *See also* governance
Binance 74, 75, 101, 106, 109–112, 137, 158–165, 176, 397, 522, 532.
 See also crypto exchanges

Index

Index

J

JP Morgan 165, 204, 471, 539

K

Know Your Customer. *See* KYC
KoreConX 259–261, 275–279
Kraken 137, 162, 193, 241. *See also* crypto exchanges
KYC 74, 138, 162, 264, 275, 278, 279, 534. *See also* regulations

L

Libra 65, 66, 93, 549. *See also* consortia / working groups
Lighting Network 410. *See also* performance/scalability solutions
liquid immersion cooling 395, 534
Litecoin 126, 160, 161, 515. *See also* cryptocurrencies
Long, Caitlin 5, 13, 24, 193

M

Mancone, Roberto 270–272
McCaleb, Jed 162, 174, 226, 227, 235–241, 243–258
meritocracy 65, 67, 534, 546. *See also* governance
Merkle 57, 58, 117-119, 146, 410, 433, 486, 516, 518, 531, 534, 549
Microsoft 18, 24, 25, 40, 83, 96, 134, 185, 200, 321, 336, 360, 375, 387, 497, 499, 544, 559
minimal viable ecosystem. *See* MVE
mining 45, 77, 78, 84, 109, 111, 127, 145, 146, 158, 161, 176–178, 196, 198, 232, 233, 392–403, 410, 528, 529, 534–537, 541, 542
mining pool 400, 535, 537, 542
mission 17, 18, 70–72, 86, 89, 92, 182, 184, 185, 235, 261, 262, 285, 299, 310–312, 331, 412, 435, 457, 484
Monero 76, 77, 108, 126, 166, 167, 420–422, 539. *See also* anonymity
money laundering 113, 138, 197, 225, 515, 535

Q

QR 289, 293, 295, 301, 304, 319, 340, 543, 544

quantum computing 316, 392, 396, 404, 503, 543. *See also* cybersecurity threats

Quick Response. *See* QR

Quorum 80, 81, 100–102, 126, 134, 179, 180, 242, 304, 413, 418, 424, 436, 539, 544, 545.
    See also permissioned blockchain code bases

R

R3 134, 182, 424, 428, 520, 539, 545. *See also* consortia /working groups

Raft 521, 544, 545. *See also* consensus protocols

Raiden Network 411, 545. *See also* performance/scalability solutions

Regenor, James 310–318, 456, 471, 472

regulations

    AML (anti-money laundering) 74, 138, 162, 234, 264, 278, 515, 535

    CFTC (US Commodity Futures Trading Commission) 164, 194, 196

    GDPR (General Data Protection Regulation) 348

    Howey Test 195, 235

    IRS (US Internal Revenue Service) 194, 210

    KYC (Know Your Customer) 74, 138, 162, 275, 534

    SEC (US Securities and Exchange Commission) 74, 168, 194, 210, 227

    State of Wyoming 18, 155, 191, 210, 298

    US Federal Reserve 108, 109, 193, 220

representative meritocracy 65, 67, 546. *See also* governance

rights of overrides 70, 83, 86, 89, 92, 484

rights of participation 70, 75, 86, 89, 92, 448, 484

rights of use 101, 106, 113, 147, 519

rights of validation 70, 75, 86, 89, 92, 448, 484

Ripple 76, 78, 101, 103, 126, 134, 159, 174, 215–217, 226–235, 239–242, 249, 250, 262, 289,
    397, 424, 435, 472, 533, 539

Rogers, Everett 450–463, 480

Ro, Sandra 25, 185, 497

RSA 516, 546. *See also* cryptography

Index

S

sandbox 133, 192, 490, 546

Santander 85, 227, 229, 230, 253, 259–279

Satoshi Nakamoto. *See* Nakamoto, Satoshi

scalability 36, 78, 92, 167, 182, 278, 304, 317, 353, 391, 392, 405, 406, 409, 411–413, 493, 520, 526, 546, 550

SEC (US Securities and Exchange Commission) 74, 75, 168, 192, 194, 195, 220, 227, 235. *See also* regulations

Security Token Offering. *See* STO

Segregated Witness. *See* SegWit

SegWit (Segregated Witness) 122, 145, 409, 410, 546. *See also* performance/scalability solutions

self-sovereign identity. *See* SSI

SHA-256 117, 118, 161, 530, 547. *See also* cryptography

sharding 409, 411, 547. *See also* performance/scalability solutions

sidechains/relays 428, 433, 547. *See also* interoperability

Silk Road 422, 547, 548

Simple Payment Verification. *See* SPV

smart contract 73–75, 82–86, 92, 101, 107, 108, 113, 114, 131–133, 169, 170, 187, 234, 243, 245, 249, 265, 272, 309, 357, 379, 380, 398, 399, 406, 411, 418, 426, 428, 433, 486, 520–522, 527, 531, 532, 544, 545, 549

SmartResume 327, 333, 334, 346–359, 465, 477

Solana 49, 75, 77, 101, 126, 159

Sovrin Network 337, 339, 341, 342, 343, 344, 345, 346

SPDI (Special Purpose Depository Institution) 192, 193, 210, 223

Special Purpose Depository Institution. *See* SPDI

SPV (Simple Payment Verification) 426, 433, 434, 549. *See also* interoperability

SSI (self-sovereign identity) 20, 31, 42, 50, 52, 184, 327–341, 345, 359, 509, 523, 547

stable coins 49, 106, 107, 154, 155, 159, 163, 249. *See also* cryptocurrencies

stakeocracy 65, 549. *See also* governance

State of Wyoming 18, 155, 191, 298. *See also* regulations

steering committee 65, 67, 68, 69, 94, 346. *See also* governance

Index

Y

Z